OXFORD ~~ENGLISH DRAMA~~

General Edito

Associate General Editors: ~~~~

THE WIDOWIN

AND (

GW00643385

D. H. LAWRENCE, playwright, poet, novelist, and essayist, was born into a pitman's family in the Nottinghamshire mining village of Eastwood in 1885. Five of his early poems were published in the *English Review* in 1909 and his first novel, *The White Peacock*, followed in 1911. In 1912 Lawrence took up writing full time, and eloped to Italy with a married woman, Frieda Weekley. Much of his early writing took dramatic form, including *A Collier's Friday Night* and *The Widowing of Mrs Holroyd*, completed in 1909, and *The Daughter-in-Law* and *The Fight for Barbara*, in 1912. His plays did not meet the theatrical tastes of the time, and later works in the form, including *Touch and Go* (1918), also went largely unnoticed. It was as a novelist that Lawrence achieved recognition in his own lifetime, for works such as *Sons and Lovers* (1913), *The Rainbow* (1915), *Women in Love* (1920), and *Lady Chatterley's Lover* (1928). Lawrence died of tuberculosis on 2 March 1930. His plays only began to win recognition in the live theatre during the late 1960s, with a sequence of productions and revivals by Peter Gill at the Royal Court Theatre in London. The first three, based on his own experiences of life in a pit village, have won posthumous recognition as precursors of the working-class drama which established itself at that theatre during the previous decade.

SIMON TRUSSLER has edited or co-edited over one hundred issues of *Theatre Quarterly* and its successor, *New Theatre Quarterly*, since founding the journal in 1971. He is author or editor of numerous books on drama and theatre including *Theatre at Work* (1967), *New Theatre Voices of the Seventies* (1981), *Shakespearean Concepts* (1989), *The Cambridge Illustrated History of British Theatre* (1994), and the 'Writer-File' and 'Swan Theatre Plays' series.

MICHAEL CORDNER is Reader in the Department of English and Related Literature at the University of York. He has edited George Farquhar's *The Beaux' Stratagem*, the *Complete Plays* of Sir George Etherege, *Four Comedies* of Sir John Vanbrugh, and, for Oxford English Drama, *Four Restoration Marriage Plays* and Sheridan's *The School for Scandal and Other Plays*. He is writing books on *The Comedy of Marriage* and *Shakespeare and the Actor*.

PETER HOLLAND is Professor of Shakespeare Studies and Director of the Shakespeare Institute, University of Birmingham.

MARTIN WIGGINS is a Fellow of the Shakespeare Institute and Lecturer in English at the University of Birmingham.

OXFORD ENGLISH DRAMA

J. M. Barrie
Peter Pan and Other Plays

Aphra Behn
The Rover and Other Plays

George Farquhar
The Recruiting Officer and Other Plays

John Ford
'Tis Pity She's a Whore and Other Plays

Ben Jonson
The Alchemist and Other Plays

D. H. Lawrence
*The Widowing of Mrs Holroyd and
Other Plays*

Christopher Marlowe
Doctor Faustus and Other Plays

John Marston
The Malcontent and Other Plays

Thomas Middleton
*A Mad World, My Masters and
Other Plays*

Richard Brinsley Sheridan
*The School for Scandal and
Other Plays*

J. M. Synge
*The Playboy of the Western World and
Other Plays*

John Webster
*The Duchess of Malfi and
Other Plays*

Oscar Wilde
*The Importance of Being Earnest and
Other Plays*

William Wycherley
The Country Wife and Other Plays

Court Masques,
ed. David Lindley

Four Jacobean Sex Tragedies
ed. Martin Wiggins

Four Restoration Marriage Plays
ed. Michael Cordner

Four Revenge Tragedies
ed. Katharine Maus

Five Romantic Plays 1768–1821
ed. Paul Baines and
Edward Burns

*The New Woman and
Other Emancipated Woman Plays*
ed. Jean Chothia

OXFORD WORLD'S CLASSICS

D. H. LAWRENCE

A Collier's Friday Night
The Widowing of Mrs Holroyd
The Daughter-in-Law
The Fight for Barbara
Touch and Go

Edited with an Introduction and Notes by
SIMON TRUSSLER

General Editor
MICHAEL CORDNER

Associate General Editors
PETER HOLLAND · MARTIN WIGGINS

OXFORD
UNIVERSITY PRESS

OXFORD

UNIVERSITY PRESS

Great Clarendon Street, Oxford OX2 6DP

Oxford University Press is a department of the University of Oxford.
It furthers the University's objective of excellence in research, scholarship,
and education by publishing worldwide in

Oxford New York

Athens Auckland Bangkok Bogotá Buenos Aires Calcutta
Cape Town Chennai Dar es Salaam Delhi Florence Hong Kong Istanbul
Karachi Kuala Lumpur Madrid Melbourne Mexico City Mumbai
Nairobi Paris São Paulo Shanghai Singapore Taipei Tokyo Toronto Warsaw

with associated companies in Berlin Ibadan

Oxford is a registered trade mark of Oxford University Press
in the UK and in certain other countries

Published in the United States
by Oxford University Press Inc., New York

British Library Cataloguing in Publication Data

Data available

Library of Congress Cataloging in Publication Data

Data available

ISBN 0-19-283314-6

1 3 5 7 9 10 8 6 4 2

Typeset in Ehrhardt
by Country Setting, Kingsdown, Kent CT14 8ES
Printed in Great Britain by
Cox & Wyman Ltd.
Reading, Berkshire

CONTENTS

ACKNOWLEDGEMENTS

I am grateful to Michael Cordner and Martin Wiggins for their support and guidance as General Editors of the series, and to Roberta Barker, of the Shakespeare Institute, Stratford-upon-Avon, for her careful reading of the final proofs against the copy texts. Sadly, the volume of *The Plays* in 'The Cambridge Edition of the Works of D. H. Lawrence' did not appear until late in 1999, when this collection was already at an advanced stage of preparation; none the less, I have been indebted to its editors, Hans-Wilhelm Schwarze and John Worthen, for their scrupulous scholarship and many critical insights. I am as ever thankful to my younger children, Jonathan and Meryl, for bearing with an eccentric and often preoccupied father, and to my older children, Nicholas and Anna, for their graceful acceptance of excuses about pressure of work. I am grateful to my grand-daughter Phoebe for being my grand-daughter Phoebe. This collection could only be dedicated to Peter Gill, to whom the world owes a lasting debt for his rediscovery of Lawrence's plays for the live theatre.

INTRODUCTION

Lawrence's Life and Literary Career

D. H. Lawrence was born in the Nottinghamshire mining village of Eastwood—'of about three thousand souls, about eight miles from Nottingham'—in 1885. He was the fourth child of an ill-fated marriage between a local pitman, illiterate and unambitious, and a better educated woman whose early infatuation with his rough virtues (and unexpected merits as a dancing partner) soon turned to fretful disappointment when he showed no interest in improving himself. As her husband increasingly neglected his family for the rough camaraderie of the public house, her ambitions were duly transferred to her offspring—and in particular to the academically bright young David Herbert, who at the age of thirteen won a scholarship to Nottingham High School.

Leaving school at sixteen, Lawrence was stricken with pneumonia soon after starting work in a factory. During his convalescence he met Jessie Chambers, the original of Miriam in his autobiographical novel *Sons and Lovers*. It was she who encouraged him to write during the training and apprenticeship as a teacher he then undertook; and he had probably completed the first draft of his earliest play, *A Collier's Friday Night*, before gaining his teacher's certificate in 1908, when he left Eastwood for a post in the outer London suburb of Croydon. The year which followed the death of his mother in December 1910 was, in Lawrence's own words, one in which 'everything collapsed'—his relationship with Jessie and, following a further bout of pneumonia, his teaching career besides. But it was also the year in which his first novel, *The White Peacock*, was published, and he determined to take up writing full time: his second novel, *The Trespasser*, followed in 1912, and 'slowly the world came back, or I myself returned: but to another world'.

This was the world of his tumultuous love affair with Frieda Weekley, the German wife of a Nottingham professor, with whom Lawrence eloped to Italy. Here he set about completing *Sons and Lovers*, which was eventually published in 1913, to be followed a year later by his second play, *The Widowing of Mrs Holroyd*. *The Daughter-in-Law* and *The Fight for Barbara* were also products of this period, as were two attempts at comedy, *The Merry-Go-Round* and *The Married Man*: but none of these found a publisher or producer; and when a return to England was enforced on Lawrence by the outbreak of the First World War, his energies were concentrated on the linked novels of provincial life which became *The Rainbow* (1915) and *Women in Love* (1920).

In chauvinistic wartime Britain, the Lawrences—a non-combatant husband with a newly-divorced wife of German origin—inevitably met with a hostile reception, and the couple returned to Italy in 1919, later journeying further afield in Lawrence's quest for physical health and spiritual refreshment. The post-war novels—notably *Kangaroo* (1923), *The Plumed Serpent* (1926), and *Lady Chatterley's Lover* (1928)—are sustained rather by a philosophical than an autobiographical drive; and in the one further play he completed, the ersatz biblical epic *David* (1925), he deployed or deftly imitated the cadences of the Authorized Version to retell the Old Testament story in the light of his evolving conception of a lost cosmic religion. Following Lawrence's early death in 1930, it was as a novelist, short-story writer, and poet that he was to be remembered, until productions of the three mining plays brought him posthumous fame as a dramatist almost forty years later.

The Sources of the Plays in Lawrence's Life and Art

Keith Sagar called his biography of Lawrence *Life into Art* (1985), and wrote from the premise that Lawrence's intention was always, 'consciously or unconsciously, to explore, clarify, objectify, and generalize his own most pressing problems and most vivid experiences' (p. 2). Yet one of the distinctive features of Lawrence's plays is that, while most indeed have their roots in his life experience—sometimes even down to the dates of events or ages of characters—a craftsmanlike distance can be felt between the creator and the work. It is as if the poet's or novelist's omnipresence, whether overt or implicit, is giving way with dignity before characters who speak in their own persons. I have taken it as no part of my purpose in the present collection, therefore, to distract attention from the intrinsic theatrical qualities of the plays by giving extensive attention to their roots; but in the present section I shall touch briefly on the personal associations of each play, in order to identify such features as might confuse or detract from its theatrical appreciation. For those whose interests lie in the ways in which Lawrence transmuted his life into his dramatic art, Sagar's biography and the scholarly Cambridge Edition of *The Plays* will provide detailed guidance.

While characters' names are almost always changed from their originals—though often barely disguised—Lawrence's practice with the names of places (streets, collieries, pubs) varies; but even when a changed name leaves no phonetic clue to its source, other facets of the play usually clarify its origins. All the characters of *A Collier's Friday Night* have their identifiable originals: Maggie Pearson is clearly drawn from Lawrence's friend Jessie Chambers, and even the minor characters are recognizable from real life—Nellie Lambert being based on Lawrence's younger sister Lettice Ada, and her visiting friends Gertie and Beatrice on actual Eastwood neighbours.

The play explores in its few microcosmic hours the same territory, physical and emotional, as Lawrence's novel *Sons and Lovers* (in terms of the events portrayed, Chapter 8 of the novel is most directly analogous). A would-be intellectual son is worshipped by an ambitious mother, who now feels excluded from their relationship by a girl with whom he can more fully share his intellectual interests. Both despise the inarticulate miner husband and father, who has come to prefer the company and consolation of the public house. The only atypicality on this particular Friday night is the burning of the bread which the two young people have been left to watch, the quarrel thus precipitated, and the almost oedipal reconciliation between mother and son with which the play concludes. One of the play's strengths is that none of its indebtedenss to Lawrence's experience is necessary knowledge for its appreciation—apart, perhaps, from the disquieting intensity of the mother–son relationship, which might otherwise appear out of proportion to the quotidian reality which the play so effectively conveys.

The Widowing of Mrs Holroyd also has its equivalent in Lawrence's prose fiction—the short story 'The Odour of Chrysanthemums' (1911). Here, though, the biographical analogies are less direct. Lawrence's own uncle, like Holroyd in the play, was killed in a pit accident at Brinsley Colliery, and also left his widow with two small children. Although this was five years before Lawrence was born, Brinsley was only two miles from Eastwood, and the young Lawrence was a frequent visitor at his aunt's cottage—which, as in the play, was close to both the New Inn and the Prince of Wales public houses. The catalytic presence of Blackmore as Mrs Holroyd's lover is Lawrence's invention, as is the tipsy intrusion of Clara and Laura—though Mrs Holroyd's original attraction to her husband for his qualities as a dancing partner rekindles a spark of Lawrence's own parents' relationship.

The Daughter-in-Law drifts further from a direct connection with Lawrence's life, though the names of its characters and the locations mentioned usually have their Eastwood origins. Of all three of the colliery plays, it is this in which the 'local colour' of pit-village life rather than the specifics of plot depend upon Lawrence's personal experience.

The closely contemporaneous *The Fight for Barbara*, set in an Italian villa drawn to resemble the one in which Lawrence and Frieda Weekley spent their first winter together, is, however, the most directly auto-biographical of his plays. Sending off the manuscript to his friend and mentor Edward Garnett, Lawrence noted that he did so at Frieda's urging, though 'She says I have glorified myself beyond recognition, and put her in rags.' Years later, after Lawrence's death, Frieda claimed that the play had been written 'when he was in a rage with me', and that she 'did *not* wobble' in her allegiance to him, as does Barbara in the play; but she confirms that the play is 'a record of the vivid hours with Lawrence full of hope and gaiety on the Lago di Garda'. Thus, Frieda's father and mother did indeed visit the couple here, in the hope of persuading their daughter to return; and Frieda claimed that the plaintive figure of Tressider is made to echo her estranged husband Ernest's 'very words'. Knowledge of such real-life origins is more helpful here than for the earlier plays precisely in so far as the immediacy of the feelings and the specificity of the events remain less than fully transmuted into purposeful dramatic action.

The problem with *Touch and Go* is rather a failure of the novelist to adapt his raw materials to the art of the dramatist—for in his novel *Women in Love*, completed in 1916, Lawrence had already repurposed the Eastwood pit-owning family Barber under the name of Crich. That novel was still unpublished when a year or so later he began work on the play, in which the Barbers become the Barlows – whose son Gerald has had a doomed affair with a sculptress, Anabel, just as the Gerald of the novel has with the sculptress Gudrun. The problem is that Lawrence seems to assume for his dramatic characters their pre-existence in the novel; and, to complicate matters further, their complex pasts now have to be filtered (through none too fine a mesh) to serve his didactic purpose of exploring the relationship between capital and labour. In conse-quence, the theme of industrial conflict seems to float on the surface of a play in which the real action is taking place in murky and unexplored waters far below.

The Contemporary Theatrical Background

Lawrence's love of the stage began early, to judge from the scattered but affectionate references to the rough touring companies of his youth—the 'blood-tubs', as he calls them in *The White Peacock*, where melodrama played alongside potted Shakespeare in makeshift spaces to makeshift audiences. Although his first recorded visit to a 'real' theatre was to see

Sarah Bernhardt at the Theatre Royal, Nottingham, in June 1908, by then he had long been a member of an informal grouping of friends who called themselves 'the Pagans', and whose regular activities included play-readings and theatre visits—one of these to Galsworthy's *Strife*. But the Pagans tempered their intellectual activities with improvised theatricals, and in these (to judge from the memories of such fellow-members as Jessie Chambers and Louise Burrows) Lawrence delighted in displaying his gift for mimicry. William Hopkin—the original of Willie Houghton in *Touch and Go*—also recalls Lawrence's insistence on charades whenever a gathering felt in party mood.

Sylvia Sklar, in *The Plays of D. H. Lawrence*—the single full-length study of this aspect of Lawrence's work—collects a wide range of references and recollections in support of her assertion that 'it was Lawrence's whole early intention to be a playwright'. And the evidence of *The White Peacock* certainly suggests a young man in love with the 'tumult of wild feeling' the theatre could evoke. There, Lawrence describes his characters as 'stunned' by a visit to *Carmen*—'she with tears in her eyes, he with a strange wild beating of his heart'. Yet this is not at all the feeling with which one leaves any of his own plays: and what perhaps lay between the enthusiast's raw emotions and the craftsman's solid achievements were all those evenings spent among the Pagans, reading and discussing the works of the great European writers then in intellectual (but not popular) fashion.

According to Jessie Chambers, it was Lawrence who introduced Ibsen to the Pagans. The great Norwegian dramatist had died full of years in 1906, but his plays remained relatively neglected in Britain, despite the championship of Bernard Shaw. (For Shaw himself, the only English dramatist of the time on whom posterity has bestowed undisputed honours, Lawrence appears to have felt personal respect but professional detachment.) However, in a later judgement of Strindberg's plays as 'unnatural, forced, a bit indecent', he bracketed Ibsen with Strindberg as 'a bit wooden . . . a bit skin-erupty'.

Following his move to Croydon, Lawrence had ready access to the theatrical offerings of London's West End—yet he seems to have been every bit as pleased that the school where he was teaching had a tradition (for that time surprising) of theatrical activity, and no less proud of a school production of *Ali Baba and the Forty Thieves* than of his own class's play-reading of *The Tempest*. Following his bout of pneumonia in 1912, former colleagues at the school presented Lawrence with a volume of Chekhov's plays, and though later in life this influence also appears to have been rejected, at the time he wrote enthusiastically of 'a new thing in drama'; and a little later, in his call for 'a reaction against Shaw and Galsworthy and Barker', he exempted Chekhov along with the Irish dramatist J. M. Synge when stressing the need to 'get free from the authority' of oppressive contemporaries.

The nature of this 'authority' as it affected Lawrence is, however, not immediately clear. The 'reaction' he calls for appears to be against prevailing English varieties of naturalism and realism—the subtle distinctions between which need not concern us here—yet his early plays appear to be, precisely, distinctive English expressions of those modes. Where he differs from the contemporaries he names is in the working-class idiom and assumptions which underlie his own work. On the Continent, Gorky in Russia, Hauptmann in Germany, and the Théâtre Libre of Antoine in France had all experimented with ways of giving the working classes a 'realistic' dramatic voice; but few English dramatists in Lawrence's lifetime even attempted to treat working-class concerns, and even fewer to create convincing working-class characters. Some, with the egregious Henry Arthur Jones, simply felt that 'the epitaph on . . . all this realistic business will be—it does not matter what happens in kitchen-middens'. Others, such as Sir Arthur Pinero, more apologetically asserted that the lower orders simply lacked the articulacy needful to be granted a stage voice. This was a view apparently shared in practice even by such a professed socialist as Shaw, whose proletarian characters draw on venerable stereotypes, from the 'wily servant' embodied by Enery Straker in *Man and Superman* to the 'professional parasite' perpetuated by Alfred Dolittle in *Pygmalion* (even the names are redolent of their theatrical ancestry—as also arguably of their creator's snobbery). The popular melodrama of the previous century had simply inverted this typology, asserting the dignity of honest labour but, it has to be said, with very little attempt at dramatic complexity.

The 'new wave' of English drama associated first with the Vedrenne–Barker management of the Court Theatre in London from 1904 to 1907, and subsequently with the 'Manchester School' which enjoyed the patronage of Annie Horniman at the Gaiety Theatre from 1908, did acknowledge the desirability of representing ordinary people on the stage. But whether in Galsworthy's well-intentioned but doom-laden strikers, convicts, and petty ne'er-do-wells, or in the more workaday but none the less mildly risible northerners of Harold Brighouse or Stanley Houghton, the feeling is of a well-heeled dramatist conducting his audience through the more decorous fringes of a slum. Lawrence, alone among the English playwrights of his time, wrote of the working classes from within, from experience, and from the heart. And in consequence his plays did not get produced.

Despite a reception—from friends and advisors as much as from within the theatrical profession—that ranged from polite indifference to outright hostility, he none the less persisted in revising his plays, soliciting their production, and continuing to write in the genre. Even as late as 1913, when he had published three novels, against these may be set an output of six plays. Yet his contemporaries, instead of welcoming so original a theatrical voice, found themselves puzzled by its accent. If Lawrence had been working in the cultural climate in which his plays at last reached the professional stage in the 1960s, we could conjecture that his whole career might have been directed towards the drama rather than the novel—or that he might at least, like his near-contemporaries Somerset Maugham and J. B. Priestley, have found equal fame in both these forms.

Those who dubbed the emergent working-class drama of the late 1950s 'kitchen sink' presumably intended an ironic contrast with the more familiar 'drawing-rooms' of middle-class drama. Yet whereas such drawing rooms were merely convenient central locations for an action which assumed (and sometimes explored) a large surrounding house and grounds, the kitchen truly was the focus for much working-class family life. If there were also a 'front room'—as in *A Collier's Friday Night*, whence the piano–playing is heard—it remained largely inviolate. This was partly to keep it 'special'—free from coal-dust for weddings, funerals, and perhaps Sunday lunches—but was mainly to economize on heating a house probably riddled with jerry-built dampness (upstairs as well as down, as old Lambert's trousers bear their steaming witness).

It is easy to forget that theatrical taste-makers of Lawrence's time— the occupants of the dress circle and stalls of central London theatres— would have found a theatrical presentation of such domestic life entirely alien to their experience. The enforced intimacies of a two-up, two-down existence would have felt unbearably claustrophobic to members of a society who left the running of their own extensive households to a network of servants, and who avoided the care of (or even much intimacy with) their own children, at first through the surrogacy of nannies and nurseries, then through the more decisive separation of the boarding school system.

London's higher intellectual circles, with which Lawrence became increasingly involved after his enforced separation from the simple pleasures of school drama in Croydon, were themselves largely drawn from such a background, however much the political consciousness of some may have turned them against it. They would also have been contemptuous of most West End fare, recognizing with Lawrence that it existed 'mainly in the interests of fashion rather than of art'. Both circumstances would have helped to turn Lawrence's ambitions towards the novel. His largely itinerant existence after the elopement with Frieda in 1912 made continuing contacts with London managements impractical, while during the First World War audiences displayed even less appetite for seriousness of any sort. In the aftermath of the war, Lawrence continued to seek outlets for his plays, but during his lifetime only two of the plays ever reached the stage, in exceedingly small-scale productions—*The Widowing of Mrs Holroyd* in 1916 in Los Angeles and in 1920 in Manchester; and *David* in London in 1927—and only one other, *Touch and Go*, joined them in achieving the dignity of publication.

The Mining Background

Although some grinders at the wheel of critical fashion now question George Orwell's motives for his forays into pre-war working-class experience, it has to be said that anyone wanting to get an imaginative feeling for the experience of being a pitman will do better to read Orwell's short essay, 'Down the Mine', published in *The Road to Wigan Pier* (1937), than any or all of the plays of D. H. Lawrence. I strike this cautionary note because the term 'the mining plays' (I have even seen 'the mining trilogy') is sometimes used as a shorthand description for the first three plays in this volume. But they are not plays about mining: they are plays about working-class family life in a pit village, and in each the emphasis is rather on the wives, mothers, and dependants of pitmen, with the breadwinner's mode of work very much a 'given' of the action.

Indeed, when an event down the pit affects the action of a play, Lawrence seems unsure of himself in dealing with it. This does not matter very much with Joe's minor injury in *The Daughter-in-Law*, since it is of the essence that it was caused by his fooling about, not while he was working; yet even a pit fatality—the death of Holroyd in *The Widowing of Mrs Holroyd*—is needlessly muddled by Rigley's reference to 'after-damp', a poisonous methane gas, as having hopefully shortened the victim's suffering. For methane was formed following an explosion: and in this case there has been a collapse, not an explosion. Perhaps, argue the Cambridge editors, 'Rigley is using a technical term to divert attention from the actual cause of death'—but this would only argue for Lawrence's ineptitude in expecting an audience first to recognize the term, and then to catch the implications of its 'deliberate' misuse.

The truth is that Lawrence's experience of the actualities of mining began at the pithead, and ended at the kitchen range, where the home-coming pitman warmed and cleansed himself. What he also well knew, of course, were both the emotions and the economics of belonging to a pitman's family; and it is this territory that the dramatist treads with assurance. So, in *A Collier's Friday Night*, we hear and learn from the financial dealings between old Lambert, Barker and Carlin a good deal about the 'butty' system peculiar to the Midlands coalfields, where it survived into the 1930s. 'Butties' were themselves working miners, who had contracted with the pit-owners to be responsible for working a section of the coal-face, themselves setting the expected pace for the pitmen they sub-contracted. These daymen would be paid out of what the butties received for the tonnage hewed each week—the butties then sharing among themselves whatever had been cut in excess of the agreed minimum. Thus, Lambert, Barker and Carlin put aside what is due to the daymen before their own share-out—Lambert no doubt keeping anything left over (as does Morel in *Sons and Lovers*), his evident seniority indicated also by such nice touches as the fountain pen his colleagues so admire.

The Eastwood collieries were owned by Barber, Walker and Company, and at the time of the national coal strike of 1912 employed some three thousand men. Strikes, of course, had a severe impact upon family economics and family dynamics—but the workers' solidarity they reinforced remained strong in the coalfields, until the Thatcher government crushed first the souls and then the livelihoods of the miners in the 1980s. In *The Daughter-in-Law*, it is thus Joe and Luther's night-time foiling of the blacklegs which effectively reunites the family, though earlier there has been concern over how the household will manage for the duration. In this respect, according to *The Times*, during the 1912 strike there was some implicit collusion with the bosses: the owners apparently did not press for the payment of rent on colliery-owned cottages during the strike, 'knowing from past experience that the debts will be discharged in full'. And this strike ended with both sides able to claim a victory—a Minimum Wages Act was passed, but the owners successfully insisted on settlement by district. Meanwhile the local 'Co-op' would extend credit for groceries, in part from political sympathy, but also because it too was confident that it would get its money in the end.

Such compromises, which maintained a fragile sense of community even at times of confrontation, were part of an unspoken consensus that old Barlow in *Touch and Go* knows to have vanished—not least owing to the impact of increasing mechanization. Blackmore in *The Widowing of Mrs Holroyd* is thus clearly set aside from the rest of the underground fraternity: for as an electrician he services the new cutting machinery which had for long been resisted—as much by traditionalist owners for its expense as by the miners for the threat it posed to their craft, if not to their jobs. Because of the eccentricity of Barlow (and all his clan), this comes through less clearly than it might in *Touch and Go*—just as the issue of whether the pitmen are truly supporting the office-workers or using them for their own ends also remains fudged.

The roots of trade unionism in the Nottingham coalfields, according to their historian Alan Griffin, were Methodist rather than socialist: no wonder, perhaps, that Lawrence viewed trade unionism as equivocally as his own Congregationalist background—on the one hand as a stimulus to nonconformity, on the other as a sect with its own rigidities and repressions. In *Touch and Go*, he seemed to be setting up a dialectic of character and ideology to explore if not resolve his equivocation— between the humanitarian socialist Willie Houghton and the interestingly flawed union leader, Job Arthur Freer. But the characters pursue their own parallel courses, and as for the watching crowd, they might be the mob from Shakespeare's *Julius Caesar* for all the judgement they show, or authorial sympathy they receive.

The Theatrical Recovery of the Plays

Critical reconsiderations of Lawrence's plays have followed rather than encouraged their recognition on stage. One of the few assessments prior to the Royal Court productions of the 1960s, by Arthur E. Waterman, damned with faint praise, making the astonishing claim that 'Lawrence didn't take his dramatic work very seriously'. And such misconceptions were not limited to those whose interests lay primarily in the novels. I would count Eric Bentley and Raymond Williams as probably the two foremost critical influences upon my own generation, as we began to look for ways of discussing plays as works for the stage rather than the page; yet Bentley, in his influential *The Playwright as Thinker* (1948), placed Lawrence among other novelists who had 'fancied himself as a dramatist with largely unhappy consequences' (p. 64); while Williams, in the first edition of his own major study, *Modern Drama from Ibsen to Eliot* (1952), cited several of Lawrence's more general artistic pronouncements, but made no reference to his plays whatsoever. Yet when Williams came to revise the volume—also significantly retitling it *Modern Drama from Ibsen to Brecht*—he added a complete section on

Lawrence's plays, paying special attention to *The Daughter-in-Law*. It can have been no accident that the new edition was published in 1968, just a year after that play had received its belated premiere at the Royal Court. Within a further year, Williams had contributed an important introduction to the Penguin collection which brought the three 'mining plays' accessibly into print.

It was ironic that Lawrence the novelist should have gained his post-humous recognition as a playwright at the Royal Court—where, barely a decade earlier, a well-intentioned management had launched the new English Stage Company by seeking out novelists in what turned out to be the vain hope that they could readily turn their hands to plays. In the event, of course, the success of John Osborne's *Look Back in Anger* in 1956 brought dedicated playwrights aplenty onto its own and other stages, though in all that flurry of new theatrical energy it was the Court which long retained for itself a distinctive role as the home of chal-lenging new writing.

Philip Roberts's *The Royal Court Theatre 1965–1972* (1986) includes a chapter on *The Daughter-in-Law*, which opens with a rather charming description of the chain of events through which Peter Gill—then a young actor and playwright needing to prove himself as assistant to the theatre's artistic director—came upon Lawrence's plays. As early as 1958, he had seen the television adaptation of *The Widowing of Mrs Holroyd*, and when, in 1965, the need arose to earn his directorial spurs with a one-night production, he came across 'this little green book' which was the first, 1934 edition of *A Collier's Friday Night*. Even while the play was in rehearsal, Heinemann had published and Gill had pur-chased the 'Phoenix Edition' of *The Complete Plays of D. H. Lawrence*, and the young director found himself transfixed alike by 'the extra-ordinary last scene in *Holroyd*' and by the whole of *The Daughter-in-Law*—the latter, of course, still unperformed.

Gill was later asked to direct the Court premiere of *The Daughter-in-Law*, and in the February of 1967 paid a visit to Eastwood with his set designer, John Gunter. They came across 'a group of cottages that were incredibly poor', one of which they were allowed to explore—and it was on this actual interior that Gunter decided to base his designs. (As Gill recalls, 'The man next door showed me a copy that his sister had given him of *Collier's Friday Night* in that same green cover.') The 'confined space' Gunter had discovered, and within which he felt the play needed to be set, was in some ways analogous to the 'confined space' of the Court, with its notoriously difficult sight-lines and limited wing-space. At that stage, the only part already cast was Joe Gascoigne, to be played by Victor Henry—an actor of mercurial genius and unpredictable temperament, uncannily cast not to 'type' but to absolute individuality.

The production was a quiet but distinct success, and in the following year *The Widowing of Mrs Holroyd* was brought into a season of all three plays to be directed by Gill. In the event the strain proved too great, and others took over while he was hospitalized; but all three productions still bore his distinct imprint—of scrupulous attention to detail, and of truth to the rhetorical, emotional, and economic life that Lawrence was portraying. Indeed, Gill felt that Lawrence 'seemed to be a completely Royal Court writer'; and other early critics of the plays—'early', that is, in the time of the plays' theatrical reception, not their creation—were also inclined to suggest their anticipation of the neo-naturalism of the late 1950s and 1960s. Comparisons might indeed be made with Arnold Wesker's East End tenements, Norfolk tied cottage, or the workaday location of *The Kitchen*—or with the more laddish settings of a David Storey, whose fascination with the routines of work put the rigging of a marquee on stage in *The Contractor* and saw the playing out of all the rituals and rivalries of a Rugby League game in *The Changing Room*. The umbrella of neo-naturalism is not in itself important, for that has cast a pervasive shadow over a good deal of twentieth-century British drama: what matters is the shared recognition that work, the effects of work, and the economics of work necessarily play a larger part in the lives of the poor than of even the moderately affluent, with whose emotional upsets the vast majority of plays of the time were still concerned.

Slowly, others of Lawrence's plays have found productions—*The Fight for Barbara* at the Mermaid Theatre, London, as early as 1967, when its director, Robin Midgeley, sought parallels between Lawrence's Jimmy Wesson and Osborne's Jimmy Porter in *Look Back in Anger*. In so far as both plays are at one level about a poor man with a wife or lover from a wealthy family, and some of the tensions that result, the comparison was not without interest, and was more helpful than gilding the autobiographical elements which are evident enough already. Peter Gill tried to make something of *The Merry-Go-Round* for the Royal Court in 1973, but his willingness to cut and otherwise adapt the play suggested that he felt less confident of its viability than in his earlier productions, where he had insisted on the integrity of what Lawrence had written. In the same year, *Touch and Go* received a production from one of the most prestigious amateur companies in Britain, the Questors in Ealing, and finally its professional premiere at the Oxford Playhouse in 1979; while *The Married Man* reached the stage in 1997, almost ninety years after its composition, in a student production by the Royal Academy of Dramatic

Art. None of these productions achieved any notable success, and only the 'mining plays' seem to have established for themselves a permanent place in the repertoire of the British theatre. But given Lawrence's previous neglect as a playwright, and his inexperience in the practical aspects of the craft, that in itself is an astonishing achievement—and the time-lag between the composition of the plays and their 'discovery' unique in the annals of the theatre.

A Collier's Friday Night

According to Frieda Lawrence, in her autobiographical *Not I But the Wind* (1934), Lawrence told her later in life that 'I would write a different *Sons and Lovers* now; my mother was wrong and I thought she was absolutely right.' Even at the time when he still believed in his mother's absolute rightness, Lawrence had already written a very different *Sons and Lovers*: it was called *A Collier's Friday Night*.

Lawrence claimed to have written the play in the autumn or winter of 1906, at the age of twenty-one—the same age as his *persona* in the play, Ernest Lambert. But Jessie Chambers claimed that he had never mentioned the play to her before September 1909, and references to the deaths of Meredith and Swinburne in the single surviving manuscript confirm a final revision while Lawrence was teaching in Croydon, shortly after that date. Granted at least a period of gestation over the previous few years, this would have been concurrent with the writing of the verses he was later to compartmentalize as his 'rhyming poems', of several short stories, and of the novel *Laetitia* which was soon to be transformed into *The White Peacock*. At this time Lawrence wanted to become simply a 'writer' rather than specifically a poet, novelist, or dramatist, and was dabbling in all these forms. But the play shows a decidedly maturer craft and (as he was later to put it) 'metaphysics' than his other early work, which is often flawed by sentiment or a shallow fatalism, and would have suggested that, if anywhere, it was in the drama that his future as a writer most promisingly lay. It was not to be: around the time of the play's completion Ford Madox Hueffer published five of Lawrence's poems in his *English Review*, and *The White Peacock* reached print in 1911—but *A Collier's Friday Night* remained unpublished until 1934 and unperformed until 1939.

In her chapter on the play, Sylvia Sklar devotes a great deal of space to demonstrating that Lawrence was conflating incidents from different periods of his student life into this single Friday evening, as if the burning of bread and the argument over a son's right to love a woman other than his mother were just too existential to have possibly been contingent. All that matters, of course, is that the incidents should seem to follow: that the impression is of the flow of happenstance—of tiny domestic crises precipitating major confrontations, as they do so often in life. At the opposite critical pole are those accustomed to the worked-up crises and peripeteia of the 'well-made' play, who therefore complain that nothing of significance really *happens*. Rather than having too contrived a structure or no adequate structure at all, Lawrence had simply hit on a balance appropriate to his subject.

Thus, although *A Collier's Friday Night* is often discussed as if it were a cameo version of *Sons and Lovers*, perhaps its most accomplished attribute is Lawrence's recognition that this *is* a play, with quite different generic requirements and expectations from a novel. We should remind ourselves that at its worst the 'well-made' play was prone to compress into its three hours' traffic all the turning-points of a lifetime, employing longueurs of exposition to clarify the past and convenient coincidences to compress the present; and who likelier to write a well-made play at its worst than a prentice writer with a novel's worth of angst in his head? Yet Lawrence maintains a strict neoclassical unity of time in taking us through an evening that is maybe not quite typical, but does not seem in the least contrived, or bloated in the issues it raises, and which finally eases the characters back into their usual, necessary night-time routines. These stake out no orthodox 'dramatic' climax—just the time when everybody needs to get to bed: in Lawrence, whatever the strains and stresses, nobody forgets to riddle and stoke the range before they retire.

Indeed, whatever the events of this particular Friday evening, its pace is determined by regular expectations and rituals—the various arrivals home, the supper that is fragmented by these arrivals and fought over for its few delicacies, the various neighbours 'dropping in', the visit of Lambert's fellow 'butties' for the weekly reckoning and their subsequent departure for the pub, the trips into town for Friday-evening shopping—and, of course, the understated, indeed implicit courtship of the young people who are then left alone in the house.

In this sense, *A Collier's Friday Night* might not unkindly be called a 'slice-of-life' drama; and while some have suggested that its title pays homage to Burns's whimsical ode to rustic toil and domestic virtue, 'The Cotter's Saturday Night', to me it appears rather to align itself with then-recent 'slice-of-life' plays such as Gorky's *The Lower Depths* (1902), set in a Russian doss-house, and Hauptmann's *The Weavers* (1893)—the latter, with its focus on the effects of industrial struggle on a small community, being closer in theme if not in tenor to the later

Touch and Go. For there is no industrial struggle in this play, even though its very setting on a Friday rather than a Saturday night was due to the recent achievement by the miners of a five-day working week, following hard on the heels of their successful fight for an eight-hour day. *A Collier's Family's Friday Night* would be a more accurate title.

And yet, as Raymond Williams well expressed it, the working-class family forms 'an evident and mutual economic unit, within which both rights and responsibilities are uncertainly contained'; and the play is full of the uncertainties of that mutuality. When Mrs Lambert claims to her husband of her beloved son, 'That lad works ten times as hard as you do,' the context makes it clear that he does not—he's having fun, showing off to the girls, slacking a bit, and what work he does do he has chosen and enjoys. Old Lambert is right, in his own eyes, in claiming that he is helping to keep his son for 'doing nothing'—for 'doing nothing' means bringing no money into the household, while still commanding its resources. This was inevitable when a child wished to be 'educated out' of class expectations (to follow his father down the mine, or into some menial factory job); and the resulting tensions were to become a familiar feature of working-class family life as merit came slowly to counter-balance money, and allow poorer children their chance to join the educated elite. Some hard-up parents were happy to see children rise 'above their station', despite the strains of delayed wage-earning; others were grudging in the economies this imposed upon them, or simply refused to make the sacrifice; and others again were divided—as is the Lambert household—between one acceptive and one dismissive parent.

Lawrence's play in this respect anticipates a long-running theme of mid-century literature—notably as those of the generation which had benefited from the Education Act of 1944 came to draw up the spiritual profit-and-loss accounts of their declassing. Typical is *In Celebration* (1969), in which David Storey, himself the son of a miner, shows the three brothers of a humble household returning for their parents' fortieth wedding anniversary, for the inevitable reopening and hopeful healing of old wounds. Yet Lawrence's play less expectedly anticipates also the proto-feminism of Arnold Wesker's *Roots* (1959), in which Beatie Bryant, who has come to feel as oppressed by the tutelage of an educated boy-friend as by the ingrained servility of her parents, exultantly cuts the cords that have bound her. Maggie, in Lawrence's play, appears to have no such ambition, and to be content with subservience; but the arrogance of Ernest is patriarchal as well as intellectual, and, despite his autobiographical proximity to his creator, that arrogance is conveyed with both clarity and honesty.

And while this is far from being a feminist play, it is the women who make the lasting impressions—even the two visiting pitmen either have domestic chores to perform or, in Barker's case, aspire to the 'feminine' accomplishment of piano-playing (his efforts being duly mocked, though he is later said in a stage direction to play Grieg 'with real sympathy'). Indeed, for a play eponymously concerned with the masculine business of being a collier, both male Lamberts are much set about with women. Apart from the central relationship with his mother, Ernest Lambert has to cope not only with the intellectually aspirant and hero-worshipping Maggie, but with the no-nonsense briskness of his sister Nellie, and the intrusions of the propitiatory Gertie and the caustic, mischief-making Beatrice (with Barker, one of the few characters to share her name with her counterpart in *Sons and Lovers*).

Against Sylvia Sklar's belief in the symbolic importance of Mrs Lambert's constant concern with provisioning—making tea, baking bread, departing to shop for the next week's groceries—one may set the thought that, on a normal Friday evening, such concerns would simply have been part of the trivial round—as on every evening of the week was the making of the family supper and the preparation of tomorrow's 'snap-bag' for her husband's sustenance in the pit. Giving preference to Ernest over Nellie, and to Nellie over her husband, in the allocation of the choicer morsels is not 'symbolic' but emotional prioritizing. She is doling out the food as she doles out her affections. And doling out food forms a large part of her everyday life.

None of the younger women, apart from Maggie, are, from a 'well-made' standpoint, essential to the action. Yet it takes the visiting Gertie Coomber to soften the edges of the 'futile ferocity' which is old Lambert's only way of responding to Nellie's jibes. His family has his measure, and knows how to pit its feelings against him to best effect—Mrs Lambert with a residual but exasperated affection, Nellie with 'cold contempt', Ernest with sublime condescension. Old Lambert, neither articulate nor subtle, can none the less respond to the simpler social lubrication which Gertie offers. If, at his lowest, he is 'between anger and shame and sorrow, of which an undignified rage is predominant', this is because undignified rage is the feeling that his own family has encouraged him to cultivate.

Although in production the play may benefit from the verisimilitudinous re-creation of the kitchen of a pitman's cottage, we need to remind ourselves that *A Collier's Friday Night* was first seen at the Royal Court in a Sunday-evening production without décor—or, more precisely, was somehow squeezed within the set of John Osborne's *A Patriot for Me*, then running during the rest of the week. Wesker's *The Kitchen*, despite the detailed 'behind-the-scenes' view it appears to require, had a similarly makeshift first performance, and has been most memorably revived in a style more akin to expressionism than realism. In creative hands, then, no play need be limited by the seeming dictates of its stylistic trappings, and Lawrence's characteristically precise opening stage directions, even down to listing the books on the shelves, are in this respect as optional as Shaw's (who was inclined to allow his directions to drift into a discursive but prescriptive vein way beyond the playwright's province). We may regret that no writer's dramatic imagination (apart, arguably, from Georg Büchner's in *Woyzeck*) had yet allowed itself the free scenic range of an Edward Bond, who in *Saved* (1965) was among the first to allow his scenes to ebb and flow as incident and character dictated (deriving the freedom in roughly equal measure from Brechtian theory and the influence of TV drama, at last freeing itself from studio sets). Yet here, the disadvantages of the action being confined to that single kitchen set are probably outweighed by the advantages—less in terms of the scenic embellishments that may or may not be offered than of the emotional confinement that must be evoked.

The Widowing of Mrs Holroyd

The Widowing of Mrs Holroyd appears to have been been written and completed in the year before November 1910, when Lawrence began circulating it in manuscript. But despite encouragement from Granville Barker and much early talk of productions, its theatrical success in his lifetime was limited to a premiere in Los Angeles in 1916, an amateur production in Manchester in 1920, and just three London performances in 1926. It was, however, the first of Lawrence's plays to be published, in 1914. The publication is unsurprising, in that *The Widowing of Mrs Holroyd* has at least the semblance of the 'well-made' structure then expected—a beginning which sets the scene and initiates the action, a middle which develops a crisis of character and of conscience, and an end which delivers a strong climax, the death of a major character.

The incidents of the first act which bring before us the unhappy state of the Holroyds' relationship also tie in surely but unobtrusively with the events of the last. The arrival of the electrician Blackmore at Mrs Holroyd's home clarifies a relationship whose essence, at this stage, is its very lack of clarity. Blackmore would like to compensate for the physical intimacy he cannot broach by encouraging emotional dependency, but is only allowed to perform such small favours as replacing the broken globe of an oil lamp. Yet the two children clearly like him, and he probably offers just the kind of solid, stolid support the family needs.

However, a drunken husband and father stands in the way, and his latest goings-on in the pub are prattled back to us by the children—with a good deal less clumsiness, it must be said, than such necessary exposition was often handled by Lawrence's contemporaries. Holroyd has, we learn, been dancing with a group of visiting women from Nottingham in 'paper bonnets' (dancing, of course, being an accomplishment of Lawrence's own father—who said, according to Lawrence in a rare mention of him to Jessie Chambers, that 'one ought to be able to dance on a threepenny bit'. Maybe young Jack Holroyd's reluctant admiration for his father's dancing skills reflects something of the feelings of Lawrence and his mother towards the once physically attractive young man with whom Mrs Lawrence, like Mrs Holroyd, fell in love).

When Clara and Laura, an ebullient pair of tipsy females, overflow with Charles Holroyd from the pub, the tenor of the first act changes. Yet Lawrence gives even this odd couple a kind of precarious dignity, tempering the garrulity of their arrival as we glean a little incidental knowledge of the sad lives from which they are seeking escape—Clara being a widow and a pub landlady, as Mrs Holroyd might well have been had she not spurned her guardian–uncle's wish that she should join him behind the bar. Clara's self-defensive remark as she sobers up, 'You know, my husband was a brute to me—an' I was in bed three month after he died', reminds us of what she shares with Mrs Holroyd; and perhaps the memory returns to us—and to her—at the end of the play as she contemplates her future. Holroyd, truculent after the departure of his now dispirited pick-ups, returns to the pub.

The second act, two hours later, sees Blackmore accompanying the incapably drunk Holroyd back home. There is a strained declaration of love over the husband's comatose body, and plans are laid for flight. But in the third act Holroyd's mother arrives to report that he is missing, and in a sequence that is at once dream-like and horribly reminiscent of such moments of delayed realization of one's worst fears, Holroyd's body is brought back home after the pit-fall that has killed him, left alone at the end of his shift. The two women grieve together as they prepare to lay out the corpse.

If, as she declares to Blackmore, her husband's death is 'a judgement on us,' it is—as such judgements in tragedy often are—a matter of the fortuitous collision of events: of Holroyd's death occurring as if it were in response to his wife's decision to leave him, a decision complicated by what is really the only awkward dramatic device in the play, the matter of the money Mrs Holroyd's uncle has conveniently left her. (Shaw called such intrusions 'Scribean', after the French writer who recurrently employed them.) This has evidently not yet cleared probate, and the practical Mrs Holroyd is more concerned than her would-be lover that she should have this little security behind her if she is to leave. Like all Lawrence's strong women in these early plays, whatever the depths of her feelings Mrs Holroyd remains intensely practical.

The force of the play falls precisely between the dramatic resolution it offers and the emotional resolution it denies. The conventions of the time would have had a recovered Holroyd, 'brought to his senses' by his brush with death, climactically reconciled with his wife, the 'other man' removed (perhaps to some self-imposed colonial exile), and the wife recognizing that her duty was to be an understanding spouse rather than a 'new woman'. What actually happens is—in terms of tragedy rather than of such fashionable problem plays—no less conventional, but full of teasing moral ambiguities. What might have happened between Blackmore and Mrs Holroyd but for the physical presence of the inert body separating them in Act Two—a presence so much more forceful on stage than page? After Holroyd's death, what reception awaits Blackmore when he fulfils his promise to 'come tomorrow'? And is Mrs Holroyd doomed by guilt to prove more faithful to the memory of her husband than to his living presence? There are no answers, because there is no reality beyond the boundaries set by the play to deliver them; but Lawrence's craftsmanship in shaping a tragic action which purposefully denies us the comfort of catharsis is masterful.

And it does seem to me that *The Widowing of Mrs Holroyd* is that rare creature, often enough declared extinct, a modern tragedy. For if Holroyd's death is the judgement his wife declares it, it is the judgement not of the Christian God she assumes, but of the cruel gods of classical tragedy—the gods of the underworld where Holroyd meets his death. Neither chronologically nor thematically is it coincidental that the sense of inevitability about this death is reminiscent of J. M. Synge's tragedy in miniature, *Riders to the Sea*, first performed in Dublin in 1904 and published in England in the following year. For Synge was one of those few excluded from Lawrence's contempt for his more prosaic contemporaries—and he described Synge's *Riders to the Sea* as 'about the genuinest bit of dramatic tragedy, English, since Shakespeare'.

The tiny fishing community on the Aran Islands which Synge was portraying shared many characteristics with the tight-knit mining communities of which Lawrence wrote, not least its sense of the omnipresence of death. The Grandmother's lament—'Eh, they'll bring 'im 'ome, I know they will, smashed up an' broke! An' one of my sons they've burned down pit till the flesh dropped off 'im, an' one was shot till 'is shoulder was all of a mosh, an' they brought 'em 'ome to me. An' now there's this' (Act 3, lines 242–6)—is strongly reminiscent of Maurya's for her own lost sons in *Riders*. (Shortly after his mother's death Lawrence recalled his own grandmother's words concerning Jack Holroyd's original: 'Like a blessed smiling babe he looked—he did that.')

It is worth noting that as critics came to declare tragedy a genre that was unviable for the modern age, these two adherents to the form both ignored and overcame (as had Büchner in *Woyzeck*) the alleged impossibility of allowing working-class or peasant characters the dignity of tragic heroism. On a more mundane level (which does nothing to rob either play of its tragic dignity) there is here, too, the peasant concern with both the private necessities and the public face of death, typified in the Grandmother's shock that her daughter-in-law has not got a set of laying-out clothes at the ready—so 'he'll have to have his father's'. And when she returns with the clothes but without the father, who has made dutiful noises but could not be bothered to 'come up', she declares with unconscious irony: 'You don't know what it is to live with a man that has no feeling.' Across that void, the mutual incomprehension of the sexes bridges generations, while across the body of the dead son and husband, the two women reach a shared understanding of the nature of love.

Strangely, the one less than satisfactory feature of the play is the character of the lover, Blackmore, about whom Lawrence seems to care little—though the name suggests dark, hidden depths of emotion that the novelist in him might better have evoked. Yet Mrs Holroyd also appears equivocal towards Blackmore, other than as a means of escape. He seems to stride in as if from another play, then to wander out again, and somehow lacks the stature which even the two tipsy dancers assert. Of all the characters, he is the least integral to the action, other than as a dramatic device to tempt Mrs Holroyd's escape, and the least comfortable within it. Perhaps in a tragedy one just cannot afford to be well-meaning but ordinary.

Bernard Shaw saw the play, and was deeply impressed, declaring that the 'vividly effective dialogue' made his own 'seem archaic in comparison'. And Esmé Percy reported Shaw to have said after the performance, 'Compared with that, my prose is machine-made lace. You can hear the typewriter in it.' Even when Shaw was putting himself down, he did so with the self-satisfaction of his own wit: for all that, there is an honesty in his recognition of Lawrence's dramatic genius which was shared by few others at the time.

The Daughter-in-Law

Although *The Daughter-in-Law* was written in 1913, and sent off to Lawrence's mentor Edward Garnett, it failed to find a producer: indeed, it would have proved as intractable at that time for actors whose regional dialects, if any, would long since have been drilled out of them as for audiences unaccustomed to finding the provincial proletariat a fit subject for drama. When, in 1936, a version of the play reached the stage, it was clearly hoped that it might ride on the rare West End success of a play about working-class life, Walter Greenwood's adaptation of his own novel *Love on the Dole*. Greenwood was duly asked to work over what was then billed as Lawrence's 'unrevised play', which, somewhat melodramatized and retitled *My Son's My Son*, opened under their joint attribution at the Playhouse Theatre in May 1936. But its success was distinctly modest, and the play seems to have attracted no subsequent public notice until it finally reached print in the *Complete Plays* of 1965. Thanks to Peter Gill and the Royal Court, the rest is stage history.

Despite the aspects of class and dialect which made it unacceptable in its time, the play shows Lawrence increasingly confident in his dramatic technique. And the supposed 'difficulty' of the dialogue should not be overstated—as does Sylvia Sklar, in suggesting that 'the "unintelligibility" of the dialect makes us look elsewhere than to the spoken words for meaning. Its very difficulty and obscurity indicate that the words people use are less significant than the thoughts these words mask.' This, I can't help feeling, would be rather more true of the sophisticated deflections of a Noël Coward than the down-the-line exchanges of Mrs Gascoigne and Mrs Purdy. The practical problems faced by actors and director in this play have more to do with pace and emphasis—notably, how to sustain interest in an eponymous character and her husband who do not even appear until a good third of the way into the action, except through reports of their respective misbehaviour—Minnie Gascoigne's ideas beyond her station, ruthlessly derided by her mother-in-law, and Luther's dalliance with Mrs Purdy's daughter, who is now with child and must be provided for. (As Gill found, the need for an abrupt change of setting from mother-in-law's to daughter-in-law's household can also pose scenographic problems.)

Yet the pace of that first scene is masterful. We learn just about as much as we want about Joe Gascoigne and his self-inflicted accident to understand the guarded mother–son relationship, in which Joe evidently enjoys as much and as little independence as serves his needs. Mrs Purdy's arrival then decisively determines the direction of the play, in a way that would certainly have shocked a morally upright audience when it was written; for in conventional dramatic terms, an illegitimate pregnancy betokened imminent banishment or suicide or both. Lawrence's characters, however, display none of the moral repugnance or judgemental repudiation which even the humane Dickens, barely half a century earlier, felt to be the lot of the 'fallen woman'. Here there is displeasure and disappointment, but largely a quiet pragmatism, based on shared assumptions between the mothers that speak of long if casual acquaintance and a sense of what proprieties are and are not required to save face within the community: 'It's neither a cryin' nor a laughin' matter, but it's a matter of a girl wi' child an' a man six week married.' Mrs Gascoigne none the less relishes the probable effects upon her daughter-in-law: 'It'll take her down a peg or two, and, my sirs, she wants it, my sirs, she needs it.'

Minnie has scarcely had time to establish her presence in the second scene—combining her clear physical attraction towards Luther with the familiar despair of such strong Lawrentian women at their husbands' inertial weight—before she has be hustled out of the way for the negotiations with Mrs Purdy. But if the very title of the play defines Minnie Gascoigne as a function of her mother-in-law's perception—which is indeed how that long first scene presents her—the rest of the action shows her struggle to assert her independence, albeit with the Scribean assistance of her uncle's money (for here is another woman who has had a falling out with a pub-keeping guardian, but been remembered in his will). We see Minnie first shaking off her assigned role, then redefining it—not as Mrs Gascoigne's daughter-in-law but as Luther Gascoigne's wife and her own woman.

As for the hapless Luther, he cuts a pathetic figure in pleading mitigation: it 'wor an off-chance' whenever he has been with other women and, despite his thirty years, 'I niver been much wi' anybody.' Yet it is the brotherhood of Luther and Joe that gives us for the first and only time in Lawrence's dramatic work a feeling for the strength of that other fraternity—loyalty to a trade union, now especially needful in the face of military support for the bosses. The brothers display an unquestioning—and in Joe's case at least, not unreasoning—support for the strike, which leads to their overnight disappearance and the successful thwarting of the blacklegs. The last act confrontation between wife and mother as they await Luther's return is reminiscent of that between the two Mrs Holroyds, albeit over a feared rather than an actual death—though the mother manages to persuade herself that pit deaths are a sort of revenge on women: 'They get huffed up, they bend down their faces, and they say to theirselves: "Now I'll get myself hurt, an' she'll be sorry," else: "Now I'll get myself killed, an' she'll ha'e nobody to sleep wi' 'er, an' nobody to nag at",' and she can imagine Luther thinking, 'If I'm killed, then *she* maun lay me out.'

A sort of understanding is reached between the women, and, following the brothers' return and Mrs Gascoigne's departure with Joe, comes a sort of reconciliation between Minnie and Luther. This is none the less poignant for its understatement and its calculated ambiguity. In the earlier plays it is clear that the closely analogous marriages of the Lamberts and the Holroyds were doomed to fail. Both husbands need, in Grandmother Holroyd's term, 'managing' by women readier to make allowances for the sheer daily toil their men undergo, and for their essential ordinariness. They also want a little human kindness—such as old Lambert gets from Gertie Coomber, and such as her little daughter commends to Mrs Holroyd (''Appen if you said something nice to him, mother, he'd happen go to bed, and not shout'). Here, one's sympathies in performance will depend as much on a mix of one's personal politics of sexuality and the choices made by actors and director as on Lawrence's text or subtext; and whether one feels that Minnie and Luther will survive together depends, too, on one's own and the actors' feelings towards Lawrence's mystical belief in the darker reaches of desire, and, if these are shared, how successfully they are conveyed to an audience.

In a letter to Edward Garnett, it is almost certain that it was of *The Daughter-in-Law* that Lawrence wrote, 'It is neither a tragedy nor a comedy—just ordinary.' The truth of this does not make the play better or worse than the indisputably tragic *Widowing of Mrs Holroyd*—just different. What in a 'well-made' play might be condemned as contradictions are here of the essence of the 'ordinary'—ordinariness itself being rather extraordinary in a play written in 1913. For example, no connection is made between Minnie's allegation that Luther has no 'go' and his later demonstration to the contrary: and perhaps none is intended, for neat cause-and-effect connections are here seldom pushed, increasing our sense that the life in the play is being lived, not organized.

The Fight for Barbara

Describing the play as a 'comedy', Lawrence sent *The Fight for Barbara* to Edward Garnett from Italy, where he had completed it in a three-day break from work on the novel that became *Sons and Lovers*. 'Much of it', he wrote to Garnett, 'is word for word true.' Both the speed of composition and the unmediated verisimilitude show through, making this an interesting piece for the autobiographical reasons already discussed, but not an intrinsically satisfying one. Neither, for that matter, is it more than intermittently comic.

In the event, *The Fight for Barbara* remained unstaged and unpublished in Lawrence's lifetime, and first saw print in 1933 in the middlebrow literary magazine *Argosy*, where it was retitled, less dramatically but more accurately, *Keeping Barbara*. For there is no real 'fight', physical or otherwise, in this play: quite apart from our biographical knowledge of who is going to 'keep' Barbara, even her brief flirtation with returning to her husband seems primarily a flirtation with Wesson's feelings: for this is a woman who acts out of passion rather than fleeting pity. Despite this, there is little sense of the open delight in each other's sexuality whence Barbara's preference for Wesson over Tressider derives. Of course the official censorship and theatrical codes would not have permitted much in the way of a physicalized relationship, and this is no *Lady Chatterley's Lover*; but Lawrence finds no alternative means to dramatize or verbalize the intensity of the couple's feelings beyond the bedroom. There are no glimpses of dark sexual desires such as Minnie Gascoigne finds in Luther's lips in his coal-blackened face, nor even the hints of attraction to a well-looking fellow who could 'dance on a halfpenny'. Despite the play's brevity and the residual excitements of the elopement, there is something settled and, well, *married* about these sparring partners.

Even here, as in the 'mining plays', it is the intrusion of mothers and fathers which provides a catalyst for the shifting conflicts and reconciliations. Tressider, Barbara's cast-off husband, seems almost irrelevant, a hanger-on to the coat-tails of his in-laws. (No more than Tressider did Ernest Weekley commit suicide; yet Frieda's hold over him was enduring, for after Lawrence's death the then 65-year-old Weekley asked her to remarry him. She refused, though she did later get married again, to a much younger man.) Yet there is something touching about Tressider's strivings to express, in an emotional realm unfamiliar to him, the pathos of unreciprocated love—even when it is reduced to the bathos of his declaring, 'I would have shed my blood on every paving stone in Bromley for you' (one of the few few genuinely funny lines in the play).

Some of the embarrassments derived from differences in class and manners between Wesson and the visitors are amusing, though they also hint at possible unease to come—at Barbara's incapacity for housekeeping, and at the all-consuming nature of Wesson's desire that threatens to 'swallow' Barbara (as, in an interesting sexual turnaround,

Ernest felt Maggie threatened to do in *A Collier's Friday Night*—though Barbara, one feels, would be a distinctly tougher morsel to digest). There is, too, an undoubted element of class superiority in Barbara's taunting of Wesson for his 'writhing' attempts at *politesse* during her mother's first visit—and some justification for the taunts in the felt gap between his prior avowals of independence and his actual sloping off to bring an unwanted tray of snacks.

For all the doubts about the play, it is important to remember that it was written barely a decade after the almost invariable solution to all drama in which a 'new woman' asserted her independence was a reconciliation to hearth, home, and husband by the fall of the curtain; and even those writers who dared to cross such moral boundaries—notably Ibsen in *A Doll's House* (1879)—did so in full recognition of the force with which society wished to preserve them. (When Henry Arthur Jones offered a version to English audiences in 1884, under the title *Breaking a Butterfly*, he used an alternative ending in which Nora, who in the original leaves her husband, dutifully gives him another chance.) But here the boundaries have already been shamelessly, almost cheerfully overstepped, as a 'given' of the action—indeed, for the two main characters such boundaries barely exist, for they are concerned with emotional loyalties, not societal expectations, though they are wryly aware that they constitute a 'scandal' in the eyes of others. (It is a nice touch that, when Barbara is talking of leaving Wesson, and he does not wish her to go to a hotel where she is known to the landlady, this is clearly out of concern for his own self-esteem, not to keep up moral proprieties.)

Even the reactions of the parents and the 'injured husband' seem morally transitional (in socio-theatrical rather than biographical terms). Far from the outright disavowal of an adulterous daughter and wife, there is proffered forgiveness and the best that can be done to 'hush up' the scandal, if only Barbara will return. And as Barbara briefly hesitates between her men, even Lady Charlcote recommends that she'd 'better stick to the one you can live with, and not to the one you can do without.' Of course, this is partly self-defensive on the part of Lawrence as author and seducer of another man's wife; but it is also reasonably consistent with the character of Lady Charlcote as we have it—altogether brisker and more down-to-earth than her husband's or son-in-law's. Yet the play's interestingly transitional morality never quite meshes with the more traditional nature of its comedy, which has Barbara and Wesson conversing in a highly mannered style in their togetherness no less than Barbara and Tressider, more understandably, do in their separation. 'Word for word true', maybe, but surely not feeling for feeling.

Touch and Go

Touch and Go reached print more speedily than any other of Lawrence's plays—written in 1918, his first play for five years, it was published two years later, the second in a series conceived by the left-wing writer Douglas Goldring of 'Plays for a People's Theatre'. That it was not the first, as originally intended, was probably due to Goldring's recognition that the play itself was not very left-wing, nor did its Preface suggest that Lawrence had much sympathy for a 'people's theatre'.

The Preface is a curious and really rather reactionary document, quite apart from its pointless quibbling over the definition of a 'people's theatre'. Written as the play was in the economic aftermath of the First World War, its assertion that 'The proletariat isn't poor. Everybody is poor except Capital and Labour', either displays unforgivable ignorance of social realities, or have a meaning entirely personal to Lawrence which is never made clear. His image of Capital and Labour as bejowled bulldog and dissatisfied mongrel scrapping over a bone is so obviously reductive that he quickly abandons it in favour of Labour wanting its 'pound of flesh'—the implication being that, once this is taken, the victim will bleed to death. He then limps sideways into a new metaphor, of a squabble over a ship which each party would scuttle to spite the other. The level of ideology and imagery alike are reminiscent of a *Punch* political cartoon of the period—incomprehensibly simplistic for a writer of Lawrence's background and sensitivity.

His attempt at a definition of tragedy—'the working out of some immediate passional problem within the soul of man'—might be worth debating if it had any relevance to the play which follows; but it is scarcely exemplified by Gerald's assertion that his hatred is 'a cleansing process—like Aristotle's Katharsis'. Whatever this displays of Gerald's knowledge of Aristotle, it shows very little knowledge of himself; and by the end of the play hatred has been shown on both sides to be a very dirtying process indeed.

If we did not know better, we might believe from its structure that *Touch and Go* was among the first of Lawrence's plays rather than among the last. Its muddling of novelish characters and dramatic materials shows him unlearning a great deal that he had previously seemed to grasp instinctively. Or perhaps he was setting out to produce a commercially successful play about middle-class people with middle-class romantic entanglements and motor cars—though this would make it all the more ironic that he was ostensibly writing for a 'people's theatre'. Indeed, given the kind of naturalistic staging on which the play seems to be predicated, the requirement for a working motor car on stage scarcely seems to justify the problems it would cause; and while the casual call for 'bicycles to sweep past' for a few seconds in the third act might prove less expensive for the props department, it would not be much less stressful to put into practice.

Anachronistically, such demands would seem more appropriate to a television script—and the shifts of focus from private to public in the market-place scenes also seem filmic rather than theatrical. They are typical, too, of the problems that the play fails to resolve—between its presentation of the 'public' conflict between pitmen and bosses and the 'private' conflict between Anabel and Gerald (not to mention Oliver's ambiguous relationship with them both); and, within the family, of the generational conflict between Gerald, his garrulously impotent father, and his demented mother—whose 'black fate' reminds me irreverently of the matriarch in Stella Gibbons's *Cold Comfort Farm* (1932), holding a family to ransom with memories of 'something nasty in the woodshed'.

As Raymond Williams pointed out in *Culture and Society* (1958), it is important to remember that Lawrence was not observing the mining industry from afar, but had himself been caught up in it: 'It is only by hard fighting, and, further, by the fortune of fighting on a favourable front, that anyone born into the industrial working class escapes his function of replacement.' What Lawrence seemed unable to sustain was a commitment to those less able and less lucky than himself, as he became increasingly contemptuous of the class whence he sprang.

One of the problems with the play is its inexplicit but none the less pervasive identification of industrialism and materialism, a theme more fully expanded in Lawrence's essay on 'Democracy' (unpublished until 1936). Here, he argues that the workers have become as habituated to the ugliness imposed upon them as 'the moneyed classes and promoters of industry' who have condemned them to it. He rejects political 'solutions' which appear rooted not in a desire to restore the 'human intuitive faculty' but in mere envy of material wealth—the 'forcing of all human energy into a competition of mere acquisition'.

This is the *reductio ad absurdum* of the political thinking behind *Touch and Go*, which ideologically is pivoted between the early Lawrence who respected an individualism based on the recognition of material needs, and the later Lawrence, flirting with fascistic calls for submission to the leadership of 'superior' beings. Whatever we feel politically or emotionally about the Barlow family and its acolytes, it is not only from the retrospect of a new millennium that we recognize their decadence—as Chekhov had already recognized the decadence of the class about which he wrote. But Lawrence seems to present the Barlows as a class destined, for better or worse, to rule in perpetuity—or to fall to the forces of Labour no less dedicated to the impoverishment of the human spirit.

Any more complex dialectic is thwarted not only by the sheer eccentricity of the bosses' representatives, but by the lack of coherent opposition to their viewpoint. For the workers are barely more than glimpsed: even the clerks, as they mumble their embarrassed obeisances to Gerald and Anabel, are permitted more articulacy than the colliers, who merely heckle, threaten, and eventually act as an undifferentiated mob—these, the men whose voices and idiom Lawrence best knew and remembered of all those he portrays. The self-regardingly distant Willie Houghton, despite our knowledge that his original was indeed a soap-box orator, here becomes a lone voice who begins to despair of his own sanity in the industrial wilderness. And Job Arthur Freer is ultimately presented as a rabble-rousing opportunist, moved more by Gerald's insults than his own beliefs, though his earlier apparent duplicity could also be interpreted as the necessary tactics of compromise.

As for the minor characters, Anabel, though supposedly 'artistic', is not much more than a sounding-board for others, activating or initiating nothing; while Oliver belies his facade of vague benignity with his nostalgia for the lock-out—as 'lively and gay' as a fox-hunt. What the play *says*, in the end, is said through Oliver—that there must be a 'better way', a scarcely startling revelation which gets nobody anywhere. But what it *shows*, in the end, is that Capital, as embodied by Gerald—a calculating boor lacking in self-control—is ruthless in pushing its own interests, while Labour, a dissonant chorus of nameless voices, can be easily manipulated and turned to violence by ideologues and rogues.

But ultimately the problem with *Touch and Go* lies in its umbilical connection with *Women in Love*, and the density of raw material in Lawrence's head that he draws on for the play. If there is a more recent analogue to *Touch and Go*, it is with such a play as John Whiting's *Saint's Day* (1951)—another piece in which a past of personal and societal conflict broods over an action that is contingent on so much that is uncertain and unspoken, unknown and (in the context offered by the dramatist) unknowable. Yet where *Saint's Day* resonates with its multiple ambiguities and richness of texture, too often *Touch and Go* only irritates and puzzles.

NOTE ON THE TEXTS

D. H. Lawrence lived during the first great age of 'Collected Plays'. The likes of Shaw, Galsworthy, J. M. Barrie, Stanley Houghton, and St John Hankin all saw their plays raised from the indignity of the functional acting editions which was all most Victorian dramatists achieved to the high literary status to which Ben Jonson laid claim in the edition of his own plays published in 1616, and which Heminge and Condell claimed on Shakespeare's behalf when they assembled the First Folio of 1623.

But where most of Lawrence's contemporary dramatists followed in Jonson's footsteps and either oversaw (scrupulously in Shaw's case) or at least authorized the publication of their work, Lawrence comes closer to Shakespeare, in having won only posthumous recognition for much of his dramatic output, just three of his plays having been published in his lifetime. The original manuscript of *The Widowing of Mrs Holroyd* has not survived, so the extent to which Lawrence revised it for publication in 1914 is uncertain, though in later life he talked of having rewritten the play 'almost entirely on the proofs'. This edition has become by default the 'copy text', used for all later editions of the play. Of the other plays published in his lifetime, it is unlikely that Lawrence saw proofs of *Touch and Go* (1920), while *David* (1926) is not included in this collection.

In choosing a copy text for the remainder of Lawrence's dramatic canon, editors are left disputing alternative kinds of authority. *Had* the manuscript of *Mrs Holroyd* survived, and *had* the play been performed before publication, and *had* Lawrence made further corrections to the printed text, which version should be preferred? The play as Lawrence laid down his pen? The performance script as hacked about and revised in rehearsal—as almost all new plays are? Or the version further tidied up, 'improved', and house-styled for publication?

The debate over such conflicting kinds of 'authority' rages, and becomes the more relevant to this 'Note' because the editors of the Cambridge Edition of *The Plays*—published late in 1999, when this collection was already at an advanced stage of preparation—have done valiant scholarly work in retrieving and collating available manuscripts, and the various typescripts made from them by agents and secretaries, which they regard as having an authority superior to that of the only previous edition of the *Complete Plays*, published by Heinemann in 1964.

However, it was either in this edition or in the misleadingly titled *Plays of D. H. Lawrence*—which included only *Mrs Holroyd*, *Touch and Go*, and *David*—published earlier by Heinemann, in 1934, that Peter Gill, in effectively discovering D. H. Lawrence for the live theatre, first read the plays; and these were the editions he used for his productions during the 1960s. Accordingly, they have the authority of stage performance, as also does the version of *The Fight for Barbara* used for the *Complete Plays*, which reprints the text first published in *Argosy* in 1933. The Cambridge editors prefer the manuscript text of 1912, noting that Lawrence's agents expressed surprise when they saw that the play had been published under the title *Keeping Barbara*, and deduce that 'it can be assumed that the cuts had also not been agreed'. But one might deduce precisely the opposite: if there was concern over a mere change of title, would not anger at substantive cuts also have been made explicit?

Simply, we do not know whether the typescripts made by the agents for publication in *Argosy*, which have not survived, incorporated cuts or other changes made by Lawrence. And whether the shorter or longer version of this rather inchoate play is the better is a matter for argument. I have chosen to retain the shorter version here, in part to put into print the evidence for that argument, in part because the choice is in line with my decision elsewhere to include the versions of the plays which have actually been staged. This is partly, again, so that alternative versions may remain available—but also in the belief that the authority of the theatrical performance does in general supersede that of the author's immaculate conception, unmidwived by actors and directors, whose wisdom in these matters most dramatists readily acknowledge. The *Complete Works* of 1964 has therefore been used as copy text, with some corrections of evident misprints or mistranscriptions—a number of the latter brought to my attention by the Cambridge editors, to whom my grateful acknowledgements.

In addition to having edited texts of many plays from the sixteenth through the twentieth centuries over the past thirty years, I also earn a fair proportion of my present living from transforming living authors' typescripts or disks into typeset text, so am well aware of all the accidental and deliberate changes that take place when texts are undergoing continuous revision between conception and opening night. When the texts have been transmitted as accidentally and haphazardly as those of D. H. Lawrence—or Shakespeare—many more complications abound, but should not too much concern or depress us. Lawrence, much more than Shakespeare, would simply have wished to have seen his plays in print, and thankfully a choice of editions now accords them that dignity.

SELECT BIBLIOGRAPHY

The texts of Lawrence's complete dramatic output are to be found in Hans-Wilhelm Schwarze and John Worthen (eds.), *The Plays*, in 'The Cambridge Edition of the Works of D. H. Lawrence' (Cambridge: Cambridge University Press, 1999). This valuably annotated scholarly edition, though priced beyond the reach of all but the most dedicated student, should be available in institutional libraries, along with the earlier volumes of the same edition, which include seven volumes of *The Letters of D. H. Lawrence*, edited by James T. Boulton *et al.* (1979–93). However, for the novels, poems, and better known non-fictional writing, the full range of inexpensive Penguin editions will serve most purposes.

For the period during which Lawrence's 'mining plays' were written, John Worthen's *D. H. Lawrence: the Early Years, 1885–1912* (Cambridge: Cambridge University Press, 1991) is especially valuable, while Keith Sagar's *D. H. Lawrence: Life into Art* (Harmondsworth: Penguin, 1985), despite its larger scope, pays fuller attention to the plays than most other biographies. Of these, Harry T. Moore's *The Intelligent Heart* (London: Heinemann, 1955) was for long the 'standard' life. Jessie Chambers, writing as 'E.T.', published her own reminiscences in *D. H. Lawrence: a Personal Record* (London: Cape, 1935), as did Frieda Lawrence in *Not I, But the Wind* (Santa Fe: Rydal Press, 1934). Edward Nehls (ed.), *D. H. Lawrence: a Composite Biography* (Madison: University of Wisconsin Press, 1957–9) assembles in three volumes an intriguing collage of Lawrence's life.

While there is a prolific (almost overwhelming) secondary literature dealing with Lawrence's novels, there is a relative dearth of critical writing about the plays. Sylvia Sklar's *The Plays of D. H. Lawrence: a Biographical and Critical Study* (London: Vision Press, 1975) is, valiantly, still the only full-length study; while Arthur E. Waterman's 'The Plays of D. H. Lawrence', in *D. H. Lawrence: a Collection of Critical Essays* (Englewood Cliffs, N. J.: Prentice-Hall, 1963) has been influential from its anthologizing in 'casebook' format. The section on *The Widowing of Mrs Holroyd* in Raymond Williams, *Drama from Ibsen to Brecht* (London: Chatto and Windus, 1968) and his 'Introduction' to *Three Plays by D. H. Lawrence* (Harmondsworth: Penguin, 1969) are still well worth seeking out.

Two useful reference works are Warren Roberts, *A Bibliography of D. H. Lawrence* (Cambridge: Cambridge University Press, second ed., 1982), and Keith Sagar (ed.), *A D. H. Lawrence Handbook* (Manchester: Manchester University Press, 1982). Charles A. Carpenter's *Modern Drama Scholarship and Criticism, 1966–1980* (Toronto: University of Toronto Press, 1986), which has been annually updated since 1981 in the Summer issues of the scholarly journal *Modern Drama*, helps to sift the (still scanty) materials on Lawrence's plays from the massive output of other material on the writer.

A CHRONOLOGY OF D. H. LAWRENCE

1885   David Herbert Lawrence born at Eastwood, Nottingham, 11 September.

1898   Attends Nottingham High School on a scholarship, until 1901.

1901   First attack of pneumonia, shortly after beginning a factory job.

1902   Attended University College, Nottingham, as pupil-teacher, until 1908.

1908   Began to teach at Davidson Road School, Croydon.

1909   Five poems published in the *English Review*, and *A Collier's Friday Night* and *The Widowing of Mrs Holroyd* completed.

1910   *The Merry-Go-Round* written. Death of his mother (December).

1911   Publication of his first novel, *The White Peacock*. Meets Edward Garnett. Further attack of pneumonia (November).

1912   Resigns his teaching job (February). Meets Frieda Weekley in March, and they elope to Germany in May. *The Married Man* written and the novel *The Trespasser* published. Settles with Frieda near Lago di Garda, Italy. Writes *The Fight for Barbara* and completes *The Daughter-in-Law*.

1913   Publication of the autobiographical novel, *Sons and Lovers*.

1914   Publication of *The Widowing of Mrs Holroyd*. Marriage to Frieda (July). Outbreak of First World War (August).

1915   Settles in Cornwall. Publication of *The Rainbow* banned by court order.

1917   Unsettled after enforced departure from Cornwall.

1918   Writes *Touch and Go* and publishes *New Poems*. End of First World War.

1919   Returns to Italy.

1920   Private publication of *Women in Love*. The novel *The Lost Girl* published.

1921   Published *Psychoanalysis and the Unconscious*, and the travel book, *Sea and Sardinia*.

1922   Visits Ceylon and Australia. Settles in New Mexico (September, to March 1923). The novel *Aaron's Rod* and the collection of short stories *England, My England* published.

1923   Publishes the critical *Studies in Classic American Literature*, the novel *Kangaroo*, and the book of verses, *Birds, Beasts, and Flowers*. Travelling widely in America and Europe.

1925   Completes his last play, *David*. Travelling in England and Italy until 1928.

1926   Publishes the novel *The Plumed Serpent*. *David* performed in New York, and three performances of *The Widowing of Mrs Holroyd* in London.

1927   *David* performed in London. *Mornings in Mexico* published.

1928   Travelling in Switzerland and France. *Collected Poems* published, and private publication in Florence of the novel *Lady Chatterley's Lover*.

1929   Police raid an exhibition of his paintings in London. Manuscript of his book of verse *Pansies* seized in the post, but subsequently published.

1930   Dies in France, 2 March.

A COLLIER'S FRIDAY NIGHT

CHARACTERS

MRS LAMBERT
LAMBERT
NELLIE LAMBERT
ERNEST LAMBERT
MAGGIE PEARSON
GERTIE COOMBER
BEATRICE WYLD
BARKER
CARLIN

The action of the play takes place in the kitchen of the Lamberts' house

Act 1

*The kitchen or living-room of a working-man's house. At the back
the fireplace, with a large fire burning. On the left, on the oven
side of the stove,° a woman of some fifty-five years sits in a wooden
rocking-chair, reading. Behind her and above her, in the recess
made by the fireplace, four shelves of books, the shelf-covers being
of green serge, with woollen ball fringe, and the books being ill-
assorted school books, with an edition of Lessing, florid in green
and gilt,° but tarnished. On the left, a window looking on a garden
where the rain is dripping through the first twilight. Under the
window, a sofa, the bed covered with red chintz. By the side of the
window, on the wall near the ceiling, a quiver clothes-horse is
outspread with the cotton articles which have been ironed, hanging
to air. Under the outspread clothes is the door which communicates
with the scullery and with the yard. On the right side of the
fireplace, in the recess equivalent to that where the bookshelves
stand, a long narrow window, and below it, a low, brown, fixed
cupboard, whose top forms a little sideboard, on which stand a
large black enamel box of oil-colours, and a similar japanned
box of water-colours, with Reeve's silver trade-mark.° There is
also on the cupboard top a tall glass jar containing ragged pink
chrysanthemums. On the right is a bookcase upon a chest of
drawers. This piece of furniture is of stained polished wood in
imitation of mahogany. The upper case is full of books, seen
through the two flimsy glass doors: a large set of the* World's
Famous Literature° *in dark green at the top—then on the next
shelf prize-books in calf and gold, and imitation soft leather
poetry- books, and a Nuttall's dictionary° and Cassell's French,
German and Latin dictionaries. On each side of the bookcase are
prints from water-colours, large, pleasing and well framed in oak.
Between the little brown cupboard and the bookcase, an arm-chair,
small, round, with many little staves; a comfortable chair such as
is seen in many working-class kitchens; it has a red chintz cushion.
There is another Windsor chair° on the other side of the bookcase.
Over the mantelpiece, which is high, with brass candlesticks and
two 'Coronation' tumblers in enamel, hangs a picture of Venice,
from one of Stead's Christmas Numbers°—nevertheless,
satisfactory enough.*

*The woman in the rocking-chair is dressed in black, and wears a
black sateen apron. She wears spectacles, and is reading* The
New Age.° *Now and again she looks over her paper at a piece of* 40
*bread which stands on a hanging bar before the fire, propped up
by a fork, toasting. There is a little pile of toast on a plate on the
boiler hob beside a large saucepan; the kettle and a brown teapot
are occupying the oven-top near the woman. The table is laid for
tea, with four large breakfast-cups in dark-blue willow-pattern,* 45
*and plates similar. It is an oval mahogany table, large enough
to seat eight comfortably. The woman sees the piece of bread
smoking, and takes it from the fire. She butters it and places it on
the plate on the hob, after which she looks out of the window, then,
taking her paper, sits down again in her place.* 50
*Someone passes the long narrow window, only the head being seen,
then quite close to the large window on the left. There is a noise as
the outer door opens and is shut, then the kitchen door opens, and a
girl enters. She is tall and thin, and wears a long grey coat and a
large blue hat, quite plain. After glancing at the table, she crosses* 55
*the room, drops her two exercise-books on the wooden chair by the
bookcase, saying*

NELLIE LAMBERT Oh! I am weary.

MOTHER You are late.

NELLIE I know I am. It's Agatha Karton—she is a great gaby.° There's 60
always something wrong with her register,° and old Tommy gets in
such a fever, the great kid.

> *She takes off her hat, and going to the door on right, stands in the
> doorway, hanging it up with her coat on the pegs in the passage,
> just by the doorway* 65

And I'm sure the youngsters have been regular little demons; I could
have killed them.

MOTHER I've no doubt they felt the same towards you, poor little
wretches.

NELLIE (*with a short laugh*) I'll bet they did, for I spanked one or two of 70
'em well.

MOTHER Trust you, trust you! You'll be getting the mothers if you're
not careful.

NELLIE (*contemptuously*) I had one old cat this afternoon. But I told her
straight. I said: 'If your Johnny, or Sammy, or whatever he is, is a 75
nuisance, he'll be smacked, and there's an end of it.' She was mad, but
I told her straight; I didn't care. She can go to Tommy if she likes:
I know he'll fuss her round, but I'll tell *him* too. Pah! he fusses the
creatures up!—I *would!*

She comes towards the table, pushing up her hair with her fingers.   80
It is heavy and brown, and has been flattened by her hat. She
glances at herself in the little square mirror which hangs from a nail
under the right end of the mantelpiece, a mere unconscious glance
which betrays no feeling, and is just enough to make her negligently
touch her hair again. She turns a trifle fretfully to the table   85

NELLIE Is there only potted meat?° You know I can't bear it.

MOTHER (*conciliatorily*) Why, I thought you'd like it, a raw day like
this—and with toast.

NELLIE You know I don't. Why didn't you get some fruit?—a little tin
of apricots—   90

MOTHER I thought you'd be sick of apricots—I know Ernest is.

NELLIE Well, I'm not—you know I'm not. Pappy potted meat!
She sits down on the sofa wearily. Her Mother pours out two cups
of tea, and replaces the pot on the hob

MOTHER Won't you have some, then?   95

NELLIE (*petulantly*) No, I don't want it.
The Mother stands irresolute a moment, then she goes out. Nellie
reaches over to the bookshelves and takes a copy of The Scarlet
Pimpernel,° *which she opens on the table, and reads, sipping her*
tea but not eating. In a moment or two she glances up, as the   100
Mother passes the window and enters the scullery. There is the
sound of the opening of a tin

NELLIE Have you fetched some?—Oh, you are a sweetling!
The Mother enters, with a little glass dish of small tinned apricots.
They begin tea   105

MOTHER Polly Goddard says her young man got hurt in the pit this
morning.

NELLIE Oh—is it much? (*She looks up from her book*)

MOTHER One of his feet crushed. Poor Polly's very sad. What made her
tell me was Ben Goddard going by. I didn't know he was at work   110
again, but he was just coming home, and I asked her about him, and
then she went on to tell me of her young man. They're all coming
home from Selson,° so I expect your father won't be long.

NELLIE Goodness!—I hope he'll let us get our tea first.

MOTHER Well, you were late. If he once gets seated in the Miner's Arms   115
there's no telling when he comes.

NELLIE I don't care when he does, so long as he doesn't come yet.

MOTHER Oh, it's all very well!
They both begin to read as they eat. After a moment another girl
runs past the window and enters. She is a plump, fair girl, pink   120
and white. She has just run across from the next house

5

GERTIE COOMBER Hello, my duck, and how are you?

NELLIE (*looking up*) Oh, alright, my bird.

GERTIE Friday to-night. No Eddie for you! Oh, poor Nellie! Aren't
I glad, though! (*She snaps her fingers quaintly*)   125
    The Mother laughs

NELLIE Mean cat!

GERTIE (*giggling*) No, I'm not a mean cat. But I like Friday night; we can
go jinking off up town and wink at the boys. I like market night. (*She
puts her head on one side in a peculiar, quaint, simple fashion*)   130
    The Mother laughs

NELLIE *You* wink! If she so much as sees a fellow who'd speak to her, she
gets behind me and stands on one foot and then another.

GERTIE I don't! No, I don't, Nellie Lambert. I go like this: 'Oh, good
evening, *how* are you? I'm sure I'm very pleased.' (*She says this in a*   135
*very quaint 'prunes-and-prisms' manner,° with her chin in the air and her
hand extended. At the end she giggles*)
    The Mother, with her cup in her hand, leans back and laughs.
    Nellie, amused in spite of herself, smiles shortly

NELLIE You are a daft object! What about last week, when David   140
Thompson—
    Gertie puts her hand up and flips the air with affected contempt

GERTIE David Thompson! A bacon sawyer!° Ph!

NELLIE You brazen madam! He's as good as you. And then Johnny
Grocock.   145

GERTIE What a name! Not likely. Mrs Grocock! (*She giggles*) Oh dear
no, nothing short of Mrs Carooso.° (*She holds back the skirts of her long
pinafore with one hand and affects the Gibson bend°*)

MOTHER (*laughing heartily*) Caruso! Caruso! A great fat fellow—!

GERTIE Besides, a collier! I'm not going to wash stinking pit-things.   150

NELLIE You don't know what you'll do yet, my girl. I never knew such
cheek! I should think you want somebody grand, you do.

GERTIE I do that. Somebody who'll say, 'Yes, dear. Oh *yes*, dear! Certainly, certainly!'
    She simpers across the room, then giggles   155

NELLIE You soft cat, you! But look here, Gert, you'll get paid out,
treating Bernard Hufton as you do.

GERTIE (*suddenly irritated*) Oh, I can't abide him. I always feel as if I
could smack his face. He thinks himself slikey.° He always makes my—
    A head passes the narrow side window   160
Oh, glory! there's Mr Lambert. I'm off!
    *She draws back against the bookcase. A man passes the large
    window. The door opens and he enters. He is a man of middling*

stature, a miner, black from the pit. His shoulders are pushed up
because he is cold. He has a bushy iron-grey beard. He takes from   165
his pocket a tin bottle and a knotted 'snap' bag—his food bag of
dirty calico—and puts them with a bang on the table. Then he
drags his heavily-shod feet to the door on right; he limps slightly,
one leg being shorter than the other. He hangs up his coat and cap
in the passage and comes back into the living-room. No one speaks.   170
He wears a grey-and-black neckerchief and, being coatless, his
black arms are bare to the elbows, where end the loose dirty sleeves
of his flannel singlet. The Mother rises and goes to the scullery,
carrying the heavy saucepan. The man gets hold of the table and
pulls it nearer the fire, away from his daughter   175

NELLIE Why can't you leave the table where it was! We don't *want* it
stuck on top of the fire.

FATHER Ah dun, if you dunna.°
He drags up his arm-chair and sits down at the table full in front
of the fire   180
'An yer got a drink for me?
The Mother comes and pours out a cup of tea, then goes back to
the scullery
It's a nice thing as a man as comes home from th' pit parched up canna
ha'e a drink got 'im. (*He speaks disagreeably*)   185

MOTHER Oh, you needn't begin! I know you've been stopping, drinking.

FATHER Dun yer?—Well, yer know too much, then. You wiser than
them as knows, you are!
There is a general silence, as if the three listeners were shrugging
their shoulders in contempt and anger. The Father pours out his   190
tea into his saucer, blows it and sucks it up. Nellie looks up from
her book and glowers at him with ferocity. Gertie puts her hand
before her mouth and giggles behind his back at the noise. He does
not drink much, but sets the cup back in the saucer and lays his
grimed arms wearily along the table. The Mother enters with a   195
plate of cabbage

MOTHER Here, that's a clean cloth.
She does not speak unkindly

FATHER (*brutally*) You should put a dotty 'un° on, then.
The Mother takes a newspaper and spreads it over the cloth before   200
him. She kneels at the oven, takes out a stew-jar, and puts meat
and gravy on the plate with the cabbage, and sets it before him.
He does not begin at once to eat. The Mother puts back her chair
against the wall and sits down

MOTHER Are your trousers wet?   205

7

FATHER (*as he eats*) A bit.

MOTHER Then why don't you take them off?

FATHER (*in a tone of brutal authority*) Fetch my breeches an' wa's'coat down, Nellie.

NELLIE (*continuing to read, her hands pushed in among her hair*) You can 210
ask me properly.

> *The Father pushes his beard forward and glares at her with futile*
> *ferocity. She reads on. Gertie Coomber, at the back, shifts from*
> *one foot to the other, then coughs behind her hand as if she had a*
> *little cold. The Mother rises and goes out by door on right* 215

FATHER You lazy, idle bitch, you let your mother go!

NELLIE (*shrugging her shoulders*) You can shut up. (*She speaks with cold contempt*)

> *Gertie sighs audibly. The tension of the scene will not let her run*
> *home. Nellie looks up, flushed, carefully avoiding her Father* 220

NELLIE Aren't you going to sit down, Gert?

GERTIE No, I'm off.

NELLIE Wait a bit and I'll come across with you. I don't want to stop *here*.

> *The Father stirs in his chair with rage at the implication. The* 225
> *Mother comes downstairs and enters with a pair of black trousers,*
> *from which the braces are trailing, and a black waistcoat lined*
> *with cream and red lining. She drops them against her husband's*
> *chair*

MOTHER (*kindly, trying to restore the atmosphere*) Aren't you going to sit 230
down, Gertie? Go on the stool.

> *Gertie takes a small stool on the right side of fireplace, and sits*
> *toying with the bright brass tap of the boiler. The Mother goes out*
> *again on right, and enters immediately with five bread tins and a*
> *piece of lard paper.° She stands on the hearthrug greasing the tins.* 235
> *The Father kicks off his great boots and stands warming his*
> *trousers before the fire, turning them and warming them*
> *thoroughly*

GERTIE Are they cold, Mr Lambert?

FATHER They are that! Look you, they steaming like a sweating hoss.° 240

MOTHER Get away, man! The driest thing in the house would smoke if
you held it in front of the fire like that.

FATHER (*shortly*) Ah, I know I'm a liar. I knowed it to begin wi'.

NELLIE (*much irritated*) Isn't he a nasty-tempered kid!

GERTIE But those front bedrooms are clammy. 245

FATHER (*gratified*) They h'are, Gertie, they h'are.

8

GERTIE (*turning to avoid Nellie's contempt and pottering the fire°*) I know
  the things I bring down from ours, they fair damp in a day.

FATHER They h'are, Gertie, I know it. And I wonder how 'er'd like to
  clap 'er arse into wet breeches.   250

  He goes scrambling off to door on right, trailing his breeches

NELLIE (*fiercely*) Father!

  *Gertie puts her face into her hands and laughs with a half-audible
  laugh that shakes her body*

I can't think what you've got to laugh at, Gertie Coomber.   255

  *The Mother, glancing at her irate daughter, laughs also. She
  moves aside the small wooden rocking-chair, and, drawing forth a
  great panchion° of dough from the corner under the book-shelves,
  begins to fill the bread tins. She sets them on the hearth—which
  has no fender, the day being Friday, when the steel fender is put   260
  away, after having been carefully cleaned to be saved for Saturday
  afternoon. The Father enters, the braces of his trousers dangling,
  and drops the heavy moleskin pit breeches in corner on right*

NELLIE I wonder why you can't put them in the scullery; the smell of
  them's hateful.   265

FATHER You mun° put up wi' it, then. If you were i' th' pit you'd niver
  put your nose up at them again.

  *He sits down and recommences eating. The sound further irritates
  his daughter, who again pushes her fingers into her hair, covering
  her ears with her palms. Her Father notices, and his manners   270
  become coarser. Nellie rises, leaving her book open on the table*

NELLIE Come on, Gert! (*She speaks with contemptuous impatience*)

  *The Father watches them go out. He lays his arms along the
  newspaper, wearily*

FATHER I'm too tired ter h'eat.   275

MOTHER (*sniffing, and hardening a little*) I wonder why you always have
  to go and set her off in a tantrum as soon as you come in.

FATHER A cheeky bitch; 'er wants a good slap at th' side o' th' mouth!

MOTHER (*incensed*) If you've no more sense than that, I don't wonder—

FATHER You don't wonder—you don't wonder! No, I know you don't   280
  wonder. It's you as eggs 'em on against me, both on 'em.

MOTHER (*scornfully*) You set them against yourself. You do your best
  for it, every time they come in.

FATHER Do I, do I! I set 'em against me, do I? I'm going to stand 'em
  orderin' me about, an' turnin' their noses up, am I?   285

MOTHER You shouldn't make them turn their noses up, then. If you do
  your best for it, what do you expect?

9

FATHER A jumped-up monkey! An' it's you as 'as made 'em like it, the pair on 'em. There's neither of 'em but what treats me like a dog. I'm not daft! I'm not blind! I can see it.   290

MOTHER If you're so clever at seeing it, I should have thought you'd have sense enough not to begin it and carry it on as you do.

FATHER Me begin it! When do I begin it? You niver hear me say a word to 'em, till they've snapped at me as if I was a—as if I was a—No, it's you as puts 'em on in. It's you, you blasted—   295

> *He bangs the table with his fist. The Mother puts the bread in the oven, from which she takes a rice pudding; then she sits down to read. He glares across the table, then goes on eating. After a little while he pushes the plate from him. The Mother affects not to notice for a moment*   300

'An yer got any puddin'?

MOTHER Have you finished?

> *She rises, takes a plate and, crouching on the hearth, gives him his pudding. She glances at the clock, and clears the tea-things from her daughter's place. She puts another piece of toast down, there   305
> remaining only two pieces on the plate*

FATHER (*looking at the rice pudding*) Is this what you'n had?

MOTHER No; we had nothing.

FATHER No, I'll bet you non 'ad this baby pap.

MOTHER No, I had nothing for a change, and Nellie took her dinner.   310

FATHER (*eating unwillingly*) Is there no other puddin' as you could 'a made?

MOTHER Goodness, man, are you so mightily particular about your belly? This is the first rice pudding you've had for goodness knows how long, and—No, I couldn't make any other. In the first place, it's   315
Friday, and in the second, I'd nothing to make it with.

FATHER You wouldna ha'e, not for me. But if you 'a wanted—

MOTHER (*interrupting*) You needn't say any more. The fact of the matter is, somebody's put you out at the pit, and you come home to vent your spleen on us.   320

FATHER (*shouting*) You're a liar, you're a liar! A man comes home after a hard day's work to folks as 'as never a word to say to 'im, as shuts up the minute 'e enters the house, as 'ates the sight of 'im as soon as 'e comes in th' room—!

MOTHER (*with fierceness*) We've had quite enough, we've had quite   325
enough! Our Ernest'll be in in a minute and we're not going to have this row going on; he's coming home all the way from Derby, trailing from college to a house like this, tired out with study and all this journey: we're not going to have it, I tell you.

Her husband stares at her dumbly, betwixt anger and shame and   330
sorrow, of which an undignified rage is predominant. The Mother
carries out some pots to the scullery, re-enters, takes the slice of
toast and butters it

FATHER It's about time as we had a light on it; I canna see what I'm eatin'.
The Mother puts down the toast on the hob, and having fetched   335
a dustpan from the scullery, goes out on right to the cellar to turn
on the gas and to bring coals. She is heard coming up the steps
heavily. She mends the fire, and then lights the gas at a brass
pendant hanging over the table. Directly after there enters a
young man of twenty-one, tall and broad, pale, clean-shaven,   340
with the brownish hair of the 'ginger' class, which is all ruffled
when he has taken off his cap, after having pulled various books
from his pockets and put them on the little cupboard top. He takes
off his coat at door right as his sister has done

ERNEST (*blowing slightly through pursed lips*) Phew! It is hot in here!   345
FATHER (*bluntly, but amiably*) Hot! It's non hot! I could do wi' it ten
  times hotter.
MOTHER Oh, you! You've got, as I've always said, a hide like a hippo-
  potamus. You ought to have been a salamander.
FATHER Oh ah, I know tha'll ha'e summat ter say.   350
MOTHER Is it raining now, Ernest?
ERNEST Just a drizzle in the air, like a thick mist.
MOTHER Ay, isn't it sickening? You'd better take your boots off.
ERNEST (*sitting in his sister's place on the sofa*) Oh, they're not wet.
MOTHER They must be damp.   355
ERNEST No, they're not. There's a pavement all the way. Here, look at
  my rose! One of the girls in Coll. gave it me, and the tan-yard girls
  tried to beg it. They are brazen hussies! 'Gi'e's thy flower. Sorry;
  gi'e's thy buttonhole'—and one of them tried to snatch it. They have
  a bobby° down by the tan-yard brook every night now. Their talk   360
  used to be awful, and it's so dark down there, under the trees. Where's
  Nellie?
MOTHER In Coombers'.
ERNEST Give me a bit of my paper, Father. You know the leaf I want:
  that with the reviews of books on.   365
FATHER Nay, I know nowt about reviews o' books. Here t'art. Ta'e it.
Father hands the newspaper to his son, who takes out two leaves
and hands the rest back
ERNEST Here you are; I only want this.
FATHER Nay, I non want it. I mun get me washed. We s'll ha'e th' men   370
  here directly.

ERNEST I say, Mater, another seven-and-six° up your sleeve?

MOTHER I'm sure! And in the middle of the term, too! What's it for *this* time?

ERNEST *Piers the Ploughman*,° that piffle, and two books of Horace:°   375
Quintus Horatius Flaccus, dear old chap.

MOTHER And when have you to pay for them?

ERNEST Well, I've ordered them, and they'll come on Tuesday. I'm sure I don't know what we wanted that *Piers Ploughman* for—it's sheer rot, and old Beasley could have gassed on it without making us buy it,   380
if he'd liked. Yes, I did feel wild. Seven-and-sixpence!

FATHER I should non get 'em, then. You needna buy 'em unless you like. Dunna get 'em, then.

ERNEST Well, I've ordered them.

FATHER If you 'anna the money you canna 'a'e 'em, whether or not.   385

MOTHER Don't talk nonsense. If he has to have them, he has. But the money you have to pay for books, and they're no good when you've done with them!—I'm sure it's really sickening, it is!

ERNEST Oh, never mind, Little;° I s'll get 'em for six shillings. Is it a worry, Mütterchen?°   390

MOTHER It is, but I suppose if it has to be, it has.

ERNEST Old Beasley is an old chough.° While he was lecturing this afternoon Arnold and Hinrich were playing nap;° and the girls always write letters, and I went fast asleep.

FATHER So that's what you go'n to Collige for, is it?   395

ERNEST (*nettled*) No, it isn't. Only old Beasley's such a dry old ass, with his lectures on Burke.° He's a mumbling parson, so what do you expect?

> *The Father grunts, rises and fetches a clean new bucket from the scullery. He hangs this on the top of the boiler, and turns on the*   400
> *water. Then he pulls off his flannel singlet and stands stripped to the waist, watching the hot water dribble into the bucket. The pail half-filled, he goes out to the scullery on left*

Do you know what Professor Staynes said this morning, Mother? He said I'd got an instinct for Latin—and you know he's one of the   405
best fellows in England on the classics: edits Ovid° and whatnot. An instinct for Latin, he said.

MOTHER (*smiling, gratified*) Well, it's a funny thing to have an instinct for.

ERNEST I generally get an alpha plus. That's the highest, you know,   410
Mater. Prof. Staynes generally gives me that.

MOTHER Your grandfather was always fond of dry reading: economics

and history. But I don't know where an instinct for Latin comes
from—not from the Lamberts, that's a certainty. Your Aunt Ellen
would say, from the Vernons.   415

> *She smiles ironically as she rises to pour him another cup of tea,*
> *taking the teapot from the hob and standing it, empty, on the*
> *Father's plate*

ERNEST Who are the Vernons?

MOTHER (*smiling*) It's a wonder your Aunt Ellen or your Aunt Eunice   420
has never told you . . .

ERNEST Well, they haven't. What is it, Mütter?

MOTHER (*sniffing*) A parcel of nonsense . . . .

ERNEST Oh, go on, Ma, you are tantalizing! You hug it like any blessed
girl.   425

MOTHER Yes, your Aunt Ellen always said she would claim the peacock
and thistle° for her crest, if ever . . .

ERNEST (*delighted*) The Peacock and Thistle! It sounds like the name of
a pub.

MOTHER My great-great-grandfather married a Lady Vernon—so they   430
say. As if it made any matter—a mere tale!

ERNEST Is it a fact though, Matoushka?° Why didn't you tell us before?

MOTHER (*sniffing*) What should I repeat such—

FATHER (*shouting from the scullery, whence has come the noise of his*
washing) 'An yer put that towil ter dry?   435

MOTHER (*muttering*) The towel's dry enough.

> *She goes out and is heard taking the roller towel from behind the*
> *outer door. She returns, and stands before the fire, holding the*
> *towel to dry. Ernest Lambert, having frowned and shrugged his*
> *shoulders, is reading*   440

MOTHER I suppose you won't have that bit of rice pudding?

> *Her son looks up, reaches over and takes the brown dish from the*
> *hearth. He begins to eat from the dish*

ERNEST I went to the Savoy to-day.

MOTHER I shouldn't go to that vegetable place. I don't believe there's   445
any substance in it.

ERNEST Substance! Oh, lord! I had an asparagus omelette, I believe they
called it; it was too much for me! A great stodgy thing! But I like the
Savoy, generally. It was—

> *Somebody comes running across the yard. Nellie Lambert enters*   450
> *with a rush*

NELLIE Hello! have you done?

FATHER (*from the scullery*) Are you going to shut that doo-ar! (*Shouting*)

NELLIE (*with a quick shrug of the shoulders*) It *is* shut. (*Brightly, to her brother*) Who brought this rose? It'll just do for me. Who gave it 455
you?—Lois?

ERNEST (*flushing*) What do you want to know for? You're always saying 'Lois'. I don't care a button about Lois.

NELLIE Keep cool, dear boy, keep cool.

> *She goes flying lightly round, clearing the table. The Father, drip-* 460
> *ping, bending forward almost double, comes hurrying from the*
> *scullery to the fire. Nellie whisks by him, her long pinafore rustling*

FATHER (*taking the towel*) 'Ow she goes rushin' about, draughtin'.° (*Rubs his head, sitting on his heels very close to the fire*)

NELLIE (*smiling contemptuously, to herself*) Poor kid! 465

FATHER (*having wiped his face*) An' there isn't another man in th' kingdom as 'ud stan' i' that scullery stark naked. It's like standin' i' t' cowd watter.

MOTHER (*calmly*) Many a man stands in a colder.

FATHER (*shortly*) Ah, I'll back;° I'll back there is! Other men's wives 470
brings th' puncheon on to th' 'earthstone, an' gets the watter for 'em, an' —

MOTHER Other men's wives may do: more fools them: you won't catch me.

FATHER No, you wunna; you may back your life o' that! An' what if you 475
'ad to?

MOTHER Who'd make me?

FATHER (*blustering*) Me.

MOTHER (*laughing shortly*) Not half a dozen such.

> *The Father grunts. Nellie, having cleared the table, pushes him* 480
> *aside a little and lets the crumbs fall into hearth*

FATHER A lazy, idle, stinkin' trick!

> *She whisks the tablecloth away without speaking*

An' tha doesna come waftin' in again when I'm washin' me, tha
remembers. 485

ERNEST (*to his Mother, who is turning the bread*) Fancy! Swinburne's dead.°

MOTHER Yes, so I saw. But he was getting on.

FATHER (*to Nellie, who has come to the boiler and is kneeling, getting a lading-can° full of water*) Here, Nellie, gie my back a wash. 490

> *She goes out, and comes immediately with flannel and soap. She*
> *claps the flannel on his back*

(*Wincing*) Ooo! The nasty bitch!

> *Nellie bubbles with laughter. The Mother turns aside to laugh*

NELLIE   You great baby, afraid of a cold flannel!   495
         She finishes washing his back and goes into the scullery to wash
         the pots. The Father takes his flannel shirt from the bookcase
         cupboard and puts it on, letting it hang over his trousers. Then he
         takes a little blue-striped cotton bag from his pit trousers' pocket
         and throws it on the table to his wife   500
FATHER   Count it. (*He shuffles upstairs*)
         The Mother counts the money, putting it in little piles, checking it
         from two white papers. She leaves it on the table. Ernest goes into
         the scullery to wash his hands and is heard talking to his sister,
         who is wiping the pots. A knock at the outer door   505
ERNEST   Good evening, Mr Barker.
A VOICE Good evenin', Ernest.
         A miner enters: pale, short, but well-made. He has a hard-looking
         head with short black hair. He lays his cap on a chair
         Good evenin', Missis. 'Asn't Carlin come? Mester upstairs?   510
MOTHER   Yes, he'll be down in a minute. I don't expect Mr Carlin will
         be many minutes. Sit down, Mr Barker. How's that lad of yours?
BARKER   Well, 'e seems to be goin' on nicely, thank yer. Dixon took th'
         splints off last wik.
MOTHER   Oh, well, that's better. He'll be alright directly. I should think 515
         he doesn't want to go in the pit again.
BARKER   'E doesna. 'E says 'e shall go farmin' wi' Jakes; but I shanna let
         'im. It's nowt o' a sort o' job, that.
MOTHER   No, it isn't. (*Lowering her voice*) And how's missis?
BARKER   (*also lowering his voice*) Well, I don't know. I want ter get back 520
         as soon as I'n got a few groceries an' stuff in. I sent for Mrs Smalley
         afore I com'n out. An' I'm come an' forgot th' market bag.
MOTHER   (*going into the scullery*) Have mine, have mine. Nay, I've got
         another. (*Brings him a large carpet bag with leather handles*)
BARKER   Thank yer, Missis. I can bring it back next wik. You sure you   525
         wunna want it?
         Another knock. Enter another man, fair, pale, smiling, an
         inconsiderable man
CARLIN   Hgh! Tha's bested° me then? Good evenin', Missis.
BARKER   Yes, I'n bet° thee.   530
         Enter the Father. He has put on a turn-down collar and a black
         tie, and his black waistcoat is buttoned, but he wears no coat. The
         other men take off the large neckerchiefs, grey and white silk, in
         fine check, and show similar collars. The Father assumes a slight
         tone of superiority   535

FATHER Well, you've arrived, then! An' 'ow's the missis by now, Joe?

BARKER Well, I dun know, Walter. It might be any minnit.

FATHER (*sympathetically*) Hu! We may as well set to, then, an' get it done.
        *They sit at the table, on the side of the fire. Ernest Lambert comes
        in and takes an exercise-book from the shelves and begins to do*   540
        algebra, using a text-book. He writes with a fountain-pen

CARLIN They gran' things, them fountain-pens.

BARKER They are that!

CARLIN What's th' mak on it, Ernest?

ERNEST It's an Onoto.°   545

BARKER Oh-ah! An' 'ow *dun* yer fill it? They says as it hold wi' a vacum.

ERNEST It's like this: you push this down, put the nib in th' ink, and
   then pull it out. It's a sort of a pump.

BARKER Um! It's a canny thing, that!

CARLIN It is an' a'.   550

FATHER Yes, it's a very good idea. (*He is slightly condescending*)

MOTHER Look at the bread, Ernest.

ERNEST Alright, Mater.
        *She goes upstairs, it being tacitly understood that she shall not
        know how much money falls to her husband's share as chief 'butty'*°   555
        in the weekly reckoning

BARKER Is it counted?

FATHER Yes. It's alright, Ernest?

ERNEST (*not looking up*) Yes.
        They begin to reckon, first putting aside the wages of their day   560
        *men;° then the Father and Barker take four-and-threepence, as
        equivalent to Carlin's rent, which has been stopped; then the
        Father gives a coin each, dividing the money in that way. It is
        occasionally a puzzling process and needs the Ready Reckoner*°
        from the shelf behind.   565
        End of Act I

Act 2

Scene, as before: the men are just finishing reckoning.
Barker and Carlin, talking in a mutter, put their money in their
pockets. Ernest Lambert is drawing a circle with a pair of
compasses. Carlin rises

CARLIN Well, I might as well be shiftin'.　5

BARKER Ay, I mun get off.

Enter Nellie, who has finished washing the pots, drying her hands
on a small towel. She crosses to the mirror hanging at the right
extremity of the mantelpiece

CARLIN Well, Nellie!　10

NELLIE (*very amiably, even gaily*) Good evening, Mr Carlin. Just off ?

CARLIN Yes—ah mun goo.

BARKER An 'ow's th' instrument by now, Nellie?

NELLIE The instrument? Oh, the piano! Ours is a tinny old thing. Oh,
yes, you're learning. How are you getting on?　15

BARKER Oh, we keep goin' on, like. 'Ave you got any fresh music?

FATHER Ah, I bet 'er 'as. Ow's gerrin' some iv'ry day or tow.°

NELLIE I've got some Grieg°—lovely! Hard, though. It is funny—ever
so funny.

BARKER An' yer iver 'eared that piece 'The Maiden's Prayer'? °　20

NELLIE (*turning aside and laughing*) Yes. Do you like it? It is pretty, isn't
it?

BARKER I 'ad that for my last piece.

NELLIE Did you? Can you play it?

BARKER (*with some satisfaction*) Yes. I can do it pretty fair. 'An yer got th'　25
piece?

NELLIE Yes. Will you play it for us? Half a minute.

She finishes stroking her hair up with her side-combs, and, taking
the matches from the mantelpiece, leads the way to the door

Come on.　30

FATHER Yes, step forward, Joe.

Barker goes out after Nellie. Through the open door comes the
crashing sound of the miner's banging through The Maiden's
Prayer *on an old sharp-toned piano. Carlin stands listening,*
and shakes his head at the Father, who smiles back, glancing at　35
the same time nervously at his son, who has buried his hands in
his hair

CARLIN Well, are ter comin' down, George? (*He moves towards the door*)

FATHER (*lighting his pipe—between the puffs*) In about quarter of an hour, Fred.   40

CARLIN Good night, then. Good night, Ernest. (*He goes out*)
>   *The Mother is heard coming downstairs. She glances at her son, and shuts the passage door. Then she hurries to the oven and turns the bread. As she moves away again her husband thrusts out his hand and gives her something*   45

FATHER (*going towards the passage door*) I know it's a bad wik. (*He goes out*)

MOTHER (*counts the money he has given her, gives a little rapid clicking with her tongue on the roof of her mouth, tossing her head up once*) Twenty-eight shillings!° (*Counts again*) Twenty-eight shillings! (*To her son*) 50
And what was the cheque?

ERNEST (*looking up, with a frown of irritation*) Eight pounds one and six, and stoppages.

MOTHER And he gives me a frowsty twenty-eight . . . and I've got his club° to pay, and you a pair of boots. . . . Twenty-eight! . . . I wonder 55
if he thinks the house is kept on nothing . . . . I'll take good care he gets nothing extra, I will, too. . . . I knew it, though—I knew he'd been running up a nice score° at the Tunns'—that's what it is. There's rent, six-and-six, and clubs seven shillings, besides insurance and gas and everything else. I wonder how he thinks it's done—I wonder if he 60
thinks we live on air?

ERNEST (*looking up with pain and irritation*) Oh, Mater, don't bother! What's the good? If you worry for ever it won't make it any more.

MOTHER (*softened, conquering her distress*) Oh, yes, it's all very well for you, but if I didn't worry what would become of us I should like to 65
know?
>   *Gertie Coomber runs in. She is wearing a large blue felt hat and a Norfolk costume;° she is carrying a round basket. From the parlour comes the sound of Grieg's* Anitra's Tanz, *and then* Ase's Tod,° *played well, with real sympathy*   70

GERTIE (*with a little shy apprehension*) Who's in the parlour?

MOTHER It's only Mr Barker. (*Smiling slightly*) He wanted to show Nellie how well he could play 'The Maiden's Prayer'.°
>   *Gertie suddenly covers her mouth and laughs*

GERTIE (*still laughing*) He, he! I'll bet it was a thump! Pomp! Pomp! 75
(*Makes a piano-thumping gesture*) Did you hear it, Ernest?

ERNEST (*not looking up*) Infernal shindy.
>   *Gertie puts up her shoulders and giggles, looking askance at the student who, she knows, is getting tired of interruptions*

MOTHER Yes, I wish he'd go—(*almost whispering*)—and his wife is   80
expecting to go to bed any minute.

> *Gertie puts her lower lip between her teeth and looks serious. The*
> *music stops. Barker and Nellie are heard talking, then the Father.*
> *There is a click of boots on the tiled passage and they enter*

NELLIE What did you think of Mr Barker, Mother?—don't you think   85
it's good? I think it's wonderful—don't you, Ernest?

ERNEST (*grunting*) Um—it is.

> *Gertie Coomber suddenly hides behind her friend and laughs*

MOTHER (*to Barker*) Yes, I'm sure you get on wonderfully—wonderfully—considering.   90

BARKER Yes, ah's non done so bad, I think.

FATHER Tha 'asna, Joe, tha 'asna, indeed!

MOTHER Don't forget the bag, Mr Barker—I know you'll want it.

BARKER Oh, thank yer. Well, I mun goo. Tha'rt comin' down, George?

FATHER Yes, I'm comin' down, Joe. I'll just get my top-coat on, an'   95
then—(*He struggles awkwardly into his overcoat*)

> *Barker resumes his grey muffler*

BARKER Well, good night, everybody; good night, Ernest—an' thank
yer, Missis.

MOTHER I hope things will be—(*She nods significantly*)—alright.   100

BARKER Ah, thank yer, I hope it will. I expect so: there's no reason why
it shouldn't. Good night.

ALL Good night, Mr Barker.

> *The Father and Barker go out. Immediately Nellie flings her*
> *arms round Gertie's neck*   105

NELLIE Save me, Gert, save me! I thought I was done for that time. . . .
I gave myself up! The poor piano! Mother, it'll want tuning now, if it
never did before.

MOTHER (*with slight asperity, half-amused*) It may want at it, then.

GERTIE (*laughing*) You're done, Nellie, you're done brown! If it's like   110
dropping a saucepan-lid—no—you've got to put up with it!

NELLIE I don't care. It couldn't be much worse than it is, rotten old
thing. (*She pulls off her pinafore and hangs it over the back of a chair,*
then goes to the mirror, once more to arrange her hair)

GERTIE Oh, come on, Nellie, Cornell's will be crammed.   115

NELLIE Don't worry, my dear. What are you going to fetch? Anything
nice?

GERTIE No, I'm not—only bacon and cheese; they send you any stuff:
cat and candles—any muck!

> *The Mother takes the little stool and sits down on it on the*   120
> *hearthrug, lacing up her boots*

19

MOTHER I suppose you're not going out, Ernest?

ERNEST No.

MOTHER Oh—so you can look after the bread. There are two brown
loaves at the top; they'll be about half an hour; the white one's nearly   125
done. Put the other in as soon as they come out. Don't go and forget
them, now.

ERNEST No.

MOTHER He says 'No!' (*She shakes her head at him with indulgent, proud
affection*)   130

NELLIE (*as if casually, yet at once putting tension into the atmosphere*) Is
Mag coming down?

> *He does not answer immediately*

MOTHER I should think not, a night like this, and all the mud there is.

ERNEST She said she'd come and do some French. Why?   135

NELLIE (*with a half-smile, off-handedly*) Nothing.

MOTHER You'd never think she'd trapse through all this mud. . . .

NELLIE Don't bother. She'd come if she had to have water-wings to flop
through.

> *Gertie begins to giggle at the idea. The Mother sniffs*   140

ERNEST (*satirically*) Just as you'd flounder to your Eddie.

> *Gertie lifts her hands with a little sharp gesture as if to say, 'Now
> the fun's begun!'*

NELLIE (*turning suddenly, afire with scorn*) Oh, should I? You'd catch me
running after anybody!   145

MOTHER (*rising*) There, that'll do. Why don't you go up town, if you're
going?

> *Nellie Lambert haughtily marches off and puts on a dark coat
> and a blue hat*

NELLIE Is it raining, Gert?   150

GERTIE No, it's quite fine.

NELLIE I'll bet it's fine!

GERTIE Well, you asked me. It *is* fine; it's not raining.

> *The Mother re-enters from the passage, bringing a bonnet and a
> black coat*   155

NELLIE Want me to bring anything, Mater?

MOTHER I shall leave the meat for you.

NELLIE Alright. Come on, Gert.

> *They go out*

MOTHER (*she dreads that her son is angry with her and, affecting care-*   160
lessness, puts the question to him, to find out) Should we be getting a few
Christmas-tree things for little Margaret? I expect Emma and Joe

will be here for Christmas: it seems nothing but right, and it's only six
weeks now.

ERNEST (*coldly*) Alright.   165

> *He gets up and takes another book from the shelf without looking
> at her. She stands a moment suspended in the act of putting a pin
> through her bonnet*

MOTHER Well, I think we ought to make a bit of Christmas for the little
thing, don't you?   170

ERNEST Ay. You gave our things to the lads, didn't you? (*He still does not
look up from his books*)

MOTHER (*with a sound of failure in her voice*) Yes. And they've kept them
better than ever I thought they would. They've only broken your blue
bird—the one you bought when you were quite little.   175

> *There is a noise of footsteps and a knock at the door. The Mother
> answers*

(*Trying to be affable, but diffident, her gorge having risen a little*) Oh, is
it you, Maggie? Come in. How ever have you got down, a night like
this? Didn't you get over the ankles in mud?   180

> *She re-enters, followed by a ruddy girl of twenty, a full-bosomed,
> heavily-built girl, of medium stature and handsome appearance,
> ruddy and black. She is wearing a crimson tam-o'-shanter° and a
> long grey coat. She keeps her head lowered, and glancing only
> once splendidly at Ernest, replies with a strange, humble defiance* 185

MAGGIE No—oh, it's not so bad: besides, I came all round by the road.

MOTHER I should think you're tired, after school.

MAGGIE No; it's a relief to walk in the open; and I rather like a black
night; you can wrap yourself up in it. Is Nellie out?

MOTHER (*stiffly*) Yes; she's gone up town.   190

MAGGIE (*non-significantly*) Ah, I thought I passed her. I wasn't sure.
She wouldn't notice me; it *is* dark over the fields.

MOTHER Yes, it is. I'm sure *I'm* awful at recognizing people.

MAGGIE Yes—and so am I, generally. But it's no good bothering. If they
like to take offence, they have to. . . . I can't help it.   195

> *The Mother sniffs slightly. She goes into the passage and returns
> with a string net bag. She is ready to go out*

MOTHER (*still distantly*) Won't you take your things off? (*Looks at the
bread once more before going*)

MAGGIE Ah, thanks, I will.   200

> *She takes off her hat and coat and hangs them in the passage. She
> is wearing a dark blue cloth 'pinafore-dress', and beneath the blue
> straps and shoulder pieces a blouse of fine woollen stuff with a*

*small intricate pattern of brown and red. She is flushed and
handsome; her features are large, her eyes dark, and her hair falls*   205
*in loose profusion of black tendrils about her face. The coil at the
back is coming undone; it is short and not heavy. She glances
supremely at Ernest, feeling him watching her*

MOTHER (*at the oven*) You hear, Ernest? This white cake° will be done
in about five minutes, and the brown loaves in about twenty.   210

ERNEST Alright, my dear.

This time it is she who will not look at him

MAGGIE (*laughing a low, short laugh*) My hair!—is it a sight? I have to
keep my coat collar up, or it would drop right down—what bit of it
there is.   215

*She stands away from the mirror, pinning it up, but she cannot
refrain from just one glance at herself.*

*Ernest Lambert watches her, and then turns to his Mother, who is
pulling on a pair of shabby black gloves. Mrs Lambert, however,
keeps her eyes consciously averted; she is offended, and is a woman*   220
of fierce pride

MOTHER Well, I expect I shall see you again, Maggie.

MAGGIE (*with a faint, grave triumph*) It depends what time you come
back. I shan't have to be late.

MOTHER Oh, you'll be here when I get back.   225

MAGGIE (*submissive, but with minute irony*) Very well.

MOTHER And don't forget that bread, Ernest.

*She picks her bag off the table and goes out, without having looked
at either of them*

ERNEST (*affectionately*) No, Little, I won't.   230

*There is a pause for a moment. Maggie Pearson sits in the
arm-chair opposite him, who is on the sofa, and looks straight
at him. He raises his head after a moment and smiles at her*

MAGGIE Did you expect me?

ERNEST (*nodding*) I knew you'd come. You know, when you feel as cer-   235
tain as if you couldn't possibly be mistaken. But I *did* swear when I
came out of Coll. and found it raining.

MAGGIE So did I. Well, not swear, but I was mad. Hasn't it been a horrid
week?

ERNEST Hasn't it?—and I've been so sick of things.   240

MAGGIE Of what?

ERNEST Oh, of fooling about at College—and everything.

MAGGIE (*grimly*) You'd be sicker of school.

ERNEST I don't know. At any rate I should be doing something real,
whereas, as it is—oh, Coll.'s all foolery and flummery.   245

MAGGIE I wish I had a chance of going. I feel as if they'd been pulling things away from me all week—like a baby that has had everything taken from it.

ERNEST (*laughing*) Well, if school pulls all your playthings and pretty things away from you, College does worse: it makes them all silly and idiotic, and you hate them—and—what then—!   250

MAGGIE (*seriously*) Why? How?

ERNEST Oh, I don't know. You have to fool about so much, and listen when you're not interested, and see old professors like old dogs walking round as large as life with ancient bones they've buried and   255
scratched up again a hundred times; and they're just as proud as ever. It's such a farce! And when you see that farce, you see all the rest: all the waddling tribe of old dogs with their fossil bones—parsons and professors and councillors—wagging their tails and putting their paws on the bones and barking their important old barks—and all the   260
puppies yelping loud applause.

MAGGIE (*accepting him with earnestness*) Ay! But are they all alike?

ERNEST Pretty well. It makes you a bit sick. I used to think men in great places were great—

MAGGIE (*fervently*) I know you did.   265

ERNEST — and then to find they're no better than yourself—not a bit—

MAGGIE Well, I don't see why they should be.

ERNEST (*ignoring her*) — it takes the wind out of your sails. What's the good of anything if that's a farce?

MAGGIE What?   270

ERNEST The folks at the top. By Jove, if you once lose your illusion of 'great men', you're pretty well disillusioned of everything—religion and everything.

> *Maggie sits absorbedly, sadly biting her forefinger: an act which
> irritates him*   275

(*Suddenly*) What time did Mother go out?

MAGGIE (*starting*) I don't know—I never noticed the time.

ERNEST (*rising and going to the oven, picking up the oven-cloth from the hearth*) At any rate I should think it's five minutes.

> *He goes to the oven door, and takes from the lower shelf a 'cake'*   280
> *loaf, baked in a dripping-pan, and, turning it over, taps it with
> his knuckles*

ERNEST I should think it's done. I'll give it five minutes to soak.°

> *He puts the bread in the oven shelf, turns the brown loaves, and
> shuts the oven door. Then he rises and takes a little notebook from*   285
> *the shelf*

Guess what I've been doing.

23

MAGGIE (*rising, dilating, reaching towards him*) I don't know. What?
ERNEST (*smiling*) Verses.
MAGGIE (*putting out her hand to him, supplicating*) Give them to me!   290
ERNEST (*still smiling*) They're such piffle.
MAGGIE (*betwixt supplication and command*) Give them to me.
> *He hands her the little volume, and goes out to the scullery.*
> *She sits down and reads with absorption.*
> *He returns in a moment, his hands dripping with clear water, and,*   295
> *pulling forward the panchion from the corner, takes out the last*
> *piece of white dough, scrapes the little pieces together, and begins to*
> *work the mass into a flattish ball, passing it from hand to hand.*
> *Then he drops the dough into the dripping-pan, and leaves it*
> *standing on the hearth. When he rises and looks at her, she looks*   300
> *up at him swiftly, with wide, brown, glowing eyes, her lips parted.*
> *He stands a moment smiling down at her*
ERNEST Well, do you like them?
MAGGIE (*nodding several times, does not reply for a second*) Yes, I do.
ERNEST They're not up to much, though.   305
MAGGIE (*softly*) Why not?
ERNEST (*slightly crestfallen at her readiness to accept him again*) Well, are
   they?
MAGGIE (*nodding again*) Yes, they are! What makes you say they're not?
   I think they're splendid.   310
ERNEST (*smiling, gratified, but not thinking the same himself*) Which do
   you like best?
MAGGIE (*softly and thoughtfully*) I don't know. I think this is so lovely,
   this about the almond tree.
ERNEST (*smiling*) And you under it.   315
> *She laughs up at him a moment, splendidly*
But that's not the best.
MAGGIE (*looking at him expectantly*) No?
ERNEST That one, 'A Life History', is the best.
MAGGIE (*wondering*) Yes?   320
ERNEST (*smiling*) It is. It means more. Look how full of significance it is,
   when you think of it. The profs. would make a great long essay out of
   the idea. Then the rhythm is finer: it's more complicated.
MAGGIE (*seizing the word to vindicate herself when no vindication is
   required*) Yes, it is more complicated: it is more complicated in every   325
   way. You see, I didn't understand it at first. It is best. Yes, it is. (*She
   reads it again*)
> *He takes the loaf from the oven and puts the fresh one in*
ERNEST What have you been doing?

MAGGIE (*faltering, smiling*) I? Only—only some French.   330

ERNEST What, your diary?

MAGGIE (*laughing, confused*) Ah—but I don't think I want you to see it.

ERNEST Now, you know you wrote it for me! Don't you think it was a
good idea, to get you to write your diary in French? You'd never have
done any French at all but for that, and you'd certainly never have   335
told me. . . . You never tell me *your* side.

MAGGIE There's nothing to tell.

ERNEST (*shaking his finger excitedly*) That's just what you say, that's just
what you say! As many things happen for you as for me.

MAGGIE Oh, but you go to Derby every day, and you see folks, and I—   340

ERNEST (*flinging his hand at her*) Piffle! I tell you—do I tell you the train
was late? Do I—?

MAGGIE (*interrupting, laughing in confusion and humility*) Yes, you do—
ah!

      He has stopped suddenly with tremendous seriousness and   345
      excitement

ERNEST When?

MAGGIE (*nervous, apologizing, laughing*) On Sunday—when you told me
you'd have—

ERNEST (*flinging her words aside with excited gesture*) There you are!—   350
you're raking up a trifle to save you from the main issue. Just like a
woman! What I said was (*He becomes suddenly slow and fierce*) you
never tell me about you, and you drink me up, get me up like a cup
with both hands and drink yourself breathless—and—and there you
are—you, you never pour me any wine of yourself—   355

MAGGIE (*watching him, fascinated and a little bit terror-struck*) But isn't it
your fault?

      He turns on her with a fierce gesture. She starts

ERNEST How can it be, when I'm always asking you—? (*He scratches his
head with wild exasperation*)   360

MAGGIE (*almost inaudibly*) Well—

      He blazes at her so fiercely, she does not continue, but drops her
      head and looks at her knee, biting her finger

ERNEST (*abruptly*) Come on—let's see what hundreds of mistakes . . .

      She looks at him; dilates, laughs nervously, and goes to her coat,   365
      returning with a school exercise-book, doubled up.
      He sits on the sofa, brings her beside him with a swift gesture. Then
      he looks up at the fire, and starts away round the table

ERNEST (*going into the scullery and crossing the room with dustpan*) I must
mend the fire. There's a book of French verse with my books. Be   370
looking at that while I . . .

His voice descends to the cellar, where he is heard hammering the
coal. He returns directly.
She stands at the little cupboard, with her face in a book. She is
very short-sighted.   375
He mends the fire without speaking to her, and goes out to wash
his hands

ERNEST (*returning*) Well, what do you think of it? I got it for fourpence.

MAGGIE I like it ever so much.

ERNEST You've hardly seen it yet. Come on.   380

They sit together on the sofa and read from the exercise-book, she
nervously

(*Suddenly*) Now, look here—Oh, the poor verbs! I don't think
anybody dare treat them as you do! Look here!

She puts her head closer.   385

He jerks back his head, rubbing his nose frantically, laughing

Your hair did tickle me!

She turns her face to his, laughing, with open mouth. He breaks
the spell

Well, have you seen it?   390

MAGGIE (*hesitating, peering across the lines*) No-o-o.

ERNEST (*suddenly thrusting his finger before her*) There! I wonder it
doesn't peck your nose off. You *are* a—

She has discovered her mistake and draws back with a little
vibrating laugh of shame and conviction   395

You hussy, what should it have been?

MAGGIE (*hesitating*) Eurent?

ERNEST (*sitting suddenly erect and startling her up too*) What! The
preterite? The *preterite*? And you're talking about going to school!

She laughs at him with nervous shame; when he glares at her, she   400
dilates with fine terror

(*Ominously*) Well—?

MAGGIE (*in the depths of laughing despair, very softly and timidly*) I don't
know.

ERNEST (*relaxing into pathetic patience*) Verbs of motion take *être*, and if   405
you do a thing frequently, use the imperfect. You are—Well, you're
inexpressible!

They turn to the diary: she covered with humiliation, he
aggrieved. They read for a while, he shaking his head when
her light springing hair tickles him again   410

(*Softly*) What makes you say that?

MAGGIE (*softly*) What?

26

ERNEST That you are 'un enfant de Samedi'—a Saturday child?

MAGGIE (*mistrusting herself so soon*) Why—it's what they say, you know.

ERNEST (*gently*) How?   415

MAGGIE Oh—when a child is serious; when it doesn't play except on Saturdays, when it is quite free.

ERNEST And you mean you don't play?
> *She looks at him seriously*

No, you haven't got much play in you, have you?—I fool about so   420
much.

MAGGIE (*nodding*) That's it. You can forget things and play about. I always think of Francis Thompson's *Shelley*,° you know—how he made paper boats . . .

ERNEST (*flattered at the comparison*) But I don't make paper boats. I tell   425
you, you think too much about me. I tell you I have got nothing but a gift of coloured words. And do I teach you to play?—not to hold everything so serious and earnest? (*He is very serious*)
> *She nods at him again. He looks back at the paper. It is finished.*
> *Then they look at one another, and laugh a little laugh, not of*   430
> *amusement*

ERNEST Ah, your poor diary! (*He speaks very gently*)
> *She hides her head and is confused*

I haven't marked the rest of the mistakes. Never mind—we won't bother, shall we? You'd make them again, just the same.   435
> *She laughs. They are silent a moment or two; it is very still*

You know (*He begins sadly, and she does not answer*)—you think too much of me—you do, you know.
> *She looks at him with a proud, sceptical smile*

(*Suddenly wroth*) You are such a flat,° you won't believe me! But   440
I know—if I don't, who does? It's just like a woman, always aching to believe in somebody or other, or something or other.
> *She smiles*

I say, what will you have? Baudelaire?°

MAGGIE (*not understanding*) What?   445

ERNEST Baudelaire.

MAGGIE (*nervous, faltering*) But who's—?

ERNEST Do you mean to say you don't know who Baudelaire is?

MAGGIE (*defensively*) How should I?

ERNEST Why, I gassed to you for half an hour about him, a month   450
back—and now he might be a Maori—!

MAGGIE It's the names—being foreign.

ERNEST Baudelaire—Baudelaire—it's no different from Pearson!

MAGGIE (*laughing*) It sounds a lot better.

ERNEST (*laughing, also, and opening the book*) Come on! Here, let's have 455
'Maîtresse des Maîtresses';° should we?

MAGGIE (*with gentle persuasiveness*) Yes. You'll read it?

ERNEST *You* can have a go, if you like.

> *They both laugh. He begins to read 'Le Balcon'° in tolerably bad*
> *French, but with some genuine feeling. She watches him all the*   460
> *time. At the end, he turns to her in triumph, and she looks back*
> *in ecstasy*

There! isn't that fine?

> *She nods repeatedly*

That's what they can do in France. It's so heavy and full and volup- 465
tuous: like oranges falling and rolling a little way along a dark-blue
carpet; like twilight outside when the lamp's lighted; you get a sense
of rich, heavy things, as if you smelt them, and felt them about you in
the dusk: isn't it?

> *She nods again*   470

Ah, let me read you 'The Albatross'.° This is one of the best—anybody would say so—you see, fine, as good as anything in the world.
(*Begins to read*)

> *There is a light, quick step outside, and a light tap at the door,*
> *which opens.*   475
> *They frown at each other, and he whispers*

ERNEST Damn! (*Aloud*) Hell, Beat!

> *There enters a girl of twenty-three or four; short, slight, pale,*
> *with dark circles under her rather large blue eyes, and with dust-*
> *coloured hair. She wears a large brown beaver hat and a long*   480
> *grey-green waterproof coat*

BEATRICE WYLD Hello, Ernest, how are ter? Hello, Mag! Are they all
out?

ERNEST (*shutting up the book and drawing away from Maggie. The action*
is reciprocal—Beatrice Wyld seats herself in the armchair opposite) 485
They've gone up town. I don't suppose Nellie will be long.

BEATRICE (*coughing, speaking demurely*) No, she won't see Eddie to-
night.

ERNEST (*leaning back*) Not till after ten.

BEATRICE (*rather loudly, sitting up*) What! Does he come round after 490
they shut up shop?

ERNEST (*smiling ironically*) Ay, if it's getting on for eleven—!

BEATRICE (*turning in her chair*) Good lawk!°—are they that bad? Isn't it
fair sickenin'?

28

ERNEST He gets a bit wild sometimes.   495

BEATRICE I should think so, at that price. Shall you ever get like that, Mag?

MAGGIE Like what, Beatrice?

BEATRICE Now, Maggie Pearson, don't pretend to be 'ormin'.° She knows as well as I do, doesn't she, Ernest?   500

MAGGIE Indeed I don't. (*She is rather high-and-mighty, but not impressive*)

BEATRICE Garn!° We know you, don't we, Ernie? She's as bad as anybody at the bottom, but she pretends to be mighty 'ormin'.

MAGGIE I'm sure you're mistaken, Beatrice.   505

BEATRICE Not much of it, old girl. We're not often mistaken, are we, Ernie? Get out; we're the 'dead certs'°—aren't we, Willie? (*She laughs with mischievous exultance, her tongue between her teeth*)

MAGGIE (*with great but ineffectual irony*) Oh, I'm glad somebody is a 'dead cert'. I'm very glad indeed! I shall know where to find one now.   510

BEATRICE You will, Maggie.

      There is a slight, dangerous pause

BEATRICE (*demurely*) I met Nellie and Gertie, coming.

ERNEST Ay, you would.

MAGGIE (*bitterly*) Oh, yes.   515

BEATRICE (*still innocently*) She had got a lovely rose. I wondered —

ERNEST Yes, she thought Eddie would be peeping over the mousetraps and bird-cages. I bet she examines those drowning-mouse engines° every time she goes past.

BEATRICE (*with vivacity*) Not likely, not likely! She marches by as if   520
there was nothing but a blank in the atmosphere. You watch her. Eyes *Right!*—but she nudges Gert to make her see if he's there.

ERNEST (*laughing*) And then she turns in great surprise.

BEATRICE No, she doesn't. She keeps 'Eyes Front', and smiles like a young pup—and the blushes!—Oh, William, too lov'ly f'r anyfing!   525

ERNEST I'll bet the dear boy enjoys that blush.

BEATRICE Ra-ther! (*Artlessly revenant à son mouton°*) And he'll have the rose and all, to rejoice the cockles of his heart this time.

ERNEST (*trying to ward it off*) Ay. I suppose you'll see him with it on Sunday.   530

BEATRICE (*still innocently*) It *was* a beauty, William! Did you bring it for her?

ERNEST I got it in Derby.

BEATRICE (*unmasking*) Did you? Who *gave* it you, Willie?

ERNEST (*evasively, pretending to laugh*) Nay, it wouldn't do to tell.   535

BEATRICE Oh, William, *do* tell us! Was it the Dark, or the Athletics?°

ERNEST What if it was neither?

BEATRICE Oh, Willie, *another!* Oh, it *is* shameful! Think of the poor things, what damage you may do them.

ERNEST (*uneasily*) Yes, they are delicate pieces of goods, women. Men   540
have to handle them gently; like a man selling millinery.

BEATRICE (*hesitating, then refraining from answering this attack fully*) It's the hat-pins, Willie dear. But *do* tell us. Was it the Gypsy?—Let's see, you generally call it her in German, don't you?—What's the German for gypsy, Maggie?—But was it the Gypsy, or the Athletic Girl that   545
does Botany?

ERNEST (*shaking his head*) No. It was an Erewhonian.°

BEATRICE (*knitting her brows*) Is that the German for another? Don't say so, William! (*Sighs heavily*) 'Sigh no more, ladies'°—Oh, William! And these two are quite fresh ones, and all. Do you *like* being a   550
mutton-bone, William?—one bitch at one end and one at the other? Do *you* think he's such a juicy bone to squabble for, Maggie?

MAGGIE (*red and mortified*) I'm sure I don't think anything at all about it, Beatrice.

BEATRICE No; we've got more sense, we have, Maggie. We know him   555
too well—he's not worth it, is he?

> *Maggie Pearson does not reply.*
> *Beatrice Wyld looks at her dress, carefully rubbing off some spot*
> *or other; then she resumes*

BEATRICE But surely it's not another, Willie?   560

ERNEST What does it matter who it is? Hang me, I've not spoken to—I've hardly said ten words—you said yourself, I've only just known them.

BEATRICE Oh, Willie, I'm sure I thought it was most desperate—from what you told me.   565

> *There is another deadly silence. Beatrice resumes innocently, quite*
> *unperturbed*

Has he told *you*, Maggie?

MAGGIE (*very coldly*) I'm sure I don't know.

BEATRICE (*simply*) Oh, he can't have done, then. You'd never have   570
forgot. There's one like a Spaniard—or was it like an Amazon, Willie?

ERNEST Go on. Either'll do.

BEATRICE A Spanish Amazon, Maggie—olive-coloured, like the colour of a young clear bit of sea-weed, he said—and, oh, I know!   575
'great free gestures'—a cool clear colour, not red. Don't you think she'd be lovely?

MAGGIE I do indeed.

BEATRICE Too lovely f'r anyfing?—And the other. Oh, yes: 'You should see her run up the college stairs! She can go three at a time, like a hare running uphill.'—And she was top of the Inter. list° for Maths and Botany. Don't you wish you were at college, Maggie? 580

MAGGIE For some things.

BEATRICE *I* do. We don't know what he's up to when he's there, do we?

MAGGIE I don't know that we're so very anxious— 585

BEATRICE (*convincingly*) We're not, but he thinks we are, and I believe he makes it all up. I bet the girls just think: 'H'm. Here's a ginger-and-white fellow; let's take a bit of the conceit out of him'—and he thinks they're gone on him, doesn't he?

MAGGIE Very likely. 590

BEATRICE He *does*, Maggie; that's what he does. And I'll bet, if we could hear him—the things he says about us! I'll bet he says there's a girl with great brown eyes—

ERNEST Shut up, Beat! you little devil—you don't know when to stop.

BEATRICE (*affecting great surprise*) William! Maggie! Just *fancy*!! 595
        There is another silence, not ominous this time, but charged with
        suspense
What am I a devil for? (*Half timidly*)

ERNEST (*flushing up at the sound of her ill-assurance*) Look here; you may just as well drop it. It's stale, it's flat. It makes no mark, don't flatter 600 yourself—we're sick of it, that's all. It's a case of *ennui*. Vous m'agacez les nerfs. Il faut aller au diable.° (*He rises, half laughing, and goes for the dust-pan*)

BEATRICE (*her nose a trifle out of joint*) Translate for us, Maggie.
        Maggie shakes her head, without replying. She has a slight 605
        advantage now.
        Ernest crosses the room to go to coal-cellar.
        Beatrice coughs slightly, adjusts her tone to a casual, disinterested
        conversation, and then says, from sheer inability to conquer her
        spite 610
You *do* look well, Maggie. I don't think I've seen anybody with such a colour. It's fair fine.
        Maggie laughs and pulls a book towards her. There is silence.
        Ernest's steps are heard descending to the cellar and hammering
        the coal. Presently he re-mounts. The girls are silent, Maggie 615
        pretending to read; Beatrice staring across the room, half smiling,
        tapping her feet

ERNEST (*hurrying in and putting the coal on the hob*) Begum, what about the bread?

MAGGIE (*starting up and dilating towards him with her old brilliance*) Oh,   620
    what have we—? Is it—? Oh!
>   *Ernest has forestalled her at the oven. There issues a great puff*
>   *of hot smoke. He draws back a little, and Maggie utters a quick,*
>   *tremulous 'Oh!'*

BEATRICE (*with concern*) Hel-lo, Ernest! that smells a bit thick!   625
>   *He pulls out the loaves one after another. There is one brown loaf*
>   *much blackened, one in tolerable condition, and the white 'cake'*
>   *very much scorched on one side.*
>   *Beatrice begins to laugh, in spite of her sympathy at the dismay;*
>   *he is kneeling on the hearth, the oven door open, the oven-cloth in*   630
>   *his hand, and the burnt bread toppled out of its tins on the hearth*
>   *before him. Maggie is bending over his shoulder, in great concern.*
>   *Beatrice sputters with more laughter. Ernest looks up at her, and*
>   *the dismay and chagrin on his face change also to an irresistible*
>   *troubled amusement at the mishap, and he laughs heartily.*   635
>   *Maggie joins in, strainedly at first, then with natural shaking,*
>   *and all three laugh with abandonment, Beatrice putting her*
>   *hand up over her face, and again doubling over till her head*
>   *touches her knees*

ERNEST No—no! Won't Ma be wild, though!—What a beastly shame!   640
>   *Beatrice breaks out afresh, and he, though grieved, bubbles again*
>   *into grudging laughter*
Another day and the rotten fire would burn slow, but to-night it's
ramped like—

BEATRICE Hell, Ernie!   645
>   *She goes off again into a wild tossing of laugher, hesitating a*
>   *moment to watch him as he lugubriously picks up the worst loaf*
>   *and eyes it over*

ERNEST (*grimly*) It's black bread now, that they talk about. (*He sniffs the*
    loaf)   650
>   *Beatrice resumes her mad, interrupted laughter. Maggie sits down*
>   *on the sofa and laughs till the tears come.*
>   *Ernest taps the loaf with his finger*

BEATRICE Are you trying to see if it's done, William? (*From naïve irony*
    she departs into laughter)   655

ERNEST (*answers, his lugubrious soul struggling with laughter, the girls laugh-*
    ing the while) No, I was listening if it sounded hollow. Hark!
>   *They listen. Laughter*
It sounds cindery. I wonder how deep it goes. (*In a spirit of curiosity,*
    he rises and fetches a knife, and, pulling a newspaper over the hearth,   660

begins to cut away the burnt crust. The bread–charcoal falls freely on the paper. He looks at the loaf) By Jove, there *is* a lot! It's like a sort of fine coke.

> *The girls laugh their final burst, and pant with exhaustion, their hands pressed in their sides*   665

It's about done for, at any rate. (*Puts it down and takes another brown loaf; taps it*) This is not so bad, really, is it? (*Sadly*) It sounds a bit desiccated, though. Poor Ma! (*He laughs*) She'll say it's your fault, Mag.

MAGGIE (*with astonished, incredulous laughter*) Me?   670

BEATRICE She will, Mag, she will! She'll say if you hadn't been here making a fuss of him—

MAGGIE (*still laughing*) I'd better go before she comes.

BEATRICE You want to scrape that with the nutmeg-grater,° Ernest. Where is it? Here, give it me.   675

> *She takes the loaf, and Ernest goes out and returns with the grater. She begins to grate the loaf.*
> *Maggie takes up the white 'cake' and feels the pale side, tapping the bottom*

MAGGIE (*with decision*) This isn't done. It's no good cutting it off till it's   680
all finished. I may as well put it in again. (*She feels the heat of the two shelves, and puts the loaf on the upper*)

> *Ernest picks up the ruined loaf*

ERNEST What will she say when she sees this?

MAGGIE Put it on the fire and have done with it.   685

> *They look at her in some astonishment at the vandalism of the remark*

ERNEST But . . . (*He looks at the loaf on all sides*)

MAGGIE It's no good, and it'll only grieve their poor hearts if they see it. 'What the heart doesn't . . .'   690

BEATRICE Ay, put it on, William. What's it matter? Tell 'em the cat ate it.

ERNEST (*hesitating*) Should I?

BEATRICE (*nudging his elbow*) Ay, go on.

> *He puts the loaf on the fire, which is not yet mended, and they stand watching the transparent flames lick it up*   695

ERNEST (*half sad, whimsically, repentant*) The Staff of Life!

MAGGIE It's a faggot now, not a staff.

ERNEST Ah, well! (*He slides all the cinders and Beatrice's scrapings together in the newspaper and pours them in the fire*)

BEATRICE (*holding up her scraped loaf*) It doesn't show, being brown.   700
You want to wrap it in a damp cloth now. Have you got a cloth?

ERNEST What?—a clean tea-towel?

BEATRICE Ay, that'll do. Come here; let's go and wet it.

> *She goes out, and re-enters directly with the towel screwed up. She* 705
> *folds it round the loaf, the others watching. She sets the shrouded*
> *loaf on the table, and they all sit down. There is a little pause*

Have you given over coming down to chapel now, Maggie?

MAGGIE N-no. I don't know that I have. Why?

BEATRICE You don't often put in an appearance now.

MAGGIE (*a trifle petulantly*) Don't I? Well, I don't feel like it, I suppose. 710

BEATRICE William, you have something to answer for, my boy. (*She speaks portentously*)

ERNEST Shall I? Ne'er mind; I'll say 'adsum'° every time. Recording Angel: 'Ernest Lambert.'—'Adsum!'

BEATRICE But you don't know what the little Mas say about you, my lad. 715

ERNEST The dear little Mas! They will be gossiping about—

BEATRICE (*springing from her chair*) Look out! there's Nellie. Take that in th' pantry, William. Come out!

> *She thrusts the towelled loaf into Ernest's hands, and he hurries*
> *away with it, while she hastily shoots the coal on the fire, and,* 720
> *putting down the dust-pan by the boiler, sits in her chair and*
> *looks "ormin'.'*
>
> *Enter Nellie Lambert and Gertie Coomber, blinking*

NELLIE (*bending her head to shield her eyes*) Hasn't Ma come? I never saw her. Hullo, Maggie, you've *not* gone yet, you see. (*She sniffs and goes* 725
straight to the oven) Goodness, what a smell of burning! Have you been and forgotten the bread? (*She kneels and looks in the oven*)

BEATRICE (*very quietly and negligently*) Ernest forgot that one. It's only a bit caught.

> *Nellie peeps in the panchion where the other loaves are—those* 730
> *baked by the Mother*

NELLIE He generally forgets if Maggie's here.

> *Beatrice bursts out laughing*

MAGGIE (*rising, indignant*) Why, Nellie, when has it ever been burnt before? 735

NELLIE (*smiling a careless smile*) Many a time.

MAGGIE Not when I've been here.

NELLIE Aren't you going to sit down a bit, Gert?

GERTIE No, I'm off. Our Frances'll be wanting her ducks. (*She laughs, but does not go*) 740

> *Maggie, her head hanging, goes to put on her hat and coat. The*
> *other girls smile, meaningly, at one another*

Are you going, then, Maggie?

MAGGIE (*distantly*) Yes, it's getting late. I've a long walk, you see.

GERTIE You have! I'm glad I've not got it. I often wonder how you dare   745
go through those woods on a pitch-dark night.

BEATRICE I daresn't. (*She laughs at herself*)

MAGGIE I'd rather go through our wood than through Nottingham
Road, with the people—!

BEATRICE I'm glad you would, for I wouldn't.   750
> *Ernest Lambert pulls on his overcoat and his cap. He gathers
> certain books. He looks at Maggie, and she at him*

MAGGIE Well, good night, everybody. I shall have to go. (*She hesitates,
finding it difficult to break away*)

BEATRICE AND NELLIE Good night.   755

GERTIE Good night, Maggie. I hope it won't be too muddy for you.
> *Maggie laughs slightly*

NELLIE (*as the two go through the door, loudly*) And don't be ever so late
back, our Ernest!
> *They do not reply. As their steps are heard passing the wide win-   760
> dow, Beatrice flings up her arms and her feet in an ungraceful,
> exultant glee, flicking her fingers with noiseless venom*

BEATRICE (*in an undertone*) I gave her beans!

NELLIE (*turning, with a smile, and lighting up*) Did you? What did you
say?   765

GERTIE (*amused, giggling, but shamefaced*) *Did* you?

BEATRICE (*exultant*) Oh, lum! ° I'll bet her cheeks are warm!
> *End of Act 2*

Act 3

The same room, half an hour later.
Beatrice Wyld sits in the arm-chair, and Nellie Lambert on the
sofa, the latter doing drawn-thread work° on a white tray-cloth,
part of which is fixed in a ring: at this part Nellie is stitching

BEATRICE Ah, it makes you grin! the way she used to talk before she had   5
him!

NELLIE She did. She thought nobody was as good as her Arthur. She's
found her mistake out.

BEATRICE She *has* an' all! He wanted some chips for his supper the
other night, when I was there. 'Well,' I said, 'it's not far to Fretwell's,   10
Arthur.' He did look mad at me. 'I'm not going to fetch chips,'
he said, a cocky little fool; and he crossed his little legs till I should
'a liked to have smacked his mouth. I said to her, 'Well, Mabel, if
you do, you're a fool!'—in her state, and all the men that were about!
He's not a bit of consideration. You never saw anybody as fagged° as   15
she looks.

NELLIE She does. I felt fair sorry for her when I saw her last Sunday but
one. She doesn't look like she used.

BEATRICE By Jove, she doesn't! He's brought her down a good many
pegs. I shouldn't wonder if she wasn't quite safe, either. She told   20
me she had awful shooting pains up her side, and they last for five
minutes.

NELLIE (*looking up*) Oh?

BEATRICE Ay! I'm glad I'm not in her shoes. They may talk about getting married as they like! Not this child!   25

NELLIE Not to a thing like him.

BEATRICE I asked her if she didn't feel frightened, an' she said she
didn't care a scrap. I should care, though—and I'll bet she does, at the
bottom.

The latch clicks. The Mother enters, carrying a large net° full of   30
purchases, and a brown-paper parcel. She lets these fall heavily
on the table, and sits on the nearest chair, panting a little, with
evident labour of the heart

MOTHER Yes, my lady!—you called for that meat, didn't you?

NELLIE (*rising and going to look in the parcels*) Well, my duck, I looked for   35
you downtown; then when I was coming back, I forgot all about it.

MOTHER And I—was silly enough—to lug it myself—

36

NELLIE (*crossing to her Mother, all repentant*) Well, what *did* you for?—
you *knew* I could fetch it again! You do do such ridiculous things!
(*She begins to take off her Mother's bonnet*)   40

MOTHER Yes! We know your fetching it—again. If I hadn't met little
Abel Gibson—I really don't think I should have got home.

BEATRICE (*leaning forward*) If Nellie forgets it, you should forget it,
Mrs Lambert. I'm sure you ought not to go lugging all those things.

MOTHER But I met young Abel Gibson just when I was thinking I   45
should have to drop them—and I said: 'Here, Abel, my lad, are you
going home?' and he said he was, so I told him he could carry my bag.
He's a nice little lad. He says his father hasn't got much work, poor
fellow. I believe that woman's a bad manager. She'd let that child
clean up when he got home—and he said his Dad always made the   50
beds. She's not a nice woman, I'm sure. (*She shakes her head and begins
to unfasten her coat*)

> Nellie, seeing her Mother launched into easy gossip, is at ease on
> her score, and returns to the bags

You needn't go looking; there's nothing for you.   55

NELLIE (*petulantly*) You always used to bring us something—

MOTHER Ay, I've no doubt I did . . . (*She sniffs and looks at Beatrice
Wyld*)

NELLIE (*still looking, unconvinced*) Hello! Have a grape, Beatrice. (*She
offers Beatrice a white paper-bag of very small black grapes*)   60

MOTHER They want washing first, to get the sawdust out. Our Ernest
likes those little grapes, and they *are* cheap: only fourpence.

BEATRICE (*looking up from the bag*) Oh, they are cheap. No, I won't have
any, Nellie, thanks.

NELLIE I'll wash them.   65

MOTHER Just let the tap run on them—and get a plate.

NELLIE Well, as if I shouldn't get a plate! The little Ma thinks we're all
daft.

MOTHER (*sniffing—it is her manner of winking*) Is all the bread done?

NELLIE Yes. I took the last out about a quarter of an hour ago.   70

MOTHER (*to Beatrice*) Was Maggie Pearson gone when you came?

BEATRICE No—she's only been gone about three-quarters of an hour.

MOTHER (*tossing her head and lowering her tone confidentially*) Well,
really! I stopped looking at a man selling curtains a bit longer than
I should, thinking she'd be gone.   75

BEATRICE Pah!—it makes you sick, doesn't it?

MOTHER It does. You wouldn't think she'd want to come trailing down
here in weather like this, would you?

37

BEATRICE You wouldn't. I'll bet you'd not catch me!—and she knows
what you think, alright.   80

MOTHER Of course she does.

BEATRICE She wouldn't care if the Old Lad° was here, scowling at her;
she'd come.

MOTHER If that lad was at home.

BEATRICE (*scornfully*) Ay!   85

> *The Mother rises and goes out with her coat.*
> *Nellie enters, with a plate of wet black grapes*

NELLIE Now, Beat! (*Offering the grapes*)

BEATRICE No, Nellie, I don't think I'll have any.

NELLIE Go on—have some! Have some—go on! (*Speaks rather im-*   90
peratively.)

> *Beatrice takes a few grapes in her hand*

What a scroddy° few! Here, have some more.

BEATRICE (*quietly*) No, Nellie, thanks, I won't have any more. I don't
think they'd suit me.   95

> *Nellie sits down and begins to eat the grapes, putting the skins*
> *on a piece of paper.*
> *The Mother re-enters. She looks very tired. She begins carrying*
> *away the little parcels*

NELLIE Don't you put those away, Mother; I'll do it in a minute.   100

> *The Mother continues. Nellie rises in a moment or two, frowning*

You *are* a persistent little woman! Why don't you wait a bit and let me
do it?

MOTHER Because your father will be in in a minute, and I don't want
him peeking and prying into everything, thinking I'm a millionaire. 105
(*She comes and sits down in her rocking-chair by the oven*)

> *Nellie continues to carry away the goods, which have littered the*
> *table, looking into every parcel*

NELLIE Hello! what are these little things?

MOTHER Never you mind.   110

NELLIE Now, little woman, don't you try to hug yourself and be sec-
retive. What are they?

MOTHER They're pine-kernels. (*Turning to Beatrice*) Our Ernest's
always talking about the nut-cakes he gets at Mrs Dacre's; I thought
I'd see what they were like. Put them away; don't let him see them. 115
I shan't let him know at all, if they're not up to much. I'm not going
to have him saying Mother Dacre's things are better than mine.

BEATRICE I wouldn't—for I'm sure they're not.

MOTHER Still, I rather like the idea of nuts. Here, give me one; I'll try it.

>*They each eat a pine-kernel with the air of a connoisseur in*   120
>   *flavours*

(*Smiling to herself*) Um—aren't they oily!

BEATRICE They *are!* But I rather like them.

NELLIE So do I. (*Takes another*)

MOTHER (*gratified*) Here, put them away, miss!   125
>   *Nellie takes another. The Mother rises and snatches them away*
>   *from her, really very pleased*

There won't be one left, I know, if I leave them with *her*. (*She puts them away*)

NELLIE (*smiling and nodding her head after her Mother; in a whisper*) Isn't   130
she fussy?
>   *Beatrice puts out her tongue and laughs*

MOTHER (*returning*) I tried a gelatine sponge last week. He likes it much better than cornflour. Mrs Dacre puts them in mincemeat, instead of suet—the pine-kernels. I must try a bit.   135

BEATRICE Oh! it *sounds* better.

MOTHER (*seating herself*) It does. (*She looks down at the bread*)
>   *Beatrice puts up her shoulders in suspense*

I think you let this one dry up.

NELLIE No, I didn't. It was our Ernest who let it burn.   140

MOTHER Trust him! And what's he done? (*She begins to look round*)
>   *Beatrice pulls a very wry face, straightens it quickly and says*
>   *calmly*

BEATRICE Is your clock right, Mrs Lambert?

MOTHER (*looking round at the clock*) Ten minutes—ten minutes fast.   145
Why, what time is it?

BEATRICE Good lack! (*Rising suddenly*) It's half-past ten! Won't our Pa rave! 'Yes, my gel—it's turning out time again. We're going to have a stop put to it.' And our mother will recite! Oh, the recitations!— there's no shutting her up when she begins. But at any rate, she shuts   150 our Pa up, and he's a nuisance when he thinks he's got just cause to be wrath.—Where did I put my things?

MOTHER I should think that Nellie's put hers on top. (*She looks at Nellie*) Don't sit there eating every one of those grapes. You know our Ernest likes them.   155

NELLIE (*suddenly incensed*) Good gracious! I don't believe I've had more than half a dozen of the things!

MOTHER (*laughing and scornful*) Half a dozen!

NELLIE Yes, half a dozen.—Beatrice, we can't have a thing in this house—everything's for our Ernest.   160

MOTHER   What a story! What a story! But he *does* like those little grapes.

NELLIE   And everything else.

MOTHER (*quietly, with emphasis*)   He gets a good deal less than you.

NELLIE (*withdrawing from dangerous ground*)   I'll bet.

> *Gertie Coomber runs in*   165

BEATRICE   Hello, Gert, haven't you seen John?

GERTIE (*putting up her chin*)   No.

BEATRICE   A little nuisance!—fancy!

GERTIE   Eh, I don't care—not me.

NELLIE   No, it's her fault. She never does want to see him. I wonder any   170
fellow comes to her.

GERTIE (*nonchalantly*)   Um—so do I.

BEATRICE   Get out, Gert; you know you're fretting your heart out 'cause
he's not come.

GERTIE (*with great scorn*)   Am I? Oh, *am* I? Not me! If I heard him   175
whistling this moment, I wouldn't go out to him.

NELLIE   Wouldn't you! I'd shove you out, you little cat!

GERTIE (*with great assumption of amusing dignity*)   Oh, would you,
indeed!

> *They all laugh.*   180
> *Beatrice pins on her hat before the mirror*

You haven't got Ernest to take you home to-night, Beat. Where is he?
With Maggie Pearson? Hasn't he come back yet?

MOTHER (*with some bitterness*)   He hasn't. An' he's got to go to college
to-morrow. Then he reckons he can get no work done.   185

GERTIE   Ha!—they're all alike when it suits them.

MOTHER   I should thank her not to come down here messing every
Friday and Sunday.

NELLIE   Ah, she's always here. I should be ashamed of *myself*.

BEATRICE   Well—our Pa! I must get off. Good night, everybody. See   190
you to-morrow, Nell.

NELLIE   I'll just come with you across the field.

> *She fetches a large white cashmere shawl and puts it over her*
> *head. She disposes it round her face at the mirror.*
> *Beatrice winks at the Mother*   195

GERTIE   She's going to look for Eddie.

NELLIE (*blushing*)   Well, what if I am? Shan't be many minutes, Ma.

MOTHER (*rather coldly*)   I should think not! I don't know what you want
at all going out at this time o' night.

> *Nellie shrugs her shoulders, and goes out with Beatrice Wyld, who*   200
> *laughs and bids another good night*

40

MOTHER (*when they have gone*) A silly young hussy, gadding to look for
    him. As if she couldn't sleep without seeing him.

GERTIE Oh, he always says, 'Come and look for me about eleven.' I bet
    he's longing to shut that shop up.   205

MOTHER (*shortly*) Ha! he's softer than she is, and I'm sure that's not
    necessary. I can't understand myself how folks can be such looneys.
    I'm sure I was never like it.

GERTIE And I'm sure I never should be. I often think, when John's
    coming, 'Oh, hang it, I wish he'd stay away!'   210

MOTHER Ah, but that's too bad, Gertie. If you feel like that you'd better
    not keep it on any longer.—Yet I used to be about the same myself.
    I was born with too much sense for that sort of slobber.

GERTIE Yes, isn't it hateful? I often think, 'Oh, get off with you!' I'm
    sure I should never be like Nellie.—Isn't Ernest late? You'll have Mr   215
    Lambert in first.

MOTHER (*bitterly*) He *is* late. He must have gone every bit of the way.

GERTIE Nay, I bet he's not—that.

    There is silence a moment.

    The Mother remembers the bread   220

MOTHER (*turning round and looking in the panchion*) Well, there ought to
    be two more brown loaves. What have they done with them, now?
    (*Turns over the loaves, and looks about*)

GERTIE (*laughing*) I should think they've gone and eaten them, between
    them.   225

MOTHER That's very funny.

    She rises, and is going to look round the room. There is a whistle
    outside

GERTIE (*turning her head sharply aside*) Oh, *hang* it! I'm not going—I'm
    not!   230

MOTHER Who is it? John?

GERTIE It is, and I'm *not* going.

    The whistle is heard again

    He can shut up, 'cause I'm not going!

MOTHER (*smiling*) You'll have to just go and speak to him, if he's waiting   235
    for you.

    The whistle is heard louder

GERTIE Isn't it hateful! I don't care. I'll tell him I was in bed. I should be
    if my father wasn't at the Ram.

MOTHER (*sighing*) Ay! But you may guess he's seen Nellie, and she's   240
    been saying something to him.

GERTIE Well, she needn't, then!

The whistle goes again.
Gertie cannot resist the will of the other, especially as the Mother
bids her go. She flings her hand, and turns with great impatience   245
He can shut up! What's he want to come at this time for? Oh, *hang*
him!
She goes out slowly and unwillingly, her lips closed angrily. The
Mother smiles, sighs, and looks sad and tired again
MOTHER (*to herself*) It's a very funny thing!   250
She wanders round the room, looking for the bread. She lights a
taper and goes into the scullery
(*Re-passing, she repeats*) A *very* remarkable thing!
She goes into the pantry on right, and after a moment returns with
the loaf in the damp cloth, which she has unfolded. She stands   255
looking at the loaf, repeating a sharp little sound against her
palate with her tongue, quickly vibrating her head up and down
(*To herself*) So this is it, is it? It's a nice thing!—And they put it down
there, thinking I shouldn't see it. It's a nice thing! (*Goes and looks in*
the oven, then says bitterly) I always said she was a deep one. And he   260
thinks he'll stop out till his father comes!—And what have they done
with the other?—Burnt it, I should think. That's what they've done.
It's a nice thing—a nice thing! (*She sits down in the rocking-chair,*
perfectly rigid, still overdone with weariness and anger and pain)
After a moment, the garden gate is heard to bang back, and a   265
heavy step comes up the path, halting, punctuated with the scratch
and thrust of a walking-stick, rather jarring on the bricked yard
The Father enters. He also bends his head a little from the light,
peering under his hat-brim.
The Mother has quickly taken the withered loaf and dropped it in   270
among the others in the panchion.
The Father does not speak, but goes straight to the passage, and
hangs up his hat, overcoat, and jacket, then returns and stands
very near the fire, holding his hands close down to the open ruddy
grate. He sways slightly when he turns, after a moment or two,   275
and stands with his hands spread behind his back, very near
the fire.
The Mother turns away her head from him.
He remains thus for a minute or so, then he takes a step forward,
and, leaning heavily on the table, begins to pick the grapes from   280
the plate, spitting out the skins into his right hand and flinging
them at random towards the fire behind his back, leaning all the
time heavily with the left hand on the table.

After a while this irritates the Mother exceedingly

MOTHER You needn't eat all those grapes. There's somebody else!   285

FATHER (*speaking with an exaggerated imitation of his son's English*) 'Somebody else!' Yes, there *is* 'somebody else'! (*He pushes the plate away and the grapes roll on the table*) I know they was not bought for me! I know it! I know it! (*His voice is rising*) Somebody else! Yes, there *is* somebody else! I'm not daft! I'm not a fool. Nothing's got for me.   290
No–o. You can get things for them, you can.

The Mother turns away her head, with a gesture of contempt
(*Continues with maddening tipsy, ironic snarl*) I'm not a fool! I can see it! I can see it! I'm not daft! There's nothing for me, but you begrudge me every bit I put in my mouth.   295

MOTHER (*with cold contempt*) You put enough down your own throat. There's no need for anybody else. You take good care you have your share.

FATHER I have my share. Yes, I do, I do!

MOTHER (*contemptuously*) Yes, you do.   300

FATHER Yes, I do. But I shouldn't if you could help it, you begrudging bitch. What did you put away when I came in, so that I shouldn't see it? Something! Yes! Something you'd got for them! Nobody else. Yes! *I* know you'd got it for somebody else!

MOTHER (*quietly, with bitter scorn*) As it happens, it was nothing.   305

FATHER (*his accent is becoming still more urban. His O's are A's, so that 'nothing' is 'nathing'*) Nathing! Nathing! You're a liar, you're a liar. I heard the scuffle. You don't think I'm a fool, do you, woman?

She curls her lips in a deadly smile

FATHER I know, I know! Do *you* have what you give me for dinner? No,   310
you don't. You take good care of it!

MOTHER Look here, you get your good share. Don't think *you* keep the house. Do you think I manage on the few lousy shillings you give me? No, you get as much as you deserve, if any man did. And if *you* had a rice pudding, it was because *we* had *none*. Don't come here talking.   315
You look after *yourself*, there's no mistake.

FATHER An' I mean to, an' I mean to!

MOTHER Very well, then!

FATHER (*suddenly flaring*) But I'm not going to be treated like a dog in my own house! I'm *not*, so don't think it! I'm master in this house, an'   320
I'm *going* to be. I tell you, I'm master of this house.

MOTHER You're the only one who thinks so.

FATHER I'll stop it! I'll put a stop to it. They can go—they can go!

MOTHER You'd be on short commons if they did.

FATHER What? What? Me! You saucy bitch, I can keep myself, an' you   325
as well, an' him an' all as holds his head above me—am doing—an' I'll
stop it, I'll stop it—or they can go.

MOTHER Don't make any mistake—*you* don't keep us. You hardly keep
yourself.

FATHER. Do I?—do I? And who does keep 'em, then?   330

MOTHER I do—and the girl.

FATHER You do, do you, you snappy little bitch! You do, do you? Well,
keep 'em yourself, then. Keep that lad in his idleness yourself, then.

MOTHER Very willingly, very willingly. And that lad works ten times as
hard as you do.   335

FATHER Does he? I should like to see him go down th' pit every day!
I should like to see him working every day in th' hole. No, he won't
dirty his fingers.

MOTHER Yes, you wanted to drag all the lads into the pit, and you only
begrudge them because I wouldn't let them.   340

FATHER (*shouting*) You're a liar—you're a liar! I never wanted 'em in th'
pit.

MOTHER (*interrupting*) You did your best to get the other two there,
anyway.

FATHER (*still shouting*) You're a liar—I never did anything of the sort.   345
What other man would keep his sons doing nothing till they're
twenty-two? Where would you find another? Not that I begrudge it
him—I don't, bless him . . .

MOTHER Sounds like it.

FATHER I don't. I begrudge 'em nothing. I'm willing to do everything   350
I can for 'em, and 'ow do they treat me? Like a dog, I say, like a dog!

MOTHER And whose fault is it?

FATHER Yours, you stinking hussy! It's you as makes 'em like it. They're
like you. You teach 'em to hate me. You make me like dirt for 'em: you
set 'em against me . . .   355

MOTHER You set them yourself.

FATHER (*shouting*) You're a liar! (*He jumps from his chair and stands
bending towards her, his fist clenched and ready and threatening*) It's you.
It always 'as been you. You've done it—

    Enter Ernest Lambert   360

ERNEST (*pulling off his cap and flashing with anger*) It's a fine row you're
kicking up. I should bring the neighbours in!

FATHER I don't care a damn what I do, you sneering devil, you! (*He turns
to his son, but remains in the same crouching, threatening attitude*)

ERNEST (*flaring*) You needn't swear at me, either.   365

44

FATHER I shall swear at who the devil I like. Who are you, you young
    hound—who are you, you measley little—

ERNEST At any rate, I'm not a foul-mouthed drunken fool.

FATHER (*springing towards him*) What! I'll smite you to the ground if you
    say it again, I will, I *will*!   370

ERNEST Pah!

> *He turns his face aside in contempt from the fist brandished near
> his mouth*

FATHER (*shouting*) What! Say it! I'll drive my fist through you!

ERNEST (*suddenly tightening with rage as the fist is pushed near his face*) 375
    Get away, you spitting old fool!

> *The Father jerks nearer and trembles his fist so near the other's
> nose that he draws his head back, quivering with intense passion
> and loathing, and lifts his hands*

MOTHER Ernest, Ernest, don't!   380

> *There is a slight relaxation*

(*Lamentable, pleading*) Don't say any more, Ernest! Let him say what
he likes. What should I do if . . .

> *There is a pause.*
>
> *Ernest continues rigidly to glare into space beyond his Father.* 385
> *The Father turns to the Mother with a snarling movement, which
> is nevertheless a movement of defeat. He withdraws, sits down in
> the arm-chair, and begins, fumbling, to get off his collar and tie,
> and afterwards his boots.*
>
> *Ernest has taken a book, and stands quite motionless, looking at* 390
> *it. There is heard only the slash of the Father's bootlaces. Then
> he drags off the boot, and it falls with a loud noise.*
>
> *Ernest, very tense, puts down the book, takes off his overcoat,
> hangs it up, and returns to the side of the sofa nearest the door,
> where he sits, pretending to read.* 395
>
> *There is silence for some moments, and again the whip of
> boot-laces. Suddenly a snarl breaks the silence*

FATHER But don't think I'm going to be put down in my own house! It
    would take a better man than you, you white-faced jockey°—or your
    mother either—or all the lot of you put together! (*He waits awhile*) 400
    I'm not daft—I can see what she's driving at. (*Silence*) I'm not a fool,
    if you think so. I can pay you yet, you sliving° bitch! (*He sticks out his
    chin at his wife*)

> *Ernest lifts his head and looks at him*

(*Turns with renewing ferocity on his son*) Yes, and you either. I'll stand 405
no more of your chelp.° I'll stand no *more*! Do you hear me?

MOTHER Ernest!
>   *Ernest looks down at his book.*
>   *The Father turns to the Mother*

FATHER Ernest! Ay, prompt him! Set him on—you know how to do it—   410
you know how to do it!
>   *There is a persistent silence*

I know it! I know it! I'm not daft, I'm not a fool! (*The other boot falls to the floor*)

>   *He rises, pulling himself up with the arms of the chair, and,*   415
>   *turning round, takes a Waterbury watch° with a brass chain from*
>   *the wall beside the bookcase: his pit watch that the Mother hung*
>   *there when she put his pit-trousers in the cupboard—and winds it*
>   *up, swaying on his feet as he does so. Then he puts it back on the*
>   *nail, and a key swings at the end of the chain. Then he takes a*   420
>   *silver watch from his pocket, and, fumbling, missing the keyhole,*
>   *winds that up also with a key, and, swaying forward, hangs it up*
>   *over the cupboard. Then he lurches round, and, limping pitiably,*
>   *goes off upstairs.*
>   *There is a heavy silence. The Waterbury watch can be heard*   425
>   *ticking*

ERNEST I would kill him, if it weren't that I shiver at the thought of touching him.

MOTHER Oh, you mustn't! Think how awful it would be if there were anything like that. I couldn't bear it.   430

ERNEST He is a damned, accursed fool!
>   *The Mother sighs. Ernest begins to read.*
>   *There is a quick patter of feet, and Gertie Coomber comes*
>   *running in*

GERTIE Has Mr Lambert come?   435

MOTHER Ay—in bed.

GERTIE My father hasn't come yet. Isn't it sickening?

MOTHER It is, child. They want horsewhipping, and those that serve them, more.

GERTIE I'm sure we haven't a bit of peace of our lives. I'm sure when   440
Mother was alive, she used to say her life was a burden, for she never knew when he'd come home, or how.

MOTHER And it is so.

GERTIE Did you go far, Ernest?

ERNEST (*not looking up*) I don't know. Middling.   445

MOTHER He must have gone about home, for he's not been back many minutes.

GERTIE There's our Frances shouting!
>   *She runs off*

MOTHER (*quietly*) What did you do with that other loaf?   450

ERNEST (*looking up, smiling*) Why, we forgot it, and it got all burned.

MOTHER (*rather bitterly*) Of course you forgot it. And where is it?

ERNEST Well, it was no good keeping it. I thought it would only grieve
>   your heart, the sight of it, so I put it on the fire.

MOTHER Yes, I'm sure! That was a nice thing to do, I must say! . . . Put   455
>   a brown loaf on the fire, and dry the only other one up to a cinder!
>   *The smile dies from his face, and he begins to frown*
>   (*She speaks bitterly*) It's always alike, though. If Maggie Pearson's
>   here, nobody else matters. It's only a laughing matter if the bread gets
>   burnt to cinders and put on the fire. (*Suddenly bursts into a glow of*   460
>   *bitterness*) It's all very well, my son—you may talk about caring for
>   me, but when it comes to Maggie Pearson it's very little you care for
>   me—or Nellie—or anybody else.

ERNEST (*dashing his fingers through his hair*) You talk *just* like a woman!
>   As if it makes any difference! As if it makes the least difference!   465

MOTHER (*folding her hands in her lap and turning her face from him*) Yes,
>   it does.

ERNEST (*frowning fiercely*) It doesn't. Why should it? If I like apples,
>   does it mean I don't like—bread? You know, Ma, it doesn't make any
>   difference.   470

MOTHER (*doggedly*) *I* know it does.

ERNEST (*shaking his finger at her*) But why should it, why should it? You
>   know you wouldn't be interested in the things we talk about: you
>   know you wouldn't.

MOTHER Why shouldn't I?   475

ERNEST Should you, now? Look here: we talked about French poetry.
>   Should you care about that?
>   *No answer*
>   You know you wouldn't! And then we talked about those pictures
>   at the Exhibition°—about Frank Brangwyn°—about Impression-   480
>   ism°—for ever such a long time. You would only be bored by that—

MOTHER Why should I? You never tried.

ERNEST But you wouldn't. You wouldn't care whether it's Impres-
>   sionism or pre-Raphaelitism.° (*Pathetically*)

MOTHER I don't see why I shouldn't.   485

ERNEST (*ruffling his hair in despair; after a pause*) And, besides, there are
>   lots of things you can't talk to your own folks about, that you would
>   tell a stranger.

MOTHER (*bitterly*) Yes, I know there are.

ERNEST (*wildly*) Well, I can't help it—can I, now?   490

MOTHER (*reluctantly*) No—I suppose not—if you say so.

ERNEST But you know!

MOTHER (*turning aside again with some bitterness and passion*) I do know, my boy—I *do* know!

ERNEST But I can't help it.   495

> *His Mother does not reply, but sits with her face averted*

Can I, now? Can I?

MOTHER You say not.

ERNEST (*changing the position again*) And you wouldn't care if it was Alice, or Lois, or Louie. You never row me if I'm a bit late when I've   500
been with them. . . . It's just Maggie, because you don't like her.

MOTHER (*with emphasis*) No, I *don't* like her—and I *can't* say I do.

ERNEST But why not? Why not? She's as good as I am—and I'm sure you've nothing against her—have you, now?

MOTHER (*shortly*) No, I don't know I've anything against her.   505

ERNEST Well, then, what do you get so wild about?

MOTHER Because I don't like her, and I never shall, so there, my boy!

ERNEST Because you've made up your mind not to.

MOTHER Very well, then.

ERNEST (*bitterly*) And you did from the beginning, just because she   510
happened to care for me.

MOTHER (*with coldness*) And does nobody else care for you, then, but her?

ERNEST (*knitting his brows and shaking his hands in despair*) Oh, but it's not a question of that.   515

MOTHER (*calmly, coldly*) But it is a question of that.

ERNEST (*fiercely*) It isn't! You know it isn't! I care just as much for you as ever—you know I do.

MOTHER It looks like it, when night after night you leave me sitting up here till nearly eleven—and gone eleven sometimes—   520

ERNEST Once, Mother, once—and that was when it was her birthday.

MOTHER (*turning to him with the anger of love*) And how many times is it a quarter to eleven, and twenty to?

ERNEST But you'd sit up just the same if I were in; you'd sit up reading—you know you would.   525

MOTHER You don't come in to see.

ERNEST When I am in, do you go to bed before then?

MOTHER I do.

ERNEST Did you on Wednesday night, or on Tuesday, or on Monday?

MOTHER No; because you were working.   530

ERNEST I was *in*.

MOTHER I'm not going to go to bed and leave you sitting up, and I'm not going to go to bed to leave you to come in when you like . . . so there!

ERNEST (*beginning to unfasten his boots*) Alright—I can't help it, then.

MOTHER You mean you won't.   535

> There is a pause. ERNEST *hangs his head, forgetting to unlace his boot further*

ERNEST (*pathetically*) You don't worry our Nellie. Look, she's out now. You never row her.

MOTHER I do. I'm always telling her.   540

ERNEST Not like this.

MOTHER I do! I called her all the names I could lay my tongue to last night.

ERNEST But you're not nasty every time she goes out to see Eddie, and you don't for ever say nasty things about *him*. . . .   545

> There is a moment of silence, while he waits for an answer

ERNEST And I always know you'll be sitting here working yourself into a state if I happen to go up to Herod's Farm.°

MOTHER Do I?—and perhaps you would, if you sat here waiting all night—   550

ERNEST But, Ma, you don't care if Nellie's out.

MOTHER (*after brooding awhile; with passion*) No, my boy, because she doesn't mean the same to me. She has never understood—she has not been—like you. And now—you seem to care nothing—you care for *any*thing more than home: you tell me nothing but the little   555 things: you used to tell me everything; you used to come to me with everything; but now—I don't *do* for you now. You have to find somebody else.

ERNEST But I can't help it. I can't help it. I have to grow up—and things are different to us now.   560

MOTHER (*bitterly*) Yes, things *are* different to us now. They never used to be. And you say I've never tried to care for her. I have—I've tried and tried to like her, but I can't, and it's no good.

ERNEST (*pathetically*) Well, my dear, we shall have to let it be, then, and things will have to go their way. (*He speaks with difficulty*) You know,   565 Mater—I don't care for her—really—not half as I care for you. Only, just now—well, I can't help it, I can't help it. But I care just the same—for you—I do.

MOTHER (*turning with a little cry*) But I thought you didn't!

> *He takes her in his arms, and she kisses him, and he hides his face*   570
> *in her shoulder. She holds him closely for a moment; then she*
> *kisses him and gently releases him. He kisses her. She gently*
> *draws away, saying, very tenderly*

MOTHER There!—Nellie will be coming in.

ERNEST (*after a pause*) And you do understand, don't you, Mater?   575

MOTHER (*with great gentleness, having decided not to torment him*) Yes,
I understand now. (*She bluffs him*)

> *Ernest takes her hand and strokes it a moment. Then he bends*
> *down and continues to unfasten his boots. It is very silent*

I'm sure that hussy ought to be in—just look at the time!   580

ERNEST Ay, it's scandalous!

> *There are in each of their voices traces of the recent anguish, which*
> *makes their speech utterly insignificant. Nevertheless, in thus*
> *speaking, each reassures the other that the moment of abnormal*
> *emotion and proximity is passed, and the usual position of careless*   585
> *intimacy is reassumed*

MOTHER (*rising*) I shall have to go and call her—a brazen baggage!

> *There is a rattle of the yard gate, and Nellie runs in, blinking very*
> *much*

NELLIE (*out of breath; but very casually*) Hello, our Ernest, you home?   590

MOTHER Yes, miss, and been home long ago. I'll not have it, my lady, so
you needn't think it. You're not going to be down there till this time
of night! It's disgraceful. What will his mother say, do you think,
when he walks in at past eleven?

NELLIE She can say what she likes. Besides, she'll be in bed.   595

MOTHER She'll hear him, for all that. I'd be ashamed of myself, that I
would, standing out there slobbering till this time of night! I don't
know how anyone can be such a fool!

NELLIE (*smiling*) Perhaps not, my dear.

MOTHER (*slightly stung*) No, and I should be sorry. I don't know what he   600
wants running up at this time of a night.

NELLIE Oh, Mother, don't go on again! We've heard it a dozen times.

MOTHER And you'll hear it two dozen.

> *Ernest, having got off his shoes, begins to take off his collar and tie*
> *Nellie sits down in the arm-chair.*   605

NELLIE (*dragging up the stool and beginning to unlace her boots*) I could
hear my father carrying on again. Was he a nuisance?

MOTHER Is he ever anything else when he's like that?

NELLIE He *is* a nuisance. I wish he was far enough! Eddie could hear every word he said.   610

ERNEST Shame! Shame!

NELLIE (*in great disgust*) It is! *He* never hears anything like that. Oh, I was wild. I could have killed him!

MOTHER You should have sent him home; then he'd not have heard it at all.   615

NELLIE He'd only just come, so I'm sure I wasn't going to send him home then.

ERNEST So you heard it all, to the mild-and-bitter end?

NELLIE No, I didn't. And I felt such a fool!

ERNEST You should choose your spot out of earshot, not just by the   620
garden gate. What did you do?

NELLIE I said, 'Come on, Eddie, let's get away from this lot.' I'm sure I shouldn't have wondered if he'd gone home and never come near again.

MOTHER (*satirically*) What for?   625

NELLIE Why—when he heard that row.

MOTHER I'm sure it was very bad for him, poor boy.

NELLIE (*fiercely*) How should you like it?

MOTHER I shouldn't have a fellow there at that time at all.

ERNEST You thought a father-in-law that kicked up a shindy was   630
enough to scare him off, did you? Well, if you choose your girl, you can't choose your father-in-law—you'll have to tell him that.

> *Nellie has taken off her shoes. She stands in front of the mirror and uncoils her hair, and plaits it in a thick plait which hangs down her back*   635

MOTHER Come, Ernest; you'll never want to get up in the morning.

NELLIE (*suddenly*) Oh! There now! I never gave him that rose. (*She looks down at her bosom and lifts the head of a rather crushed rose*) What a nuisance!

ERNEST The sad history of a rose between two hearts: 640

> *Rose, red rose, that burns with a low flame,*
> > *What has broken you?*
> *Hearts, two hearts caught up in a game*
> > *Of shuttlecock—Amen!*°

NELLIE (*blushing*) Go on, you soft creature! (*Looks at the rose*)   645

ERNEST Weep over it.

NELLIE Shan't!

ERNEST And pickle it, like German girls do.

NELLIE Don't be such a donkey.

ERNEST Interesting item: final fate of the rose.   650

> *Nellie goes out; returns in a moment with the rose in an egg-cup in one hand, and a candle in the other.*
>
> *The Mother rises*

ERNEST I'll rake, Mother.

> *Nellie lights her candle, takes her shawl off the table, kisses her*   655
> *Mother good night, and bids her brother good night as he goes out to the cellar.*
>
> *The Mother goes about taking off the heavy green table-cloth, disclosing the mahogany, and laying a doubled table-cloth half across. She sets the table with a cup and saucer, plate, knife,*   660
> *sugar-basin, brown-and-white teapot and tea-caddy. Then she fetches a tin bottle and a soiled snapbag, and lays them together on the bare half of the table. She puts out the salt and goes and drags the pit-trousers from the cupboard and puts them near the fire*
>
> *Meanwhile Ernest has come from the cellar with a large lump of*   665
> *coal, which he pushes down in the fireplace so that it shall not lodge and go out*

MOTHER You'll want some small bits.—And bring a few pieces for him in the morning.

ERNEST (*returning to the cellar with the dust-pan*) Alright! I'll turn the   670
gas out now.

> *The Mother fetches another candle and continues her little tasks. The gas goes suddenly down and dies slowly out.*
>
> *Ernest comes up with his candlestick on a shovelful of coal. He puts the candle on the table, and puts some coal on the fire, round*   675
> *the 'raker'.° The rest he puts in the shovel on the hearth. Then he goes to wash his hands.*
>
> *The Mother, leaving her candle in the scullery, comes in with an old iron fire-screen which she hangs on the bars of the grate, and the ruddy light shows over and through the worn iron top.*   680
> *Ernest is heard jerking the roller-towel. He enters, and goes to his Mother, kissing her forehead, and then her cheek, stroking her cheek with his finger-tips*

ERNEST Good night, my dear.

MOTHER Good night.—Don't you want a candle?   685

ERNEST No—blow it out. Good night.

MOTHER (*very softly*) Good night.

> *There is in their tones a dangerous gentleness—so much gentleness that the safe reserve of their souls is broken.*

52

Ernest goes upstairs. His bedroom door is heard to shut.   690
The Mother stands and looks in the fire. The room is lighted by the
red glow only. Then in a moment or two she goes into the scullery,
and after a minute—during which running of water is heard—she
returns with her candle, looking little and bowed and pathetic, and
crosses the room, softly closing the passage door behind her.   695
End of Act 3

THE WIDOWING
OF MRS HOLROYD

MRS HOLROYD
HOLROYD
BLACKMORE
JACK HOLROYD
MINNIE HOLROYD
GRANDMOTHER
RIGLEY
CLARA
LAURA
MANAGER
TWO MINERS

The action of the play takes place in the Holroyds' cottage

Act 1 Scene 1

The kitchen of a miner's small cottage. On the left is the fireplace,
with a deep, full red fire. At the back is a white-curtained window,
and beside it the outer door of the room. On the right, two white
wooden stairs intrude into the kitchen below the closed stair-foot
door. On the left, another door.   5
The room is furnished with a chintz-backed sofa under the
window, a glass-knobbed painted dresser on the right, and in the
centre, toward the fire, a table with a red and blue check tablecloth.
On one side of the hearth is a wooden rocking-chair, on the other
an armchair of round staves. An unlighted copper-shaded lamp   10
hangs from the raftered ceiling. It is dark twilight, with the
room full of warm fireglow. A woman enters from the outer door.
As she leaves the door open behind her, the colliery rail can be
seen not far from the threshold, and, away back, the headstocks°
of a pit.   15
The woman is tall and voluptuously built. She carries a basket
heaped full of washing, which she has just taken from the clothes-
lines outside. Setting down the basket heavily, she feels among the
clothes. She lifts out a white heap of sheets and other linen, setting
it on the table; then she takes a woollen shirt in her hand   20

MRS HOLROYD (*aloud, to herself*) You know they're not dry even now,
   though it's been as fine as it has. (*She spreads the shirt on the back of her*
   rocking-chair, which she turns to the fire)

VOICE (*calling from outside*) Well, have you got them dry?

    Mrs Holroyd starts up, turns and flings her hand in the direction   25
   of the open door, where appears a man in blue overalls, swarfed°
   and greased. He carries a dinner-basket

MRS HOLROYD You— you—I don't know what to call you! The idea
   of shouting at me like that—like the Evil One out of the darkness!

BLACKMORE I ought to have remembered your tender nerves. Shall   30
   I come in?

MRS HOLROYD No—not for your impudence. But you're late, aren't
   you?

BLACKMORE It's only just gone six. We electricians, you know, we're the
   gentlemen on a mine: ours is gentlemen's work. But I'll bet Charles   35
   Holroyd was home before four.

MRS HOLROYD (*bitterly*) Ay, and gone again before five.

BLACKMORE But mine's a lad's job, and I do nothing!—Where's he gone?

MRS HOLROYD (*contemptuously*) Dunno! He'd got a game on some- 40
where—toffed himself up to the nines, and skedaddled off as brisk as
a turkey-cock. (*She smirks in front of the mirror hanging on the chimney-
piece, in imitation of a man brushing his hair and moustache and admiring
himself*)

BLACKMORE Though turkey-cocks aren't brisk as a rule. Children 45
playing?

MRS HOLROYD (*recovering herself, coldly*) Yes. And they ought to be in.
> *She continues placing the flannel garments before the fire, on the
> fender and on chair-backs, till the stove is hedged in with a
> steaming fence; then she takes a sheet in a bundle from the table,* 50
> *and goes up to Blackmore, who stands watching her*

Here, take hold, and help me fold it.

BLACKMORE I shall swarf it up.°

MRS HOLROYD (*snatching back the sheet*) Oh, you're as tiresome as everybody else. 55

BLACKMORE (*putting down his basket and moving to door on right*) Well, I
can soon wash my hands.

MRS HOLROYD (*ceasing to flap and fold pillow-cases*) That roller-towel's
ever so dirty. I'll get you another. (*She goes to a drawer in the dresser,
and then back toward the scullery, from which comes the sound of water*) 60

BLACKMORE Why, bless my life, I'm a lot dirtier than the towel. I don't
want another.

MRS HOLROYD (*going into the scullery*) Here you are.

BLACKMORE (*softly, now she is near him*) Why did you trouble now?
Pride, you know, pride, nothing else. 65

MRS HOLROYD (*also playful*) It's nothing but decency.

BLACKMORE (*softly*) Pride, pride, pride!
> *A child of eight suddenly appears in the doorway*

JACK Oo, how dark!

MRS HOLROYD (*hurrying agitated into the kitchen*) Why, where have you 70
been—what have you been doing now?

JACK (*surprised*) Why—I've only been out to play.

MRS HOLROYD (*still sharply*) And where's Minnie?
> *A little girl of six appears by the door*

MINNIE I'm here, mam, and what do you think—? 75

MRS HOLROYD (*softening, as she recovers equanimity*) Well, and what
should I think?

JACK Oh, yes, mam—you know my father—?

MRS HOLROYD (*ironically*) I should hope so.

MINNIE We saw him dancing, mam, with a paper bonnet.   80

MRS HOLROYD What——?

JACK There's some women at New Inn, what's come from Nottingham—

MINNIE An' he's dancin' with the pink one.

JACK Shut up, our Minnie. An' they've got paper bonnets on—

MINNIE All colours, mam!   85

JACK (*getting angry*) Shut up, our Minnie! An' my dad's dancing with her.

MINNIE With the pink-bonnet one, mam.

JACK Up in the club-room over the bar.

MINNIE An' she's a lot littler than him, mam.   90

JACK (*piteously*) Shut up, our Minnie—An' you can see 'em go past the window, 'cause there isn't no curtains up, an' my father's got the pink-bonnet one—

MINNIE An' there's a piano, mam—

JACK An' lots of folk outside watchin', lookin' at my dad! He can dance,   95
can't he, mam?

MRS HOLROYD (*she has been lighting the lamp, and holds the lamp-glass*)
And who else is there?

MINNIE Some more men—an' *all* the women with paper bonnets on.

JACK There's about ten, I should think, an' they say they came in a   100
brake from Nottingham.

> *Mrs Holroyd, trying to replace the lamp-glass° over the flame,*
> *lets it drop on the floor with a smash*

JACK There, now—now we'll have to have a candle.

BLACKMORE (*appearing in the scullery doorway with the towel*) What's   105
that—the lamp-glass?

JACK I never knowed Mr Blackmore was here.

BLACKMORE (*to Mrs Holroyd*) Have you got another?

MRS HOLROYD No. (*There is silence for a moment*) We can manage with
a candle for to-night.   110

BLACKMORE (*stepping forward and blowing out the smoky flame*) I'll see if
I can't get you one from the pit. I shan't be a minute.

MRS HOLROYD Don't—don't bother—I don't want you to.

> *He, however, unscrews the burner and goes*

MINNIE Did Mr Blackmore come for tea, mam?   115

MRS HOLROYD No; he's had no tea.

JACK I bet he's hungry. Can I have some bread?

MRS HOLROYD (*she stands a lighted candle on the table*) Yes, and you can
get your boots off to go to bed.

JACK It's not seven o'clock yet.   120

MRS HOLROYD It doesn't matter.

MINNIE What do they wear paper bonnets for, mam?

MRS HOLROYD Because they're brazen hussies.

JACK I saw them having a glass of beer.

MRS HOLROYD A nice crew!   125

JACK They say they are old pals of Mrs Meakins. You could hear her
    screaming o' laughin', an' my dad says: 'He-ah, missis—here—a
    dog's-nose° for the Dachess—hopin' it'll smell samthing'—What's a
    dog's-nose?

MRS HOLROYD (*giving him a piece of bread and butter*) Don't ask me,   130
    child. How should I know?

MINNIE Would she eat it, mam?

MRS HOLROYD Eat what?

MINNIE Her in the pink bonnet—eat the dog's-nose?

MRS HOLROYD No, of course not. How should I know what a dog's-   135
    nose is?

JACK I bet he'll never go to work to-morrow, mother—will he?

MRS HOLROYD Goodness knows. I'm sick of it—disgracing me. There'll
    be the whole place cackling° *this* now. They've no sooner finished
    about him getting taken up° for fighting than they begin on this. But 140
    I'll put a stop to it some road° or other. It's not going on, if I know it:
    it isn't.

    She stops, hearing footsteps, and Blackmore enters

BLACKMORE Here we are then—got one all right.

MINNIE Did they give it you, Mr Blackmore?   145

BLACKMORE No, I took it.

    *He screws on the burner and proceeds to light the lamp. He is a
    tall, slender, mobile man of twenty-seven, brown-haired, dressed
    in blue overalls. Jack Holroyd is a big, dark, ruddy, lusty lad.
    Minnie is also big, but fair*   150

MINNIE What do you wear blue trousers for, Mr Blackmore?

BLACKMORE They're to keep my other trousers from getting greasy.

MINNIE Why don't you wear pit-breeches, like dad's?

JACK 'Cause he's a 'lectrician. Could you make me a little injun what
    would make electric light?   155

BLACKMORE I will, some day.

JACK When?

MINNIE Why don't you come an' live here?

BLACKMORE (*looking swiftly at Mrs Holroyd*) Nay, you've got your own
    dad to live here.   160

MINNIE (*plaintively*) Well, you could come as well. Dad shouts when
we've gone to bed, an' thumps the table. He wouldn't if you was here.

JACK He dursn't—

MRS HOLROYD Be quiet now, be quiet. Here, Mr Blackmore. (*She again
gives him the sheet to fold*) 165

BLACKMORE Your hands *are* cold.

MRS HOLROYD Are they?—I didn't know.

  Blackmore puts his hand on hers

MRS HOLROYD (*confusedly, looking aside*) You must want your tea.

BLACKMORE I'm in no hurry. 170

MRS HOLROYD Selvidge to selvidge.° You'll be quite a domestic man,
if you go on.

BLACKMORE Ay.

  They fold the two sheets

BLACKMORE They are white, your sheets! 175

MRS HOLROYD But look at the smuts on them—look! This vile hole! I'd
never have come to live here, in all the thick of the pit-grime, and
lonely, if it hadn't been for him, so that he shouldn't call in a public-
house on his road home from work. And now he slinks past on the
other side of the railway, and goes down to the New Inn instead of 180
coming in for his dinner. I might as well have stopped in Bestwood.

BLACKMORE Though I rather like this little place, standing by itself.

MRS HOLROYD Jack, can you go and take the stockings in for me?
They're on the line just below the pigsty. The prop's near the apple-
tree—mind it. Minnie, you take the peg-basket. 185

MINNIE Will there be any rats, mam?

MRS HOLROYD Rats—no. They'll be frightened when they hear you, if
there are.

  The children go out

BLACKMORE Poor little beggars! 190

MRS HOLROYD Do you know, this place is fairly alive with rats. They
run up that dirty vine in front of the house—I'm always at him to cut
it down—and you can hear them at night overhead like a regiment of
soldiers tramping. Really, you know, I *hate* them.

BLACKMORE Well—a rat is a nasty thing! 195

MRS HOLROYD But I s'll get used to them. I'd give anything to be out of
this place.

BLACKMORE It *is* rotten, when you're tied to a life you don't like. But
I should miss it if you weren't here. When I'm coming down the line
to the pit in the morning—it's nearly dark at seven now—I watch the 200
firelight in here. Sometimes I put my hand on the wall outside where

61

the chimney runs up to feel it warm. There isn't much in Bestwood, is there?

MRS HOLROYD There's less than nothing if you can't be like the rest of them—as common as they're made.

BLACKMORE It's a fact—particularly for a woman—But this place is cosy—God love me, I'm sick of lodgings.

MRS HOLROYD You'll have to get married—I'm sure there are plenty of nice girls about.

BLACKMORE Are there? I never see 'em. (*He laughs*)

MRS HOLROYD Oh, come, you can't say that.

BLACKMORE I've not seen a single girl—an unmarried girl—that I should want for more than a fortnight—not one.

MRS HOLROYD Perhaps you're very particular.

She puts her two palms on the table and leans back. He draws near to her, dropping his head

BLACKMORE Look here!

He has put his hand on the table near hers

MRS HOLROYD Yes, I know you've got nice hands—but you needn't be vain of them.

BLACKMORE No—it's not that—But don't they seem—(*He glances swiftly at her; she turns her head aside; he laughs nervously*)—they sort of go well with one another. (*He laughs again*)

MRS HOLROYD They *do*, rather—

They stand still, near one another, with bent heads, for a moment. Suddenly she starts up and draws her hand away

BLACKMORE Why—what is it?

She does not answer. The children come in—Jack with an armful of stockings, Minnie with the basket of pegs

JACK I believe it's freezing, mother.

MINNIE Mr Blackmore, could you shoot a rat an' hit it?

BLACKMORE (*laughing*) Shoot the lot of 'em, like a wink.

MRS HOLROYD But you've had no tea. What an awful shame to keep you here!

BLACKMORE Nay, I don't care. It never bothers me.

MRS HOLROYD Then you're different from most men.

BLACKMORE All men aren't alike, you know.

MRS HOLROYD But do go and get some tea.

MINNIE (*plaintively*) Can't you stop, Mr Blackmore?

BLACKMORE Why, Minnie?

MINNIE So's we're not frightened. Yes, do. Will you?

BLACKMORE Frightened of what?

MINNIE 'Cause there's noises, an' rats—an' perhaps dad'll come home and shout.

BLACKMORE But he'd shout more if I was here.   245

JACK He doesn't when my uncle John's here. So you stop, an' perhaps he won't.

BLACKMORE Don't you like him to shout when you're in bed?

> *They do not answer, but look seriously at him.*

CURTAIN   250

Act 1 Scene 2

> *The same scene, two hours later. The clothes are folded in little piles on the table and the sofa. Mrs Holroyd is folding a thick flannel undervest or singlet which her husband wears in the pit and which has just dried on the fender*

MRS HOLROYD (*to herself*) Now, thank goodness, they're all dried. It's   5
only nine o'clock, so he won't be in for another two hours, the nuisance. (*She sits on the sofa, letting her arms hang down in dejection. After
a minute or two she jumps up, to begin rudely dropping the piles of washed
clothes in the basket*) I don't care, I'm not going to let him have it all *his*
way—no! (*She weeps a little, fiercely, drying her eyes on the edge of her*   10
white apron) Why should *I* put up with it all?—*He* can do what he
likes. But I don't care, no, I don't—

> *She flings down the full clothes-basket, sits suddenly in the
> rocking-chair, and weeps. There is the sound of coarse, bursting
> laughter, in vain subdued, and a man's deep guffaws. Footsteps*   15
> *draw near. Suddenly the door opens, and a little, plump, pretty
> woman of thirty, in a close-fitting dress and a giddy, frilled bonnet
> of pink paper, stands perkily in the doorway. Mrs Holroyd springs
> up; her small, sensitive nose is inflamed with weeping, her eyes are
> wet and flashing. She fronts° the other woman*   20

CLARA (*with a pert smile and a jerk of the head*) Good evenin'!

MRS HOLROYD What do you want?

CLARA (*she has a Yorkshire accent*) Oh, we've not come beggin'—this is
a visit.

> *She stuffs her handkerchief in front of her mouth in a little*   25
> *snorting burst of laughter. There is the sound of another woman
> behind going off into uncontrollable laughter, while a man guffaws*

MRS HOLROYD (*after a moment of impotence—tragically*) What—!

CLARA (*faltering slightly, affecting a polite tone*) We thought we'd just call— 30
　　　　She stuffs her handkerchief in front of her explosive laughter—
　　　　the other woman shrieks again, beginning high, and running down
　　　　the scale

MRS HOLROYD What do you mean?—What do you want here?

CLARA (*she bites her lip*) We don't want anything, thanks. We've just 35
　　called. (*She begins to laugh again—so does the other*) Well, I don't think
　　much of the manners in this part of the country. (*She takes a few*
　　hesitating steps into the kitchen)

MRS HOLROYD (*trying to shut the door upon her*) No, you are not coming
　　in.

CLARA (*preventing her closing the door*) Dear me, what a to-do! (*She* 40
　　struggles with the door. The other woman comes up to help; a man is seen
　　in the background)

LAURA My word, aren't we good enough to come in?
　　　　Mrs Holroyd, finding herself confronted by what seems to her
　　　　excitement a crowd, releases the door and draws back a little— 45
　　　　almost in tears of anger

MRS HOLROYD You have no business here. What do you want?

CLARA (*putting her bonnet straight and entering in brisk defiance*) I tell you
　　we've only come to see you. (*She looks round the kitchen, then makes a*
　　gesture toward the arm-chair) Can I sit here? (*She plumps herself down*) 50
　　Rest for the weary.
　　　　A woman and a man have followed her into the room. Laura is
　　　　highly coloured, stout, some forty years old, wears a blue paper
　　　　bonnet, and looks like the landlady of a public-house. Both she
　　　　and Clara wear much jewellery. Laura is well dressed in a blue 55
　　　　cloth dress. Holroyd is a big blond man. His cap is pushed back,
　　　　and he looks rather tipsy and lawless. He has a heavy blond
　　　　moustache. His jacket and trousers are black, his vest grey, and
　　　　he wears a turn-down collar with dark bow

LAURA (*sitting down in a chair on right, her hand on her bosom, panting*) 60
　　I've laughed till I feel fair bad.

CLARA 'Aven't you got a drop of nothink to offer us, mester? Come, you
　　are slow. I should 'ave thought a gentleman like you would have been
　　out with the glasses afore we could have got breaths to ask you.

HOLROYD (*clumsily*) I dunna believe there's owt in th' 'ouse but a bottle 65
　　of stout.

CLARA (*putting her hand on her stomach*) It feels as if th' kettle's going to
　　boil over.
　　　　She stuffs her handkerchief in front of her mouth, throws back
　　　　her head, and snorts with laughter, having now regained her 70

*confidence. Laura laughs in the last state of exhaustion, her hand
  on her breast*

HOLROYD Shall ta ha'e it then?

CLARA What do you say, Laura—are you having a drop?

LAURA (*submissively, and naturally tongue-tied*) Well—I don't mind—   75
  I will if *you* do.

CLARA (*recklessly*) I think we'll 'ave a drop, Charlie, an' risk it. It'll
  'appen hold the rest down.

> *There is a moment of silence, while Holroyd goes into the scullery.
> Clara surveys the room and the dramatic pose of Mrs Holroyd*   80
> *curiously*

HOLROYD (*suddenly*) Heh! What, come 'ere—!

> *There is a smash of pots, and a rat careers out of the scullery.
> Laura, the first to see it, utters a scream, but is fastened to her
> chair, unable to move*   85

CLARA (*jumps up to the table, crying*) It's a rat—Oh, save us! (*She
  scrambles up, banging her head on the lamp, which swings violently*)

MRS HOLROYD (*who, with a little shriek, jerks her legs up on to the sofa,
  where she was stiffly reclining, now cries in despairing falsetto, stretching
  forth her arms*) The lamp—mind, the lamp!   90

> *Clara steadies the lamp, and holds her hand to her head*

HOLROYD (*coming from the scullery, a bottle of stout in his hand*) Where is
  he?

CLARA I believe he's gone under the sofa. My, an' he's a thumper,° if you
  like, as big as a rabbit.   95

> *Holroyd advances cautiously toward the sofa*

LAURA (*springing suddenly into life*) Hi, hi, let me go—let me go—Don't
  touch him—Where is he? (*She flees and scrambles on to Clara's arm-
  chair, catching hold of the latter's skirts*)

CLARA Hang off—do you want to have a body down—Mind, I tell you.   100

MRS HOLROYD (*bunched up on the sofa, with crossed hands holding her arms,
  fascinated, watches her husband as he approaches to stoop and attack the
  rat; she suddenly screams*) Don't, he'll fly at you.

HOLROYD He'll not get a chance.

MRS HOLROYD He will, he will—and they're poisonous! (*She ends on   105
  a very high note. Leaning forward on the sofa as far as she dares, she
  stretches out her arms to keep back her husband, who is about to kneel and
  search under the sofa for the rat*)

HOLROYD Come off, I canna see him.

MRS HOLROYD I won't let you; he'll fly at you.   110

HOLROYD I'll settle him—

MRS HOLROYD Open the door and let him go.

HOLROYD I shonna. I'll settle him. Shut thy claver.° He'll non come anigh thee.

> *He kneels down and begins to creep to the sofa. With a great*   115
> *bound, Mrs Holroyd flies to the door and flings it open. Then*
> *she rushes back to the couch*

CLARA There he goes!

HOLROYD (*simultaneously*) Hi!—Ussza! (*He flings the bottle of stout out*
of the door)   120

LAURA (*piteously*) Shut the door, do.

> *Holroyd rises, dusting his trousers knees, and closes the door.*
> *Laura heavily descends and drops in the chair*

CLARA Here, come an' help us down, Charlie. Look at her; she's going off.   125

> *Though Laura is still purple-red, she sinks back in the chair.*
> *Holroyd goes to the table. Clara places her hands on his shoulders*
> *and jumps lightly down. Then she pushes Holroyd with her*
> *elbow*

Look sharp, get a glass of water.   130

> *She unfastens Laura's collar and pulls off the paper bonnet. Mrs*
> *Holroyd sits up, straightens her clothing, and tries to look cold and*
> *contemptuous. Holroyd brings a cup of water. Clara sprinkles her*
> *friend's face. Laura sighs and sighs again very deeply, then draws*
> *herself up painfully*   135

CLARA (*tenderly*) Do you feel any better—shall you have a drink of water?

> *Laura mournfully shakes her head; Clara turns sharply to*
> *Holroyd*

She'll 'ave a drop o' something.   140

> *Holroyd goes out. Clara meanwhile fans her friend with a hand-*
> *kerchief. Holroyd brings stout. She pours out the stout, smells the*
> *glass, smells the bottle—then finally the cork*

Eh, mester, it's all of a work—it's had a foisty cork.

> *At that instant the stairfoot door opens slowly, revealing the*   145
> *children—the girl peering over the boy's shoulder—both in white*
> *nightgowns. Everybody starts. Laura gives a little cry, presses her*
> *hand on her bosom, and sinks back, gasping*

CLARA (*appealing and anxious, to Mrs Holroyd*) You don't 'appen to 'ave a drop of brandy for her, do you, missis?   150

> *Mrs Holroyd rises coldly without replying, and goes to the stair-*
> *foot door where the children stand*

MRS HOLROYD (*sternly to the children*) Go to bed!

JACK What's a matter, mother?

MRS HOLROYD Never you mind, go to bed!   155

CLARA (*appealingly*) Be quick, missis.

> *Mrs Holroyd, glancing round, sees Laura going purple, and runs*
> *past the children upstairs. The boy and girl sit on the lowest stair.*
> *Their father goes out of the house, shamefaced. Mrs Holroyd runs*
> *downstairs with a little brandy in a large bottle*   160

CLARA Thanks, awfully. (*To Laura*) Come on, try an' drink a drop,
there's a dear.

> *They administer brandy to Laura. The children sit watching,*
> *open-eyed. The girl stands up to look*

MINNIE (*whispering*) I believe it's blue bonnet.   165

JACK (*whispering*) It isn't—she's in a fit.

MINNIE (*whispering*) Well, look under th' table—(*Jack peers under*)—
there's 'er bonnet. (*Jack creeps forward*) Come back, our Jack.

JACK (*returns with the bonnet*) It's all made of paper.

MINNIE Let's have a look—it's stuck together, not sewed.   170

> *She tries it on. Holroyd enters—he looks at the child*

MRS HOLROYD (*sharply, glancing round*) Take that off!

> *Minnie hurriedly takes the bonnet from her head. Her father*
> *snatches it from her and puts it on the fire*

CLARA There, you're coming round now, love.   175

> *Mrs Holroyd turns away. She sees Holroyd's eyes on the brandy-*
> *bottle, and immediately removes it, corking it up*

MRS HOLROYD (*to Clara*) You will not need this any more?

CLARA No, thanks. I'm very much obliged.

MRS HOLROYD (*does not unbend, but speaks coldly to the children*) Come,   180
this is no place for you—come back to bed.

MINNIE No, mam, I don't want to.

MRS HOLROYD (*contralto*) Come along!

MINNIE I'm frightened, mam.

MRS HOLROYD Frightened, what of?   185

MINNIE Oo, there *was* a row.

MRS HOLROYD (*taking Minnie in her arms*) Did they frighten you, my
pet? (*She kisses her*)

JACK (*in a high whisper*) Mother, it's pink bonnet and blue bonnet, what
was dancing.   190

MINNIE (*whimpering*) I don't want to go to bed, mam, I'm frightened.

CLARA (*who has pulled off her pink bonnet and revealed a jug-handle*
coiffure°) We're going now, duckie—you're not frightened of us, are
you?

Mrs Holroyd takes the girl away before she can answer. Jack   195
lingers behind

HOLROYD   Now then, get off after your mother.

JACK (*taking no notice of his father*)   I say, what's a dog's-nose?

Clara ups with her handkerchief and Laura responds with a faint
giggle   200

HOLROYD   Go thy ways upstairs.

CLARA   It's only a small whiskey with a spoonful of beer in it, my duck.

JACK   Oh!

CLARA   Come here, my duck, come on.

Jack curious, advances   205

CLARA   You'll tell your mother we didn't mean no harm, won't you?

JACK (*touching her earrings*)   What are they made of?

CLARA   They're only earrings. Don't you like them?

JACK   Um! (*He stands surveying her curiously. Then he touches a bracelet*
made of many little mosaic brooches) This is pretty, isn't it?   210

CLARA (*pleased*)   Do you like it?

She takes it off. Suddenly Mrs Holroyd is heard calling, 'Jack, Jack!'
Clara starts

HOLROYD   Now then, get off!

CLARA (*as Jack is reluctantly going*)   Kiss me good night, duckie, an' give   215
this to your sister, shall you?

She hands Jack the mosaic bracelet. He takes it doubtfully. She
kisses him. Holroyd watches in silence

LAURA (*suddenly, pathetically*)   Aren't you going to give me a kiss, an' all?

Jack yields her his cheek, then goes   220

CLARA (*to Holroyd*)   Aren't they nice children?

HOLROYD   Ay.

CLARA (*briskly*)   Oh, dear, you're very short, all of a sudden. Don't answer
if it hurts you.

LAURA   My, isn't he different?   225

HOLROYD (*laughing forcedly*)   I'm no different.

CLARA   Yes, you are. You shouldn't 'ave brought us if you was going to
turn funny over it.

HOLROYD   I'm not funny.

CLARA   No, you're not. (*She begins to laugh. Laura joins in in spite of*   230
herself) You're about as solemn as a roast potato. (*She flings up her*
hands, claps them down on her knees, and sways up and down as she laughs,
Laura joining in, hand on breast) Are you ready to be mashed? (*She goes*
off again—then suddenly wipes the laughter off her mouth and is solemn)

68

But look 'ere, this'll never do. Now I'm going to be quiet. (*She prims* 235
herself)

HOLROYD Tha'd 'appen better.

CLARA Oh, indeed! You think I've got to pull a mug° to look decent?
You'd have to pull a big un, at that rate.

> *She bubbles off, uncontrollably—shaking herself in exasperation* 240
> *meanwhile. Laura joins in. Holroyd leans over close to her*

HOLROYD Tha's got plenty o' fizz in thee, seemly.

CLARA (*putting her hand on his face and pushing it aside, but leaving her*
hand over his cheek and mouth like a caress) Don't, you've been drinking. (*She begins to laugh*) 245

HOLROYD Should we be goin' then?

CLARA Where do you want to take us?

HOLROYD Oh—you please yourself o' that! Come on wi' me.

CLARA (*sitting up prim*) Oh, indeed!

HOLROYD (*catching hold of her*) Come on, let's be movin'—(*He glances* 250
apprehensively at the stairs)

CLARA What's your hurry?

HOLROYD (*persuasively*) Yi,° come on wi' thee.

CLARA I don't think. (*She goes off, uncontrollably*)

HOLROYD (*sitting on the table, just above her*) What's use o' sittin' 'ere? 255

CLARA I'm very comfy: I thank thee.

HOLROYD Tha'rt a baffling little 'ussy.

CLARA (*running her hand along his thigh*) Aren't you havin' nothing, my
dear? (*Offers him her glass*)

HOLROYD (*getting down from the table and putting his hand forcibly on her* 260
shoulder) No. Come on, let's shift.

CLARA (*struggling*) Hands off!

> *She fetches him a sharp slap across the face. Mrs Holroyd is heard*
> *coming downstairs. Clara, released, sits down, smoothing herself.*
> *Holroyd looks evil. He goes out to the door* 265

CLARA (*to Mrs Holroyd, penitently*) I don't know what you think of us,
I'm sure.

MRS HOLROYD I think nothing at all.

CLARA (*bubbling*) So you fix your thoughts elsewhere, do you? (*Suddenly*
changing to seriousness) No, but I *have* been awful to-night. 270

MRS HOLROYD (*contralto, emphatic*) I don't want to know anything about
you. I shall be glad when you'll go.

CLARA Turning-out time, Laura.

LAURA (*turtling*) I'm sorry, I'm sure.

CLARA Never mind. But as true as I'm here, missis, I should never ha' 275
come if I'd thought. But I had a drop—it all started with your husband sayin' he wasn't a married man.

LAURA (*laughing and wiping her eyes*) I've never knowed her to go off like
it—it's after the time she's had.

CLARA You know, my husband was a brute to me—an' I was in bed three 280
month after he died. He was a brute, he was. This is the first time I've
been out; it's a'most the first laugh I've had for a year.

LAURA It's true, what she says. We thought she'd go out of 'er mind. She
never spoke a word for a fortnight.

CLARA Though he's only been dead for two months, he was a brute to 285
me. I was as nice a young girl as you could wish when I married him
and went to the Fleece Inn—I was.

LAURA Killed hisself drinking. An' she's that excitable, she is. We s'll
'ave an awful time with 'er tomorrow, I know.

MRS HOLROYD (*coldly*) I don't know why I should hear all this. 290

CLARA I know I must 'ave seemed awful. An' them children—aren't
they nice little things, Laura?

LAURA They are that.

HOLROYD (*entering from the door*) Hanna you about done theer?

CLARA My word, if this is the way you treat a lady when she comes to see 295
you. (*She rises*)

HOLROYD I'll see you down th' line.°

CLARA You're not coming a stride with us.

LAURA We've got no hat, neither of us.

CLARA We've got our own hair on our heads, at any rate. (*Drawing* 300
herself up suddenly in front of Mrs Holroyd) An' I've been educated at a
boarding school as good as anybody. I can behave myself either in the
drawing-room or in the kitchen as is fitting and proper. But if you'd
buried a husband like mine, you wouldn't feel you'd much left to be
proud of—an' you might go off occasionally. 305

MRS HOLROYD I don't want to hear you.

CLARA (*bobbing a curtsy*) Sorry I spoke.

She goes out stiffly, followed by Laura

HOLROYD (*going forward*) You mun mind th' points down th' line.

CLARA'S VOICE I thank thee, Charlie—mind thy own points. 310

He hesitates at the door—returns and sits down. There is silence
in the room. Holroyd sits with his chin in his hand. Mrs Holroyd
listens. The footsteps and voices of the two women die out. Then
she closes the door. Holroyd begins to unlace his boots

HOLROYD (*ashamed yet defiant, withal anxious to apologize*) Wheer's my   315
slippers?

> *Mrs Holroyd sits on the sofa with face averted and does not*
> *answer*

HOLROYD Dost hear? (*He pulls off his boots, noisily, and begins to hunt*
under the sofa) I canna find the things. (*No answer*) Humph!—then I'll   320
do be 'out 'em. (*He stumps about in his stockinged feet; going into the*
scullery, he brings out the loaf of bread; he returns into the scullery)
Wheer's th' cheese? (*No answer—suddenly*) God blast it! (*He hobbles*
into the kitchen) I've trod on that broken basin, an' cut my foot open.
(*Mrs Holroyd refuses to take any notice. He sits down and looks at his*   325
sole—he pulls off his stocking and looks again) It's lamed me for life.
(*Mrs Holroyd glances at the wound*) Are 'na ter goin' ter get me owt
for it?

MRS HOLROYD Psh!

HOLROYD Oh, a' right then. (*He hops to the dresser, opens a drawer, and*   330
pulls out a white rag; he is about to tear it)

MRS HOLROYD (*snatching it from him*) Don't tear that!

HOLROYD (*shouting*) Then what the deuce am I to do? (*Mrs Holroyd sits*
stonily) Oh, a' right then! (*He hops back to his chair, sits down, and begins*
to pull on his stocking) A' right then—a' right then. (*In a fever of rage*   335
he begins pulling on his boots) I'll go where I *can* find a bit o' rag.

MRS HOLROYD Yes, that's what you want! All you want is an excuse to
be off again—'a bit of rag'!

HOLROYD (*shouting*) An' what man'd want to stop in wi' a woman sittin'
as fow° as a jackass, an' canna get a word from 'er edgeways.   340

MRS HOLROYD Don't expect me to speak to you after to-night's show.
How dare you bring them to my house, how dare you?

HOLROYD They've non hurt your house, have they?

MRS HOLROYD I wonder you dare to cross the doorstep.

HOLROYD I s'll do what the deuce I like. They're as good as you are.   345

MRS HOLROYD (*stands speechless, staring at him; then low*) Don't you come
near me again—

HOLROYD (*suddenly shouting, to get his courage up*) She's as good as you
are, every bit of it.

MRS HOLROYD (*blazing*) Whatever I was and whatever I may be, don't   350
you ever come near me again.

HOLROYD What! I'll show thee. What's the hurt to you if a woman
comes to the house? They're women as good as yourself, every whit
of it.

MRS HOLROYD Say no more. *Go* with them then, and don't come back. 355

HOLROYD What! Yi, I will go, an' you s'll see. What! You think you're something, since your uncle left you that money, an' Blackymore puttin' you up to it. I can see your little game. I'm not as daft as you imagine. I'm no fool, I tell you.

MRS HOLROYD No, you're not. You're a drunken beast, that's all you 360
are.

HOLROYD What, what—I'm what? I'll show you who's gaffer, though.
(*He threatens her*)

MRS HOLROYD (*between her teeth*) No, it's not going on. If *you* won't go,
I will. 365

HOLROYD Go then, for you've always been too big for your shoes, in my
house—

MRS HOLROYD Yes—I ought never to have looked at you. Only you showed a fair face then.

HOLROYD What! What! We'll see who's master i' this house. I tell you, 370
I'm goin' to put a stop to it. (*He brings his fist down on the table with a bang*) It's going to stop. (*He bangs the table again*) I've put up with it long enough. Do you think I'm a dog in the house, an' not a man, do you—

MRS HOLROYD A dog would be better. 375

HOLROYD Oh! Oh! Then we'll see. We'll see who's the dog and who isna. We're goin' to see. (*He bangs the table*)

MRS HOLROYD Stop thumping that table! You've wakened those children once, you and your trollops.

HOLROYD I shall do what the deuce I like! 380

MRS HOLROYD No more, you won't, no more. I've stood this long enough. Now I'm going. As for you—you've got a red face where she slapped you. Now go to her.

HOLROYD What? What?

MRS HOLROYD For I'm sick of the sights and sounds of you. 385

HOLROYD (*bitterly*) By God, an' I've known it a long time.

MRS HOLROYD You have, and it's true.

HOLROYD An' I know who it is th'rt hankerin' after.

MRS HOLROYD I only want to be rid of you.

HOLROYD I know it mighty well. But *I* know him! 390

> *Mrs Holroyd, sinking down on the sofa, suddenly begins to sob
> half-hysterically. Holroyd watches her. As suddenly, she dries
> her eyes*

MRS HOLROYD Do you think I care about what you say? (*Suddenly*) Oh,
I've had enough. I've tried, I've tried for years, for the children's sakes. 395
Now I've had enough of your shame and disgrace.

HOLROYD Oh, indeed!

MRS HOLROYD (*her voice is dull and inflexible*) I've had enough. Go out
again after those trollops—leave me alone. I've had enough. (*Holroyd
stands looking at her*) Go, I mean it, go out again. And if you never   400
come back again, I'm glad. I've had enough. (*She keeps her face
averted, will not look at him, her attitude expressing thorough weariness*)

HOLROYD All right then!

> *He hobbles, in unlaced boots, to the door. Then he turns to look
> at her. She turns herself still farther away, so that her back is*   405
> *towards him. He goes.*
> CURTAIN

Act 2

The scene is the same, two hours later. The cottage is in darkness,
save for the firelight. On the table is spread a newspaper. A cup
and saucer, a plate, a piece of bacon in the frying tin are on the
newspaper ready for the miner's breakfast. Mrs Holroyd has gone
to bed. There is a noise of heavy stumbling down the three steps 5
outside

BLACKMORE'S VOICE Steady, now, steady. It's all in darkness. Missis!—
Has she gone to bed?
    He tries the latch—shakes the door

HOLROYD'S VOICE (*he is drunk*) Her's locked me out. Let me smash 10
that bloody door in. Come out—come out—ussza! (*He strikes a heavy*
blow on the door. There is a scuffle)

BLACKMORE'S VOICE Hold on a bit—what're you doing?

HOLROYD'S VOICE I'm smashing that blasted door in.

MRS HOLROYD (*appearing and suddenly drawing the bolts, flinging the door* 15
open) What do you think you're doing?

HOLROYD (*lurching into the room, snarling*) What? What? Tha thought
tha'd play thy monkey tricks on me, did ter? (*Shouting*) But I'm going
to show thee. (*He lurches at her threateningly; she recoils*)

BLACKMORE (*seizing him by the arm*) Here, here—! Come and sit down 20
and be quiet.

HOLROYD (*snarling at him*) What?—What? An' what's thaigh° got ter
do wi' it. (*Shouting*) What's thaigh got ter do wi' it?

BLACKMORE Nothing—nothing; but it's getting late, and you want
your supper. 25

HOLROYD (*shouting*) I want nowt. I'm allowed nowt in this 'ouse.
(*Shouting louder*) 'Er begrudges me ivry morsel I ha'e.

MRS HOLROYD Oh, what a story!

HOLROYD (*shouting*) It's the truth, an' you know it.

BLACKMORE (*conciliatory*) You'll rouse the children. You'll rouse the 30
children, at this hour.

HOLROYD (*suddenly quiet*) Not me—not if I know it. *I* shan't disturb
'em—bless 'em.
    He staggers to his arm-chair and sits heavily

BLACKMORE Shall I light the lamp? 35

MRS HOLROYD No, don't trouble. Don't stay any longer, there's no
need.

74

BLACKMORE (*quietly*) I'll just see it's all right.

> *He proceeds in silence to light the lamp. Holroyd is seen dropping forward in his chair. He has a cut on his cheek. Mrs Holroyd is in an old-fashioned dressing-gown. Blackmore has an overcoat buttoned up to his chin. There is a very large lump of coal on the red fire* 40

MRS HOLROYD Don't stay any longer.

BLACKMORE I'll see it's all right. 45

MRS HOLROYD I shall be all right. He'll go to sleep now.

BLACKMORE But he can't go like that.

MRS HOLROYD What has he done to his face?

BLACKMORE He had a row with Jim Goodwin.

MRS HOLROYD What about? 50

BLACKMORE I don't know.

MRS HOLROYD The beast!

BLACKMORE By Jove, and isn't he a weight! He's getting fat, must be—

MRS HOLROYD He's big made—he has a big frame.

BLACKMORE Whatever he is, it took me all my time to get him home. 55
I thought I'd better keep an eye on him. I knew you'd be worrying.
So I sat in the smoke-room° and waited for him. Though it's a dirty
hole—and dull as hell.

MRS HOLROYD Why did you bother?

BLACKMORE Well, I thought you'd be upset about him. I had to drink 60
three whiskies—had to, in all conscience—(*Smiling*)

MRS HOLROYD I don't want to be the ruin of you.

BLACKMORE (*smiling*) Don't you? I thought he'd pitch forward on to
the lines and crack his skull.

> *Holroyd has been sinking farther and farther forward in drunken sleep. He suddenly jerks too far and is awakened. He sits upright, glaring fiercely and dazedly at the two, who instantly cease talking* 65

HOLROYD (*to Blackmore*) What are thaigh doin' 'ere?

BLACKMORE Why, I came along with you. 70

HOLROYD Thou'rt a liar, I'm only just come in.

MRS HOLROYD (*coldly*) He is no liar at all. He brought you home
because you were too drunk to come yourself.

HOLROYD (*starting up*) Thou'rt a liar! I niver set eyes on him this night,
afore now. 75

MRS HOLROYD (*with a 'Pf' of contempt*) You don't know what you *have*
done to-night.

HOLROYD (*shouting*) I s'll not ha'e it, I tell thee.

MRS HOLROYD Psh!

HOLROYD I s'll not ha'e it. I s'll ha'e no carryin's i' my 'ouse—   80

MRS HOLROYD (*shrugging her shoulders*) Talk when you've got some sense.

HOLROYD (*fiercely*) I've as much sense as thaigh. Am I a fool? Canna I see? What's *he* doin' here then, answer me that. What?

MRS HOLROYD Mr Blackmore came to bring *you* home because   85
you were *too drunk* to find your own way. And this is the thanks he gets.

HOLROYD (*contemptuously*) Blackymore, Blackymore. It's him tha cuts thy cloth by,° is it?

MRS HOLROYD (*hotly*) You don't know what you're talking about, so   90
keep your tongue still.

HOLROYD (*bitingly*) I don't know what I'm talking about—I don't know what I'm talking about—don't I? An' what about him standing there then, if I don't know what I'm talking about?—What?

BLACKMORE You've been to sleep, Charlie, an' forgotten I came in with   95
you, not long since.

HOLROYD I'm not daft, I'm not a fool. I've got eyes in my head and sense. You needn't try to get over me. I know what you're up to.

BLACKMORE (*flushing*) It's a bit off to talk to me like that, Charlie, I must say.   100

HOLROYD I'm not good enough for 'er. She wants Mr Blackmore. He's a gentleman, he is. Now we have it all; now we understand.

MRS HOLROYD I wish you understood enough to keep your tongue still.

HOLROYD What? What? I'm to keep my tongue still, am I? An' what   105
about *Mr Blackymore?*

MRS HOLROYD (*fiercely*) Stop your mouth, you—you vulgar, low-minded brute.

HOLROYD Am I? Am I? An' what are you? What tricks are you up to, an' all? But that's all right—that's all right. (*Shouting*) That's all right, if   110
it's *you.*

BLACKMORE I think I'd better go. You seem to enjoy—er—er—calumniating your wife.

HOLROYD (*mockingly*) Calamniating—calamniating—I'll give you calamniating, you mealy-mouthed jockey: I'll give you calamniating.   115

BLACKMORE I think you've said about enough.

HOLROYD 'Ave I, 'ave I? Yer flimsy jack°—'ave I? (*In a sudden burst*) But I've not done wi' thee yet?

BLACKMORE (*ironically*) No, and you haven't.

HOLROYD (*shouting—pulling himself up from the arm-chair*) I'll show   120
  thee—I'll show thee.

> *Blackmore laughs*

HOLROYD Yes!—yes, my young monkey. It's thaigh, is it?

BLACKMORE Yes, it's *me*.

HOLROYD (*shouting*) An' I'll ma'e thee wish it worn't, I will. What—?   125
  What? Tha'd come slivin'° round here, would ta? (*He lurches forward
  at Blackmore with clenched fist*)

MRS HOLROYD Drunken, drunken fool—oh, don't.

HOLROYD (*turning to her*) What?

> *She puts up her hands before her face. Blackmore seizes the*   130
> *upraised arm and swings Holroyd round*

BLACKMORE (*in a towering passion*) Mind what tha'rt doing!

HOLROYD (*turning fiercely on him—incoherent*) Wha'—wha'—!

> *He aims a heavy blow. Blackmore evades it, so that he is struck on*
> *the side of the chest. Suddenly he shows his teeth. He raises his fists*   135
> *ready to strike Holroyd when the latter stands to advantage*

MRS HOLROYD (*rushing upon Blackmore*) No, no! Oh, no!

> *She flies and opens the door, and goes out. Blackmore glances after*
> *her, then at Holroyd, who is preparing, like a bull, for another*
> *charge. The young man's face lights up*   140

HOLROYD Wha'—wha—!

> *As he advances, Blackmore quickly retreats out-of-doors.*
> *Holroyd plunges upon him, Blackmore slips behind the door-jamb,°*
> *puts out his foot, and trips Holroyd with a crash upon the brick*
> *yard*   145

MRS HOLROYD Oh, what has he done to himself?

BLACKMORE (*thickly*) Tumbled over himself.

> *Holroyd is seen struggling to rise, and is heard incoherently*
> *cursing*

MRS HOLROYD Aren't you going to get him up?   150

BLACKMORE What for?

MRS HOLROYD But what shall we do?

BLACKMORE Let him go to hell.

> *Holroyd, who has subsided, begins to snarl and struggle again*

MRS HOLROYD (*in terror*) He's getting up.   155

BLACKMORE All right, let him.

> *Mrs Holroyd looks at Blackmore, suddenly afraid of him also*

HOLROYD (*in a last frenzy*) I'll show thee—I'll—

He raises himself up, and is just picking his balance when
Blackmore, with a sudden light kick, sends him sprawling again.   160
He is seen on the edge of the light to collapse into stupor

MRS HOLROYD He'll kill you, he'll kill you!
Blackmore laughs short

MRS HOLROYD Would you believe it! Oh, isn't it awful! (*She begins to*
weep in a little hysteria; Blackmore stands with his back leaning on the   165
doorway, grinning in a strained fashion) Is he hurt, do you think?

BLACKMORE I don't know—I should think not.

MRS HOLROYD I wish he was dead; I do, with all my heart.

BLACKMORE Do you? (*He looks at her quickly; she wavers and shrinks; he*
begins to smile strainedly as before) You don't know *what* you wish, or   170
what you want.

MRS HOLROYD (*troubled*) Do you think I could get past him to come
inside?

BLACKMORE I should think so.
Mrs Holroyd, silent and troubled, manoeuvres in the doorway,   175
stepping over her husband's feet, which lie on the threshold

BLACKMORE Why, you've got no shoes and stockings on!

MRS HOLROYD No.
She enters the house and stands trembling before the fire

BLACKMORE (*following her*) Are you cold?   180

MRS HOLROYD A little—with standing on the yard.

BLACKMORE What a shame!
She, uncertain of herself, sits down. He drops on one knee,
awkwardly, and takes her feet in his hands

MRS HOLROYD Don't—no, don't!   185

BLACKMORE They are frightfully cold. (*He remains, with head sunk, for*
some moments, then slowly rises) Damn him!
They look at each other; then, at the same time, turn away

MRS HOLROYD We can't leave him lying there.

BLACKMORE No—no! I'll bring him in.   190

MRS HOLROYD But—!

BLACKMORE He won't wake again. The drink will have got hold of him
by now. (*He hesitates*) Could you take hold of his feet—he's so heavy.

MRS HOLROYD Yes.
They go out and are seen stooping over Holroyd   195

BLACKMORE Wait, wait, till I've got him—half a minute.
Mrs Holroyd backs in first. They carry Holroyd in and lay him
on the sofa

MRS HOLROYD Doesn't he look awful?

BLACKMORE It's more mark than mar.° It isn't much, really.   200

He is busy taking off Holroyd's collar and tie, unfastening the waistcoat, the braces and the waist buttons of the trousers; he then proceeds to unlace the drunken man's boots

MRS HOLROYD (*who has been watching closely*) I shall never get him upstairs.   205

BLACKMORE He can sleep here, with a rug or something to cover him. *You* don't want him—upstairs?

MRS HOLROYD Never again.

BLACKMORE (*after a moment or two of silence*) He'll be all right down here. Have you got a rug?   210

MRS HOLROYD Yes.

She goes upstairs. Blackmore goes into the scullery, returning with a ladling can° and towel. He gets hot water from the boiler. Then, kneeling down, he begins to wipe the drunken man's face lightly with the flannel, to remove the blood and dirt   215

MRS HOLROYD (*returning*) What are you doing?

BLACKMORE Only wiping his face to get the dirt out.

MRS HOLROYD I wonder if he'd do as much for you.

BLACKMORE I hope not.

MRS HOLROYD Isn't he horrible, horrible—   220

BLACKMORE (*looks up at her*) Don't look at him then.

MRS HOLROYD I can't take it in, it's too much.

BLACKMORE He won't wake. I will stay with you.

MRS HOLROYD (*earnestly*) No—oh, no.

BLACKMORE There will be the drawn sword between us.° (*He indicates   225
the figure of Holroyd, which lies, in effect, as a barrier between them*)

MRS HOLROYD (*blushing*) Don't!

BLACKMORE I'm sorry.

MRS HOLROYD (*after watching him for a few moments lightly wiping the sleeping man's face with a towel*) I wonder you can be so careful over him.   230

BLACKMORE (*quietly*) It's only because he's helpless.

MRS HOLROYD But why should you love him ever so little?

BLACKMORE I don't—only he's helpless. Five minutes since I could have killed him.

MRS HOLROYD Well, I don't understand you men.   235

BLACKMORE Why?

MRS HOLROYD I don't know.

BLACKMORE I thought as I stood in that doorway, and he was trying to get up—I wished as hard as I've ever wished anything in my life—

MRS HOLROYD What?   240

BLACKMORE That I'd killed him. I've never wished anything so much in my life—if wishes were anything.

MRS HOLROYD Don't, it *does* sound awful.

BLACKMORE I *could* have done it, too. He ought to be dead.

MRS HOLROYD (*pleading*) No, don't! You know you don't mean it, and   245
you make me feel so awful.

BLACKMORE I do mean it. It is simply true, what I say.

MRS HOLROYD But don't say it.

BLACKMORE No?

MRS HOLROYD No, we've had enough.   250

BLACKMORE Give me the rug.

   She hands it him, and he tucks Holroyd up

MRS HOLROYD You only do it to play on my feelings.

BLACKMORE (*laughing shortly*) And now give me a pillow—thanks.

   There is a pause—both look at the sleeping man   255

BLACKMORE I suppose you're fond of him, really.

MRS HOLROYD No more.

BLACKMORE You *were* fond of him?

MRS HOLROYD I was—yes.

BLACKMORE What did you like in him?   260

MRS HOLROYD (*uneasily*) I don't know.

BLACKMORE I suppose you really care about him, even now?

MRS HOLROYD Why are you so sure of it?

BLACKMORE Because I think it is so.

MRS HOLROYD I did care for him—now he has destroyed it—   265

BLACKMORE I don't believe he can destroy it.

MRS HOLROYD (*with a short laugh*) Don't you? When you are married
you try. You'll find it isn't so hard.

BLACKMORE But what did you like in him—because he was good-
looking, and strong, and that?   270

MRS HOLROYD I liked that as well. But if a man makes a nuisance of
himself, his good looks are ugly to you, and his strength loathsome.
Do you think I *care* about a man because he's got big fists, when he is
a coward in his real self?

BLACKMORE Is he a coward?   275

MRS HOLROYD He *is*—a pettifogging, paltry one.

BLACKMORE And so you've really done with him?

MRS HOLROYD I have.

BLACKMORE And what are you going to do?

MRS HOLROYD I don't know.   280

BLACKMORE I suppose nothing. You'll just go on—even if you've done
with him—you'll go on with him.

   There is a long pause

BLACKMORE But was there nothing else in him but his muscles and his good looks to attract you to him? 285

MRS HOLROYD Why? What does it matter?

BLACKMORE What did you *think* he was?

MRS HOLROYD Why must we talk about him?

BLACKMORE Because I can never quite believe you.

MRS HOLROYD I can't help whether you believe it or not. 290

BLACKMORE Are you just in a rage with him, because of to-night?

MRS HOLROYD I know, to-night finished it. But it was never right between us.

BLACKMORE Never?

MRS HOLROYD Not once. And then to-night—no, it's too much; I can't 295 stand any more of it.

BLACKMORE I suppose he got tipsy. Then he said he wasn't a married man—vowed he wasn't, to those paper bonnets. They found out he was, and said he was frightened of his wife getting to know. Then he said they should all go to supper at his house—I suppose they came 300 out of mischief.

MRS HOLROYD He did it to insult me.

BLACKMORE Oh, he was a bit tight—you can't say it was deliberate.

MRS HOLROYD No, but it shows how he feels toward me. The feeling comes out in drink. 305

BLACKMORE How does he feel toward you?

MRS HOLROYD He wants to insult me, and humiliate me, in every moment of his life. Now I simply despise him.

BLACKMORE You really don't care any more about him?

MRS HOLROYD No. 310

BLACKMORE (*hesitates*) And you would leave him?

MRS HOLROYD I would leave him, and not care *that* about him any more. (*She snaps her fingers*)

BLACKMORE Will you come with me?

MRS HOLROYD (*after a reluctant pause*) Where? 315

BLACKMORE To Spain: I can any time have a job there, in a decent part. You could take the children.

The figure of the sleeper stirs uneasily—they watch him

BLACKMORE Will you?

MRS HOLROYD When would you go? 320

BLACKMORE To-morrow, if you like.

MRS HOLROYD But why do you want to saddle yourself with me and the children?

BLACKMORE Because I want to.

81

MRS HOLROYD But you don't love me?   325
BLACKMORE Why don't I?
MRS HOLROYD You don't.
BLACKMORE I don't know about that. I don't know anything about love.
    Only I've gone on for a year, now, and it's got stronger and stronger—
MRS HOLROYD What has?   330
BLACKMORE This—this wanting you, to live with me. I took no notice
    of it for a long time. Now I can't get away from it, at no hour and
    nohow. (*He still avoids direct contact with her*)
MRS HOLROYD But you'd *like* to get away from it.
BLACKMORE I hate a mess of any sort. But if you'll come away with   335
    me—you and the children—
MRS HOLROYD But I couldn't—you don't love me—
BLACKMORE I don't know what you mean by I don't love you.
MRS HOLROYD I can feel it.
BLACKMORE And do you love *me?* (*A pause*)   340
MRS HOLROYD I don't know. Everything is so—so—
        There is a long pause
BLACKMORE How old are you?
MRS HOLROYD Thirty-two.
BLACKMORE I'm twenty-seven.   345
MRS HOLROYD And have you never been in love?
BLACKMORE I don't think so. I don't know.
MRS HOLROYD But you must know. I must go and shut that door that
    keeps clicking.
        She rises to go upstairs, making a clatter at the stairfoot door. The   350
        noise rouses her husband. As she goes upstairs, he moves, makes
        coughing sounds, turns over, and then suddenly sits upright,
        gazing at Blackmore. The latter sits perfectly still on the sofa, his
        head dropped, hiding his face. His hands are clasped. They remain
        thus for a minute   355
HOLROYD Hello! (*He stares fixedly*) Hello! (*His tone is undecided, as if he*
    mistrusts himself) What are—who are ter? (*Blackmore does not move;*
    Holroyd stares blankly; he then turns and looks at the room) Well, I
    dunna know.
        He staggers to his feet, clinging to the table, and goes groping to   360
        the stairs. They creak loudly under his weight. A door-latch is
        heard to click. In a moment Mrs Holroyd comes quickly downstairs
BLACKMORE Has he gone to bed?
MRS HOLROYD (*nodding*) Lying on the bed.
BLACKMORE Will he settle now?   365

MRS HOLROYD I don't know. He is like that sometimes. He will have delirium tremens if he goes on.

BLACKMORE (*softly*) You can't stay with him, you know.

MRS HOLROYD And the children?

BLACKMORE We'll take them.   370

MRS HOLROYD Oh!

> *Her face puckers to cry. Suddenly he starts up and puts his arms round her, holding her protectively and gently, very caressingly. She clings to him. They are silent for some moments*

BLACKMORE (*struggling, in an altered voice*) Look at me and kiss me.   375

> *Her sobs are heard distinctly. Blackmore lays his hand on her cheek, caressing her always with his hand*

BLACKMORE My God, but I hate him! I wish either he was dead or me. (*Mrs Holroyd hides against him; her sobs cease; after a while he continues in the same murmuring fashion*) It can't go on like it any more. I feel as   380
if I should come in two. I can't keep away from you. I simply can't. Come with me. Come with me and leave him. If you knew what a hell it is for me to have you here—and to see him. I can't go without you, I can't. It's been hell every moment for six months now. You say I don't love you. Perhaps I don't, for all I know about it. But oh, my   385
God, don't keep me like it any longer. Why should *he* have you—and I've never had anything.

MRS HOLROYD Have you never loved anybody?

BLACKMORE No—I've tried. Kiss me of your own wish—will you?

MRS HOLROYD I don't know.   390

BLACKMORE (*after a pause*) Let's break clear. Let's go right away. Do you care for me?

MRS HOLROYD I don't know. (*She loosens herself; rises dumbly*)

BLACKMORE When do you think you *will* know?

> *She sits down helplessly*   395

MRS HOLROYD I don't know.

BLACKMORE Yes, you do know, really. If he was dead, should you marry me?

MRS HOLROYD Don't say it—

BLACKMORE Why not? If wishing of mine would kill him, he'd soon be   400
out of the way.

MRS HOLROYD But the children!

BLACKMORE I'm fond of them. I shall have good money.

MRS HOLROYD But he's their father.

BLACKMORE What does that mean—?   405

MRS HOLROYD Yes, I know—(*A pause*) but—

BLACKMORE Is it *him* that keeps you?

MRS HOLROYD No.

BLACKMORE Then come with me. Will you? (*He stands waiting for her;
then he turns and takes his overcoat; pulls it on, leaving the collar turned
up, ceasing to twist his cap*) Well—will you tell me to-morrow?   410

    *She goes forward and flings her arms round his neck. He suddenly
kisses her passionately*

MRS HOLROYD But I ought not. (*She draws away a little; he will not let
her go*)   415

BLACKMORE Yes, it's all right. (*He holds her close*)

MRS HOLROYD Is it?

BLACKMORE Yes, it is. It's all right.

    *He kisses her again. She releases herself but holds his hand. They
keep listening*   420

MRS HOLROYD Do you love me?

BLACKMORE What do you ask for?

MRS HOLROYD Have I hurt you these months?

BLACKMORE *You* haven't. And I don't care what it's been if you'll come
with me. (*There is a noise upstairs and they wait*) You *will* soon, won't   425
you?

    She kisses him

MRS HOLROYD He's not safe. (*She disengages herself and sits on the sofa*)

BLACKMORE (*takes a place beside her, holding her hand in both his*) You
should have waited for me.   430

MRS HOLROYD How wait?

BLACKMORE And not have married him.

MRS HOLROYD I might never have known you—I married him to get
out of my place.

BLACKMORE Why?   435

MRS HOLROYD I was left an orphan when I was six. My Uncle John
brought me up, in the Coach and Horses at Rainsworth. He'd got
no children. He was good to me, but he drank. I went to Mansfield
Grammar School. Then he fell out with me because I wouldn't wait
in the bar, and I went as nursery governess to Berryman's. And I felt   440
I'd nowhere to go, I belonged to nowhere, and nobody cared about
me, and men came after me, and I hated it. So to get out of it, I
married the first man that turned up.

BLACKMORE And you never cared about him?

MRS HOLROYD Yes, I did. I did care about him. I wanted to be a wife to   445
him. But there's nothing at the bottom of him, if you know what
I mean. You can't *get* anywhere with him. There's just his body and
nothing else. Nothing that keeps him, no anchor, no roots, nothing

satisfying. It's a horrible feeling there is about him, that nothing is
safe or permanent—nothing is anything—   450

BLACKMORE And do you think you can trust me?

MRS HOLROYD I think you're different from him.

BLACKMORE Perhaps I'm not.

MRS HOLROYD (*warmly*) You are.

BLACKMORE At any rate, we'll see. You'll come on Saturday to   455
London?

MRS HOLROYD Well, you see, there's my money. I haven't got it yet. My
uncle has left me about a hundred and twenty pounds.

BLACKMORE Well, see the lawyer about it as soon as you can. I can let
you have have some money if you want any. But don't let us wait after   460
Saturday.

MRS HOLROYD But isn't it wrong?

BLACKMORE Why, if you don't care for him, and the children are
miserable between the two of you—which they are—

MRS HOLROYD Yes.   465

BLACKMORE Well, then I see no wrong. As for him—he would go one
way, and only one way, whatever you do. Damn him, he doesn't
matter.

MRS HOLROYD No.

BLACKMORE Well, then—have done with it. Can't you cut clean of   470
him? Can't you now?

MRS HOLROYD And then—the children—

BLACKMORE They'll be all right with me and you—won't they?

MRS HOLROYD Yes—

BLACKMORE Well, then. Now, come and have done with it. We can't   475
keep on being ripped in two like this. We need never hear of him any
more.

MRS HOLROYD Yes—I love you. I do love you—

BLACKMORE Oh, my God! (*He speaks with difficulty—embracing her*)

MRS HOLROYD When I look at him, and then at you—ha—(*She gives a*   480
short laugh)

BLACKMORE He's had all the chance—it's only fair—Lizzie—

MRS HOLROYD My love.

> There is silence. He keeps his arm round her. After hesitating, he
> picks up his cap   485

BLACKMORE I'll go then—at any rate. Shall you come with me?

> She follows him to the door

MRS HOLROYD I'll come on Saturday.

BLACKMORE Not now?

> CURTAIN   490

Act 3

Scene, the same. Time, the following evening, about seven o'clock.
The table is half-laid, with a large cup and saucer, plate, etc.,
ready for Holroyd's dinner, which, like all miners, he has when he
comes home between four and five o'clock. On the other half of the
table Mrs Holroyd is ironing. On the hearth stand newly baked 5
loaves of bread. The irons° hang at the fire. Jack, with a bowler
hat hanging at the back of his head, parades up to the sofa, on
which stands Minnie engaged in dusting a picture. She has a soiled
white apron tied behind her, to make a long skirt

JACK Good mornin', missis. Any scissors or knives to grind? 10

MINNIE (*peering down from the sofa*) Oh, I can't be bothered to come
    downstairs. Call another day.

JACK I shan't.

MINNIE (*keeping up her part*) Well, I can't come down now. (*Jack stands
    irresolute*) Go on, you have to go and steal the baby.° 15

JACK I'm not.

MINNIE Well, you can steal the eggs out of the fowl-house.

JACK I'm not.

MINNIE Then I shan't play with you.

> *Jack takes off his bowler hat and flings it on the sofa; tears come* 20
> *in Minnie's eyes*

Now I'm *not* friends. (*She surveys him ruefully; after a few moments of*
silence she clambers down and goes to her mother) Mam, he won't play
    with me.

MRS HOLROYD (*crossly*) Why don't you play with her? If you begin 25
    bothering, you must go to bed.

JACK Well, I don't want to play.

MRS HOLROYD Then you must go to bed.

JACK I don't want to.

MRS HOLROYD Then what do you want, I should like to know? 30

MINNIE I wish my father'd come.

JACK I do.

MRS HOLROYD I suppose he thinks he's paying me out. This is the
    third time this week he's slunk past the door and gone down to Old
    Brinsley instead of coming in to his dinner. He'll be as drunk as a lord 35
    when he does come.

> *The children look at her plaintively*

MINNIE Isn't he a nuisance?

JACK I hate him. I wish he'd drop down th' pit-shaft.

MRS HOLROYD Jack!—I never heard such a thing in my life! You 40
mustn't say such things—it's wicked.

JACK Well, I do.

MRS HOLROYD (*loudly*) I won't have it. He's your father, remember.

JACK (*in a high voice*) Well, he's always comin' home an' shoutin' an'
bangin' on the table. (*He is getting tearful and defiant*) 45

MRS HOLROYD Well, you mustn't take any notice of him.

MINNIE (*wistfully*) 'Appen if you said something nice to him, mother,
he'd happen go to bed, and not shout.

JACK I'd hit him in the mouth.

MRS HOLROYD Perhaps we'll go to another country, away from him— 50
should we?

JACK In a ship, mother?

MINNIE In a ship, mam?

MRS HOLROYD Yes, in a big ship, where it's blue sky, and water and
palm-trees, and— 55

MINNIE An' dates—?

JACK When should we go?

MRS HOLROYD Some day.

MINNIE But who'd work for us? Who should we have for father?

JACK You don't want a father. I can go to work for us. 60

MRS HOLROYD I've got a lot of money now, that your uncle left me.

MINNIE (*after a general thoughtful silence*) An' would my father stop
here?

MRS HOLROYD Oh, he'd be all right.

MINNIE But who would he live with? 65

MRS HOLROYD I don't know—one of his paper bonnets, if he likes.

MINNIE Then she could have her old bracelet back, couldn't she?

MRS HOLROYD Yes—there it is on the candlestick, waiting for her.

*There is a sound of footsteps—then a knock at the door. The
children start* 70

MINNIE (*in relief*) Here he is.

Mrs Holroyd goes to the door. Blackmore enters

BLACKMORE It is foggy to-night—Hello, aren't you youngsters gone
to bed?

MINNIE No, my father's not come home yet. 75

BLACKMORE (*turning to Mrs Holroyd*) Did he go to work then, after last
night?

MRS HOLROYD I suppose so. His pit things were gone when I got up.
I never thought he'd go.

BLACKMORE And he took his snap° as usual? 80

87

MRS HOLROYD Yes, just as usual. I suppose he's gone to the New Inn. He'd say to himself he'd pay me out. That's what he always does say, 'I'll pay thee out for that bit—I'll ma'e thee regret it.'

JACK We're going to leave him.

BLACKMORE So you think he's at the New Inn?   85

MRS HOLROYD I'm sure he is—and he'll come when he's full. He'll have a bout now, you'll see.

MINNIE Go and fetch him, Mr Blackmore.

JACK My mother says we shall go in a ship and leave him.

BLACKMORE (*after looking keenly at Jack: to Mrs Holroyd*) Shall I go   90
and see if he's at the New Inn?

MRS HOLROYD No—perhaps you'd better not—

BLACKMORE Oh, he shan't see me. I can easily manage that.

JACK Fetch him, Mr Blackmore.

BLACKMORE All right, Jack. (*To Mrs Holroyd*) Shall I?   95

MRS HOLROYD We're always pulling on you—But yes, do!

            Blackmore goes out

JACK I wonder how long he'll be.

MRS HOLROYD You come and go to bed now: you'd better be out of the
way when he comes in.   100

MINNIE And you won't say anything to him, mother, will you?

MRS HOLROYD What do you mean?

MINNIE You won't begin of him—row him.

MRS HOLROYD Is he to have all his own way? What *would* he be like, if
I didn't row him?   105

JACK But it doesn't matter, mother, if we're going to leave him—

MINNIE But Mr Blackmore'll come back, won't he, mam, and dad
won't shout before him?

MRS HOLROYD (*beginning to undress the children*) Yes, he'll come back.

MINNIE Mam—could I have that bracelet to go to bed with?   110

MRS HOLROYD Come and say your prayers.

            They kneel, muttering in their mother's apron

MINNIE (*suddenly lifting her head*) Can I, mam?

MRS HOLROYD (*trying to be stern*) Have you finished your prayers?

MINNIE Yes.   115

MRS HOLROYD If you want it—beastly thing! (*She reaches the bracelet
down from the mantelpiece*) Your father must have put it up there—I
don't know where I left it. I suppose he'd think I was proud of it and
wanted it for an ornament.

            Minnie gloats over it. Mrs Holroyd lights a candle and they go   120
            upstairs. After a few moments the outer door opens, and there

enters an old woman. She is of middling stature and wears a large
grey shawl over her head. After glancing sharply round the room,
she advances to the fire, warms herself; then, taking off her shawl,
sits in the rocking-chair. As she hears Mrs Holroyd's footsteps, she   125
folds her hands and puts on a lachrymose expression, turning down
the corners of her mouth and arching her eyebrows

MRS HOLROYD Hello, mother, is it you?

GRANDMOTHER Yes, it's me. Haven't you finished ironing?

MRS HOLROYD Not yet.   130

GRANDMOTHER You'll have your irons red-hot.

MRS HOLROYD Yes, I s'll have to stand them to cool. (*She does so, and*
moves about at her ironing)

GRANDMOTHER And you don't know what's become of Charles?

MRS HOLROYD Well, he's not come home from work yet. I supposed he   135
was at the New Inn—Why?

GRANDMOTHER That young electrician come knocking asking if I
knew where he was. 'Eh,' I said, 'I've not set eyes on him for over a
week—nor his wife neither, though they pass th' garden gate every
time they go out. I know nowt on 'im.' I axed him what was the   140
matter, so he said Mrs Holroyd was anxious because he'd not come
home, so I thought I'd better come and see. Is there anything up?

MRS HOLROYD No more than I've told you.

GRANDMOTHER It's a rum 'un, if he's neither in the New Inn nor the
Prince o' Wales. I suppose something you've done's set him off.   145

MRS HOLROYD It's nothing I've done.

GRANDMOTHER Eh, if he's gone off and left you, whativer shall we do!
Whativer 'ave you been doing?

MRS HOLROYD He brought a couple of bright daisies° here last night—
two of those trollops from Nottingham—and I said I'd not have it.   150

GRANDMOTHER (*sighing deeply*) Ay, you've never been able to agree.

MRS HOLROYD We agreed well enough except when he drank like a fish
and came home rolling.

GRANDMOTHER (*whining*) Well, what can you expect of a man as 'as
been shut up i' th' pit all day? He must have a bit of relaxation.   155

MRS HOLROYD He can have it different from that, then. At any rate,
I'm sick of it.

GRANDMOTHER Ay, you've a stiff neck, but it'll be bowed by you're my
age.

MRS HOLROYD Will it? I'd rather it were broke.   160

GRANDMOTHER Well—there's no telling what a jealous man will do.
(*She shakes her head*)

MRS HOLROYD Nay, I think it's my place to be jealous, when he brings a brazen hussy here and sits carryin' on with her.

GRANDMOTHER He'd no business to do that. But you know, Lizzie, he's   165
got something on *his* side.

MRS HOLROYD What, pray?

GRANDMOTHER Well, I don't want to make any mischief, but you're my son's wife, an' it's nothing but my duty to tell you. They've been saying a long time now as that young electrician is here a bit too often.   170

MRS HOLROYD He doesn't come for my asking.

GRANDMOTHER No, I don't suppose he wants for asking. But Charlie's not the man to put up with that sort o' work.

MRS HOLROYD Charlie put up with it! If he's anything to say, why doesn't he say it, without going to other folks . . . ?   175

GRANDMOTHER Charlie's never been near me with a word—nor 'as he said a word elsewhere to my knowledge. For all that, this is going to end with trouble.

MRS HOLROYD In this hole, every gossiping creature thinks she's got the right to cackle about you—sickening! And a parcel of lies.   180

GRANDMOTHER Well, Lizzie, I've never said anything against you. Charlie's been a handful of trouble. He made my heart ache once or twice afore you had him, and he's made it ache many, many's the time since. But it's not all on his side, you know.

MRS HOLROYD (*hotly*) No, I don't know.   185

GRANDMOTHER You thought yourself above him, Lizzie, an' you know he's not the man to stand it.

MRS HOLROYD No, he's run away from it.

GRANDMOTHER (*venomously*) And what man wouldn't leave a woman that allowed him to live on sufferance in the house with her, when he   190
was bringing the money home?

MRS HOLROYD 'Sufferance!'—Yes, there's been a lot of letting him live on 'sufferance' in the house with me. It is *I* who have lived on sufferance, for his service and pleasure. No, what he wanted was the drink and the public house company, and because he couldn't get   195
them here, he went out for them. That's all.

GRANDMOTHER You have always been very clever at hitting things off, Lizzie. I was always sorry my youngest son married a clever woman. He only wanted a bit of coaxing and managing, and you clever women won't do it.   200

MRS HOLROYD He wanted a slave, not a wife.

GRANDMOTHER It's a pity your stomach wasn't too high for him, before you had him. But no, you could have eaten him ravishing° at one time.

MRS HOLROYD It's a pity you didn't tell me what he was before I had
    him. But no, he was all angel. You left me to find out what he really   205
    was.

GRANDMOTHER Some women could have lived with him happy
    enough. An' a fat lot you'd have thanked me for my telling.

      There is a knock at the door, Mrs Holroyd opens

RIGLEY They tell me, missus, as your mester's not hoom yet.   210

MRS HOLROYD No—who is it?

GRANDMOTHER Ask him to step inside. Don't stan' there lettin' the
    fog in.

      Rigley steps in. He is a tall, bony, very roughly hewn collier

RIGLEY Good evenin'.   215

GRANDMOTHER Oh, is it you, Mr Rigley? *(In a querulous, spiteful tone
    to Mrs Holroyd)* He butties° along with Charlie.

MRS HOLROYD Oh!

RIGLEY An' han yer seen nowt on 'im?

MRS HOLROYD No—was he all right at work?   220

RIGLEY Well, e' wor nowt to mention. A bit short, like: 'adna much to
    say, I canna ma'e out what 'e's done wi' 'issen. *(He is manifestly uneasy,
    does not look at the two women)*

GRANDMOTHER An' did 'e come up i' th' same bantle° wi' you?

RIGLEY No—'e didna. As Ah was comin' out o' th' stall,° Ah shouted,   225
    'Art comin', Charlie? We're a' off.' An' 'e said, 'Ah'm comin' in a
    minute.' 'E wor just finishin' a stint,° like, an' 'e wanted ter get it set.
    An' 'e'd been a bit roughish in 'is temper, like, so I thowt 'e didna want
    ter walk to th' bottom° wi' us . . .

GRANDMOTHER *(wailing)* An' what's 'e gone an' done to himself?   230

RIGLEY Nay, missis, yo' munna ax me that. 'E's non done owt as Ah
    know on. On'y I wor thinkin', 'appen summat 'ad 'appened to 'im,
    like, seein' as nob'dy had any knowings of 'im comin' up.

MRS HOLROYD What is the matter, Mr Rigley? Tell us it out.

RIGLEY I canna do that, missis. It seems as if 'e niver come up th' pit—   235
    as far as we can make out. 'Appen a bit o' stuff's fell an' pinned 'im.

GRANDMOTHER *(wailing)* An' ave you left 'im lying down there in the
    pit, poor thing?

RIGLEY *(uneasily)* I couldna say for certain where 'e is.

MRS HOLROYD *(agitated)* Oh, it's very likely not very bad, mother!   240
    Don't let us run to meet trouble.

RIGLEY We 'ave to 'ope for th' best, missis, all on us.

GRANDMOTHER *(wailing)* Eh, they'll bring im 'ome, I know they will,
    smashed up an' broke! An' one of my sons they've burned down pit

till the flesh dropped off 'im, an' one was shot till 'is shoulder was all   245
of a mosh,° an' they brought 'em 'ome to me. An' now there's this . . .

MRS HOLROYD (*shuddering*) Oh, don't, mother. (*Appealing to Rigley*)
You don't know that he's hurt?

RIGLEY (*shaking his head*) I canna tell you.

MRS HOLROYD (*in a high hysterical voice*) Then what is it?   250

RIGLEY (*very uneasy*) I canna tell you. But yon young electrician—Mr
Blackmore—'e rung down to the night deputy,° an' it seems as though
there's been a fall or summat . . .

GRANDMOTHER Eh, Lizzie, you parted from him in anger. You little
knowed how you'd meet him again.   255

RIGLEY (*making an effort*) Well, I'd 'appen best be goin' to see what's
betide.

    He goes out

GRANDMOTHER I'm sure I've had my share of bad luck, I have. I'm sure
I've brought up five lads in the pit, through accidents and troubles,   260
and now there's this. The Lord has treated me very hard, very hard.
It's a blessing, Lizzie, as you've got a bit of money, else what would
'ave become of the children?

MRS HOLROYD Well, if he's badly hurt, there'll be the Union-pay, and
sick-pay—we shall manage. And perhaps it's *not* very much.   265

GRANDMOTHER There's no knowin' but what they'll be carryin' him to
die 'i th' hospital.

MRS HOLROYD Oh, don't say so, mother—it won't be so bad, you'll see.

GRANDMOTHER How much money have you, Lizzie, comin'?

MRS HOLROYD I don't know—not much over a hundred pounds.   270

GRANDMOTHER (*shaking her head*) An' what's that, what's that?

MRS HOLROYD (*sharply*) Hush!

GRANDMOTHER (*crying*) Why, what?

    *Mrs Holroyd opens the door. In the silence can be heard the
    pulsing of the fan engine,° then the driving engine° chuffs rapidly:*   275
    there is a skirr of brakes° on the rope as it descends

MRS HOLROYD That's twice they've sent the chair° down—I wish we
could see. . . . Hark!

GRANDMOTHER What is it?

MRS HOLROYD Yes—it's stopped at the gate. It's the doctor's.   280

GRANDMOTHER (*coming to the door*) What, Lizzie?

MRS HOLROYD The doctor's motor. (*She listens acutely*) Dare you stop
here, mother, while I run up to the top an' see?

GRANDMOTHER You'd better not go, Lizzie, you'd better not. A woman's
best away.   285

MRS HOLROYD It is unbearable to wait.

GRANDMOTHER Come in an' shut the door—it's a cold that gets in your bones.

> *Mrs Holroyd goes in*

MRS HOLROYD Perhaps while he's in bed we shall have time to change   290
him. It's an ill wind brings no good. He'll happen be a better man.

GRANDMOTHER Well, you can but try. Many a woman's thought the same.

MRS HOLROYD Oh, dear, I wish somebody would come. He's never been hurt since we were married.   295

GRANDMOTHER No, he's never had a bad accident, all the years he's been in the pit. He's been luckier than most. But everybody has it, sooner or later.

MRS HOLROYD (*shivering*) It *is* a horrid night.

GRANDMOTHER (*querulous*) Yes, come your ways in.   300

MRS HOLROYD Hark!

> *There is a quick sound of footsteps. Blackmore comes into the light of the doorway*

BLACKMORE They're bringing him.

MRS HOLROYD (*quickly putting her hand over her breast*) What is it?   305

BLACKMORE You can't tell anything's the matter with him—it's not marked him at all.

MRS HOLROYD Oh, what a blessing! And is it much?

BLACKMORE Well—

MRS HOLROYD What is it?   310

BLACKMORE It's the worst.

GRANDMOTHER Who is it?—What does he say?

> *Mrs Holroyd sinks on the nearest chair with a horrified expression. Blackmore pulls himself together and enters the room. He is very pale*   315

BLACKMORE I came to tell you they're bringing him home.

GRANDMOTHER And you said it wasn't very bad, did you?

BLACKMORE No—I said it was—as bad as it could be.

MRS HOLROYD (*rising and crossing to her mother-in-law, flings her arms round her; in a high voice*) Oh, mother, what shall we do? What shall   320
we do?

GRANDMOTHER You don't mean to say he's dead?

BLACKMORE Yes.

GRANDMOTHER (*staring*) God help us, and how was it?

BLACKMORE Some stuff fell.   325

GRANDMOTHER (*rocking herself and her daughter-in-law—both weeping*)
Oh, God have mercy on us! Oh, God have mercy on us! Some stuff
fell on him. An' he'd not even time to cry for mercy; oh, God spare

him! Oh, what shall we do for comfort? To be taken straight out of his
sins. Oh, Lizzie, to think he should be cut off in his wickedness. He's   330
been a bad lad of late, he has, poor lamb. He's gone very wrong of late
years, poor dear lamb, very wrong. Oh, Lizzie, think what's to become
of him now! If only you'd have tried to be different with him.

MRS HOLROYD (*moaning*) Don't, mother, don't. I can't bear it.

BLACKMORE (*cold and clear*) Where will you have him laid? The men   335
will be here in a moment.

MRS HOLROYD (*staring up*) They can carry him up to bed—

BLACKMORE It's no good taking him upstairs. You'll have to wash him
and lay him out.

MRS HOLROYD (*startled*) Well—   340

BLACKMORE He's in his pit-dirt.

GRANDMOTHER He is, bless him. We'd better have him down here,
Lizzie, where we can handle him.

MRS HOLROYD Yes.

> *She begins to put the tea things away, but drops the sugar out of*   345
> *the basin and the lumps fly broadcast°*

BLACKMORE Never mind, I'll pick those up. You put the children's
clothes away.

> *Mrs Holroyd stares witless around. The Grandmother sits rocking*
> *herself and weeping. Blackmore clears the table, putting the pots in*   350
> *the scullery. He folds the white tablecloth and pulls back the table.*
> *The door opens. Mrs Holroyd utters a cry. Rigley enters*

RIGLEY They're bringing him now, missis.

MRS HOLROYD Oh!

RIGLEY (*simply*) There must ha' been a fall directly after we left him.   355

MRS HOLROYD (*frowning, horrified*) No—no!

RIGLEY (*to Blackmore*) It fell a' back of him, an' shut 'im 'in as you
might shut a loaf i' th' oven. It never touched him.

MRS HOLROYD (*staring distractedly*) Well, then—

RIGLEY You see, it come on 'im as close as a trap on a mouse, an' gen him   360
no air, an' what wi' th' gas, it smothered him. An' it wouldna be so
very long about it neither.

MRS HOLROYD (*quiet with horror*) Oh!

GRANDMOTHER Eh, dear—dear. Eh, dear—dear.

RIGLEY (*looking hard at her*) I wasna to know what 'ud happen.   365

GRANDMOTHER (*not heeding him, but weeping all the time*) But the Lord
gave him time to repent. He'd have a few minutes to repent. Ay, I
hope he did, I hope he did, else what was to become of him. The Lord
cut him off in his sins, but He gave him time to repent.

    Rigley looks away at the wall. Blackmore has made a space in the   370
    middle of the floor

BLACKMORE If you'll take the rocking-chair off the end of the rug, Mrs
  Holroyd, I can pull it back a bit from the fire, and we can lay him on that.

GRANDMOTHER (*petulantly*) What's the good of messing about—(*She
  moves*)   375

MRS HOLROYD It suffocated him?

RIGLEY (*shaking his head, briefly*) Yes. 'Appened th' after-damp°—

BLACKMORE He'd be dead in a few minutes.

MRS HOLROYD No—oh, think!

BLACKMORE You mustn't think.   380

RIGLEY (*suddenly*) They commin'!
    Mrs Holroyd stands at bay. The Grandmother half rises. Rigley
    and Blackmore efface themselves as much as possible. A man backs
    into the room, bearing the feet of the dead man, which are shod in
    great pit boots. As the head bearer comes awkwardly past the   385
    table, the coat with which the body is covered slips off, revealing
    Holroyd in his pit-dirt, naked to the waist

MANAGER (*a little stout, white-bearded man*) Mind now, mind. Ay,
  missis, what a job, indeed, it is! (*Sharply*) Where mun they put him?

MRS HOLROYD (*turning her face aside from the corpse*) Lay him on the   390
  rug.

MANAGER Steady now, do it steady.

SECOND BEARER (*rising and pressing back his shoulders*) By Guy,° but 'e
  'ings° heavy.

MANAGER Yi, Joe, I'll back my life o' that.   395

GRANDMOTHER Eh, Mr Chambers, what's this affliction on my old
  age. You kept your sons out o' the pit, but all mine's in. And to think
  of the trouble I've had—to think o' the trouble that's come out of
  Brinsley pit to me.

MANAGER It has that, it 'as that, missis. You seem to have had more'n   400
  your share; I'll admit it, you have.

MRS HOLROYD (*who has been staring at the men*) It is too much!
    Blackmore frowns; Rigley glowers at her

MANAGER You never knowed such a thing in your life. Here's a man,
  holin' a stint,° just finishin', (*He puts himself as if in the holer's position,*   405
  gesticulating freely) an' a lot o' stuff falls behind him, clean as a whistle,
  shuts him up safe as a worm in a nut and niver touches him—niver
  knowed such a thing in your life.

MRS HOLROYD Ugh!

MANAGER It niver hurt him—niver touched him.   410

MRS HOLROYD Yes, but—but how long would he *be*—(*She makes a sweeping gesture; the Manager looks at her and will not help her out*) How long would it take—ah—to—to kill him?

MANAGER Nay, I canna tell ye. 'E didna seem to ha' strived much to get out—did he, Joe?   415

SECOND BEARER No, not as far as Ah'n seen.

FIRST BEARER You look at 'is 'ands, you'll see then. E'd non ha'e room to swing the pick.

> *The Manager goes on his knees*

MRS HOLROYD (*shuddering*) Oh, don't!   420

MANAGER Ay, th' nails is broken a bit—

MRS HOLROYD (*clenching her fists*) Don't!

MANAGER E'd be sure ter ma'e a bit of a fight. But th' gas 'ud soon get hold on 'im. Ay, it's an awful thing to think of, it is indeed.

MRS HOLROYD (*her voice breaking*) I can't bear it!   425

MANAGER Eh, dear, we none on us know what's comin' next.

MRS HOLROYD (*getting hysterical*) Oh, it's too awful, it's too awful!

BLACKMORE You'll disturb the children.

GRANDMOTHER And you don't want *them* down here.

MANAGER 'E'd no business to ha' been left, you know.   430

RIGLEY An' what man, dost think, wor goin' to sit him down on his hams an' wait for a chap as wouldna say 'thank yer' for his cump'ny? 'E'd bin ready to fall out wi' a flicker o' the candle, so who dost think wor goin' ter stop when we knowed 'e on'y kep on so's to get shut on us.

MANAGER Tha'rt quite right, Bill, quite right. But theer you are.   435

RIGLEY An' if we'd stopped, what good would it ha' done—

MANAGER No, 'appen not, 'appen not.

RIGLEY For, not knowin'—

MANAGER I'm sayin' nowt agen thee, neither one road nor t'other. (*There is a general silence—then, to Mrs Holroyd*) I should think th' inquest'll be at th' New Inn to-morrow, missis. I'll let you know.   440

MRS HOLROYD Will there have to be an inquest?

MANAGER Yes—there'll have to be an inquest. Shall you want anybody in, to stop with you to-night?

MRS HOLROYD No.   445

MANAGER Well, then, we'd best be goin'. I'll send my missis down first thing in the morning. It's a bad job, a bad job, it is. You'll be a' right then?

MRS HOLROYD Yes.

MANAGER Well, good night then—good night all.   450

ALL Good night. Good night.

The Manager, followed by the two bearers, goes out, closing the door.

RIGLEY It's like this, missis. I never should ha' gone, if he hadn't wanted us to.   455

MRS HOLROYD Yes, I know.

RIGLEY 'E wanted to come up by 's sen.

MRS HOLROYD (*wearily*) I know how it was, Mr Rigley.

RIGLEY Yes—

BLACKMORE Nobody could foresee.   460

RIGLEY (*shaking his head*) No. If there's owt, missis, as you want—

MRS HOLROYD Yes—I think there isn't anything.

RIGLEY (*after a moment*) Well—good night—we've worked i' the same stall ower four years now—

MRS HOLROYD Yes.   465

RIGLEY Well, good night, missis.

MRS HOLROYD AND BLACKMORE Good night.

The Grandmother all this time has been rocking herself to and fro, moaning and murmuring beside the dead man. When Rigley has gone Mrs Holroyd stands staring distractedly before her. She has not yet looked at her husband   470

GRANDMOTHER Have you got the things ready, Lizzie?

MRS HOLROYD What things?

GRANDMOTHER To lay the child out.

MRS HOLROYD (*she shudders*) No—what?   475

GRANDMOTHER Haven't you put him by a pair o' white stockings, nor a white shirt?

MRS HOLROYD He's got a white cricketing shirt—but not white stockings.

GRANDMOTHER Then he'll have to have his father's. Let me look at the 480
shirt, Lizzie. (*Mrs Holroyd takes one from the dresser drawer*) This'll never do—a cold, canvas thing wi' a turndown collar. I s'll 'ave to fetch his father's. (*Suddenly*) You don't want no other woman to touch him, to wash him and lay him out, do you?

MRS HOLROYD (*weeping*) No.   485

GRANDMOTHER Then I'll fetch him his father's gear. We mustn't let him set, he'll be that heavy, bless him. (*She takes her shawl*) I shan't be more than a few minutes, an' the young fellow can stop here till I come back.

BLACKMORE Can't I go for you, Mrs Holroyd?   490

GRANDMOTHER No. *You* couldn't find the things. We'll wash him as soon as I get back, Lizzie.

MRS HOLROYD All right.

>   *She watches her mother-in-law go out. Then she starts, goes in the*
>   *scullery for a bowl, in which she pours warm water. She takes a*   495
>   *flannel and soap and towel. She stands, afraid to go any further*

BLACKMORE Well!

MRS HOLROYD This is a judgment on us.

BLACKMORE Why?

MRS HOLROYD On me, it is—   500

BLACKMORE How?

MRS HOLROYD It is.

>   *Blackmore shakes his head*

MRS HOLROYD Yesterday you talked of murdering him.

BLACKMORE Well!   505

MRS HOLROYD Now we've done it.

BLACKMORE How?

MRS HOLROYD He'd have come up with the others, if he hadn't felt—
felt me murdering him.

BLACKMORE But we can't help it.   510

MRS HOLROYD It's my fault.

BLACKMORE Don't be like that!

MRS HOLROYD (*looking at him—then indicating her husband*) I daren't
see him.

BLACKMORE No?   515

MRS HOLROYD I've killed him, that is all.

BLACKMORE No, you haven't.

MRS HOLROYD Yes, I have.

BLACKMORE *We* couldn't help it.

MRS HOLROYD If he hadn't felt, if he hadn't *known*, he wouldn't have   520
stayed, he'd have come up with the rest.

BLACKMORE Well, and even if it was so, we can't help it now.

MRS HOLROYD But we've killed him.

BLACKMORE Ah, I'm tired—

MRS HOLROYD Yes.   525

BLACKMORE (*after a pause*) Shall I stay?

MRS HOLROYD I—I daren't be alone with him.

BLACKMORE (*sitting down*) No.

MRS HOLROYD I don't love him. Now he's dead. I don't love him. He
lies like he did yesterday.   530

BLACKMORE I suppose, being dead—I don't know—

MRS HOLROYD I think you'd better go.

BLACKMORE (*rising*) Tell me.

MRS HOLROYD Yes.

BLACKMORE You want me to go.   535

MRS HOLROYD No—but *do* go. (*They look at each other*)

BLACKMORE I shall come to-morrow.

> *Blackmore goes out.*
>
> *Mrs Holroyd stands very stiff, as if afraid of the dead man. Then
> she stoops down and begins to sponge his face, talking to him*   540

MRS HOLROYD My dear, my dear—oh, my dear! I can't bear it, my
dear—you shouldn't have done it. You shouldn't have done it. Oh—
I can't bear it, for you. Why couldn't I do anything for you? The
children's father—my dear—I wasn't good to you. But you shouldn't have
have done this to me. Oh, dear, oh, dear! Did it hurt you?—oh, my   545
dear, it hurt you—oh, I can't bear it. No, things aren't fair—we went
wrong, my dear. I never loved you enough—I never did. What a
shame for you! It was a shame. But you didn't—you didn't try. I *would*
have loved you—I tried hard. What a shame for you! It was so cruel
for you. You couldn't help it—my dear, my dear. You couldn't help it.   550
And I can't do anything for you, and it hurt you so! (*She weeps bitterly,
so her tears fall on the dead man's face; suddenly she kisses him*) My dear,
my dear, what can I do for you, what can I? (*She weeps as she wipes his
face gently*)

> *Enter Grandmother*   555

GRANDMOTHER (*putting a bundle on the table, and taking off her shawl*)
You're not all by yourself?

MRS HOLROYD Yes.

GRANDMOTHER It's a wonder you're not frightened. You've not
washed his face.   560

MRS HOLROYD Why should I be afraid of him—now, mother?

GRANDMOTHER (*weeping*) Ay, poor lamb, I can't think as ever you could
have had reason to be frightened of him, Lizzie.

MRS HOLROYD Yes—once—

GRANDMOTHER Oh, but he went wrong. An' he was a taking° lad, as iver 565
was. (*She cries pitifully*) And when I waked his father up and told him,
he sat up in bed staring over his whiskers, and said should he come
up? But when I'd managed to find the shirt and things, he was still in
bed. You don't know what it is to live with a man that has no feeling.
But you've washed him, Lizzie?   570

MRS HOLROYD I was finishing his head.

GRANDMOTHER Let me do it, child.

MRS HOLROYD   I'll finish that.

GRANDMOTHER   Poor lamb—poor dear lamb! Yet I wouldn't wish him
   back, Lizzie. He must ha' died peaceful, Lizzie. He seems to be   575
   smiling. He always had such a rare smile on him—not that he's
   smiled much of late—

MRS HOLROYD   I loved him for that.

GRANDMOTHER   Ay, my poor child—my poor child.

MRS HOLROYD   He looks nice, mother.   580

GRANDMOTHER   I hope he made his peace with the Lord.

MRS HOLROYD   Yes.

GRANDMOTHER   If he hadn't time to make his peace with the Lord, I've
   no hopes of him. Dear o' me, dear o' me. Is there another bit of flannel
   anywhere?   585

>   *Mrs Holroyd rises and brings a piece. The Grandmother begins to*
>   *wash the breast of the dead man*

GRANDMOTHER   Well, I hope you'll be true to his children at least,
   Lizzie. (*Mrs Holroyd weeps—the old woman continues her washing*)
   Eh—and he's fair as a lily. Did you ever see a man with a whiter   590
   skin—and flesh as fine as the driven snow. He's beautiful, he is, the
   lamb. Many's the time I've looked at him, and I've felt proud of him,
   I have. And now he lies here. And such arms on 'im! Look at the
   vaccination marks, Lizzie. When I took him to be vaccinated, he had
   a little pink bonnet with a feather. (*Weeps*) Don't cry, my girl, don't.   595
   Sit up an' wash him a' that side, or we s'll never have him done. Oh,
   Lizzie!

MRS HOLROYD (*sitting up, startled*)   What—what?

GRANDMOTHER   Look at his poor hand!

>   *She holds up the right hand. The nails are bloody*   600

MRS HOLROYD   Oh, no! Oh, no! No!

>   *Both women weep*

GRANDMOTHER (*after a while*)   We maun° get on, Lizzie.

MRS HOLROYD (*sitting up*)   I can't touch his hands.

GRANDMOTHER   But I'm his mother—there's nothing I couldn't do for   605
   him.

MRS HOLROYD   I don't care—I don't care.

GRANDMOTHER   Prithee, prithee, Lizzie, I don't want thee goin' off,
   Lizzie.

MRS HOLROYD (*moaning*)   Oh, what shall I do!   610

GRANDMOTHER   Why, go thee an' get his feet washed. He's setting stiff,
   and how shall we get him laid out?

Mrs Holroyd, sobbing, goes, kneels at the miner's feet, and begins pulling off the great boots

GRANDMOTHER There's hardly a mark on him. Eh, what a man he is! 615
I've had some fine sons, Lizzie, I've had some big men of sons.

MRS HOLROYD He was always a lot whiter than me. And he used to chaff me.

GRANDMOTHER But his poor hands! I used to thank God for my
children, but they're rods o' trouble, Lizzie, they are. Unfasten his 620
belt, child. We mun get his things off soon, or else we s'll have such a job.

Mrs Holroyd, having dragged off his boots, rises. She is weeping.
CURTAIN

THE DAUGHTER-IN-LAW

CHARACTERS

MRS GASCOIGNE
JOE
MRS PURDY
MINNIE
LUTHER
CABMAN

Act 1 Scene 1 takes place in Mrs Gascoigne's kitchen, and the remainder of the play in the kitchen of Luther Gascoigne's new home

Act 1 Scene 1

A collier's kitchen—not poor. Windsor chairs,° deal table, dresser of painted wood, sofa covered with red cotton stuff. Time: about half past two of a winter's afternoon.

A large, stoutish woman of sixty-five, with smooth black hair parted down the middle of her head: Mrs Gascoigne.

Enter a young man, about twenty-six, dark, good-looking; has his right arm in a sling; does not take off cap: Joe Gascoigne

MRS GASCOIGNE Well, I s'd ha' thought thy belly 'ud a browt thee whoam afore this.

> *Joe sits on sofa without answering*

Doesn't ter want no dinner?

JOE (*looking up*) I want it if the' is ony.

MRS GASCOIGNE An if the' isna, tha can go be out? Tha talks large, my fine jockey! (*She puts a newspaper on the table; on it a plate and his dinner*) Wheer dost reckon ter's bin?

JOE I've bin ter th' office° for my munny.

MRS GASCOIGNE Tha's niver bin a' this while at th' office.

JOE They kep' me ower an hour, an' then gen me nowt.

MRS GASCOIGNE Gen thee nowt! Why, how do they ma'e that out? It's a wik sin' tha got hurt, an' if a man wi' a broken arm canna ha' his fourteen shillin' a week° accident pay, who can, I s'd like to know?

JOE They'll gie me nowt, whether or not.

MRS GASCOIGNE An' for why, prithee?

JOE (*does not answer for some time; then, suddenly*) They reckon I niver got it while I wor at work.

MRS GASCOIGNE Then where did ter get it, might I ax? I'd think they'd like to lay it onto me.

JOE Tha talks like a fool, Mother.

MRS GASCOIGNE Tha looks like one, me lad. (*She has given him his dinner; he begins to eat with a fork*) Here, hutch up,° gammy-leg°— gammy-arm.

> *He makes room; she sits by him on the sofa and cuts up his meat for him*

It's a rum un as I should start ha'in' babies again, an' feedin' 'em wi' spoon-meat. (*Gives him a spoon*) An' now let's hear why they winna gi'e thee thy pay. Another o' Macintyre's dirty knivey dodges, I s'd think.

JOE They reckon I did it wi' foolery, an' not wi' work.

MRS GASCOIGNE Oh indeed! An' what by that?

JOE (*eating*) They wunna gie me nowt, that's a'.   40

MRS GASCOIGNE It's a nice thing! An what did ter say?

JOE I said nowt.

MRS GASCOIGNE Tha wouldna'! Tha stood like a stuffed duck, an' said thank-yer.

JOE Well, it wor raight.   45

MRS GASCOIGNE How raight?

JOE I did do it wi' foolery.

MRS GASCOIGNE Then what did ter go axin' fer pay fer?

JOE I did it at work, didna I? An' a man as gets accident at work's titled ter disability pay, isna he?   50

MRS GASCOIGNE Tha said a minnit sin' as tha got it wi' foolery.

JOE An' so I did.

MRS GASCOIGNE I niver 'eered such talk i' my life.

JOE I dunna care what ter's 'eered an' what t'asna. I wor foolin' wi' a wringer° an' a pick-heft°—ta'e it as ter's a mind.   55

MRS GASCOIGNE What, down pit?

JOE I' th' stall, at snap time.°

MRS GASCOIGNE Showin' off a bit, like?

JOE Ye'.

MRS GASCOIGNE An' what then?   60

JOE Th' wringer gen me a rap ower th'arm, an' that's a'.

MRS GASCOIGNE An' tha reported it as a h'accident?

JOE It wor accident, worn't it? I niver did it a'purpose.

MRS GASCOIGNE But a pit accident.

JOE Well, an' what else wor't? It wor a accident I got i' th' pit, i' th' sta'° 65
wheer I wor workin'.

MRS GASCOIGNE But not *while* tha wor workin'.

JOE What by that?—it wor a pit accident as I got i' th' stall.

MRS GASCOIGNE But tha didna tell 'em how it happened.

JOE I said some stuff fell on my arm, an' brok' it. An' worna that trew? 70

MRS GASCOIGNE It wor very likely trew enough, lad, if on'y they'd ha' believed it.

JOE An they would ha' believed it, but for Hewett bully-raggin'°
Bettesworth 'cos he knowed he was a chappil man.° (*He imitates the
underground manager, Hewett, and Bettesworth, a butty*) 'About this 75
accident, Bettesworth. How exactly did it occur?' 'I couldn't exactly
say for certing, sir, because I wasn't linkin'.'° 'Then tell me as near as
you can.' 'Well, Mester, I'm sure I don't know.' 'That's curious,

Bettesworth—I must have a report. Do you know anything about
it, or don't you? It happened in your stall; you're responsible for it,   80
and I'm responsible for you.' 'Well, Gaffer, what's right's right, I
suppose, ter th' mesters or th' men. An' 'e wor conjurin' a' snap-time
wi' a pick-heft an' a wringer, an' the wringer catched 'im ower th'
arm.' 'I thought you didn't know!' 'I said *for certain*—I didn't see
exactly how 'twas done.'   85

MRS GASCOIGNE Hm.

JOE Bettesworth 'ud non ha' clat-farted° but for nosy Hewett. He says,
'Yo know, Joseph, when he says to me, "Do you know anything about
that h'accident?"—then I says to myself, "Take not the word of truth
hutterly outer thy mouth." '   90

MRS GASCOIGNE If he took a bit o' slaver° outen's mouth, it 'ud do.

JOE So this mornin' when I went ter th' office, Mester Salmon he com
out an' said: ' 'Ow did this h'accident occur, Joseph?' and I said,
'Some stuff fell on't.' So he says, 'Stuff fell on't, stuff fell on't! You
mean coal or rock or what?' So I says, 'Well, it worn't a thripenny bit.'°   95
'No,' he says, 'but what was it?' 'It wor a piece o' clunch,'° I says. 'You
don't use clunch for wringers,' he says, 'do you?' 'The wringin' of the
nose bringeth forth blood,' I says—

MRS GASCOIGNE Why, you know you never did. (*She begins making a
pudding*)   100

JOE No—b'r I'd ha' meant t'r'a done.

MRS GASCOIGNE We know thee! Tha's done thysen one i' th' eye this
time. When dost think tha'll iver get ter be a butty, at this rate?
There's Luther nowt b'r a day man yet.

JOE I'd as lief be a day man as a butty, i' pits that rat-gnawed there's   105
hardly a stall worth havin'; an' a company as 'ud like yer ter scrape yer
tabs° afore you went home, for fear you took a grain o' coal.

MRS GASCOIGNE Maybe—but tha's got ter get thy livin' by 'em.

JOE I hanna. I s'll go to Australia.

MRS GASCOIGNE Tha'lt do no such thing, while I'm o' this earth.   110

JOE Ah, but though, I shall—else get married, like our Luther.

MRS GASCOIGNE A fat sight better off tha'lt be for that.

JOE You niver know, Mother, dun yer?

MRS GASCOIGNE You dunna, me lad—not till yer find yerself let in.
Marriage is like a mouse-trap, for either man or woman. You've soon   115
come to th' end o' th' cheese.

JOE Well, ha'ef a loaf's better nor no bread.

MRS GASCOIGNE Why, wheer's th' loaf as tha'd like ter gnawg a' thy life?

JOE Nay, nowhere yet.

MRS GASCOIGNE Well, dunna thee talk, then. Tha's done thysen harm   120
enow for one day, wi' thy tongue.

JOE An' good as well, Mother—I've aten my dinner, a'most.

MRS GASCOIGNE An' swilled thy belly afore that, methinks.

JOE Niver i' this world!

MRS GASCOIGNE And I've got thee to keep on ten shillin's a wik°   125
club-money,° han I?

JOE Tha needna, if ter doesna want. Besides, we s'll be out on strike
afore we know wheer we are.

MRS GASCOIGNE I'm sure. You've on'y bin in—

JOE Now, Mother, spit on thy hands an' ta'e fresh hold. We s'll be out on   130
strike in a wik or a fortnit—

MRS GASCOIGNE Strike's a' they're fit for—a pack o' slutherers° as . . .
Her words tail off as she goes into pantry

JOE (*to himself*) Tha goes chunterin' i' th' pantry when somebody's at
th' door. (*Rises, goes to door*)   135

MRS PURDY'S VOICE Is your mother in?

JOE Yi, 'er's in right enough.

MRS PURDY Well, then, can I speak to her?

JOE (*calling*) Mrs Purdy wants ter speak to thee, Mother.
Mrs Gascoigne crosses the kitchen heavily, with a dripping-pan;   140
stands in doorway

MRS GASCOIGNE Good afternoon.

MRS PURDY Good afternoon.

MRS GASCOIGNE Er—what is it?
Mrs Purdy enters. She is a little fat, red-faced body in bonnet and   145
black cape

MRS PURDY I wanted to speak to yer rather pertickler.

MRS GASCOIGNE (*giving way*) Oh, yes?
All three enter the kitchen. Mrs Purdy stands near the door

MRS PURDY (*nodding at Joe*) Has he had a h'accident?   150

MRS GASCOIGNE Broke his arm.

MRS PURDY Oh my! that's nasty. When did 'e do that?

MRS GASCOIGNE A wik sin' to-day.

MRS PURDY In th' pit?

MRS GASCOIGNE Yes—an's not goin' to get any accident pay—says as   155
'e worn't workin'; he wor foolin' about.

MRS PURDY T-t-t-t! Did iver you know! I tell you what, missis, it's a
wonder they let us live on the face o' the earth at all—it's a wonder we
don't have to fly up i' th' air like birds.

JOE There'd be a squark i' th' sky then!   160

MRS PURDY But it is indeed. It's somethink awful. They've gave my
mester a dirty job o' nights, at a guinea a week,° an' he's worked fifty
years for th' company, an' isn't but sixty-two now—said he wasn't
equal to stall-workin', whereas he has to slave on th' roads° an' comes
whoam that tired he can't put's food in's mouth.   165

JOE He's about like me.

MRS PURDY Yis. But it's no nice thing, a guinea a week.

MRS GASCOIGNE Well, that's how they're servin' 'em a' round—widders' coals° stopped—leadin'° raised to four-an'-eight°—an' ivry
man niggled down to nothink.   170

MRS PURDY I wish I'd got that Fraser strung up by th' heels—I'd ma'e
his sides o' bacon rowdy.°

MRS GASCOIGNE He's put a new manager to ivry pit, an' ivry one a
nigger-driver.

MRS PURDY Says he's got to economise—says the company's not a   175
philanthropic concern—

MRS GASCOIGNE But ta'es twelve hundred a year for hissen.

MRS PURDY A mangy bachelor wi' 'is iron-men.°

JOE But they wunna work.

MRS PURDY They say how he did but coss an' swear about them   180
American Cutters.° I should like to see one set outer 'im—they'd
work hard enough rippin's guts out—even iron's got enough sense
for that. (*She suddenly subsides*)
        There is a pause

MRS GASCOIGNE How do you like living down Nethergreen?   185

MRS PURDY Well—we're very comfortable. It's small, but it's handy,
an' sin' the mester's gone down t'a guinea—

MRS GASCOIGNE It'll do for you three.

MRS PURDY Yes.
        Another pause   190

MRS GASCOIGNE The men are comin' out again, they say.

MRS PURDY Isn't it summat sickenin'? Well, I've werritted° an' werritted till I'm soul-sick—

MRS PURDY There can be as much ache in a motherly body as in bones
an' gristle, I'm sure o' that.   195

JOE Nay, I'm more than bones an' gristle.

MRS PURDY That's true as the day.
        Another long pause

MRS GASCOIGNE An' how have yer all bin keepin'?

MRS PURDY Oh, very nicely—except our Bertha.   200

MRS GASCOIGNE Is she poorly, then?

MRS PURDY   That's what I com ter tell yer. I niver knowed a word on't till a Sat'day, nor niver noticed a thing. Then she says to me, as white as a sheet, 'I've been sick every morning, Mother,' an' it com across me like a shot from a gun. I sunk down i' that chair an' couldna fetch   205
a breath.—An' me as prided myself! I've often laughed about it, an' said I was thankful my children had all turned out so well, lads an' wenches as well, an' said it was a'cause they was all got of a Sunday— their father was too drunk a' Saturday, an' too tired o' wik-days. An' it's a fact, they've all turned out well, for I'd allers bin to chappil.   210
Well, I've said it for a joke, but now it's turned on me. I'd better ha' kep' my tongue still.

JOE   It's not me, though, missis. I wish it wor.

MRS PURDY   There's no occasions to ma'e gam' of it neither, as far as I can see. The youngest an' the last of 'em as I've got, an' a lass as I   215
liked, for she's simple, but she's good-natured, an' him a married man. Thinks I to myself, 'I'd better go to's mother, she'll ha'e more about 'er than's new wife—for she's a stuck-up piece o' goods as ever trod.'

MRS GASCOIGNE   Why, what'd yer mean?   220

MRS PURDY   I mean what I say—an' there's no denyin' it. That girl— well, it's nigh on breakin' my heart, for I'm that short o' breath. (*Sighs*) I'm sure!

MRS GASCOIGNE   Why don't yer say what yer mean?

MRS PURDY   I've said it, haven't I? There's my gal gone four month wi'   225
childt to your Luther.

MRS GASCOIGNE   Nay, nay, nay, missis! You'll never ma'e me believe it.

MRS PURDY   Glad would I be if I nedna. But I've gone through it all since Sat'day on. I've wanted to break every bone in 'er body—an' I've said I should on'y be happy if I was scraightin'° at 'er funeral—   230
an' I've said I'd wring his neck for 'im. But it doesn't alter it—there it is—an' there it will be. An' I s'll be a grandmother where my heart heaves, an' maun drag a wastrel baby through my old age. An' it's neither a cryin' nor a laughin' matter, but it's a matter of a girl wi' child, an' a man six week married.   235

MRS GASCOIGNE   But our Luther never went wi' your Bertha. How d'you make it out?

MRS PURDY   Yea, yea, missis—yea indeed.

JOE   Yi, Mother, he's bin out wi' 'er. She wor pals wi' Liza Ann Varley, as went out wi' Jim Horrocks. So Jim he passed Bertha onter our   240
Luther. Why, I've had many a glass wi' the four of 'em, i' th' Ram.

MRS GASCOIGNE   I niver knowed nowt o' *this* afore.

JOE   Tha doesna know ivrythink, Mother.

MRS GASCOIGNE An' it's well I don't, methinks.

JOE Tha doesna want, neither.   245

MRS GASCOIGNE Well, I dunno what we're goin' to do, missis. He's a
young married man.

MRS PURDY An' she's a girl o' mine.

MRS GASCOIGNE How old is she?

MRS PURDY She wor twenty-three last September.   250

MRS GASCOIGNE Well then, I sh'd 'a thought she'd ha' known better.

MRS PURDY An' what about him, missis, as goes and gets married t'r
another fine madam d'rectly after he's been wi' my long lass?

JOE But he never knowed owt about.

MRS PURDY He'd seen th' blossom i' flower, if he hadna spotted the   255
fruit a-comin'.

JOE Yi—but—

MRS GASCOIGNE Yi but what?

JOE Well—you dunna expect—ivry time yer cast yer bread on th'
wathers,° as it'll come whoam to you like.   260

MRS GASCOIGNE Well, I dunno what we're goin' to do.

MRS PURDY I thought I'd better come to you, rather than—

JOE Ah, you non want it gettin' about—an' *she'd* best not know—if it
can be helped.

MRS GASCOIGNE I can't see for why.   265

MRS PURDY No indeed—a man as plays fast an' loose first wi' one an'
then goes an' marries another stuck-up piece—

MRS GASCOIGNE An' a wench as goes sittin i' th' Ram wi' the fellers
mun expect what she gets, missis.

MRS PURDY 'Appen so, 'appen so. An' th' man maun abide by what he's   270
gi'en.

MRS GASCOIGNE I dunno *what* we're goin' to do!

JOE We'd best keep it as quiet as we can.

MRS PURDY I thinks to mysen, 'It'll non become *me* to go an' jack up° a
married couple, for if *he's* at fault, it's her as 'ud ha'e ter suffer.' An'   275
though she's haughty, I knowed her mother, as nice a body as ever
stept, an' treated scandylos by Jim Hetherington. An', thinks I, she's
a horphan, if she's got money, an' nobbut her husband i' th' world.
Thinks I to mysen, it's no good visitin' it on *'er* head, if he's a villain.
For whatever th' men does, th' women maun ma'e up for. An' though   280
I do consider as it's nowt b'r a dirty trick o' his'n to ta'e a poor lass like
my long thing, an' go an' marry a woman wi' money—

MRS GASCOIGNE Woman wi' money, an' peace go wi' 'er, 'er an' 'er
money! What she's got, she'll keep, you take my word for it, missis.

MRS PURDY Yes, an' she's right of it.   285

JOE Nay, Mother, she's non close.

MRS GASCOIGNE Isn't she?—oh, isn't she? An' what is she then? All
she wanted was as much for her money as she could get. An' when she
fun as nob'dy was for sale but our Luther, she says, 'Well, I'll take it.'

JOE Nay, it worna like that—it wor him as wor that come-day-go-day°—   290

MRS PURDY God send Sunday.

MRS GASCOIGNE An' what more can a man do, think yer, but ax a
woman? When has *thee* ever done as much?

JOE No, I hanna, 'cos I've niver seen th' women as I wanted to say
'snap'—but he slormed° an' she—   295

MRS GASCOIGNE Slormed! Thee slorm but one fiftieth part to any lass
thee likes, an' see if 'er's not all over thee afore tha's said six words.
Slormed! 'Er wor that high an' mighty, 'er wanted summat bett'
nor 'im.

JOE Nay—I reckon he niver showed the spunk of a sprat-herring to 'er.   300

MRS GASCOIGNE Did *thee* show any more? Hast iver done? Yet onybody'ud think tha wor for marryin' 'er thysen.

JOE If I'd ha' *bin* for marryin' 'er, I'd ha' gone wholesale, not ha' fudged
and haffled.°

MRS GASCOIGNE But tha *worna* for marryin' neither 'er nor nobody.   305

JOE No, I worna.

MRS GASCOIGNE No, tha worna.

> *There is a long pause. The Mother turns half apologetically, half
> explanatorily, to Mrs Purdy*

It's like this 'ere, missis, if you'll not say nothink about it—sin' it's got   310
to come out atween us. He courted Minnie Hetherington when she
wor at her uncle's, at th' Bell o' Brass, an' he wor nowt bu'r a lad o'
twenty-two, an' she twenty-one. An' he wor gone on 'er right enow.
Then she had that row wi' 'er uncle, for she wor iver overbearin' an'
chancy.° Then our Luther says to me, 'I s'll ax 'er to marry me,   315
Mother,' an' I says: 'Tha pleases thysen, but ter my thinkin' tha'rt a
sight too young an' doesna know thy own mind.' Howsoever, much
notice 'e takes o' me.

JOE He took a lot o' notice on thee, tha knows well enough.

MRS GASCOIGNE An' for what shouldn't he? Hadn't I bin a good   320
mother to 'im i' ivry shape an' form? Let *her* make him as good a wife
as I made him a mother! Well—we'll see. You'll see *him* repent the
day. But they're not to be bidden. An' so, missis, he did ax 'er, as 'e'd
said 'e should. But hoity-toity an' no thank yer, she wasna for havin'
him, but mun go an' be a nursery governess up i' Manchester. Thinks   325
I to myself, she's after a town johnny, a Bertie-Willie an' a yard o' cuffs.

But he kep' on writin' to 'er, now an' again—an' she answered—as if
she wor standin' at top of a flight of steps—

JOE An' 'appen on'y wanted fetchin' down.

MRS GASCOIGNE Wi' a kick from behint, if I'd ha' had th' doin' o't. So   330
they go mornin' on.° He sees 'er once i' a blew moon. If he goes ter
Manchester, she condescends to see him for a couple of hours. If
she comes here, she ca's i' this house wi' a 'How-do-you-do, Mrs
Gascoigne', an' off again. If they go f'r a walk—

JOE He's whoam again at nine o'clock.   335

MRS GASCOIGNE If they go for a walk it's 'Thank you, I mustn't be very
late. Good night, Luther.' I thought it ud niver come ter nothink.
Then 'er uncle dies an' leaves her a hundred pounds, which con-
siderin' th' way she'd been with 'im, was more than *I'd* ha' gen her—
an' she was a bit nicer. She writes ter Luther ter come an' see 'er an'   340
stop a couple o' days. He ta'es her to the the-etter, an's for goin' i' th'
pit at a shillin', when she says: 'It's my treat, Luther, and five shillin'
seats apiece, if you please.'

JOE An' he couldna luik at th' performance, for fear as the folks was
luikin' at 'im.   345

MRS GASCOIGNE An' after th' the-etter, it must be supper wi' a man i' a
tail-coat an' silver forks, an' she pays. 'Yes,' says I when he told me,
'that's the tricks of servants, showin' off afore decent folk.'

JOE She could do what she liked, couldn't she?

MRS GASCOIGNE Well, an' after that, he didna write, 'cept to say thank   350
yer. For it put 'im in a horkard position. That wor four years ago, an'
she's nobbut seen him three times sin' that. If she could but ha'
snapped up somebody else, it 'ud bin good-bye to Luther—

JOE As tha told him many a time.

MRS GASCOIGNE As I told him many a time, for am I to sit an' see my   355
own lad bitted an' bobbed,° tasted an' spit out by a madam i' service?
Then all of a suddin, three months back, come a letter: 'Dear Luther,
I have been thinking it over, an' have come to the opinion that we'd
better get married now, if we are ever goin' to. We've been dallying on
all these years, and we seem to get no further. So we'd better make the   360
plunge, if ever we're going to. Of course you will say exactly what you
think. Don't agree to anything unless you want to. I only want to
say that I think, if we're ever going to be married, we'd better do it
without waiting any longer.' Well, missis, he got that letter when he
com whoam fra work. I seed him porin' an' porin', but I says nowt.   365
Then he ate some o's dinner, an' went out. When he com in, it wor
about haef past ten, an' 'e wor white as a sheet. He gen me that letter,

an' says: 'What's think o' that, Mother?' Well, you could ha' knocked
me down wi' a feather when I'd read it. I says: 'I think it's tidy cheek,
my lad.' He took it back an' puts i's pocket, an' after a bit, 'e says: 370
'What should ter say, Mother?' 'Tha says what's a mind, my lad,'
I says. So he begins unlacin' 's boots. Sudden he stops, an' wi's
boot-tags rattlin', goes rummagin' for th' pen an' ink. 'What art goin'
to say?' I says. 'I'm goin' ter say, 'er can do as 'er's a mind. If 'er wants
ter be married, 'er can, an' if 'er doesna, 'er nedna.' So I thinks we   375
could leave it at that. He sits him down, an' doesna write more nor a
side an' a haef. I thinks: 'That's done it, it'll be an end between them
two now.' He niver gen th' letter to me to read.

JOE   He did to me. He says: 'I'm ready an' willin' to do what you want,
whenever yer want. I'm earnin' about thirty-five bob a week, an'   380
haven't got any money because my mother gi'es me what I ax for ter
spend. But I can have what I ask for to set up house with. Your
loving—Luther.' He says to me: 'Dost think it's a'right?' I says: 'I s'd
think so; 'er maun ma'e what 'er likes out on't.'

MRS GASCOIGNE   On th' Monday after, she wor here livin' at 'er A'nt's   385
an' th' notice was in at th' registrar.° I says: 'What money dost want?'
He says: 'Thee buy what tha thinks we s'll want.' So he tells Minnie,
an' she says: 'Not bi-out I'm theer.' Well, we goes ter Nottingham,
an' she will ha'e nowt b'r old-fashioned stuff. I says: 'That's niver *my*
mind, Minnie.' She says: 'Well, I like it, an' yo'll see it'll look nice. I'll   390
pay for it.' Which to be sure I never let her. For she'd had a mester as
made a fool of her, tellin' her this an' that, what wor good taste, what
wor bad.

JOE   An' it *does* look nice, Mother, their house.

MRS GASCOIGNE   We'll see how it looks i' ten years' time, my lad, wi' th'   395
racket an' tacket° o' children. For it's not serviceable, missis.

MRS PURDY   (*who has been a sympathetic and exclamative listener*)   Then
it's no good.

MRS GASCOIGNE   An' that's how they got married.

JOE   An' he went about wi's tail atween his legs, scared outer's life.   400

MRS GASCOIGNE   For I said no more. If he axed me owt, I did it; if
he wanted owt, I got it. But it wasn't for me to go interferin' where
I wasn't wanted.

JOE   If ever I get married, Mother, I s'll go i' lodgin's six month
aforehand.   405

MRS GASCOIGNE   Tha'd better—ter get thysen a bit case-hardened.

JOE   Yi. But I'm goin' t'r Australia.

MRS GASCOIGNE   I come wi' thee, then.

JOE Tha doesna.

MRS GASCOIGNE I dunna fret—tha'lt non go.   410

MRS PURDY Well, it was what I should call a bit off-hand, I must say.

MRS GASCOIGNE You can see now how he got married, an' who's to
blame.

JOE Nay, yo' canna ma'e 'er to blame for Bertha. Liza Ann Varley's ter
blame for th' lass goin' out o' nights.   415

MRS PURDY An' there I thought they wor both i' Varley's—not galli-
vantin'.

JOE They often was. An' Jim Horrocks is ter blame fer couplin' 'er
onter our Luther, an' him an' her's ter blame for the rest. I dunno how
you can lay it on Minnie. You might as well lay it on 'er if th' childt   420
wor mine.

MRS GASCOIGNE (*sharply*) Tha'd ha'e more sense!

JOE I'd try.

MRS GASCOIGNE But now she's played fast an' loose wi' him—twice
I *know* he axed 'er to ha'e him—now she's asked for what she's got.   425
She's put her puddin' in her mouth, an' if she's burnt herself, serve
her right.

MRS PURDY Well, I didn't want to go to court. I thought, his mother'll
be th' best one to go to—

MRS GASCOIGNE No—you mun go to him hisself—go an' tell him i'   430
front of her—an' if she wants anythink, she mun ma'e arrangements
herself.

JOE What was you thinkin' of, Missis Purdy?

MRS PURDY Well, I was thinkin', she's a poor lass—an' I didn't want 'er
to go to court, for they ax such questions—an' I thought it was such   435
a *thing*, him six wik married—though to be sure I'd no notions of
how it was—I thought, we might happen say, it was one o' them
electricians as was along when they laid th' wires under th' road down
to Batsford—and—

JOE And arrange for a lump sum, like?   440

MRS PURDY Yes—we're poor, an' she's poor—an' if she had a bit o'
money of 'er own—for we should niver touch it—it might be a
'inducement to some other young feller—for, poor long thing, she's
that simple—

MRS GASCOIGNE Well, ter my knowledge, them as has had a childt   445
seems to get off i' marriage better nor many as hasn't. I'm sure,
there's a lot o' men likes it, if they think a woman's had a baby by
another man.

MRS PURDY That's nothing to trust by, missis; you'll say so yourself.

JOE An' about how much do you want? Thirty pounds?   450

MRS PURDY We want what's fair. I got it fra Emma Stapleton; they had
forty wi' their Lucy.

JOE Forty pound?

MRS PURDY Yes.

MRS GASCOIGNE Well, then, let *her* find it. She's paid for nothing but   455
the wedding. She's got money enough, if he's none. Let *her* find it.
She made the bargain, she maun stick by it. It was her dip i' th'
bran-tub—if there's a mouse nips hold of her finger, she maun suck
it better, for nobody axed her to dip.

MRS PURDY You think I'd better go to him? Eh, missis, it's a nasty   460
business. But right's right.

MRS GASCOIGNE Right *is* right, Mrs Purdy. And you go tell him a-front
of her—that's the best thing you can do. Then iverything's straight.

MRS PURDY But for her he might ha' married our Bertha.

MRS GASCOIGNE To be sure, to be sure.   465

MRS PURDY What right had she to snatch when it pleased her?

MRS GASCOIGNE That's what I say. If th' woman ca's for th' piper, th'
woman maun pay th' tune.

MRS PURDY Not but what—

JOE It's a nasty business.   470

MRS GASCOIGNE Nasty or not, it's hers now, not mine. He's *her* husband. 'My son's my son till he takes him a wife,' an' no longer. Now
let her answer for it.

MRS PURDY An' you think I'd better go when they're both in?

MRS GASCOIGNE I should go to-night, atween six an' seven, that's what   475
I should do.

JOE I never should. If I was you, I'd settle it wi'out Minnie's knowin'—
it's bad enough.

MRS GASCOIGNE What's bad enough?

JOE Why, that.   480

MRS GASCOIGNE What?

JOE Him an' 'er—it's bad enough as it is.

MRS GASCOIGNE (*with great bitterness*) Then let it be a bit worse, let it
be a bit worse. Let her have it, then; it'll do her good. Who is she, to
trample eggs that another hen would sit warm? No—Mrs Purdy, *give*   485
it her. It'll take her down a peg or two, and, my sirs, she wants it, my
sirs, she needs it.

JOE (*muttering*) A fat lot o' good it'll do.

MRS GASCOIGNE What has thee ter say, I should like to know? Fed an'
clothed an' coddled, tha art, an' not a thing tha lacks. But wait till I'm 490
gone, my lad; tha'lt know what I've done for thee, then, tha will.

JOE For a' that, it's no good 'er knowin'.

MRS GASCOIGNE Isna it?—isna it? If it's not good for 'er, it's good for '*im*.

JOE I dunna believe it.

MRS GASCOIGNE Who asked *thee* to believe it? Tha's showed thysen a   495
    wise man *this* day, hasn't ter? Wheer should ter be terday but for me?
    Wheer should ter iver ha' bin? An' then *tha* sits up for to talk. It ud
    look better o' thee not to spit i' th' hand as holds thy bread an' butter.

JOE Neither do I.

MRS GASCOIGNE Doesn't ter! Tha has a bit too much chelp an' chunter.°   500
    It doesna go well, my lad. Tha wor blortin' an' bletherin' down at th'
    office a bit sin', an' a mighty fool tha made o' thysen. How should thee
    like to go home wi' *thy* tale o' to-day, to Minnie, might I ax thee?

JOE If she didna like it, she could lump it.

MRS GASCOIGNE It 'ud be thee as 'ud lump, my lad. But what does thee   505
    know about it? 'Er'd rip th' guts out on thee like a tiger, an' stan'
    grinnin' at thee when tha shrivelled up 'cause tha'd no inside left.

MRS PURDY She looks it, I must admit—every bit of it.

JOE For a' that, it's no good her knowing.

MRS GASCOIGNE Well, I say it *is*—an' thee, tha shifty little know-all, as   510
    blorts at one minute like a suckin' calf an' th' next blethers like a hass,
    dunna thee come layin' th' law down to me, for I know better. No,
    Mrs Purdy, it's no good comin' to me. You've a right to some com-
    pensation, an' that lass o' yours has; but let them as cooked the goose
    eat it, that's all. Let him arrange it hisself—an' if he does nothink, put   515
    him i' court, that's all.

MRS PURDY He's not goin' scot-free, you may back your life o' that.

MRS GASCOIGNE You go down to-night atween six an' seven, an' let 'em
    have it straight. You know where they live?

MRS PURDY I' Simson Street?   520

MRS GASCOIGNE About four houses up—next Holbrooks.

MRS PURDY (*rising*) Yes.

JOE An' it'll do no good. Gi'e me th' money, Mother; I'll pay it.

MRS GASCOIGNE Tha wunna!

JOE I've a right to th' money—I've addled° it.   525

MRS GASCOIGNE A'right—an' I've saved it for thee. But tha has none
    on't till tha knocks me down an' ta'es it out o' my pocket.

MRS PURDY No—let them pay themselves. It's not thy childt, is it?

JOE It isna—but the money is.

MRS GASCOIGNE We'll see.   530

MRS PURDY Well, I mun get back. Thank yer, missis.

MRS GASCOIGNE And thank *you*! I'll come down to-morrow—at dark
    hour.

MRS PURDY Thank yer.—I hope yer arm'll soon be better.
JOE Thank yer.   535
MRS GASCOIGNE I'll come down to-morrow. You'll go to-night—
    atween six an' seven?
MRS PURDY Yes—if it mun be done, it mun. He took his own way, she
    took hers, now I mun take mine. Well, good afternoon. I mun see
    about th' mester's dinner.   540
JOE And you haven't said nothink to nobody?
MRS PURDY I haven't—I shouldn't be flig,° should I?
JOE No—I should keep it quiet as long's you can.
MRS GASCOIGNE There's no need for a' th' world to know—but them
    as is concerned maun abide by it.   545
MRS PURDY Well, good afternoon.
MRS GASCOIGNE Good afternoon.
JOE Good afternoon.
        Exit Mrs Purdy
    Well, that's a winder!   550
MRS GASCOIGNE Serve her right, for tip-callin' wi'm all those years.
JOE She niver ought to know.
MRS GASCOIGNE I—I could fetch thee a wipe ower th' face, I could!
        He sulks. She is in a rage

Act 1 Scene 2

*The kitchen of Luther Gascoigne's new home. It is pretty—in
'cottage' style;° rush-bottomed chairs, black oak bureau, brass
candlesticks, delft,° etc. Green cushions in chairs. Towards five
o'clock. Firelight. It is growing dark.*
Minnie Gascoigne is busy about the fire: a tall, good-looking   5
*young woman, in a shirt-blouse and dark skirt, and apron. She
lifts lids of saucepans, etc., hovers impatiently, looks at clock,
begins to trim lamp*
MINNIE I wish he'd come. If I didn't want him, he'd be here half an hour
    since. But just because I've got a pudding that wants eating on the   10
    tick—! He—he's *never* up to the scratch; he never is. As if the day
    wasn't long enough!
        *Sound of footsteps. She seizes a saucepan, and is rushing towards
        the door. The latch has clacked. Luther appears in the doorway, in
        his pit-dirt—a collier of medium height, with fair moustache. He*   15

has a red scarf knotted round his throat, and a cap with a Union
medal.° *The two almost collide*

LUTHER My word, you're on the hop!

MINNIE (*disappearing into scullery*) You *nearly* made me drop the saucepan. Why are you so late?   20

LUTHER I'm non late, am I?

MINNIE You're twenty minutes later than yesterday.

LUTHER Oh ah, I stopped finishing a stint, an' com up wi' a'most th' last batch.

    He takes a tin bottle and a dirty calico snap-bag out of his pocket,   25
    puts them on the bureau; goes into the scullery

MINNIE'S VOICE No!

    She comes hurrying out with the saucepan. In a moment, Luther
    follows. He has taken off his coat and cap, his heavy trousers are
    belted round his hips, his arms are bare to above the elbow, because   30
    the pit-singlet of thick flannel is almost sleeveless

LUTHER Tha *art* throng!°

MINNIE (*at the fire, flushed*) Yes, and everything's ready, and will be spoiled.

LUTHER Then we'd better eat it afore I wash me.   35

MINNIE No—no—it's not nice—

LUTHER Just as ter's a mind—but there's scarce a collier in a thousand washes hissen afore he has his dinner. We niver did a-whoam.

MINNIE But it doesn't look nice.

LUTHER Eh, wench, tha'lt soon get used ter th' looks on me. A bit o'   40
dirt's like a veil on my face—I shine through th' 'andsomer. What hast got? (*He peers over her range*)

MINNIE (*waving a fork*) You're not to look.

LUTHER It smells good.

MINNIE Are you *going* to have your dinner like that?   45

LUTHER Ay, lass—just for once.

    He spreads a newspaper in one of the green-cushioned armchairs
    and sits down. She disappears into the scullery with a saucepan.
    He takes off his great pit-boots. She sets a soup-tureen on the
    table, and lights the lamp. He watches her face in the glow   50

Tha'rt non bad-luikin' when ter's a mind.

MINNIE *When* have I a mind?

LUTHER Tha's allers a mind—but when ter lights th' lamp tha'rt i' luck's way.

MINNIE Come on, then.   55

    He drags his chair to the table

LUTHER   I s'll ha'e ter ha'e a newspaper afront on me, or thy cloth'll be
a blackymoor.° (*Begins disarranging the pots*)

MINNIE   Oh, you *are* a nuisance! (*Jumps up*)

LUTHER   I can put 'em a' back again.   60

MINNIE   I know your puttings back.

LUTHER   Tha couldna get married by thysen, could ter?—so tha'lt ha'e
ter ma'e th' best on me.

MINNIE   But you're such a bother—never here at the right time—never
doing the right thing—   65

LUTHER   An' my mouth's ter wide an' my head's ter narrow. Shalt iver
ha' come ter th' end of my faults an' failin's?

MINNIE   (*giving him soup*) I wish I could.

LUTHER   An' now tha'lt snap my head off 'cos I slobber, shanna tha?

MINNIE   Then don't slobber.   70

LUTHER   I'll try my luck. What hast bin doin' a' day?

MINNIE   Working.

LUTHER   Has our Joe bin in?

MINNIE   No. I rather thought he might, but he hasn't.

LUTHER   You've not been up home?   75

MINNIE   To your mother's? No, what should I go there for?

LUTHER   Eh, I dunno what ter should go for—I thought tha 'appen
might.

MINNIE   But what for?

LUTHER   Nay—I niver thowt nowt about what for.   80

MINNIE   Then why did you ask me?

LUTHER   I dunno.
             A pause

MINNIE   Your mother can come here, can't she?

LUTHER   Ay, she can come. Tha'll be goin' up wi' me to-night—I want   85
ter go an' see about our Joe.

MINNIE   What about him?

LUTHER   How he went on about's club money. Shall ter come wi' me?

MINNIE   I wanted to do my curtains.

LUTHER   But tha's got a' day to do them in.   90

MINNIE   But I want to do them to-night—I feel like it.

LUTHER   A' right.—I shanna be long, at any rate. (*A pause*) What dost
keep lookin' at?

MINNIE   How?

LUTHER   Tha keeps thy eye on me rarely.   95

MINNIE   (*laughing*) It's your mouth—it looks *so* red and bright, in your
black face.

LUTHER   Does it look nasty to thee?

MINNIE   No—no-o.

LUTHER (*pushing his moustache, laughing*) It ma'es you look like a nigger,   100
i' your pit-dirt—th' whites o' your eyes!

MINNIE   Just. (*She gets up to take his plate; goes and stands beside him. He
lifts his face to her*) I want to see if I can see you; you look so different.

LUTHER   Tha can see me well enough. Why dost want to?

MINNIE   It's almost like having a stranger.   105

LUTHER   Would ter rather?

MINNIE   What?

LUTHER   Ha'e a stranger?

MINNIE   What for?

LUTHER   Hae—I dunno.   110

MINNIE (*touching his hair*) You look rather nice—an' your hair's so dirty.

LUTHER   Gi'e me a kiss.

MINNIE   But where? You're all grime.

LUTHER   I'm sure I've licked my mouth clean.

MINNIE (*stooping suddenly, and kissing him*) You don't look nearly such a   115
tame rabbit, in your pit-dirt.

LUTHER (*catching her in his arms*) Dunna I? (*Kisses her*) What colour is
my eyes?

MINNIE   Bluey-grey.

LUTHER   An thine's grey an' black.   120

MINNIE   Mind! (*She looks at her blouse when he releases her*)

LUTHER (*timid*) Have I blacked it?

MINNIE   A bit. (*She goes to the scullery; returns with another dish*)

LUTHER   They talkin' about comin' out again.

MINNIE (*returning*) Good laws!°—they've no need.   125

LUTHER   They are, though.

MINNIE   It's a holiday they want.

LUTHER   Nay, it isna. They want th' proper scale° here, just as they ha'e
it ivrywhere else.

MINNIE   But if the seams are thin, and the company can't afford—   130

LUTHER   They can afford a' this gret new electric plant; they can afford
to build new houses for managers, an' ter give blo—ter give Frazer
twelve hundred a year.

MINNIE   If they want a good manager to make the pits pay, they have to
give him a good salary.   135

LUTHER   So's he can clip down our wages.

MINNIE   Why, what are yours clipped down?

LUTHER   Mine isn't, but there's plenty as is.

MINNIE And will this strike make a butty of you?

LUTHER You don't strike to get made a butty on. 140

MINNIE Then how *do* you do it? You're thirty-one.

LUTHER An' there's many as owd as me as is day-men yet.

MINNIE But there's more that aren't, that are butties.

LUTHER Ay, they've had luck.

MINNIE Luck! You mean they've had some *go* in them. 145

LUTHER Why, what can I do more than I am doin'?

MINNIE It isn't what you do, it's how you do it. Sluther° through any job; get to th' end of it, no matter how. That's you.

LUTHER I hole a stint as well as any man.

MINNIE Then I back° it takes you twice as long. 150

LUTHER Nay, nor that neither.

MINNIE I *know* you're not much of a workman—I've heard it from other butties, that you never put your heart into anything.

LUTHER Who hast heard it fra?

MINNIE From those that know. And I could ha' told it *them*, for I know 155
you. You'll be a day-man at seven shillings a day till the end of your life—and you'll be satisfied, so long as you can shilly-shally through. That's what your mother did for you—mardin'° you up till you were all mard-soft.

LUTHER Tha's got a lot ter say a' of a suddin. Thee shut thy mouth. 160

MINNIE You've been dragged round at your mother's apron-strings, all the lot of you, till there isn't half a man among you.

LUTHER Tha seems fond enough of our Joe.

MINNIE He is th' best in the bunch.

LUTHER Tha should ha' married him, then. 165

MINNIE I shouldn't have had to ask *him*, if he was ready.

LUTHER I'd axed thee twice afore—tha knowed tha could ha'e it when ter wanted.

MINNIE *Axed* me! It was like asking me to pull out a tooth for you.

LUTHER Yi, an' it felt like it. 170

MINNIE What?

LUTHER Axin' thee to marry me. I'm blessed if it didna feel like axin' the doctor to pull ten teeth out of a stroke.

MINNIE And then you expect me to have you!

LUTHER Well, tha *has* done, whether or not. 175

MINNIE I—yes, I had to fetch you, like a mother fetches a kid from school. A pretty sight you looked. Didn't your mother give you a ha'penny to spend, to get you to go?

LUTHER No; she spent it for me.

MINNIE She would! She wouldn't even let you spend your own   180
   ha'penny. You'd have lost it, or let somebody take it from you.

LUTHER Yi. Thee.

MINNIE Me!—me take anything from you! Why, you've got nothing
   worth having.

LUTHER I dunno—tha seems ter think so sometimes.   185

MINNIE Oh! Shilly-shally and crawl, that's all you can do. You ought to
   have stopped with your mother.

LUTHER I should ha' done, if tha hadna hawksed° me out.

MINNIE You aren't *fit* for a woman to have married, you're not.

LUTHER Then why did thee marry me? It wor thy doin's.   190

MINNIE Because I could get nobody better.

LUTHER I'm more class than I thought for, then.

MINNIE Are you! Are you!

>   *Joe's voice is heard*

JOE I'm comin' in, you two, so stop snaggin' an' snarlin'.   195

LUTHER Come in; 'er'll 'appen turn 'er tap on thee.

>   *Joe enters*

JOE Are you eatin' yet?

LUTHER Ay—it ta'es 'er that long ter tell my sins. Tha's just come right
   for puddin'. Get thee a plate outer t' cupboard—an' a spoon outer t'   200
   basket.

JOE (*at the cupboard*) You've got ivrythink tip-top. What should ter do if
   I broke thee a plate, Minnie?

MINNIE I should break another over your head.

>   *He deliberately drops and smashes a plate. She flushes crimson*   205

LUTHER Well, I'm glad it worna me.

JOE I'm that clumsy wi' my left 'and, Minnie! Why doesna ter break
   another ower my head?

LUTHER (*rising and putting pudding on a plate*) Here, ta'e this an' sit thee
   down.   210

>   *His brother seats himself*

   Hold thy knees straight, an' for God's sake dunna thee break this.
   Can ter manage?

JOE I reckon so. If I canna, Minnie'll feed me wi' a spoon. Shonna ter?

MINNIE Why did you break my plate?   215

JOE Nay, I didna break it—it wor the floor.

MINNIE You did it on purpose.

JOE How could I? I didn't say ter th' floor: 'Break thou this plate, O
   floor!'

MINNIE You have no right.   220

JOE (*addressing the floor*) Tha'd no right to break that plate—dost hear?
I'd a good mind ter drop a bit o' puddin' on thy face.
>   *He balances the spoon; the plate slides down from his knee, smash
>   into the fender*

MINNIE (*screams*) It's my best service! (*Begins to sob*)   225

LUTHER Nay, our Joe!

JOE 'Er's no occasions ter scraight. I bought th' service an' I can get th'
plates matched. What's her grizzlin' about?

MINNIE I shan't ask you to get them matched.

JOE Dunna thee, an' then tha runs no risk o' bein' denied.   230

MINNIE What have you come here like this for?

JOE I haena come here like this. I come ter tell yer our Harriet says,
would yer mind goin' an' tellin' 'er what she can do with that childt's
coat, as she's made a' wrong. If you'd looked slippy, I'd ha' ta'en yer
ter th' Cinematograph after. But, dearly-beloved brethren, let us weep;   235
these our dear departed dinner-plates . . . Come, Minnie, drop a tear
as you pass by.

LUTHER (*to Minnie*) Tha needna fret, Minnie, they can easy be matched
again.

MINNIE You're just pleased to see him make a fool of me, aren't you?   240

LUTHER He's non made a fool o' thee—tha's made a fool o' thysen,
scraightin' an' carryin' on.

JOE It's a fact, Minnie. Nay; let me kiss thee better.
>   *She has risen, with shut face*
>   *He approaches with outstretched left arm. She swings round,*   245
>   *fetches him a blow over his upper right arm. He bites his lip*
>   *with pain*

LUTHER (*rising*) Has it hurt thee, lad? Tha shouldna fool wi' her.
>   *Minnie watches the two brothers with tears of mortification in her*
>   *eyes. Then she throws off her apron, pins on her hat, puts on her*   250
>   *coat, and is marching out of the house*

LUTHER Are you going to Harriet's?

JOE I'll come and fetch you in time for th' Cinematograph.
>   *The door is heard to bang*

JOE (*picking up broken fragments of plates*) That's done it.   255

LUTHER It's bad luck—ne'er mind. How art goin' on?

JOE Oh, all right.

LUTHER What about thy club money?

JOE They wunna gi'e't me. But, I say, sorry—tha'rt for it.

LUTHER Ay—I dunno what 'er married me for, f'r it's nowt bu' fault   260
she finds wi' me, from th' minnit I come i' th' house to th' minnit I
leave it.

JOE Dost wish tha'd niver done it?—niver got married?

LUTHER (*sulky*) I dunno—sometimes.

JOE (*with tragic emphasis*) Then it's the blasted devil!   265

LUTHER I dunno—I'm married to 'er, an' she's married to me, so she
can pick holes i' me as much as she likes—

JOE As a rule, she's nice enough wi' me.

LUTHER She's nice wi' ivrybody but me.

JOE An' dost ter care?   270

LUTHER Ay—I do.

JOE Why doesn't ter go out an' leave her?

LUTHER I dunno.

JOE By the Lord, she'd cop it if I had 'er. (*Pause*)

LUTHER I wor comin' up to-night.   275

JOE I thought tha would be. But there's Mrs Purdy comin' ter see thee.

LUTHER There's who?

JOE Mrs Purdy. Didna ter ha'e a bit of a go wi' their Bertha, just afore
Minnie wrote thee?

LUTHER Ay. Why?   280

JOE 'Er mother says she's wi' childt by thee. She come up ter my mother
this afternoon, an' said she wor comin' here tonight.

LUTHER Says what?

JOE Says as their Bertha's goin' ter ha'e a child, an' 'er lays it on ter thee.

LUTHER Oh, my good God!   285

JOE Isna it right?

LUTHER It's right if 'er says so.

JOE Then it's the blasted devil! (*A pause*) So I come on here ter see if
I could get Minnie to go up to our Harriet.

LUTHER Oh, my good God!   290

JOE I thought, if we could keep it from 'er, we might settle summat, an'
'er niver know.

LUTHER (*slowly*) My God alive!

JOE She said she'd hush it up, an' lay it ont'r a electrician as laid th'
cable, an' is gone goodness knows where—make an arrangement, for   295
forty pound.

LUTHER (*thoughtfully*) I wish I wor struck dead.

JOE Well, tha arena', an' so tha'd better think about it. My mother said
as Minnie ought to know, but I say diff'rent, an' if Mrs Purdy doesna
tell her, nobody need.   300

LUTHER I wish I wor struck dead. I wish a ton o' rock 'ud fa' on me
to-morrer.

JOE It wunna for wishin'.

LUTHER My good God!

JOE An' so—I'll get thee forty quid, an' lend it thee. When Mrs Purdy 305
comes, tell her she shall ha'e twenty quid this day week, an' twenty
quid a year from now, if thy name's niver been mentioned. I believe
'er's a clat-fart.°

LUTHER Me a childt by Bertha Purdy! But—but what's that for—now
there's Minnie? 310

JOE I dunno what it's for, but theer it is, as I'm tellin' thee. I'll stop for
another ha'ef an hour, an' if 'er doesna come, tha mun see to 'er by
thysen.

LUTHER 'Er'll be back afore ha'ef an hour's up. Tha mun go an' stop
'er . . . I—I niver meant—Look here, our Joe, I—if I—if she—if 315
she—My God, what have I done now!

JOE We can stop her from knowin'.

LUTHER (looking round) She'll be comin' back any minnit. Nay, I niver
meant t'r ha'—Joe—

JOE What? 320

LUTHER She—she—

JOE 'Er niver ne'd know.

LUTHER Ah, but though—

JOE What?

LUTHER I—I—I've done it. 325

JOE Well, it might ha' happened t'r anybody.

LUTHER But when 'er knows—an' it's me as has done it—

JOE It wouldn't ha' mattered o' anyhow, if it had bin sumb'dy else. But
tha knows what ter's got ter say. Arena' ter goin' ter wesh thee? Go an'
get th' panchion. 330

LUTHER (rising) 'Er'll be comin' in any minnit.

JOE Get thee weshed, man.

LUTHER (fetching a bucket and lading-can from the scullery, and emptying
water from the boiler) Go an' ta'e 'er somewhere, while° Mrs Purdy
goes, sholl ter? 335

JOE D'rectly. Tha heered what I telled thee?

> There is a noise of splashing in the scullery. Then a knock. Joe
> goes to the door. He is heard saying 'Come in.' Enter Mrs Purdy

MRS PURDY I hope I've not come a-mealtimes.

JOE No, they've finished. Minnie's gone up t'r our Harriet's. 340

MRS PURDY Thank the Lord for small mercies—for I didn't fancy sittin' an' tellin' her about our Bertha.

JOE We dunna want 'er ter know. Sit thee down.

MRS PURDY I'm of that mind, mester, I am. As I said, what's th' good
o' jackin' up a young married couple? For it won't unmarry 'em 345

nor ma'e things right. An' yet, my long lass oughtner ter bear a' th' brunt.

JOE Well, an' 'er isna goin' to.

MRS PURDY Is that Mester weshin'?

JOE Ah.   350

MRS PURDY 'As ter towd him?

JOE Ah.

MRS PURDY Well, it's none o' my wishin's, I'm sure o' that. Eh, dear, you've bin breakin' th' crockery a'ready!

JOE Yes, that's me, bein' wallit.°   355

MRS PURDY T-t-t! So this is 'ow she fancied it?

JOE Ah, an' it non luiks bad, does it?

MRS PURDY Very natty. Very nice an' natty.

JOE (*taking up the lamp*) Come an' look at th' parlour.

    Joe and Mrs Purdy exit right   360

MRS PURDY'S VOICE Yis—yis—it's nice an' plain. But a bit o' red plush is 'andsomer, to my mind. It's th' old-fashioned style, like! My word, but them three ornyments is gaudy-lookin'.

JOE An' they reckon they're worth five pound. 'Er mester gen 'em 'er.

MRS PURDY I'd rather had th' money.   365

JOE Ah, me an' a'.

    During this time, Luther has come hurrying out of the scullery into the kitchen, rubbing his face with a big roller-towel. He is naked to the waist. He kneels with his knees on the fender, sitting on his heels, rubbing himself. His back is not washed. He rubs his hair 370
    dry. Enter Joe, with the lamp, followed by Mrs Purdy

MRS PURDY It's uncommon, very uncommon, Mester Gaskin—and looks well, too, for them as likes it. But it hardly goes wi' my fancy, somehow, startin' wi' second-hand, owd-fashioned stuff. You dunno *who's* sotten themselves on these 'ere chairs, now, do you? 375

LUTHER It ma'es no diff'rence to me who's sot on 'em an' who 'asna.

MRS PURDY No—you get used to 'm.

LUTHER (*to Joe*) Shall thee go up t'r our Harriet's?

JOE If ter's a mind. (*Takes up his cap. To Mrs Purdy*) An' you two can settle as best you can. 380

MRS PURDY Yes—yes. I'm not one for baulkin' mysen an' cuttin' off my nose ter spite my face.

    Luther has finished wiping himself. He takes a shifting shirt° from the bureau, and struggles into it, then goes into the scullery

JOE An' you sure you'll keep it quiet, missis?   385

MRS PURDY Am I goin' bletherin' up street an' down street, think yer?

JOE An' dunna tell your Bob.

MRS PURDY I've more sense. There's not a word 'e 'ears a-whoam as is
of any count, for out it 'ud leak when he wor canned. Yes, my guy-
ney—we know what our mester is.   390

> *Re-enter Luther, in shirt and black trousers. He drops his*
> *pit-trousers and singlet beside the hearth*
> *Mrs Purdy bends down and opens his pit-trousers*

MRS PURDY Nay, if ter drops 'em of a heap, they niver goin' ter get dry
an' cosy. Tha sweats o' th' hips, as my lads did.   395

LUTHER Well, go thy ways, Joe.

JOE Ay—well—good luck. An' good night, Mrs Purdy.

MRS PURDY Good night.

> *Exit Joe. There are several moments of silence. Luther puts the*
> *broken pots on the table*   400

MRS PURDY It's sad work, Mester Gaskin, f'r a' on us.

LUTHER Ay.

MRS PURDY I left that long lass o' mine fair gaunt, fair chalked of a line,°
I did, poor thing. Not bu' what 'er should 'a 'ad more sense.

LUTHER Ah!   405

MRS PURDY But it's no use throwin' good words after bad deeds. Not
but what it's a nasty thing for yer t'r'a done, it is—an' yer can scarce
look your missis i' th' face again, I should think. (*Pause*) But I says t'r
our Bertha, 'It's his'n, an' he mun pay!' Eh, but how 'er did but
scraight an' cry. It fair turned me ower. 'Dunna go to 'm, Mother,' 'er   410
says, 'dunna go to 'm for to tell him!' 'Yi,' I says, 'right's right—tha
doesna get off wi' nowt, nor shall 'e neither. 'E wor but a scamp to do
such a thing,' I says, yes, I did. For you was older nor 'er. Not but what
she was old enough ter ha'e more sense. But 'er wor allers one o' th'
come-day-go-day sort, as 'ud gi'e th' clothes off 'er back an' niver   415
know 'er wor nek'd—a gre't soft looney as she is, an' serves 'er right
for bein' such a gaby. Yi, an' I believe 'er wor fond on thee—if a
wench can be fond of a married man. For one blessing, 'er doesna
know what 'er wor an' what 'er worn't. For they may talk o' bein' i'
love—but you non in love wi' onybody, wi'out they's a chance o' their   420
marryin' you—howiver much you may like 'em. An' I'm thinkin',
th' childt'll set 'er up again when it comes, for 'er's gone that
wezzel-brained an' doited,° I'm sure! An' it's a mort° o' trouble for
me, mester, a sight o' trouble it is. Not as I s'll be hard on 'er. She
knowed I wor comin' 'ere to-night, an's not spoke a word for hours. I   425
left 'er sittin' on th' sofey hangin' 'er 'ead. But it's a weary business,
mester, an' nowt ter be proud on. I s'd think tha wishes tha'd niver
clapt eyes on our Bertha.

LUTHER (*thinking hard*) I dunna—I dunna. An' I dunna wish as I'd
  niver seen 'er, no, I dunna. 'Er liked me, an' I liked 'er.   430
MRS PURDY An' 'appen, but for this 'ere marriage o' thine, tha'd 'a
  married 'er.
LUTHER Ah, I should. F'r 'er liked me, an' 'er worna neither nice nor
  near,° nor owt else, an' 'er'd bin fond o' me.
MRS PURDY 'Er would, an' it's a thousand pities. But what's done's done. 435
LUTHER Ah, I know that.
MRS PURDY An' as for yer missis—
LUTHER 'Er mun do as 'er likes.
MRS PURDY But tha'rt not for tellin' 'er?
LUTHER 'Er—'er'll know some time or other.   440
MRS PURDY Nay, nay, 'er nedna. You married now, lad, an' you canna
  please yoursen.
LUTHER It's a fact.
MRS PURDY An' Lizzy Stapleton, she had forty pound wi' 'er lad, an'
  it's not as if you hadn't got money. An' to be sure, we've none.   445
LUTHER No, an' I've none.
MRS PURDY Yes, you've some atween you—an'—well—
LUTHER I can get some.
MRS PURDY Then what do you say?
LUTHER I say as Bertha's welcome t'r any forty pounds, if I'd got it. 450
  For—for—missis, she wor better to me than iver my wife's bin.
MRS PURDY (*frightened by his rage*) Niver, lad!
LUTHER She wor—ah but though she wor. She thought a lot on me.
MRS PURDY An' so I'm sure your missis does. She naggles thy heart
  out, maybe. But that's just the wrigglin' a place out for hersen. She'll 455
  settle down comfortable, lad.
LUTHER (*bitterly*) Will she!
MRS PURDY Yi—yi. An' tha's done 'er a crewel wrong, my lad. An' tha's
  done my gel one as well. For, though she was old enough to know
  better, yet she's good-hearted and trustin', an' 'ud gi'e 'er shoes off 460
  'er feet. An' tha's landed 'er, tha knows. For it's not th' bad women as
  'as bastards nowadays—they've a sight too much gumption. It's fools
  like our'n—poor thing.
LUTHER I've done everything that was bad, I know that.
MRS PURDY Nay—nay—young fellers, they are like that. But it's   465
  wrong, for look at my long lass sittin' theer on that sofey, as if 'er back
  wor broke.
LUTHER (*loudly*) But I dunna wish I'd niver seen 'er, I dunna. It wor—
  it wor—she wor good to me, she wor, an' I dunna wish I'd niver
  done it.   470

MRS PURDY Then tha ought, that's a'. For I do—an' 'er does.

LUTHER Does 'er say 'er wishes 'er'd niver seen me?

MRS PURDY 'Er says nowt o' nohow.

LUTHER Then 'er doesna wish it. An' I wish I'd ha' married 'er.

MRS PURDY Come, my lad, come. Married tha art—   475

LUTHER (*bitterly*) Married I am, an' I wish I worna. Your Bertha 'er'd 'a
thought a thousand times more on me than *she* does. But I'm wrong,
wrong, wrong, i' ivry breath I take. An' I will be wrong, yi, an' I *will*
be wrong.

MRS PURDY Hush thee—there's somebody comin'.   480

> *They wait. Enter Joe and Minnie, Joe talking loudly*

MINNIE No, you've not, you've no right at all. (*To Luther*) Haven't you
even cleared away? (*To Mrs Purdy*) Good evening.

MRS PURDY Good evenin', missis. I was just goin'—I've bin sayin' it
looks very nice, th' 'ouse.   485

MINNIE Do you think so?

MRS PURDY I do, indeed.

MINNIE Don't notice of the mess we're in, shall you? He (*Pointing to
Joe*) broke the plates—and then I had to rush off up to Mrs Preston's
afore I could clear away. And he hasn't even mended the fire.   490

LUTHER I can do—I niver noticed.

MINNIE (*to Mrs Purdy*) Have a piece of cake? (*Goes to cupboard*)

MRS PURDY No, thanks, no, thanks. I mun get off afore th' Co-op° shuts
up. Thank yer very much. Well—good night, all.

> *Joe opens the door; Mrs Purdy goes out*   495

MINNIE (*bustling, clearing away as Luther comes in with coals*) Did you
settle it?

LUTHER What?

MINNIE What she'd come about.

LUTHER Ah.   500

MINNIE An' I bet you'll go and forget.

LUTHER Oh ah!

MINNIE And poor old Bob Purdy will go on just the same.

LUTHER Very likely.

MINNIE Don't let the dust all go on the hearth. Why didn't you clear   505
away? The house was like a pigsty for her to come into.

LUTHER Then I wor the pig.

MINNIE (*halting*) Why—who's trod on your tail now?

LUTHER There'd be nobody to tread on it if tha wor out.

MINNIE Oh—oh, dear o' me. (*To Joe*) I think we'd better go to the   510
Cinematograph, and leave him to nurse his sore tail.

JOE We better had.

LUTHER An' joy go with yer.

MINNIE We certainly shan't leave it at home. (*To Joe*) What time does it begin?   515

JOE Seven o'clock.

MINNIE And I want to call in Sisson's shop. Shall you go with me, or wouldn't you condescend to go shopping with me? (*She has cleared the table, brought a tray and a bowl, and is washing up the pots*)

JOE Dost think I'm daunted by Polly Sisson?   520

MINNIE You're braver than most men if you dare go in a shop. Here, take a towel and wipe these pots.

JOE How can I?

MINNIE If you were a gentleman, you'd hold the plates in your teeth to wipe them.   525

JOE Tha wouldna look very ladylike at th' end on't.

MINNIE Why?

JOE Why, hast forgot a'ready, what a shine° tha kicked up when I broke them two other plates? (*He has got a towel, and wedging a plate against his thighs, is laboriously wiping it*)   530

MINNIE I never kicked up a shine. It *is* nice of you!

JOE What?

MINNIE To do this for me.

> *Luther has begun sweeping the hearth*

JOE Tha's got two servants.   535

MINNIE But I'm sure you want to smoke while you're doing it—don't you now?

JOE Sin' tha says so. (*Fumbles in his pocket*)

MINNIE (*hastily wiping her hands, puts a cigarette between his lips—gets matches from the mantelpiece, ignoring her husband, who is kneeling sweeping the hearth—lights his cigarette*) It's so nice to have a lamed man. You feel you've got an excuse for making a fuss of him. You've got awfully nice eyes and eyebrows. I like dark eyes.   540

JOE Oh ah!

> *Luther rises hastily, goes in the passage, crosses the room quietly.*   545
> *He wears his coat, a red scarf and a cap*

MINNIE There's more go in them than in blue. (*Watches her husband go out. There is silence between the two*)

JOE He'll come round again.

MINNIE He'll have to. He'll go on sulking now. (*Her face breaks*) You—   550
you don't know how hard it is.

JOE What?

MINNIE (*crying a few fierce tears*) This—

JOE (*aghast*) What?

MINNIE Why—you don't know. You don't know how hard it is, with a   555
man as—as leaves you alone all the time.

JOE But—he niver hardly goes out.

MINNIE No, but—you don't know—he leaves me alone, he always has
done—and there's nobody—

JOE But he—   560

MINNIE He never trusts me—he leaves me so alone—and (*A little burst
of tears*) it *is* hard! (*She changes suddenly*) You've wiped your plates; my
word, you are a champion.

JOE I think so an' a'.

MINNIE I hope the pictures will be jolly—but the sad ones make me   565
laugh more, don't they you?

JOE I canna do wi' 'em.

      CURTAIN

Act 2

The same evening—eleven o'clock. Luther's house.
Minnie, alone, weeping. She gets up, fills the kettle, puts it on the
hob, sits down, weeps again; then hears somebody coming, dries her
eyes swiftly, turns the lamp low.
Enter Luther. He stands in the doorway—is rather tipsy; flings
his cap down, sits in his chair, lurching it slightly. Neither speaks
for some moments

LUTHER Well, did yer like yer pictures?

MINNIE Where have you been?

LUTHER What does it matter where I've been?

MINNIE Have you been drinking?

LUTHER What's it matter if I have?

MINNIE It matters a lot to me.

LUTHER Oh ah!

MINNIE Do you think I'm going to sleep with a man who is half-drunk?

LUTHER Nay, I non know who tha'rt goin' ter sleep wi'.

MINNIE (*rising*) I shall make the bed in the other room.

LUTHER Tha's no 'casions. I s'll do very nicely on t' sofa; it's warmer.

MINNIE Oh, you can have your own bed.

LUTHER If tha doesna sleep in it, I dunna.

MINNIE And if *you do*, I don't.

LUTHER Tha pleases thysen. Tha can sleep by thysen for iver, if ter's a mind to't.

MINNIE (*who has stood hesitating*) Oh, very well!

She goes upstairs, returns immediately with a pillow and two
blankets, which she throws on the sofa

LUTHER Thank yer kindly.

MINNIE Shall you rake?

LUTHER I'll rake.

She moves about; lays table for his morning's breakfast: a
newspaper, cup, plate, etc.—no food, because it would go dry;
rinses his tin pit-bottle, puts it and his snap-bag on the table

I could do it for mysen. Tha ned do nowt for me.

MINNIE Why this sudden fit of unselfishness?

LUTHER I niver want thee to do nowt for me, niver no more. No, not so much as lift a finger for me—not if I wor dyin'.

MINNIE You're not dying; you're only tipsy.

LUTHER Well, it's no matter to thee what I am.

MINNIE It's very comfortable for you to think so.

LUTHER I non know nowt about that.   40

MINNIE (*after a pause*) Where have you been to-night?

LUTHER There an' back, to see how far it is.

MINNIE (*making an effort*) Have you been up to your mother's?

LUTHER Where I've bin, I've bin, and where I haven't, I haven't.

MINNIE Pah!—you needn't try to magnify it and make a mountain.   45
You've been to your mother's, and then to the Ram.

LUTHER All right—if tha knows, tha knows, an' theer's an end on't.

MINNIE You talk like a fool.

LUTHER That comes o' bein a fool.

MINNIE When were you a fool?   50

LUTHER Ivry day o' my life, an' ivry breath I've ta'en.

MINNIE (*having finished work, sits down again*) I suppose you haven't got
it in you to say anything fresh.

LUTHER Why, what dost want me ter say? (*He looks at her for the first
time*)   55

MINNIE (*with a queer catch*) You might be more of a man if you said you
were sorry.

LUTHER Sorry! Sorry for what?

MINNIE You've nothing to be sorry *for*, have you?

LUTHER (*looking at her, quickly*) What art goin' ter say?   60

MINNIE It's what are *you* going to say. (*A silence*)

LUTHER (*doggedly*) I'm goin' ter say nowt.

MINNIE (*bitterly*) No, you're not *man* enough to say anything—you can
only slobber. You do a woman a wrong, but you're never man enough
to say you're sorry for it. You're *not* a man, you're not—you're some-   65
thing crawling!

LUTHER I'm glad! I'm glad! I'm glad! No, an' I wouldna ta'e 't back, no.
'Er wor nice wi' me, which is a thing tha's niver bin. An' so tha's got
it, an' mun keep it.

MINNIE Who was nice with you?   70

LUTHER *She* was—an' would ha'e bin at this minnit, but for thee.

MINNIE Pah!—you're not fit to have a wife. You only want your mother
to rock you to sleep.

LUTHER Neither mother, nor wife, neither thee nor onybody do I
want—no—no.   75

MINNIE No—you've had three cans of beer.

LUTHER An' if ter niver sleeps i' th' bed wi' me again, an' if ter niver
does a hand's turn for me niver no more, I'm glad, I'm glad. I non
want thee. I non want ter see thee.

MINNIE You mean coward. Good God! I never thought you were such 80
a mean coward as this.

LUTHER An' as for thy money—yi, I wouldna smell on't. An' neither
thine, nor our Joe's, nor my mother's will I ha'e. What I addle's my
own.° What I gi'e thee, I gi'e thee. An' she maun ha'e ten shillin's a
month, an' tha maun abide by't. 85

MINNIE What are you talking about?

LUTHER My mother wouldna gi'e me th' money. She says she's done
her share. An' tha's done thine. An' I've done mine, begod. An' what
yer canna chew yer maun swaller.

MINNIE You must be quite drunk. 90

LUTHER Must I? All right, it's Dutch courage then. A'right, then Dutch
courage it is. But I tell thee, tha does as ter's a mind. Tha can leave me,
an' go back inter service, if ter wants. What's it ter me, if I'm but a
lump o' muck i' th' 'ouse wheer tha art? Tha should ha' had our Joe—
he's got more go than me. An' I should ha' had 'er. I'd got go enough 95
for *her;* 'appen a bit too much.

MINNIE Her? Who?

LUTHER Her! An' I'm glad 'er's wi' my childt. I'm glad I did it. I'm glad!
For tha's wiped tha feet on me enough. Yi, tha's wiped thy feet on me
till what's it to me if tha does it or not? It isna! An' now—tha maun 100
abide by what ter's got, tha maun. I s'll ha'e to—an' by plenty I hadna
got I've abided. An' so—an' so—yi.

MINNIE But who is it you—who is she?

LUTHER Tha knowed a' along.

MINNIE Who is it? 105
They are both silent
Aren't you going to speak?

LUTHER What's the good?

MINNIE (*coldly*) But I must know.

LUTHER Tha does know. 110

MINNIE I can assure you I don't.

LUTHER Then assure thysen an' find out.
Another silence

MINNIE Do you mean somebody is going to have a baby by you?

LUTHER I mean what I've said, an' I mean nowt else. 115

MINNIE But you must tell me.

LUTHER I've boiled my cabbage twice a'ready, hanna I?

MINNIE Do you mean somebody is going to have a child by you?

LUTHER Tha can chew it ower, if ter's a mind.

MINNIE (*helpless*) But . . . (*She struggles with herself, then goes calm*) 120

135

LUTHER That's what I say—*but*! (*A silence*)
MINNIE And who is she?
LUTHER Thee, for a' I know.
MINNIE (*calmly, patiently*) I asked you a question.
LUTHER Ah—an' I 'eered thee.   125
MINNIE Then answer me—who is she?
LUTHER Tha knows well enow—tha knowed afore they'd towd thee—
MINNIE Nobody has told me. Who is she?
LUTHER Well, tha's seed 'er mother.
MINNIE (*numb*) Mrs Purdy?   130
LUTHER Yi.
MINNIE Their Bertha?
LUTHER Yi.
           A silence
MINNIE Why didn't you tell me?   135
LUTHER Tell thee what?
MINNIE This.
LUTHER Tha knowed afore I did.
MINNIE I know *now*.
LUTHER Me an' a'.   140
           A pause
MINNIE Didn't you know till to-night?
LUTHER Our Joe told me when tha'd just gone—I niver dreamt
    afore—an' then 'er mother . . .
MINNIE What did her mother come for?   145
LUTHER Ter see if we could hush it up a'cause o' thee, an' gi'e 'er a lump
    sum.
MINNIE Hush it up because of me?
LUTHER Ah—lay it ont'r an electrician as wor wi' th' gang as laid th'
    cable down to Balford—he's gone God knows where.   150
MINNIE But it's yours.
LUTHER I know that.
MINNIE Then why lay it onto somebody else?
LUTHER Because o' thee.
MINNIE But why because of me?   155
LUTHER To stop thee knowin', I s'd think.
MINNIE And why shouldn't I know?
LUTHER Eh, I dunno.
           A pause
MINNIE And what were you going to do to stop me knowing?   160
LUTHER 'Er axed for forty pounds down.

MINNIE And if you paid forty pounds, you got off scot-free?

LUTHER Summat so.

MINNIE And where were the forty pounds coming from?

LUTHER Our Joe said 'e'd lend 'em me. I thought my mother would, but 165
'er said 'er wouldna—neither would she gi'e't our Joe ter lend me,
she said. For I wor a married man now, an' it behoved my wife to look
after me. An' I thought tha knowed. I thought tha'd twigged, else bin
telled. An' I didna care, an' dunna care.

MINNIE And this is what you married me to! 170

LUTHER This is what tha married me to. But I'll niver ax thee for, no,
not so much as the liftin' of a finger—no—

MINNIE But when you wrote and told me you were willing to marry me,
why didn't you tell me this?

LUTHER Because—as I've telled thee—I didna know till this very 175
mortal night.

MINNIE But you knew you'd been with her.

LUTHER Ay, I knowed that.
        A pause

MINNIE And why didn't you tell me? 180

LUTHER What for should I tell thee? What good would it ha' done thee?
Tha niver towd *me* nowt.

MINNIE So that is how you look at it?

LUTHER I non care how I look at it.
        A pause 185

MINNIE And was there anybody else?

LUTHER How dost mean?

MINNIE Have you been with any other woman?

LUTHER I dunno—I might—I dunno.

MINNIE That means you have. 190

LUTHER I'm thirty.

MINNIE And who *were* they?

LUTHER I dunno. I've niver bin much wi' anybody—little, very little—
an' then it wor an off-chance. Our Joe wor more that way than me—I
worn't that way. 195
        A pause

MINNIE So—this was what I waited for you for!

LUTHER Tha niver waited for me. Tha had me a'cause tha couldna get
nobody better.

MINNIE And so— 200

LUTHER (*after a moment*) Yi, an' so. An' so, I non care what ter does. If
ter leaves me—

137

MINNIE (*in a flash*) What's the good of me leaving you? Aren't I married to you—tied to you?

LUTHER Tha could leave me whether or not. I should go t'r Australia   205
wi' our Joe.

MINNIE And what about that girl?

LUTHER I should send 'er th' money.

MINNIE And what about me?

LUTHER Tha'd please thysen.   210

MINNIE Should you *like* me to leave you, and let you go to Australia?

LUTHER 'Appen I should.

MINNIE What did you marry me for?

LUTHER 'Cos tha axed me.

MINNIE Did you never care for me?   215

He does not answer

Didn't you?

He does not answer

Didn't you?

LUTHER (*slowly*) You niver wanted me—you thought me dirt.   220

MINNIE Ha! (*A pause*) You can have the forty pounds.

LUTHER (*very doggedly*) I shanna.

MINNIE She's got to be paid.

LUTHER Tha keeps thy money.

MINNIE Then where shall you get it from?   225

LUTHER I s'll pay 'er month by month.

MINNIE But you can't. Think!

LUTHER Then I'll borrow forty quid somewhere else, an' pay it back
i' instalments. Tha keeps thy money.

MINNIE You can borrow it from me.   230

LUTHER I shall not.

MINNIE Very well. I only wanted not to have the bother of paying
month by month. I think I shall go back to my old place.

LUTHER Tha pleases thysen.

MINNIE And you can go and live with your mother again.   235

LUTHER That I should niver do—but tha pleases thysen. We've bin
married seven wik come Tuesday.

MINNIE I niver ought to ha' done it.

LUTHER What?

MINNIE Married you.   240

LUTHER No.

MINNIE For you never cared enough.

LUTHER Yi—it's my fault.

MINNIE Yes.

LUTHER It would be. Tha's niver made a fault i' thy life.   245

MINNIE Who are you, to talk about my faults!

LUTHER Well—

A pause

MINNIE I shall write to Mr Westlake to-morrow.

LUTHER Tha does as pleases thee.   250

MINNIE And if they can't take me back straight away, I shall ask him if he knows another place.

LUTHER A'right. An' we'll sell th' furniture.

MINNIE (*looking round at her home*) Yes.

LUTHER It'll non bring ha'ef tha giv for't—but it'll bring enough ter   255
ta'e me out theer.

MINNIE I'll make up what you lose by it, since I chose it.

LUTHER Tha can give ter them as'll ha'e.

MINNIE But I shall feel I owe it you.

LUTHER I've had six weeks o' married life wi' thee. I mun pay for that.   260

MINNIE You are mean, mean.

LUTHER I know—though tha'rt first as has told me so. When dost reckon tha'lt go?

MINNIE I'll go to-morrow if you want to get rid of me.

LUTHER Nay—tha does just as pleases thysen. I non want ter get rid on   265
thee. Nay, nay, it's not that. It's thee as wants ter go.

MINNIE At any rate, I s'll have a place inside a fortnight.

LUTHER (*dully*) All right.

MINNIE So I shall have to trouble you till then.

LUTHER But I dunna want thee ter do owt for me—no, I dunna.   270

MINNIE I shall keep the house, in payment for my board and lodgings. And I'll make the bed up in the back room, and I'll sleep there, because it's not furnished, and the house is yours.

LUTHER Th'art—th'art—I wish I might strike thee down!

MINNIE And I shall keep the account of every penny I spend, and you   275
must just pay the bills.

LUTHER (*rising suddenly*) I'll murder thee afore tha does.

*He goes out. She sits twisting her apron. He returns with a large
lump of coal in his hands, and rakes the fire*

MINNIE You cared more for her than for me.   280

LUTHER For who?

MINNIE For her. She was the sort of sawney° you ought to have had.
Did she think you perfect?

LUTHER (*with grim satisfaction*) She liked me.

MINNIE   And you could do just as you wanted with her?   285

LUTHER   She'd ha' done owt for me.

MINNIE   And it flattered you, did it? Because a long stalk wi' no flower
was at your service, it flattered you, did it? My word, it ought—As
for your Joe, he's not a fool like you, and that's why women think
more of him. He wouldn't want a Bertha Purdy. He'd get a woman   290
who was something—and because he knew how to appreciate her.
You—what good are you?

LUTHER   I'm no good, but to fetch an' carry.

MINNIE   And a tuppenny scullery-girl could do that as well.

LUTHER   All right.   295

MINNIE   I'll bet even Bertha Purdy thinks what a clown you are. She
never wanted you to marry her, did she?

LUTHER   She knowed I wouldn't.

MINNIE   You flatter yourself. I'll bet she never wanted you. I shouldn't
be surprised if the child isn't somebody else's, that she just foists on   300
you because you're so soft.

LUTHER   Oh ah!

MINNIE   It even flatters you to think it's yours.

LUTHER   Oh ah!

MINNIE   And quite right too—for it's the only thing you could have to   305
be proud of. And then really it's not you—

LUTHER   Oh ah!

MINNIE   If a woman has a child, and you think you're the cause, do you
think it's *your* doings?

LUTHER   If tha has one, it will be.   310

MINNIE   And is *that* anything for you to be proud of? Me whom you've
insulted and deceived and treated as no snail would treat a woman!
And then you expect me to bear your children!

LUTHER   I dunna expect thee. If tha does tha does.

MINNIE   And you gloat over it and feel proud of it!   315

LUTHER   Yi, I do.

MINNIE   No—no! I'd rather have married a tramp off the streets than
you. And—and I don't believe you *can* have children.

LUTHER   Theer tha knows tha'rt a liar.

MINNIE   I hate you.   320

LUTHER   All right.

MINNIE   And I *will* leave you, I *will*.

LUTHER   Tha's said so afore.

MINNIE   And I mean it.

LUTHER   All right.   325

MINNIE But it's your mother's doing. *She* mollycoddled and marded
    you till you weren't a man—and now—I have to pay for it.

LUTHER Oh ah!

MINNIE No, you're not a man!

LUTHER All right. They's plenty of women as would say I am.   330

MINNIE They'd be lying to get something out of you.

LUTHER Why, what could they get outer me?

MINNIE Yes—yes—what could they . . .
    She stutters to a close. He begins to take off his boots

LUTHER If tha'rt goin', tha'd better go afore th' strike begins. We should   335
    be on short commons° then—ten bob a wik.°

MINNIE There's one thing, you'd be on short commons without me.
    For nobody would keep you for ten shillings a week, unless you went
    to your mother's.

LUTHER I could live at our Harriet's, an' pay 'er off after. An' there'd be   340
    th' furniture sold.

MINNIE And you'd be delighted if there *was* a strike, so you could loaf
    about. You don't even get drunk. You only loaf. You're lazy, lazy, and
    without the stomach of a louse. You *want* a strike.

LUTHER All right.   345

MINNIE And I hope you'll get what you deserve, I do.

LUTHER Tha'rt gi'en it me.

MINNIE (*lifting her hand suddenly*) How *dare* you say so—how *dare* you!
    I'm too good for you.

LUTHER (*sullenly*) I know.   350

MINNIE Yes.
    She gets a candle, lights it, and goes to bed. He flings off his scarf
    and coat and waistcoat, throws the pillow on the hearthrug, wraps
    himself in the blankets, blows the lamp out, and lies down.
    CURTAIN   355

Act 3

*A fortnight later—afternoon. The kitchen of Luther Gascoigne's
house.*
*Mrs Gascoigne, senior, alone. Enter Minnie Gascoigne, dressed
from travelling. She is followed by a cabman carrying a bag*

MRS GASCOIGNE What—is it you!

MINNIE Yes. Didn't you get my wire? 5

MRS GASCOIGNE Thy wire! Dost mean a tallygram? No, we'n had nowt,
though th' house 'as bin shut up.

MINNIE (*to the cabman*) Thank you. How much?

CABMAN Ha'ef-a-crown.

MRS GASCOIGNE Ha'ef-a-crown for commin' from th' Midland station!° 10
Why, tha non know what's talkin' about.

MINNIE (*paying him*) Thank you.

CABMAN Thank yer. Good afternoon. (*The cabman goes out*)

MRS GASCOIGNE My word, tha knows how ter ma'e th' money fly.

MINNIE I couldn't carry a bag. 15

MRS GASCOIGNE Tha could ha' come i' th' bus ter Eastwood an' then a
man 'ud 'a browt it on.

MINNIE It is raining.

MRS GASCOIGNE Tha'rt neither sugar nor salt.

MINNIE I wonder you didn't get my telegram. 20

MRS GASCOIGNE I tell thee, th' 'ouse wor shut up last night.

MINNIE Oh!

MRS GASCOIGNE I dunno wheer 'e slep'—wi' some o's pals I should
think.

MINNIE Oh! 25

MRS GASCOIGNE Thinks I to mysen, I'd better go an' get some dinner
ready down theer. So I told our Joe ter come 'ere for's dinner as well,
but they'm neither on 'em bin in yet. That's allers t'road when it's
strike. They stop mornin'° about, bletherin' and boozin'° an' meals,
bless yer, they don't count. Tha's bin i' Manchester four days then? 30

MINNIE Yes.

MRS GASCOIGNE Ay.—Our Luther's niver bin up ter tell me. If I hadna
ha' met Mrs Pervin fra next door here, I should niver ha' knowed a
word. That wor yisterday. So I sent our Joe down. But it seems 'e's
neither bin a-whoam yesterday nor th' day afore. He slep' i' th' 'ouse 35

142

by hissen for two nights. So Mrs Sharley said. He said tha'd gone ter Manchester on business.

MINNIE Yes.

MRS GASCOIGNE But he niver come ter tell *me* nowt on't.   40

MINNIE Didn't he?

MRS GASCOIGNE It's trew what they say:

> *My son's my son till he ta'es him a wife,*
> *But my daughter's my daughter the whole of her life.*

MINNIE Do you think so?   45

MRS GASCOIGNE I'm sure. An' th' men's been out ten days now, an' such carryin's-on.

MINNIE Oh! Why—what?

MRS GASCOIGNE Meetin's ivry mornin'—crier for ever down th' street wi's bell—an' agitators. They say as Fraser dursn't venture out o' th'   50
door. Watna' pit-top's bin afire, and there's a rigiment o' soldiers drillin' i' th' statutes ground°—bits o' things they are, an' a', like a lot o' little monkeys i' their red coats—Staffordshire men. But wiry, so they say. Same as marched wi' Lord Roberts to Candyhar.° But not a man among 'em. If you watch out fra th' gardin end, you'll see 'em   55
i' th' colliers' train goin' up th' line ter Watna'—wi' their red coats jammed i' th' winders. They say as Fraser's got ten on 'em in's house ter guard him—an' they's sentinels at pit top, standin' wi' their guns, an' th' men crackin' their sides wi' laughin' at 'em.

MINNIE What for?   60

MRS GASCOIGNE Nay, that I canna tell thee. They've got the Black Watch° up at Heanor—so they says—great big Scotchmen i' kilts. They look well, ha'en them i' Heanor, wi' a' them lasses.

MINNIE And what is all the fuss about?

MRS GASCOIGNE Riotin'. I thought tha'd bobbled off ter Manchester   65
ter be i' safety.

MINNIE Oh, no—I never knew there was any danger.

MRS GASCOIGNE No more there is, as far as that goes. What's up atween you an' our Luther?

MINNIE Oh, nothing particular.   70

MRS GASCOIGNE I knowed summat wor amiss, when 'e niver come up. It's a fortnight last Tuesday, sin' 'e's set foot i' my house—an' I've niver clapt eyes on him. I axed our Joe, but he's as stubborn as a jackass, an' you canna get a word out on 'im, not for love nor money.   75

MINNIE Oh!

MRS GASCOIGNE Talks o' goin' t'r Australay. But not if I can help it. An'
hints as if our Luther—you not thinkin' of it, are you?

MINNIE No, I'm not—not that I know of.

MRS GASCOIGNE H'm! It's a rum go, when nobody seems ter know   80
where they are, nor what they're goin' ter do. But there's more blort
than bustle,° i' this world. What took thee to Manchester?

MINNIE Oh, I just wanted to go, on business.

MRS GASCOIGNE Summat about thy money, like?

MINNIE Yes.   85

MRS GASCOIGNE Our Luther wor axin' me for forty pound, th' last
time 'e wor up—but I didna see it. No—I fun' him a' as 'e wanted
for's marriage, and gen 'im ten pound i' hand, an' I thought it 'ud
suffice. An' as for forty pound—it's ter much, that's what I think.

MINNIE I don't.   90

MRS GASCOIGNE Oh, well, if tha doesna, a' well an' good. 'Appen he's
paid it, then?

MINNIE Paid it! Why, wheer was he to get it from?

MRS GASCOIGNE I thought you had it atween you.

MINNIE We haven't.   95

MRS GASCOIGNE Why, how dost mean?

MINNIE I mean we've neither of us got as much as forty pounds.

MRS GASCOIGNE Dost mean *tha* hasna?

MINNIE No, I haven't.

MRS GASCOIGNE What's a-gait° now?   100

MINNIE Nothing.

MRS GASCOIGNE What hast bin up to?

MINNIE I? Nothing. I went to Manchester to settle a little business,
that's all.

MRS GASCOIGNE And wheer did ter stop?   105

MINNIE I stayed with my old master.

MRS GASCOIGNE Wor there no missis, then?

MINNIE No—his wife is dead. You know I was governess for his grand-
children, who were born in India.

MRS GASCOIGNE H'm! So tha went to see *him*?   110

MINNIE Yes—I've always told him everything.

MRS GASCOIGNE So tha went clat-fartin' ter 'im about our Luther, did
ter?

MINNIE Well—he's the only soul in the world that I *can* go to.

MRS GASCOIGNE Hm! It doesna become thee, methinks.   115

MINNIE Well!

          Footsteps are heard

MRS GASCOIGNE Here's them lads, I s'd think.

Enter Luther and Joe

JOE (*to Minnie*) Hello! has thee come? 120

MINNIE Yes. I sent a wire, and thought someone might come to meet me.

JOE Nay, there wor no wire. We thought tha'd gone for good.

MINNIE Who thought so?

JOE Well—didna tha say so? 125

MINNIE Say what?

JOE As tha'd go, an' he could do what he liked?

MINNIE I've said many things.

MRS GASCOIGNE So that was how it stood! Tha'rt a fool, our Luther. If ter ta'es a woman at 'er word, well, tha deserves what ter gets. 130

LUTHER What am I to do, might I ax?

MRS GASCOIGNE Nay, that thy wits should tell thee. Wheer hast bin these two days?

LUTHER I walked ower wi' Jim Horrocks ter their Annie's i' Mansfield.

MRS GASCOIGNE I'm sure she'd got enough to do, without two men 135 planting themselves on her. An' how did ter get back?

LUTHER Walked.

MRS GASCOIGNE Trapsin' thy shoe-leather off thee feet, walkin' twenty miles. Hast had thy dinner?

JOE We've both had free dinners° at th' Methodist Chapel. 140

LUTHER I met Tom Heseldine i' th' Badger Box, Mother.

MRS GASCOIGNE Oh ay! Wide-mouthed as iver, I reckon.

JOE Just same. But what dost think, Mother? It's leaked out as Fraser's got a lot o' chaps to go to-morrer mornin', ter see after th' roads an' a' that. 145

MRS GASCOIGNE Th' roads wants keepin' safe, dunna they?

JOE Yi—but if th' mesters wunna ha'e th' union men, let 'em do it theirselves.

MRS GASCOIGNE Tha talks like a fool.

LUTHER What right ha' they ter get a lot of scrawdrags° an' blacklegs 150 in ter do our work? A' th' pit maun fa' in, if they wunna settle it fair wi' us.

JOE Them workin's is ours, an' th' mesters'. If th' mesters wunna treat us fair, then they mun keep 'em right theirselves. They non goin' ter ha'e no third body in. 155

MINNIE But even when it's settled, how are you going back, if the roof has come in, and the roads are gone?

JOE Tha mun ax th' mesters that. If we canna go back ter th' rotten owd pits no more, we mun look elsewhere. An' th' mesters can sit atop o' their pits an' stroke 'em. 160

LUTHER (*to Minnie*) If I got a woman in to do th' housework as tha
    wunna do for me, tha'd sit smilin', shouldn't ter?

MINNIE She could do as she liked.

LUTHER All right. Then, Mother, 'appen tha'lt boss this house. She run
    off ter Manchester, an' left me ter starve. So 'appen tha'lt come an' do   165
    for me.

MRS GASCOIGNE Nay—if ter wants owt tha mun come ter *me*.

JOE That's right. Dunna thee play blackleg i' this establishment.

MRS GASCOIGNE I s'll mind my own business.

JOE (*to Minnie*) Now, does *thee* think it right, Minnie, as th' mesters   170
    should get a lot o' crawlin' buggers in ter keep their pits i' order, when
    th' keepin' o' them pits i' order belongs by right to us?

MINNIE It belongs to whosoever the masters pay to do it.

LUTHER A'right. Then it belongs to me to ha'e any woman in ter do for
    me, as I've a mind. Tha's gone on strike, so I ha'e the right ter get any-   175
    body else.

MINNIE When have I gone on strike? I have always done your house-
    work.

LUTHER Housework—yi! But we dunna on'y keep th' roof from comin'
    in. We *get* as well. An' even th' housework tha went on strike wi'. Tha   180
    skedaddled off ter Manchester, an' left me to't.

MINNIE I went on business.

LUTHER An' we've come out on strike 'on business'.

MINNIE You've not; it's a game.

LUTHER An' the mesters'll ta'e us back when they're ready, or when   185
    they're forced to. An' same wi' thee by me.

MINNIE Oh!

JOE We got it fr' Tom Rooke—'e wor goin' ter turn 'em down. At four
    to-morrer mornin', there's ower twenty men goin' down.

MRS GASCOIGNE What a lot of fools men are! As if th' pits didn't need   190
    ter be kept tidy, ready for you to go back to 'm.

JOE They'll be kep' tidy by us, then, an' when we've a mind—an' by
    nobody else.

MRS GASCOIGNE Tha talks very high an' mighty. That's because I ha'e
    th' feedin' on thee.   195

JOE You put it like our Luther says, then. He stands for t'mesters, an'
    Minnie stands for t'men—cos 'er's gone on strike. Now becos she's
    went ter Manchester, had he got ony right ter ha'e Lizzie Charley in
    for a couple o' nights an' days?

MRS GASCOIGNE Tha talks like a fool!   200

JOE I dunna.

MINNIE He's welcome to Lizzie Charley.

JOE All right.—She's a nice gel. We'll ax 'er to come in an' manage th'
'ouse—he can pay 'er.

MINNIE What with?   205

JOE Niver you mind. Should yer like it?

MINNIE He can do just as he likes.

JOE Then should I fetch her?—should I, Luther?

LUTHER If ter's a mind.

JOE Should I, then, Minnie?   210

MINNIE If he wants her.

LUTHER I want somebody ter look after me.

JOE Right tha art. (*Puts his cap on*) I'll say as Minnie canna look after th'
house, will 'er come. That it?

LUTHER Ah.   215

MRS GASCOIGNE Dunna be a fool. Tha's had a can or two.

JOE Well—'er'll be glad o' the job.

MRS GASCOIGNE You'd better stop him, one of you.

LUTHER I want somebody ter look after me—an' tha wunna.

MRS GASCOIGNE Eh dear o' me! Dunna thee be a fool, our Joe.   220
          Exit Joe
       What wor this job about goin' ter Manchester?

LUTHER She said she wouldna live wi' me, an' so 'er went. I thought
'er'd gone for good.

MINNIE You didn't—you *knew*.   225

LUTHER I knowed what tha'd towd me—as tha'd live wi' me no longer.
Tha's come back o' thy own accord.

MINNIE I never said I shouldn't come back.

LUTHER Tha said as tha wouldna live wi' me. An' tha *didna*, neither,—
not for—   230

MRS GASCOIGNE Well, Minnie, you've brought it on your own head.
You put him off, an' you put him off, as if 'e was of no account, an'
then all of a sudden you invited him to marry you—

MINNIE Put him off! He didn't need much putting off. He never came
any faster than a snail.   235

MRS GASCOIGNE Twice, to my knowledge, he axed thee—an' what can
a man do more?

MINNIE Yes, what! A gramophone in breeches could do as much.

MRS GASCOIGNE Oh, indeed! What ailed him was, he wor in collier's
britches, i'stead o' a stool-arsed Jack's.°   240

MINNIE No—what ailed him was that *you* kept him like a kid hanging
on to you.

MRS GASCOIGNE An' tha bit thy own nose off, when ter said him nay.
For had ter married him at twenty-three, there'd ha' been none of this
trouble.   245

MINNIE And why didn't I? Why didn't I? Because he came in his half-
hearted 'I will if you like' fashion, and I despised him, yes I did.

MRS GASCOIGNE And who are *you* to be despising him, I should like to
know?

MINNIE I'm a woman, and that's enough. But I know now, it was your   250
fault. You held him, and persuaded him that what he wanted was *you*.
You kept him, like a child, you even gave him what money he wanted,
like a child. He never roughed it—he never faced out anything. You
did all that for him.

MRS GASCOIGNE And what if I did! If you made as good a wife to him   255
as I made a mother, you'd do.

MINNIE Should I? You didn't care what women your sons went with,
so long as they didn't love them. What do you care really about this
affair of Bertha Purdy? You don't. All you cared about was to keep
your sons for yourself. You kept the solid meal, and the orts and slarts° 260
any other woman could have. But I tell you, I'm *not* for having the orts
and slarts, and your leavings from your sons. I'll have a man, or
nothing, I will.

MRS GASCOIGNE It's rare to be some folks, ter pick and choose.

MINNIE I can't pick and choose, no. But what I won't have, I won't have, 265
and that is all.

MRS GASCOIGNE (*to Luther*) Have I ever kept thee from doin' as tha
wanted? Have I iver marded and coddled thee?

LUTHER Tha hasna, beguy!

MINNIE No, you haven't, perhaps, not by the look of things. But you've 270
bossed him. You've decided everything for him, really. He's depen-
ded on you as much when he was thirty as when he was three. You
told him what to do, and he did it.

MRS GASCOIGNE My word, I've never known all he did.

MINNIE You have—everything that mattered. You maybe didn't know   275
it was Bertha Purdy, but you knew it was some woman like her, and
what did you care? *She* had the orts and slarts, you kept your son. And
you want to keep him, even now. Yes—and you do keep him.

MRS GASCOIGNE We're learnin' a thing or two, Luther.

LUTHER Ay.   280
        Enter Joe

MINNIE Yes! What did you care about the woman who would have to
take some after you? Nothing! You left her with just the slarts of a
man. Yes.

MRS GASCOIGNE Indeed! I canna see as you're so badly off. You've got   285
a husband as doesn't drink, as waits on you hand and foot, as gives you
a free hand in everything. It's you as doesn't know when you're well
off, madam.

MINNIE I'd rather have had a husband who knocked me about than a
husband who was good to me because he belonged to his mother. He   290
doesn't and can't *really* care for me. You stand before him. His *real*
caring goes to *you*. Me he only wants sometimes.

JOE She'll be in in a minute.

MRS GASCOIGNE Tha'rt the biggest fool an' jackanapes, our Joe, as iver
God made.   295

MINNIE If she crosses that doorstep, then I go for good.

MRS GASCOIGNE (*bursting into fury—to Joe*) Tha see what thy bobby°
interferin' has done.

JOE Nay—that's how it stood.

MRS GASCOIGNE Tha mun go an' stop her, our Luther. Tell 'er it wor   300
our Joe's foolery. An' look sharp.

LUTHER What should *I* go for?
          Luther goes out, furious

MINNIE You see—you see! His mother's word is law to him. He'd do
what I told him, but his *feel* would be for you. He's got no *feeling* for   305
me. You keep all that.

MRS GASCOIGNE You talk like a jealous woman.

MINNIE I do! And for that matter, why doesn't Joe marry, either?
Because you keep him too. You know, in spite of his bluster, he cares
more for your little finger than he does for all the women in the   310
world—or ever will. And it's wrong—it's wrong. How is a woman
ever to have a husband, when the men all belong to their mothers?
It's wrong.

MRS GASCOIGNE Oh, indeed!—is it? You know, don't you? You know
everything.   315

MINNIE I know this, because I've suffered from it. Your elder sons you
let go, and they *are* husbands. But your young sons you've kept. And
Luther is your son, and the man that lives with me. But first, he's your
son. And Joe ought never to marry, for he'd break a woman's heart.

MRS GASCOIGNE Tha hears, lad! We're bein' told off.   320

JOE Ah, I hear. An' what's more, it's true, Mother.

MINNIE It is—it is. He only likes playing round me and getting some
pleasure out of teasing me, because he knows I'm safely married to
Luther, and can never look to him to marry me and belong to me.
He's safe, so he likes me. If I were single, he'd be frightened to death   325
of me.

JOE Happen I should.

MRS GASCOIGNE Tha'rt a fool.

MINNIE And that's what you've done to me—that's my life spoiled—
spoiled—ay, worse than if I'd had a drunken husband that knocked   330
me about. For it's dead.

MRS GASCOIGNE Tha'rt shoutin' because nowt ails thee—that's what
tha art.

JOE Nay, Mother, tha knows it's right. Tha knows tha's got me—an'll
ha'e me till ter dies—an' after that—yi.   335

MRS GASCOIGNE Tha talks like a fool.

JOE And sometimes, Mother, I wish I wor dead, I do.

MINNIE You see, you see! You see what you've done to them. It's strong
women like you, who were too much for their husbands—ah!

JOE Tha knows I couldna leave thee, Mother—tha knows I couldna.   340
An' me, a young man, belongs to thy owd age. An' there's no-wheer
for me to go, Mother. For tha'rt gettin' nearer to death an' yet I canna
leave thee to go my own road. An' I wish, yi, often, as I wor dead.

MRS GASCOIGNE Dunna, lad—dunna let 'er put these ideas i' thy head.

JOE An' I can but fritter my days away. There's no goin' forrard for me.   345

MRS GASCOIGNE Nay, lad, nay—what lad's better off than thee, dost
reckon?

JOE If I went t'r Australia, th' best part on me wouldna go wi' me.

MRS GASCOIGNE Tha wunna go t'r Australia!

JOE If I went, I should be a husk of a man. I'm allers a husk of a man,   350
Mother. There's nowt solid about me. The' isna.

MRS GASCOIGNE Whativer dost mean? You've a' set on me at once.

JOE I'm nowt, Mother, an' I count for nowt. Yi, an' I know it.

MRS GASCOIGNE Tha does. Tha sounds as if tha counts for nowt, as a
rule, doesn't ter?   355

JOE There's not much of a man about me. T'other chaps is more of
fools, but they're more of men an' a'—an' they know it.

MRS GASCOIGNE That's thy fault.

JOE Yi—an' will be—ter th' end o' th' chapter.

   Enter Luther   360

MINNIE Did you tell her?

LUTHER Yes.

MINNIE We'll have some tea, should we?

JOE Ay, let's. For it's bin dry work.

   She sets the kettle on   365

MRS GASCOIGNE I mun be goin'.

MINNIE Wait and have a cup of tea. I brought a cake.

JOE But we non goin' ter ha'e it, are we, Luther, these 'ere blacklegs goin' down interferin'.

LUTHER We arena.   370

MRS GASCOIGNE But how are you going to stop them?

JOE We s'll manage it, one road or t'other.

MRS GASCOIGNE You'll non go gettin' yourselves into trouble.

LUTHER We in trouble enow.

MINNIE If you'd have had Lizzie Charley in, what should you have paid   375
her with?

LUTHER We should ha' found the money somewhere.

MINNIE Do you know what I had to keep house on this week, Mother?

MRS GASCOIGNE Not much, sin' there wor nowt but ten shillin' strike
pay.   380

MINNIE He gave me five shillings.

LUTHER Tha could ha' had what things ter wanted on strap.°

MINNIE No—but why should you keep, to drink on, as much as you
give me to keep house on? Five shillings!

JOE Five bob's non a whackin' sight o' pocket money for a man's week.   385

MINNIE It is, if he earns nothing. It was that as finished me off.

JOE Well, *tha* niver ned go short—tha can let *him*.

MINNIE I knew that was what *he* thought. But if he wouldna have my
money for one thing, he wasn't going to for another.

MRS GASCOIGNE Why, what wouldn't he have it for?   390

MINNIE He wouldn't have that forty pounds, when I went on my knees
to beg and beseech him to.

LUTHER Tha did! Tha throwed it at me as if I wor a beggar as stank.

MINNIE And you wouldn't have it when I asked you.

LUTHER No—an wouldna ha'e it now.   395

MINNIE You can't.

LUTHER I dunna want it.

MINNIE And if you don't find money to keep the house on, we shall
both of us starve. For you've got to keep me. And I've got no money
of my own now.   400

LUTHER Why, what dost mean?

MINNIE I mean what I say.

MRS GASCOIGNE Why, what?

MINNIE I was sick of having it between us. It was but a hundred and
twenty. So I went to Manchester and spent it.   405

MRS GASCOIGNE Tha's bin an' spent a hundred and twenty pound i'
four days?

MINNIE Yes, I have.

MRS GASCOIGNE Whativer are we comin' to!

JOE That wor a stroke worth two. Tell us what tha bought.   410

MINNIE I bought myself a ring, for one thing. I thought if I ever had any
children, and they asked me where was my engagement ring, I should
have to show them something, for their father's sake. Do you like it?

Holds out her hand to Joe

JOE My word, but that's a bobby-dazzler.° Look, Mother.   415

MRS GASCOIGNE H'm.

Joe takes the ring off

JOE My word, but that's a diamond, if you like. How much did it cost?

MINNIE Thirty pounds. I've got the bill in my pocket.

MRS GASCOIGNE I only hope you'll niver come to want some day.   420

MINNIE Luther must see to that.

JOE And what else did ter buy?

MINNIE I'll show you.

Gets her bag, unlocks it, takes out three prints

JOE I dunna reckon much ter these.   425

MRS GASCOIGNE Nor me neither. An' how much has ter gen for them
apiece?

MINNIE That was twenty-five pounds. They're beautiful prints.

MRS GASCOIGNE I dunna believe a word tha says.

MINNIE I'll show you the bill. My master's a collector, and he picked   430
them for me. He says they're well worth the money. And I like them.

MRS GASCOIGNE Well, I niver seed such a job in my life. T-t-t-t! Well,
a' I can say is, I hope tha'll niver come ter want. Throwin' good
money i' th' gutter like this. Nay, I feel fair bad. Nay! T-t-t-t! Such
tricks! And such bits o' dirty paper!   435

JOE I'd rather ha'e the Co-op almanack.°

MRS GASCOIGNE So would I, any day! What dost say to't, our Luther?

LUTHER 'Er does as 'er likes.

MINNIE I had a lovely time with Mr Westlake, choosing them at the
dealer's. He *is* clever.   440

MRS GASCOIGNE Tha towd him tha wanted to get rid o' thy money, did
ter?

MINNIE No—I said I wanted some pictures for the parlour, and asked
him if he'd help me choose.

MRS GASCOIGNE Good money thrown away. Maybe the very bread of   445
your children.

MINNIE Nay, that's Luther's duty to provide.

MRS GASCOIGNE Well, a' I can say is, I hope you may never come ter
want. If our Luther died . . .

MINNIE I should go back to work.   450

MRS GASCOIGNE But what if tha'd three or four children?

MINNIE A hundred and twenty pounds wouldn't make much odds
then.

MRS GASCOIGNE Well, a' I can say, I hope tha'lt niver live ter rue the
day.   455

JOE What dost think on 'er, Luther?

LUTHER Nay, she's done as she liked with her own.

MINNIE (*emptying her purse in her lap*) I've got just seventeen shillings.
You drew your strike pay yesterday. How much have you got of that,
Luther?   460

LUTHER Three bob.

MINNIE And do you want to keep it?

LUTHER Ah.

MINNIE Very well . . . I shall spend this seventeen shillings till it's gone,
and then we shall have to live on soup-tickets.°   465

MRS GASCOIGNE I'll back my life!

JOE And who'll fetch the soup?

MINNIE Oh, I shall. I've been thinking, that big jug will do nicely. I'm in
the same boat as other men's wives now, and so I must do the same.

JOE They'll gi'e you strap at West's.   470

MINNIE I'm not going to run up bills, no, I'm not. I'll go to the free teas,
and fetch soup, an' with ten shillings a week we shall manage.

MRS GASCOIGNE Well, that's one road, lass.

MINNIE It's the only one. And now, if he can provide, he must, and if he
can't, he must tell me so, and I'll go back into service, and not be a   475
burden to him.

MRS GASCOIGNE High and mighty, high and mighty! We'll see, my lass;
we'll see.

MINNIE That's all we can do.

MRS GASCOIGNE Tha doesna care how he takes it.   480

MINNIE The prints belong to both of us. (*Hands them to Luther*) You
haven't said if you like them yet.

LUTHER (*taking them, suddenly rams them in the fire*) Tha can go to hell.

MINNIE (*with a cry*) Ah!—that's my ninety pounds gone. (*Tries to
snatch them out*)   485

MRS GASCOIGNE (*beginning to cry*) Come, Joe, let's go; let's go, my lad.
I've seen as much this day as ever my eyes want to see. Let's go, my
lad. (*Gets up, beginning to tie on her bonnet*)

MINNIE (*white and intense, to Luther*) Should you like to throw my ring
after them? It's all I've got left.   490

She holds out her hand—he flings it from him

LUTHER Yi, what do I care what I do! (*Clenching his fists as if he would strike her*)—what do I—what do I—

MRS GASCOIGNE (*putting on her shawl*) A day's work—a day's work! Ninety pound! Nay—nay, oh, nay—nay, oh, nay—nay! Let's go, Joe, 495 my lad. Eh, our Luther, our Luther! Let's go, Joe. Come.

JOE Ah, I'll come, Mother.

MRS GASCOIGNE Luther!

LUTHER What?

MRS GASCOIGNE It's a day's work, it is, wi' thee. Eh dear! Come, let's 500 go, Joe. Let's go whoam.

LUTHER An' I'll go.

MRS GASCOIGNE Dunna thee do nowt as ter'll repent of, Luther— dunna thee. It's thy mother axes thee. Come, Joe.

Mrs Gascoigne goes out, followed by Joe. Luther stands with face 505
averted from his wife; mutters something, reaches for his cap, goes
out. Minnie stands with her hand on the mantelpiece.

CURTAIN

Act 4

The following morning—about 5 a.m. A candle is burning.
Minnie sits by the fire in a dressing-gown. She is weeping.
A knock, and Mrs Gascoigne's voice. Minnie goes to open the
door; re-enters with her mother-in-law, the latter with a big
brown shawl over her head

MRS GASCOIGNE Is Luther a-whoam?

MINNIE No—he's not been in all night.

MRS GASCOIGNE T-t-t-t! Now whereiver can they be? Joe's not in neither.

MINNIE Isn't he?

MRS GASCOIGNE No. He said he might be late, so I went to bed, and slept a bit uneasy-like till about four o'clock. Then I wakes up a' of a sudden, an' says: 'I'm by mysen i' th' house!' It gave me such a turn I daresn't shout. So I gets me up an' goes ter his room, an' he'd niver bin i' bed a' night. Well, I went down, but no signs nowhere. An' 'im wi' a broken arm. An' I listened an' I listened—an' then methinks I heered a gun go off. I felt as if I should die if I stopped by mysen another minute. So I on's wi' my shawl an' nips down here. There's not a soul astir nowhere. I a'most dropped when I seed your light. Hasn't Luther bin in a' night, dost say?

MINNIE He went out with you, and he never came in again. I went to bed, thinking perhaps he'd be sleeping on the sofa. And then I came down, and he wasn't here.

MRS GASCOIGNE Well, I've seen nowt of him, for he never come up to our house.—Now I wonder what's afoot wi' th' silly fools?

MINNIE I thought he'd gone and left me.

MRS GASCOIGNE It's more like some o' this strike work. When I heered that gun, I said: 'Theer goes one o' my lads!'

MINNIE You don't think they're killed?

MRS GASCOIGNE Heaven knows what they are. But I niver thought he'd ha' served me this trick—left me by myself without telling me, and gone cutting off a' th' night through—an' him wi' a broken arm.

MINNIE Where do you think they've gone?

MRS GASCOIGNE The Lord above alone knows—but I'se warrant it's one o' these riotin' tricks—stopping them blacklegs as wor goin' down to see to th' roads.

MINNIE Do you think—?

MRS GASCOIGNE   I'll back anything. For I heered th' winding engines°
     plain as anything. Hark!
     They listen   40

MINNIE   I believe I can hear them.

MRS GASCOIGNE   Th' ingines?

MINNIE   Yes.

MRS GASCOIGNE   They're winding something down. Eh dear, what a
     dead world it seems, wi' none o' th' pits chuffin' an' no steam wavin'   45
     by day, an' no lights shinin' by night. You may back your life there
     was a gang of 'em going to stop that lot of blacklegs. And there'd be
     soldiers for a certainty. If I didn't hear a shot, I heered summat much
     like one.

MINNIE   But they'd never shoot, would they?   50

MRS GASCOIGNE   Haven't they shot men up an' down th' country?
     Didn't I know them lads was pining to go an' be shot at? I did.
     Methinks when I heard that gun, 'They'd niver rest till this had
     happened.'

MINNIE   But they're not shot, Mother. You exaggerate.   55

MRS GASCOIGNE   I niver said they wor. But if anything happens to a
     man, my lass, you may back your life, nine cases out o' ten, it's a spite°
     on th' women.

MINNIE   Oh, what a thing to say! Why, there are accidents.

MRS GASCOIGNE   Yes, an' men verily gets accidents, to pay us out, I do   60
     believe. They get huffed up, they bend down their faces, and they say
     to theirselves: 'Now I'll get myself hurt, an' she'll be sorry,' else:
     'Now I'll get myself killed, an' she'll ha'e nobody to sleep wi' 'er, an'
     nobody to nag at.' Oh, my lass, I've had a husband an' six sons.
     Children they are, these men, but, my word, they're revengeful   65
     children. Children men is a' the days o' their lives. But they're master
     of us women when their dander's up, an' they pay us back double an'
     treble—they do—an' you mun allers expect it.

MINNIE   But if they went to stop the blacklegs, they wouldn't be doing
     it to spite us.   70

MRS GASCOIGNE   Wouldn't they! Yi, but they would. My lads 'ud do it
     to spite me, an' our Luther 'ud do it to spite thee. Yes—and it's trew.
     For they'd run theirselves into danger and lick their lips for joy,
     thinking, if I'm killed, then *she* maun lay me out. Yi—I seed it in our
     mester. He got killed a' pit. An' when I laid him out, his face wor that   75
     grim, an' his body that stiff, an' it said as plain as plain: 'Now then,
     you've done for me.' For it's risky work, handlin' men, my lass, an'
     niver thee pray for sons—Not but what daughters is any good. Th'

world is made o' men, for me, lass—there's only the men for me. An' tha'rt similar. An' so, tha'lt reap trouble by the peck, an' sorrow by the bushel. For when a woman builds her life on men, either husbands or sons, she builds on summat as sooner or later brings the house down crash on her head—yi, she does.

MINNIE But it depends how and what she builds.

MRS GASCOIGNE It depends, it depends. An' tha thinks tha can steer clear o' what I've done. An' perhaps tha can. But steer clear the whole length o' th' road, tha canna, an' tha'lt see. Nay, a childt is a troublesome pleasure to a woman, but a man's a trouble pure and simple.

MINNIE I'm sure it depends what you make of him.

MRS GASCOIGNE Maybe—maybe. But I've allers tried to do my best, i' spite o' what tha said against me this afternoon.

MINNIE I didn't mean it—I was in a rage.

MRS GASCOIGNE Yi, tha meant it plain enow. But I've tried an' tried my best for my lads, I have—an' this is what owd age brings me—wi' 'em—

MINNIE Nay, Mother—nay. See how fond they are of you.

MRS GASCOIGNE Yi—an' they go now i' their mischief, yes, tryin' to get killed, to spite me. Yi!

MINNIE Nay. Nay.

MRS GASCOIGNE It's true. An' tha can ha'e Luther. Tha'lt get him, an' tha can ha'e him.

MINNIE Do you think I shall?

MRS GASCOIGNE I can see. Tha'lt get him—but tha'lt get sorrow wi' 'em, an' wi' th' sons tha has. See if tha doesna.

MINNIE But I don't care. Only don't keep him from me. It leaves me so—with nothing—not even trouble.

MRS GASCOIGNE He'll come to thee—an' he'll think no more o' me as is his mother than he will o' that poker.

MINNIE Oh, no—oh, no.

MRS GASCOIGNE Yi—I know well—an' then that other.

There is a silence—the two women listening

MINNIE If they'd been hurt, we should ha' known by now.

MRS GASCOIGNE Happen we should. If they come, they'll come together. An' they'll come to this house first.

A silence. Minnie starts

Did ter hear owt?

MINNIE Somebody got over the stile.

MRS GASCOIGNE (*listening*) Yi.

MINNIE (*listening*) It *is* somebody.

MRS GASCOIGNE I' t'street.   120

MINNIE (*starting up*) Yes.

MRS GASCOIGNE Comin'? It's Luther. (*Goes to the door*) An' it's on'y
    Luther.

> Both women stand, the Mother nearer the door. The door opens—
> a slight sluther.° Enter Luther, with blood on his face—rather   125
> shaky and dishevelled

My boy—my boy!

LUTHER Mother! (*He goes blindly*) Where's Minnie?

MINNIE (*with a cry*) Oh!

MRS GASCOIGNE Wheer's Joe?—wheer's our Joe?   130

LUTHER (*to Minnie, queer, stunned, almost polite*) It worn't 'cause I wor
    mad wi' thee I didna come whoam.

MRS GASCOIGNE (*clutching him sternly*) Where's Joe?

LUTHER He's gone up street—he thought tha might ha' wakkened.

MRS GASCOIGNE Wakkened enow.   135

> Mrs Gascoigne goes out

MINNIE Oh, what have you done?

LUTHER We'd promised not to tell nobody—else I should. We stopped
    them blacklegs—leastways—but it worn't because I—I—(*He stops
    to think*) I wor mad wi' thee, as I didna come whoam.   140

MINNIE What have you done to your head?

LUTHER It wor a stone or summat catched it. It's gev me a headache.
    Tha mun—tha mun tie a rag round it—if ter will.

> He sways as he takes his cap off. She catches him in her arms.
> He leans on her as if he were tipsy   145

Minnie—

MINNIE My love—my love!

LUTHER Minnie—I want thee ter ma'e what tha can o' me. (*He sounds
    almost sleepy*)

MINNIE (*crying*) My love—my love!   150

LUTHER I know what tha says is true.

MINNIE No, my love—it isn't—it isn't.

LUTHER But if ter'lt ma'e what ter can o' me—an' then if ter has a
    childt—tha'lt happen ha'e enow.

MINNIE No—no—it's you. It's you I want. It's you.   155

LUTHER But tha's allers had me.

MINNIE No, never—and it hurt so.

LUTHER I thowt tha despised me.

MINNIE Ah—my love!

LUTHER Dunna say I'm mean, to me—an' got no go.   160

MINNIE I only said it because you wouldn't let me love you.

LUTHER Tha didna love me.

MINNIE Ha!—it was *you*.

LUTHER Yi. (*He looses himself and sits down heavily*) I'll ta'e my boots off. (*He bends forward*)   165

MINNIE Let me do them. (*He sits up again*)

LUTHER It's started bleedin'. I'll do 'em i' ha'ef a minute.

MINNIE No—trust me—trust yourself to me. Let me have you now for my own. (*She begins to undo his boots*)

LUTHER Dost want me?   170

MINNIE (*she kisses his hands*) Oh, my love!

　　　　She takes him in her arms. He suddenly begins to cry.

　　　　CURTAIN

THE FIGHT FOR BARBARA

CHARACTERS

FRANCESCA
WESSON
BARBARA
BUTCHER
LADY CHARLCOTE
SIR WILLIAM CHARLCOTE
DR FREDERICK TRESSIDER

Scene: a villa in Italy

Act 1

*8.30 in the morning. The kitchen of an Italian villa—a big open
fireplace of stone, with a little charcoal grate—fornello—on
either side—cupboards, table, rush-bottom chairs with high
backs—many bright copper pans of all sizes hanging up
The door-bell rings in the kitchen—rings hard—after a minute   5
a door is heard to bang.
Enter Wesson, in dressing-gown and pyjamas: a young man of
about twenty-six, with thick hair ruffled from sleep. He crosses
and goes through door right. Sounds of voices. Re-enter Wesson,
followed by Italian maid-servant, Francesca, young, fair,   10
pretty—wears a black lace scarf over her head. She carries a
saucepan full of milk. On the table stand a soup-tureen and an
enamel jug*

FRANCESCA *Questa?*° (*Puts her hand on the jug*)

WESSON No, in the other. (*She pours the milk into the tureen*)   15

FRANCESCA (*smiling*) *Abondante misura!*°

WESSON What's that? *Come?*°

FRANCESCA *Abondante misura latte!*°

WESSON Oh—full measure. *Si!*°—running over!

FRANCESCA Ranning ova. (*Both laugh*)   20

WESSON Right you are—you're learning English.

FRANCESCA *Come?*

WESSON *Vous apprenez anglais—voi—inglese!*°

FRANCESCA *O—non—niente inglese!*°

WESSON Nothing English? Oh yes! Er—*fa tempo cattivo!*°   25

FRANCESCA *Tempo cattivo—si.*°

WESSON Rotten weather—

FRANCESCA *Come?*

WESSON It's all the same. (*She puts the lid on her saucepan and turns
away*) Er—what day is it?—er—*giorno che giorno?*°   30

FRANCESCA *Oggi? Domenica.*°

WESSON *Domenica!—dimanche—Sonntag*°—Sunday.

FRANCESCA *Come?*

WESSON Sunday!

FRANCESCA Sendy!   35

WESSON That's it. (*Both laugh—she blushes and turns away—bows*)

FRANCESCA *Buon giorno, Signore.*°

WESSON *Buon giorno.*

    Exit Francesca right. He drinks some milk, wipes his mouth and
    begins to whistle: 'Put me among the girls!'°—takes some   40
    branches of olive and ilex from a box near the fire—puts them in
    the fireplace. As he is so doing, enter left Barbara—age about
    twenty-six—fair—rather a fine young woman, holding her blue
    silk dressing-gown about her. She stands in the doorway left,
    holding up her finger   45

BARBARA Yes, you may well whistle that! *I* heard you, Giacometti.°

WESSON (*turning round*) And did it fetch you out of bed?

BARBARA Yes, it did. *I* heard your dulcet tones.

WESSON They were no dulcetter than usual.

BARBARA And, pray, what right had they to be *as dulcet!*—(*Draws*   50
 herself up)—to a little servant-maid, indeed!

WESSON She's awfully nice, and quite a lady.

BARBARA Yes—yes—I know you! She's pretty, is she?

WESSON Awfully pretty! (*Lighting the heap of branches in the fire*) These
 matches are the stinking devil.   55

BARBARA Aren't they! I tried to light a cigarette with them, and I
 thought I should have died!

WESSON You should have waited till the sulphur had burned away.
 (*Laughing*) And the pretty maid had got a mantilla on this morning.

BARBARA Ah! I suppose the poor thing had been to church.   60

WESSON It took my breath away when I opened the door, and I said 'Oh!'

BARBARA *Giacomo!*

WESSON *Do* call me Jimmy—I hate to be Italianized!—and she blushed
 like fury.

BARBARA Poor thing! Really, Giacometti, really, you are impossible.   65

WESSON What for?

BARBARA Fancy saying 'Oh!' to the young maid! Remember, you're a
 gentleman in her eyes.

WESSON And what's wrong with saying 'Oh!' when she's got a
 fascinating mantilla on? I can't say delicate things in Italian—and—   70
 'Oh!'—who can't say 'Oh!'—after all, what is there in it?

BARBARA What could have been more expressive! Think of the poor
 thing, how embarrassed she must feel.

    The fire blazes up in the big chimney

 Oh, how beautiful! Now that makes me *perfectly* happy. How   75
 gorgeous! How adorable! No, but, Wesson, I don't like it.

WESSON What's that, the fire?

BARBARA No, the little servant-maid. And you made her feel *so* un-
 comfortable.

WESSON I didn't.   80

BARBARA You must have done! Think—to her, at any rate, you're a
gentleman.

WESSON A thundering lot of a gentleman, when she finds me lighting
the fire and grinding the coffee—

BARBARA Yes, but no doubt she thinks that's an eccentricity.   85

WESSON There's a lot of eccentricity about living on a hundred-and-
twenty a year, the pair of us.

BARBARA And you must remember how fearfully poor these Italians
are—

WESSON It's enough for me how fearfully poor we are ourselves—you   90
in your silk dressing-gown! It'll be some time before you get such
one out of our purse.

BARBARA Well, it doesn't matter—you *are* a gentleman here. Look, this
flat is quite grand.

WESSON It will be when you have to clean it.   95

BARBARA *I* don't mind cleaning it; don't be horrid! This adorable fire!
But you won't do it, will you?

WESSON What?

BARBARA Say 'Oh!' to the little maid. It's not nice, really.

WESSON Well, you see, it popped out when I saw the mantilla. I s'll be   100
used to it another time.

BARBARA And you won't say it?

WESSON I won't say 'Oh!'; oh dear, oh no, never no more, I won't.
(*Sings*)

BARBARA (*kissing him*) Dear!   105

WESSON (*kissing her*) What d'yer want?

BARBARA I love you.

WESSON So you ought.

BARBARA Why ought I?

WESSON (*at the fire*) There you are, you see, that's how to set a fornello 110
going.

BARBARA (*teasing*) Oh—oh, is it? And now you're going to make coffee
à l'Italienne, aren't you? Oh, you wonderful person!

WESSON I am. (*Gets the coffee-mill from cupboard—grinds coffee on the
table, singing*)   115

> Johnny used to grind the coffee-mill,
> Mix the sugar with the sand;
> But he got run in and all through mixing
> His master's money with his own.

BARBARA What is that beautiful and classic song?   120
> *Wesson sings it again*

BARBARA (*laughing*) Oh, you common, common brat! Anybody could tell your father was a coal-miner.

WESSON A butty collier°—and I wish yours had been ditto—you'd ha' been more use. Think of me, Lord of Creation, getting the breakfast 125 ready. (*She takes his head between her hands, and ruffles his hair*) While you stand messing about.

BARBARA Oh, your lovely hair!—it makes waves just like the Apollo Belvedere.°

WESSON And come again to-morrer. 130

BARBARA Don't—don't laugh at yourself—or at me when I say it's nice hair. It *is*, Giacomo, it's really beautiful.

WESSON I know; it's the Apollo Belvedere, and my beautiful nose is Antinous,° and my lovely chin is Endymion°—clear out.

BARBARA You are horrid to yourself! Why won't you let me say you're 135 nice?

WESSON Because the water's boiling.

BARBARA You're not a bit nice.

WESSON Mind!—My water's boiling! (*Breaks away—making coffee in a brass jug*) If this was Pimlico or Bloomsbury,° and this was a London 140 kitchen, you wouldn't love me, would you?

BARBARA If you could do anything so horrid as to stifle me in a poor part of London, I would *not* love you—I would hate you for ever. Think of me!

WESSON But because we come careering to Italy, and the pans are of 145 copper and brass, you adore me, don't you?

BARBARA Yes—on the whole.

WESSON That is, for the first month or two. We've been here six weeks.

BARBARA Think of it—Giacomo *mio*, it seems like six minutes—it frightens me. 150

WESSON (*hesitating*) It doesn't seem three months since we left England, does it?

BARBARA I can't believe we're here yet. Giacomo, Giacomo, why is it so new, every day? Giacomo, why is it always more? It's always more, isn't it? 155

WESSON (*putting his arms round her*) You're a Judy!° (*Kisses her*)

BARBARA Do you love me?

WESSON Not a bit.

BARBARA Not a teenty° bit?

WESSON Not a scroddy° atom. (*Laughs—tightens her in his arms—kisses 160 her*)

BARBARA You're a *common* thing!

WESSON   Am I no gentleman, as Frederick said?

BARBARA   No, no one could ever accuse you of being a gentleman.

WESSON   Am I a lout?   165

BARBARA   Oh—*did* it call him a lout!

WESSON   Am I a clodhopper?

BARBARA   Now—that makes me happy! That Frederick should call *you* a clodhopper—no, that is too much joy!

WESSON   Have they called me any more names?   170

BARBARA   You forget the clumsy clown—

WESSON   That your papa would have kicked downstairs—think of the poor old winded baronet—

BARBARA   Who's had his Selma all his life! And then says you're a degraded scoundrel for running away with me.   175

WESSON   Yes—his rotten old cheek.

BARBARA   He's a failure, too, you know—Papa's a failure! Why are all people failures?

WESSON   Couldn't say.

BARBARA   It's because their women have been so rotten to them. Mama   180
treated my father badly, she did, just because of his Selma.

WESSON   You'd let *me* have a Selma, wouldn't you?

BARBARA   What! *I'd* show you—I'll show you if you try any of your little games on me. But poor Papa—everything he has done has gone wrong—his money—he had no son—   185

WESSON   So there'll be no fifth baronet—how sad—what an awful loss to society!

BARBARA   And here am I, his favourite daughter, have run away with the son of a coal-miner, from my good and loving husband.

WESSON   The right worthy Frederick Tressider, doctor of medicine.   190
Gentleman of means. Worth a dozen of me.

BARBARA   Oh, how I hated his wooden face!

WESSON   Well, you knocked spots off it pretty roughly.

BARBARA   How common, how inexpressibly common your language is.

WESSON   There goes the milk. (*Dashes to the fire*) Are you going to have   195
bregger° in the kitchen, or in the bedroom?

BARBARA   We'll have it here for once. Should we—because of this lovely fire—put some more sticks on.

WESSON   Put 'em on yourself—or, wait a minute—want eggs, or don't you?   200

BARBARA   Yes, let's have eggs.

WESSON   You're a lazy little devil.

BARBARA   Think—think how I worked yesterday!

WESSON Yes—it nearly killed you, didn't it!
Silence for a moment   205
BARBARA Poor Frederick. He *does* love me! If I'd seen it before I'd left
him—I don't think I could have done it. Why did he always hide it
from me?
WESSON He didn't. You merely never saw it.
BARBARA Oh, but it never came out!   210
WESSON What did you *want* him to do! He loved you right enough; you
merely didn't love him—and there it stands.
BARBARA But—I knew he was in love with me—but—why could I
never *feel* his love? Why could I never feel it *warm* me?
WESSON Because you never wanted to. You were non-conductive to   215
this particular form of love, that's all.
BARBARA Think, I was married to him for three years, and I was no
nearer to him than I am to that fornello.
WESSON Poor devil—it wasn't his fault.
BARBARA Yes, I have treated him badly.   220
WESSON You might have done worse by staying with him.
BARBARA But think—how he adored me! Why did it never seem
anything to me, his love? But think, Giacomo, how he must suffer—
such a highly esteemed man, and so proud and sensitive—
WESSON And we'd only known each other three weeks.   225
BARBARA Oh, Giacomo; it makes me tremble! Do you think we shall
bring it off?
WESSON We shall—if we make up our minds to. But if you keep footling
with the idea of Frederick, and your people, and duty—then we
shan't.   230
BARBARA But, Giacomo—they loved me so.
WESSON So do I.
BARBARA Yes, but they needed me more. And I belonged to them! And
they say love wears off—and if it does!
WESSON You were saying only a minute since it was always more.   235
BARBARA Giacomo, I'm frightened.
WESSON What of?
BARBARA Of everything—and sometimes I wonder—don't be cross if
I say it, will you?
WESSON Say what you like.   240
BARBARA Sometimes I wonder—it seems horrid—I wonder if I can
trust you.
WESSON Why?
BARBARA You are so queer—and I am so all alone—and if you weren't
good to me—   245

WESSON I think you needn't be mean—

BARBARA But look—you seem to want to take me away from everything and everybody. I feel as if you wanted to swallow me, and take my will away. You won't do it, will you, Giacomo?

WESSON You're fatter than I am—ask a cat not to swallow a camel.   250

BARBARA But do you think Frederick will divorce me?

WESSON You'll have to insist on it.

BARBARA No—I can't—it seems so cruel. I can't, dear. He's so cut up. You know, he says he can't publicly accuse me.

WESSON If he'd hate you and have done with it, it would be easier. Or if   255
he loved you, he would offer you divorce. But no, he messes about between one thing and another, and sentimentalizes.

BARBARA But he *does* love me, Giacomo.

WESSON And a fat lot of use it is to you. But he sees you don't clearly want a divorce and so he hangs on. Now he talks about your going to   260
live with your mother, and repenting, then he'll have you back. But you like to leave a loophole by which you could creep out and go back, don't you? Ah, you do.

BARBARA No—no—don't say it—don't say it. Only I'm frightened.

WESSON You know your people have given out you've gone into a   265
convent in France, for a little while, because you had got religious ideas or something like that. And I know they think you'll come crawling back at last—and Frederick is waiting for you—he's waiting—and you like to have it so—you do.

BARBARA (*putting her arms round his neck*) No, it's not true, Giacometti,   270
it's not true. I *do* love you, don't I?

WESSON You only don't want to belong to me.

BARBARA But I do belong to you.

WESSON You don't—you tamper with the idea of Frederick.

BARBARA He'd never do to me what you want to do.   275

WESSON What?

BARBARA Humble me, and make me nothing—and then swallow me. And it's *wrong*. It's *wrong* for you to want to swallow me. I am my-self—and you ought to leave me free.

WESSON Well, so I do.   280

BARBARA You don't. All the time you're at me. Oh, and I hate you so sometimes, Giacomo. Now you're cross with me.

WESSON I should think the eggs are done.

BARBARA (*seating herself*) I'm hungry, Giacomo—are you?

WESSON No—it makes me sick, the way you're always bleeding my   285
self-respect.

BARBARA *I! I!* Why it's I who've given you your self-respect. Think of the crumpled up, despairing, hating creature that came into Mrs Kelly's drawing-room—and now look at yourself.

WESSON   But you *won't* love me—you want to keep upper hand.   290

BARBARA (*laughing with scorn*)   There you are quite mistaken. *I* want there to be *no* upper hand. I only want both of us to be free to be ourselves—and you seem as if you *can't* have it—you want to bully me, you want to bully me inside.

WESSON   All right—eat your breakfast then.   295

BARBARA   And it makes me feel as if I want to run—I want to run from you.

WESSON   Back to Frederick.

BARBARA   Yes—poor Frederick—he never made me feel like this. I was always a free woman with him.   300

WESSON   And mightily you regretted it.

BARBARA   No—no! Not that! Your idea of marriage is like the old savages: hit a woman on the head and run off with her.

WESSON   Very well.
> *The bell rings noisily*   305
There's the butcher.
> *Goes out door right—voices—re-enter Wesson*
What do you want?

BARBARA   I don't know—what do we?

WESSON   I!—   310
> *He turns round. The butcher, a handsome young fellow of about twenty, has followed him and stands in the doorway*

BARBARA   Oh!—*Buon giorno!*°

BUTCHER   *Buon giorno, signora.*

BARBARA   *Piove?*°   315

BUTCHER   *Si.*

BARBARA   Ah!—*e il lago—?*°

BUTCHER   *È burrascoso.*°

BARBARA   Ah—*tempo cattivo per voi*—°
> *The butcher laughs.*   320

WESSON   What do you want?

BARBARA   Er—*ha vitello?*°

BUTCHER   *Si—si—quanto?*°

BARBARA   How much do we want?

WESSON   *Mezzo chilo.*°   325

BARBARA   *Mezzo chilo.*

BUTCHER (*touching his hood*)   *Grazia—buon giorno.*°
> *The door is heard to close*

BARBARA Oh, I like him, I like him—you said he wasn't nice.

WESSON He's not—look at the way he comes in.   330

BARBARA I like it. It's so decided, at any rate. I hate English people for the way they always hang fire.

WESSON Do you?

BARBARA Yes! I like him as he stands there—he looks like a wild young bull or something, peering out of his hood.   335

WESSON And you flirt with him.

BARBARA *Wesson!*

WESSON I know it's a great insult to say so. But he *is* good-looking—and see the way you stretch out your arm, and show your throat.

BARBARA But Wesson, how *can* you. I simply spoke to him. And when   340
you think of yourself with the servant maid—

WESSON I only laugh—you sort of show yourself.

BARBARA Well, really, this is too much!

WESSON True, whether or not. And you're always doing it. You always want men to think I don't *keep* you. You write to your mother like   345
that, you write to Frederick like that—always as if I didn't keep you, as if you were rather undecided, you would make up your mind to walk away from me in a little while, probably.

BARBARA How *can* you be so false? It would serve you right if I *did* leave you.   350

WESSON I know that, you've said it before.

BARBARA Really—no one but a common man would say I flirted with that butcher—

WESSON Well, I *am* common—what's the odds? You've lived with me for three months.   355

BARBARA That doesn't say I shall live with you for ever.

WESSON You can go the minute you want to go.

BARBARA Ha, could I! It's easy for you to talk. You'd see, when it came to it, how you would let me go.

WESSON I wouldn't try to stop you, if you really, really wanted to leave   360
me. But you've got to convince me of that first.

BARBARA You think there's not another like you, don't you?

WESSON For you, there isn't.

BARBARA I'm not so sure.

WESSON I am! But try, only try. Only try, and make your mistake. But   365
it'll be too late, once you've done it.

BARBARA Pooh! You needn't think you'll threaten me.

WESSON I only tell you. Can I give you anything?

BARBARA The honey.

He rises and gets it from the cupboard   370

WESSON I wait on you, yet I want to bully you.

BARBARA Yes, it's subtler than that.

WESSON If you let me wait on you, you leave yourself in my hands.

BARBARA Not a bit of it—not a bit of it! Do you think it makes any
    difference to me? Frederick would have waited on me on his knees.   375

WESSON Then it's time somebody taught you you're not as great as you
    think. You imagine you're the one and only phoenix.

BARBARA (*laughing*) And I am, aren't I, Giacometti? Say I am.

WESSON I say you're a pecky, scratchy one, at that rate.

BARBARA No—no! Say I'm nice—say I'm ever so nice.   380

WESSON On rare occasions.

BARBARA Always—say always.

WESSON It wouldn't be true.

BARBARA Yes—yes, it would, Giacomo. See, I'm ever so nice, aren't I?
    I'm ever so nice! Look at my nice arms, how they love you.   385

WESSON Better than you do.

BARBARA No—not better than I do. Come and kiss them. Come and
    give them a little kiss.

WESSON (*going and kissing her arms*) You're cruel, if you're nothing else.

BARBARA No, I'm not. Say I'm not. Kiss me!

    Wesson, laughing shakily, kisses her.—A voice is heard outside.   390
    'La posta.'°

WESSON Oh, Lord, there's the postman—he's the serpent in my Eden.

VOICE *La posta!*

    Wesson goes to the door, re-enters with letters

WESSON (*tearing open an envelope*) The serpent's left his venom.   395

BARBARA (*making a frightened face*) Is it Frederick?

WESSON And your mother.

BARBARA Oh dear! Gia, I can't stand it.

WESSON Why not?

BARBARA I can't stand it—I can't—poor Frederick. If he was ill,   400
    Giacomo?

WESSON He'd have to get better.

BARBARA He might die.

WESSON He wouldn't be such a fool. What's up in your letter?

BARBARA (*wiping her eyes*) It seems so cruel!   405

WESSON Your father's ill.

BARBARA (*starting and snatching the letter from his hand*) Papa!
    She reads, crying quietly. Wesson sits waiting—he has read
    Frederick's letter.

BARBARA (*looking up*) Is he *very* ill, Giacomo?   410

WESSON No.

BARBARA They'll say it's me.

WESSON Let 'em. It's the whisky, as a matter of fact.

BARBARA Look how cruel mama is: 'Your father is very ill, but he does not wish to see you while you continue your present mode of life. The   415 doctor says he is to be spared all strain and anxiety.'

WESSON And they're thinking of going to Harrogate,° so he's not at death's door.

BARBARA And look at Frederick's letter—'Ever since you drove a spike into my brain, on February the 24th, I have been mad.' Do you think   420 he *is* mad, Giacomo?

WESSON A bit, perhaps—but so were you when you lived with him— going clean cracked.

BARBARA He won't commit suicide, will he?

WESSON No—no more than I shall.   425

BARBARA (*reading*) 'There are some nights when I never sleep at all—I try to work, but my brain has gone.' (*Shudders*)

WESSON It *is* vile—but I can't help it. Think of the hell if you went back to him.

BARBARA (*reading—laughs*) 'Do not speak of Wesson. I do not wish to   430 hear of his existence, or to know that he exists. Only, if ever he crosses my path, I will crush him like a beetle.' How strong his feelings are!

WESSON His words, you mean.

BARBARA No, he *is* passionate—you don't know. And he *can* hate.

WESSON He can sound like it.   435

BARBARA But if he came here and killed you?

WESSON I should offer myself to the knife, of course. I must practise being 'daggeroso'° in readiness. (*Puts a pointed kitchen knife between his teeth*) So!

BARBARA Oh, you are lovely! (*Laughs*) Let me kiss you. (*He takes the   440 knife from between his teeth—she kisses him*) Oh, the way he submits! Doesn't he like it, then?

WESSON He likes it all right—but he's sick of this tragedy.

BARBARA Are you tired of me, Giacomo?

WESSON Tired of the mess we're in, that's all.   445

BARBARA Do you want to be rid of me?

WESSON I want to be sure of you.

BARBARA Well, and you are. *Do* you think Frederick will ever let me go?

WESSON You must insist on his divorcing you.

BARBARA But I daren't, Giacomo, I daren't.   450

WESSON You'd rather remain as we are?

BARBARA No—no! Only he seems something so sure—you know—like when he said: 'You have dishonoured our marriage vow, but I never will.'

WESSON That's as he pleases.   455

BARBARA But it's rather fine.

WESSON He *is* fine, in a thousand ways where I'm not. But you never loved him.

BARBARA No—I never loved him. Poor Frederick, it doesn't seem fair, does it?   460

WESSON It does not. You were rottenly unfair to him.

BARBARA In what way?

WESSON Holding him cheap. Holding his love for you lightly, when it was the biggest thing about him.

BARBARA *Why* did it never seem so much to me, till I'd left him?   465

WESSON You hated him. While he could keep you, he felt a man—but you didn't mean to be kept—you tortured him—you fought against him—you undermined him—you were killing him.

BARBARA Oh no—oh no! I never hated him. I did a lot for him.

WESSON You, perhaps, had plenty of good-will towards him—but you   470
tortured him like hell. You, with your kindness, are one of the cruel-lest things going.

BARBARA How *can* you say so, Giacomo! Am I cruel to you?

WESSON You are.

BARBARA (*laughing*) It seems to me only funny when you say I'm   475
cruel—I, who wouldn't hurt a fly.

WESSON Then I wish I was a fly, and not a man.

BARBARA Aw, did it be a man!—did it be a little man in trousers, then, did it!

WESSON It did!—I think they're getting a bit impatient, your people.   480
You'll see they'll combine forces just now to get you back.

BARBARA Even if they did, I'd be gone again in three weeks.

WESSON But if they got hold of the right handle, they'd get you back and keep you.

BARBARA What handle?   485

WESSON Oh, I dunno. Your pity, your self-sacrifice, your desire to be straight.

BARBARA Self-sacrifice! There's a lot of self-sacrifice about me. (*Laughs*) They'd find I don't work well with *that* handle.

WESSON You don't know yourself. *You* keep them dangling.   490

BARBARA Why do you hate me?

WESSON Go to hell.

BARBARA (*plaintive*) Are you cross with me? But you *are*! (*Very plaintive*) *Why* are you cross with me, Giacomo, when I love you?

WESSON You—you only love yourself.   495

BARBARA No, Giacometti, no, I don't. See how loving I am, really—see how unselfish I am—

WESSON So unselfish you'd rob Peter to pay Paul, then go back to Peter to console him.

BARBARA You're horrid to me.   500

WESSON And you are worse to me.

BARBARA But I'm not.

WESSON Hm.

BARBARA (*mocking him*) 'Hm!'—what common grunts! Kiss me (*Pleading*) Don't you *want* to kiss me?   505

WESSON No.

BARBARA (*sadly*) Aw!

WESSON (*turning and taking her in his arms*) You're a baggage.

BARBARA Do you *want* to kiss me? (*She draws back*)

WESSON Resigned, I kiss the rod.°   510

BARBARA And am I the rod? Oh, Giacomo, think of *me* as a rod.

WESSON *You* see if Frederick and your mother aren't up to some little trick just now.

BARBARA I'm frightened, Giacomo.

WESSON Then you're frightened of yourself, of your own hesitating,   515
half-and-half, neither-fish-flesh-fowl nor good-red-herring self.

    CURTAIN

Act 2

*Evening, several days after the first act. The dining-room of the
same villa—a rather large room, with piano, writing-desk and old
furniture. In the big bay window, which looks over a garden on to
the lake, is a large couch. Barbara is lying on the couch. Wesson,
without his collar and tie, sits beside her*   5

WESSON You've got a nice chin.

BARBARA Frederick used to adore it.

WESSON Then he'd no business to.

BARBARA (*putting her arms round his neck*) Dear!

WESSON Don't you wish there'd never been any Frederick—or any-   10
body else—

BARBARA Well, *you* haven't much room to talk; look what a mess your
women had got you into.

WESSON But don't you wish we could have come straight to each other,
and been married simply, before we'd knocked about?   15

BARBARA I don't trust marriage.

WESSON Because you were stupid and married wrong—that's not the
fault of marriage.

BARBARA No—but I don't trust it.

WESSON Folk are such fools, they should marry the right people.   20

BARBARA Even when the right people are *married*, they go wrong.

WESSON No—I don't believe it—and I don't believe you love me—and
whether you do or not, I *do* love you.

BARBARA Because you've decided to.

WESSON Yes, because I know. I may hate you, I may rage against you,   25
I may sneer at you—very well! It doesn't alter the fact that I love you.

BARBARA It seems to me so queer, to make up your mind that you love
anybody.

WESSON You poke holes in me—well, I'll patch 'em up—I won't give
in.   30

BARBARA Oh—oh—the dear! He's on his nice little high horse, is he?
Oh!—he should be on the roundabouts, on his wooden prancer!

WESSON Or on a round-about chicken.

BARBARA And he looks so pathetic on his chicken—the dear. (*Kisses
him*)   35

WESSON Will you stick to me, Barbara?

BARBARA Oh, did it want to be stuck to? It shall then—Oh, its nice hair!

WESSON Till death do us part—°

BARBARA Aw, is it talking about death, is it—aw!

WESSON It's ten past six. What train did your mother say—the five   40
to six?

BARBARA (*starting*) No, half past seven.

WESSON The six train has just gone.

BARBARA Are you frightened?

WESSON No—no—I'm not frightened. Only we're rather raw, really,   45
about the business. It seems funny that we're a scandal.

BARBARA Doesn't it!

WESSON I'll go and look if I can see anybody, shall I?

BARBARA Yes! Kiss me first. (*He kisses her*)

> *Exit Wesson. Barbara sits up, straightening her hair. She is in*   50
> *Bavarian peasant dress, with bare arms and throat. Wesson comes*
> *running in*

WESSON I don't think it's she—but there *is* a woman—

BARBARA Good gracious—and look at us! (*She flies out—her voice is*
heard, excited) Yes—it's she. Quick!   55

WESSON Well, I must get my collar on first.

> *In a great flurry, he ties his tie, then runs out. The stage is empty.*
> *Then voices are heard*

VOICE OF BARBARA Poor Mama!

> *They both laugh—there is silence. The door-bell rings loudly.*   60
> *Barbara rushes in and stands near the door. Wesson is heard*
> *outside*

VOICE OF WESSON Oh, how do you do! This is earlier than we thought.

VOICE OF LADY CHARLCOTE How do you do, Mr Wesson?

> *Enter Lady Charlcote—about sixty—white hair, shortish, stout,*   65
> *rather handsome—looks resentful—uglily dressed*

BARBARA Oh—Mama!

> *Runs forward, laughing shakily—does not kiss—takes her*
> *mother's hand—then stands embarrassed*

LADY CHARLCOTE (*looking round*) Yes—   70

BARBARA Take your things off—

LADY CHARLCOTE But I mustn't stay—I mustn't stay. (*Taking off her*
gloves—nervous) I want to say to you, Mr Wesson, why don't you do
something for Barbara?

WESSON (*astonished*) But I do.   75

LADY CHARLCOTE But you don't. A married woman, and you keep her
here with you as she is. It is wrong, quite wrong.

WESSON But you don't know—you don't understand.

LADY CHARLCOTE Yes, yes, I do understand. It is you who don't under-
    stand. What right have you to do it? Barbara has a husband in   80
    England, a good honest gentleman, who is going mad because of
    her. She is here, but she can go back.

BARBARA But, Mama, what I do, I do of myself. (*She is crocheting
    nervously*)

LADY CHARLCOTE Yes. (*Turning to Wesson*) You have not got even   85
    enough money to keep her. She has to have money from her sister,
    from her friends. She is the daughter of a high-born and highly
    cultured gentleman.

BARBARA But if I choose to do it, Mama, it is my own affair.

LADY CHARLCOTE No, it isn't. Think of your father—think of   90
    Frederick. (*Turning to Wesson*) And do you expect to build up hap-
    piness on the ruins of this life? You cannot. Think of your future. You
    can do nothing with my daughter. You can't put her in her own
    station, you can't even give her an honest name. Is she to live with
    you, and take money from her husband and her friends?   95

WESSON She needn't take any money from anybody.

LADY CHARLCOTE And you say you will live here. You try it for six
    months, Mr Wesson, and you will wish yourself dead, you will find it
    so dull. And Barbara is to be the servant, and she is to have no friends,
    no, not a friend in the world, but is to live buried here among these   100
    common Italians. Another man's wedding ring and engagement ring
    on her finger at this minute. The very bills of her last dresses left for
    her husband to pay.

BARBARA But, Mama, I'm not a horse that is to be kept. You don't
    consider me.   105

LADY CHARLCOTE Yes, it is you I consider. How can any man say he
    loves you, when he brings you into this shame. Where will you live?

WESSON But if there were a divorce—

LADY CHARLCOTE (*to him*) You think only of yourself. Think of her
    father. He is getting old now. Where will he go, that he can hold his   110
    head up? It is a shame that will kill him. It will kill everybody.
    (*Beginning to cry—looking in her handbag for a hanky*) We are old, and
    hoped to live at last in peace. Haven't we had trouble enough in our
    lives? And how can I sleep at night, thinking of my daughter, and
    what is to become of her? Her father does not want to see her again.   115
    (*Cries*) There is no rest, and no peace. Her husband comes, and it
    nearly kills me to see the state he is in. A woman—what is to become
    of her, what is to become of her. And you keep her here.

WESSON No—I don't keep her.

LADY CHARLCOTE Yes, you keep her here—the daughter of a highly   120
cultured gentleman, as your mistress. It is impossible. And her
husband is so good. He will have her back in spite of all, and
everything can be hushed up—

BARBARA I don't want things to be hushed up. What I do I want to be
done openly—   125

LADY CHARLCOTE Don't be a fool—you can't live on ideas.

WESSON No—I don't want people to talk—

LADY CHARLCOTE But they *will* talk. Sir William and I have come
out here because they've started—and his heart so bad! We expect
to be considered by our children, but they turn on us. It's not   130
natural that we should have all this trouble now, when we're not
expecting it. Everything begins to look comfortable, and Barbara so
well settled, when this happens. As her mother, as a woman older
than yourself, I've *got* to tell you it's wrong, absolutely wrong, and
can only end in sorrow. You will see in a few years' time where you   135
will be. It is my duty to warn you. And you must let Barbara go back
with me.

> *Wesson shakes his head—Barbara crochets nervously—there
> is silence*

BARBARA Has Papa come with you, then?   140

LADY CHARLCOTE Yes—we're staying a month with Laura in Gardone.°

WESSON (*rising*) Let me give you something to eat.

LADY CHARLCOTE No—no—I must be going at once. I must be going.
It's such a long way to the station.

WESSON Excuse me.   145

> *Exit Wesson*

BARBARA (*quietly*) How does Frederick look?

LADY CHARLCOTE Oh, poor fellow! If you saw him, you could never
do it.

BARBARA (*bending her head over her work*) Is he ill?   150

LADY CHARLCOTE Ill!—poor fellow! He is three parts mad! And he
loves you, Barbara, he loves you! How can you throw away the love of
a man like that?

BARBARA Does he really want *me*, or does he want his reputation—or
rather mine?   155

LADY CHARLCOTE Poor fellow—such a position to leave him in. And
has he ever been anything but good to you? You have had everything
you wanted—

BARBARA I haven't. He *has* been good to me—I wish he hadn't, it would
have been easier. He has been good to me, and he's given me   160

everything he could. But I haven't had what I wanted, no, and he couldn't give it me.

LADY CHARLCOTE And do you mean that this man can?

Barbara crochets in silence—they wait for each other

BARBARA Will it kill him?   165

LADY CHARLCOTE I tell him, at this rate he won't live long.

Enter Wesson with a tray, wine, biscuits, bread and butter

WESSON Will you have a glass of wine—it's 'vin du pays',° but it's—at any rate, it's all right for me, though I'm no connoisseur.

LADY CHARLCOTE No, thank you.   170

WESSON Could I make you a cup of tea?

LADY CHARLCOTE Oh no, thank you very much.

BARBARA Is Papa in Gardone?

LADY CHARLCOTE In Brescia°—but he doesn't want to see you. Oh, thank you°—But he expects you to come back in a proper state of 175
mind—I think it's all you can do, to make the best of it now. This *is* impossible. (*Neither of them answers*) And we are staying at the Monte Baldo. You will write to me, Barbara.

BARBARA Yes. Good-bye, Mama. (*They shake hands*)

LADY CHARLCOTE Good-bye. (*To Wesson*) Oh, don't you trouble to 180
come out.

WESSON I think it is no good for Barbara to go back to Frederick. It would only be misery for them both. They can't—

*Exit talking. Barbara remains alone. Her hands fall in her lap,
and she broods. There is sound of a carriage—re-enter Wesson—* 185
*he flings his cap on the table. When Barbara hears him coming
she picks up her crocheting. When he enters she looks up with a
laugh*

BARBARA Poor Mama—always full of commonsense. She was always a good one at showing the sensible side of the affair. But didn't it 190
seem common to you—like any of the women of the common people you've told me about?

WESSON Just. Only it's natural. At any rate she wasn't lofty.

BARBARA Oh no—Mama would never have been that. She would have said just the same to a Grand Duke.   195

WESSON She wouldn't—look at the money business. You *don't* need any of their money—we *can* live on what I earn.

BARBARA And *I* don't mind making your bed. I wouldn't do it for any man—no, I wouldn't. But I don't mind.

WESSON If I can't give you much money, well, I give you everything 200
I've got.

BARBARA Yes, it was mean of her, bringing that up—it's like kicking a
man when he's down.

WESSON But I suppose anybody would do it. She doesn't seem
superior, that's one thing. But I hate them! Why can't they leave us   205
alone! What do I care what the old Mrs Baronet says.

BARBARA (*laughing*) You looked as if you didn't care—the way you sat
in that chair. (*Imitates him, half crouching*)

WESSON Well—that coming all at once—

BARBARA When we'd been so happy—yes, it *was* a bit overwhelming!   210

WESSON I thought the heavens had opened and the last day come.

BARBARA You looked it—the way you sat crumpled up in that chair.
(*Laughs*)

WESSON What could I do?

BARBARA (*laughing*) You looked so frightened, so crumpled up! I   215
expected you every minute to wither away into nothing. (*Laughs uncontrollably*) I thought there'd be nothing left of you. (*Interrupted by
her laughter*) You—you seemed to get less and less—till— (*Helpless
with laughter*) I thought you'd be gone. (*Laughing*) I was frightened—
I wanted to get hold of your coat-tails (*Laugh*) to keep you.   220

WESSON Well, what could I *do*?

BARBARA I thought you were going to creep under that desk. (*Shaking
and helpless with laughter, she points to the hole under the writing desk, by
which he sits*) I thought you were going to crawl inside like a dog into a
kennel (*Helpless laughter*) and pop your head out, and look sideways   225
at her, and say 'Yap—yap' in a little, frightened voice—then rush
inside.

WESSON Well—if she'd been a man, I might have shouted—but what
else could I do?

BARBARA You looked so crumpled up, with your little tail between your   230
legs. (*Laughs*) You *did* want to get into that corner. (*Laughs help-
lessly—then rises*) Mind, let me show you. (*Laughing, she almost falls to
the floor, then creeps inside the space under the desk—pokes out her
head—falls face forward on the floor with laughter—lifts up her face,
peering sideways*) Yap—yapyap! Yap!—the little dog! (*She shrieks with*   235
laughter—he giggles from time to time—she rises again)

WESSON No—I wasn't as bad as that.

BARBARA (*shrieking*) You were, you were! I thought I should have died.
And every minute I had visions of you collapsing under the desk and
barking at Mama. (*Laughing*) Poor Mama, what would she have done   240
if you had?

WESSON I wish I had.

BARBARA I wish you had, I wish you had! (*Drying her eyes*) But no, you
sat there getting less and less. You can go so little, like a dying pig.

WESSON Well, *you* were impressed, you know you were.   245

BARBARA I wasn't—I wanted to scream. Why didn't you suddenly get
up and flap your arms like a cockerel and crow?

WESSON But what good would it have done?

BARBARA It would have been so beautiful. Or you might have got
astride on a chair and gone riding round the room, shouting.   250

WESSON I might have done a lot of things.

BARBARA Oh, you might, and you did nothing but crumple up! What a
pity! (*Beginning to laugh again*) You looked anything but a hero that
time.

WESSON I didn't feel a hero. And if I'd crowed like a cock I shouldn't   255
have looked a hero.

BARBARA Mama little thought what havoc she'd work in our little
ménage. (*Laughing*) But why do you take it so seriously?

WESSON I don't take it seriously, but I reckon it's rather rotten of her. We
thought she was coming friendlily, to help. . . . What will you eat?   260

BARBARA I don't mind a bit.

WESSON (*drinking wine*) Drink?

BARBARA Thank you. (*She drinks a little*)

WESSON I told her the only thing possible was a divorce.

BARBARA You know what a muddler she is. She blows with every wind.   265

WESSON I don't care how she blows, so long as we can get that divorce.

BARBARA If she goes and gets Frederick's back up now, God knows
when you'll get it, I tell you.

WESSON I don't care—they can all go to hell! But until you stand up in
front of me and say, 'I want definitely to go back to Frederick—you're 270
no good to me', I shall tell them to go to blazes.

BARBARA It looks as if you'll tell them a lot. Poor little dog, is his tail
coming up again? Come here and be kissed.

WESSON I don't want to be kissed. Will you eat now?

BARBARA Just as you like.   275

WESSON A tray is ready.
          Goes out—returns immediately with the supper tray

BARBARA Poor Frederick—it does twist my inside to think about him.

WESSON And a lot of good may it do you.

BARBARA Do you think he really might go mad?   280

WESSON Not unless he's weak-minded to start with.

BARBARA Well, he isn't—his mind is stronger than yours, if it came
to it.

WESSON (*rather ashamed*) I know he's not—and he won't go mad.

BARBARA But he loves me so. (*Plaintively*)   285

WESSON He should have more sense, then, for you don't love *him*.

BARBARA But I do, Giacomo.

WESSON Very well, you *do*, then.

BARBARA And I can't bear him to suffer.

WESSON You made him suffer worse underneath, twisting your   290
spear in his secret wound, before you left him, than you do now that
it's open. He can doctor an open wound. A secret one drives him
mad.

BARBARA But I didn't torture him. I was a joy to him. And think of it,
Giacomo, I was the only joy he'd ever had in his life.   295

WESSON And the only sorrow.

BARBARA Why do you want to say horrid things about me?

WESSON I don't.

BARBARA But you do! Look, you say I tortured Frederick.

WESSON So you did. So you torture me.   300

BARBARA But how?—tell me *how*, Giacomo.

WESSON You needn't laugh at me when I'm feeling a fool.

BARBARA You hate me, Giacomo.

WESSON Does it please you?

BARBARA Why should it please me? Why *should* it please me, Giacomo?   305

WESSON It appears to. You seem to exult.

BARBARA I exult because you wither away when Mama scolds you!
I assure you I don't exult in your heroic appearance *then*.

WESSON I don't ask you to.

BARBARA What does he want then—does he want me to fall at his feet   310
and worship him, does he then? (*She does so—goes on her knees at
his feet, puts her forehead to the ground—raises it up and down—in
a consoling, mocking voice*) La—di-da—di-da!—did it want to be
worshipped?

WESSON (*seizing her by the arm*) Get up, you lunatic.   315

BARBARA But don't you like to be worshipped?

WESSON (*gripping her arm*) Get up.
          She rises slowly—he grips both her arms
     You love! You love only *yourself*!

BARBARA (*putting her tongue out at him*) Tra—la-la—la!   320

WESSON Yes.

BARBARA Tra—la-la—la! (*He remains holding her—she says, almost
pleading*) Let me go.

WESSON I won't.

BARBARA I'll make you.   325
WESSON Try!
BARBARA I *will*!
WESSON Try! (*A moment of silence*)
BARBARA (*subduedly*) You hurt my arms.
WESSON (*through his teeth*) And why shouldn't I?   330
BARBARA Don't be horrid.
        Wesson puts his arms round her, fastens her close
WESSON Oh, you're not faithful to me!
        His voice is like a cry. He reaches forward, his mouth to her throat
BARBARA (*thickly*) I am.   335
        CURTAIN

Act 3 Scene 1

Morning, the next day. Barbara in walking-out dress, Wesson in an old jacket

BARBARA What time did the man say Mama would be here?

WESSON I understood she would come for you in a carriage at ten o'clock.

BARBARA And did she really say you mustn't come?

WESSON She said she wished to drive alone with you.

BARBARA Put your coat on and come, too.

WESSON No—perhaps she wants to talk to you, and to have you to her-self a bit. It's natural. You needn't do anything that you don't want to do.

BARBARA Why *should* she ask me for a drive without *you*? It's like her impudence—I *won't* go!

WESSON Yes, you'd better.

BARBARA You'd say I'd better do any miserable thing they liked to ask me.

WESSON All right.

BARBARA Why don't you say I *oughtn't* to go for a drive with Mama without you?

WESSON Because I don't care—your mother can use all her persuasions and reasons till she's sick of it.

BARBARA But why should she?

WESSON It's probably the shortest way, if we stick to ourselves all through.

BARBARA A fine lot of sticking to yourself you do, don't you? Think of the shrivelling creature whom Mama scolded yesterday.

WESSON I *was* true to myself, then—and to you.

BARBARA Were you—were you! Then I'll have another kind of fidelity, thank you.

WESSON You won't. And now you'd better go.

BARBARA Go!

WESSON For your drive. You'll find Lady Charlcote before you get to the Piazza.

BARBARA And if I don't choose to?

WESSON (*shrugging*) You'll please yourself.

BARBARA Tra—la-la—la!

WESSON I wish you'd go.

BARBARA Why do you wish I'd go? I will, then.

    Exit—the door is heard to bang. Wesson watches her

WESSON There goes the carriage, and the old lady. I should like to   40
murder the twopence-ha'penny lot of them, with their grizzling and
whining and chuffing. If they'd leave us alone we should be all right—
damn them! Miserable bits of shouters! My mother was worth
a million of 'em, for they've none of 'em the backbone of a flea—
She doesn't *want* to stick to me—she doesn't *want* to love me—she   45
won't *let* herself love me. She wants to save some rotten rag of
independence—she's afraid to let herself go and to belong to me.

    He goes to the sideboard, drinks wine, looks at a book, throws it
    down, plays a dozen chords on the piano, gets up, drinks more
    wine, sits down to write, and remains perfectly still, as if   50
    transfixed—all the time he has moved quietly—the door-bell
    rings—he does not hear—it rings louder—he starts up and goes to
    the door—is heard saying, 'How do you do? Will you come in?'
    Enter Sir William Charlcote—short, stout, a gentleman—grey
    bristling moustache   55

WESSON Will you sit down?

SIR WILLIAM (*taking a seat near the door*) Thank you.

WESSON (*offering cigarettes in a threepenny packet*) Excuse the packet.

SIR WILLIAM Thank you, I have some of my own.

    Wesson throws the packet on the table and sits on the couch   60

WESSON It's a nice day.

SIR WILLIAM Yes. (*Clearing his throat*) I called to hear from yourself an
account of what you intend to do.

WESSON (*knitting his fingers*) I intend to do nothing but what I am doing.

SIR WILLIAM And what is that?   65

WESSON Living here—working—

SIR WILLIAM And keeping my daughter under the present conditions?

WESSON Barbara stays as long as she will. I am here for her while she
wants me.

SIR WILLIAM But you have no right to be here for her to want.   70

WESSON But I say, while ever she wants me, I am here for her.

SIR WILLIAM Don't you see that is cowardly and base.

WESSON Is it the morality of it you want to discuss?

SIR WILLIAM Yes—yes—it is the *right* of it. You may perhaps think
I have no room to talk. That is like your damned impudence.   75

WESSON But that's not the point.

SIR WILLIAM A man has a right to any woman whom he can get, so long
as she's not a married woman. Go with all the unmarried women you
like. But touch a married woman, and you are a scoundrel.

WESSON So!   80

SIR WILLIAM It destroys the whole family system, and strikes at the whole of society. A man who does it is as much a criminal as a thief, a burglar, or even a murderer. You see my point?

WESSON Your point of view.

SIR WILLIAM You see so much. Then you see what you are doing: a   85
criminal act against the State, against the rights of man altogether, against Dr Tressider, and against my daughter.

WESSON So!

SIR WILLIAM And seeing *that*, only an—only a criminal by conviction can continue in what he is doing—a fellow who deserves to be locked   90
up.

WESSON If life went according to deserts.

SIR WILLIAM If you intend to behave in the least like a man, you will clear out of this place—

WESSON I've got the house on a six months' lease.   95

SIR WILLIAM I will pay the lease.

WESSON It is paid—but I like the place, and prefer to stay.

SIR WILLIAM That is, you will continue to keep my daughter in— in—in this shame and scandal—

WESSON She chooses to stay.   100

SIR WILLIAM If plain reasoning will not convince you, we must try other methods.

WESSON Very well.

SIR WILLIAM You—whom I thought to be doing a service by asking you to my house—   105
> *The bell rings*

WESSON (*rising*) Excuse me a moment.
> *Exit—voices—enter Barbara, followed by Lady Charlcote and Wesson*

BARBARA Papa!   110

SIR WILLIAM I came to speak with this man.

BARBARA But why behind my back?

SIR WILLIAM I will come when I like. I will not have women, and especially women like you, about me when I have anything to say.

BARBARA Nor more will I have men like you interfering with my affairs   115
behind my back, Papa!

LADY CHARLCOTE For shame, Barbara.

BARBARA (*turning, flashing*) What right has he to come bullying Wesson behind my back. *I* came away with him—it was *I* who suggested he should come to Italy with me when I was coming to see Laura. So   120
when you have anything to say, Papa, say it to me—if you dare.

SIR WILLIAM Dare! Dare!

BARBARA Whom are you talking to, Papa—and you of all people! I did not love Frederick, and I won't live with him—so there—and you may go.   125

SIR WILLIAM (*picking up his hat*) I never want to see you again.

LADY CHARLCOTE Barbara, you should respect your father.

BARBARA Mama—you—you—then let him respect *me*, and the man I live with.

      Exit Sir William   130

LADY CHARLCOTE What has he said?

WESSON It does not matter.

LADY CHARLCOTE Well—now you must make the best of your own affairs—for you've cut off all your own people from you, Barbara.

BARBARA I have *not* cut myself off—it's you who have left me in the   135
lurch. I was miserable with Frederick. I felt I couldn't stand it. *You* would have helped me to have had lovers, Mama. But because I come away decently and openly you all turn on me.

LADY CHARLCOTE You know it is impossible—

BARBARA Very well, I will *be* impossible!   140

LADY CHARLCOTE I shall never leave you in the lurch. (*Crying*) You are my daughter, whatever happens.

      Exit—Wesson hurries to the door after her—it is heard to close—
      he returns

BARBARA Why do you let them trample on you? *Why* do you play the   145
poor worm? It drives me *mad*!

WESSON But you don't want me to insult your father.

BARBARA But why do you let yourself be bullied and treated like dirt?

WESSON I don't.

BARBARA You do—you do—and I *hate* you for it.   150

WESSON Very well. (*She sits down on the couch, twisting her handkerchief. He seats himself beside her and takes her hand*) Never mind, they'll get over it.

BARBARA Papa won't—and I have loved him so.

WESSON He will.   155

BARBARA He won't! Oh, but I hate him—a mean funker! But he always was a funker. He had his Selma on the sly, and when Mama found him out—it positively broke him. What did he say to you?

WESSON He explained his point of view, which seems to me perfectly logical.   160

BARBARA And I suppose you agreed with him?

WESSON No; I didn't agree with him—only I understood.

BARBARA And you cringed to him, I know you did.

WESSON I don't think so.

BARBARA And now they've left me.   165

WESSON Never mind—they can slam at us, but we can stand it.

BARBARA But it's so horrible—and I have to fight for you, as if you weren't a man.

WESSON I don't think you have any need.

BARBARA Yes, but I have—and all the burden falls on me—you don't   170 take your share.

WESSON Surely I do! Never mind, I know it's horrid for you. But you will stick to me, won't you?

BARBARA I didn't think it would be so hard—I have to fight you, and them, and everybody. Not a soul in the world gives me the tiniest bit   175 of help.

WESSON That's only because you feel rotten. I love you, Barbara.

BARBARA Doesn't it make you hate me, all this horridness?

WESSON Why should it? I don't care what comes, so that we get a little closer.   180

BARBARA But it's worth it, isn't it, Giacomo?—say I'm worth it.

WESSON (putting his arms round her and kissing her) You're the only thing in life and in the world that I've got—you are.

BARBARA Are you sure?

WESSON I've got my work, which isn't life. Then there's nothing else   185 but you—not a thing—and if you leave me—well, I've done.

BARBARA How do you mean, done?

WESSON Only my effort at life. I shall feel as if I had made my big effort—put all my money down—and lost. The only thing remaining would be to go on and make the best of it.   190

BARBARA I suppose that's how Frederick feels.

WESSON I suppose it is—if only he would get a grip on and try to make the best of it.

BARBARA But it's not so easy.

WESSON No, it isn't, poor devil. But if he's got to do it, he may as well.   195

BARBARA Oh, do you love me enough, Giacomo?

WESSON I love you enough for whatever you want me for.

BARBARA Sure?

WESSON Sure! The question is, do you love me enough?

BARBARA I love you better than you love me.   200

WESSON Take your hat off, I can't kiss you.

BARBARA (obediently removing her hat) Mama told me Papa was coming—I was furious, it seemed such a mean dodge. They are mean, though, and sordid. Did he say horrid things to you?

WESSON He said he'd thrash me.   205

BARBARA (*laughing*) Fancy little Papa!

WESSON Are you miserable? Are you sorry you're done out of your
drive?

BARBARA No, I'm thankful to be back with you. If *only* they left us in
peace, we could be so happy.   210

WESSON They seem to grudge it us, don't they?

BARBARA Yes! And Mama says perhaps Frederick's coming.

WESSON At any rate we s'll have had 'em all, then.

BARBARA But I couldn't bear to see him, Giacomo!

WESSON Then don't see him.   215

BARBARA But he might do something mad.

WESSON Let him.

BARBARA No—I couldn't bear it. I couldn't bear it if anything happened to him.

WESSON Why *should* anything happen to him?   220

BARBARA And what would he do if he saw me? Would he go quite mad?

WESSON You're not such a magical person as all that.

BARBARA But you don't know him.

WESSON Quite sufficiently.

BARBARA Isn't it funny—when I was first engaged to him, and was   225
reading *Othello*, I thought what a good Othello he'd make, better than
the real one.

WESSON You feel sure he'll slay you, poor Desdemona.

BARBARA (*laughing*) Yes—he's so Othelloish.

WESSON And you so Desdemoniacal, aren't you?   230

BARBARA (*laughing*) What does that mean?

WESSON It means you sit sighing by a sycamore tree,° you poor soul.

BARBARA (*kissing him*) Oh, I love you!

WESSON Do you?

CURTAIN   235

Act 3 Scene 2

Evening of the same day. Wesson sits alone, writing. Enter
Barbara, resplendent in an evening dress, with ornament in
her hair. She stands in the doorway, looking across at herself
in a mirror

BARBARA You've never seen me in this before. (*He looks up—puts his pen*   5
between his teeth—she preens herself)

WESSON (*after a moment*) I hate it.

BARBARA (*hurt*) But why?—I look nice. Don't I look nice?

WESSON I hate it—I hate it—you belong to those others in it.

BARBARA But how nasty of you, Giacometti! It's only the dress—the   10
woman is just the same.

WESSON She's not. She's according to her frock, which is Frederick's.
You put it on for Frederick, not for me.

BARBARA I didn't. I want you to see how grand I can look. Don't you
really think I look nice?   15

WESSON No—I'd rather see you in your kitchen pinafore.

BARBARA See how you want to drag me down. But you've got an
evening suit. (*Laughing*) Does it really hurt you? (*Sits down and*
begins to play a dance on the piano—it is the 'Blue Danube'°—she breaks
off) It's the dearest dress I ever had.   20

WESSON Take it off, Barbara.

BARBARA (*slowing down—she is very quiet*) Yes.
Rises—exit slowly. He sits chewing his pen—in a moment she
rushes back, lays her hands on his shoulder

BARBARA There's Frederick!   25

WESSON Rubbish!—Where?

BARBARA At the gate—with Mama—I saw them from the bedroom
window.
Lady Charlcote's voice is heard calling 'Barbara!'

BARBARA Quick! I'll call to them from the window *I'm* coming—   30
I will—(*Moves to the window*)

WESSON What's the good? Let them go away again.

BARBARA I'll call now—

WESSON Damn!
He moves grudgingly to the door. Barbara stands with her hands   35
clasped over her bare breast, terrified—listening. The gate is
heard to bang open—voices—enter Frederick, alone—a haggard,
handsome man of forty, brown moustache, dark brown eyes,
greying at the temples. He hesitates at the door

FREDERICK (*ironically*) May I come in?   40

BARBARA (*frightened*) What do you want?

FREDERICK Merely permission to speak to you.

BARBARA You know you may speak to me.

       They hesitate—enter Wesson, followed by Lady Charlcote

WESSON Barbara, do you want me to go with Lady Charlcote to the   45
Hotel Cervo for half an hour?

BARBARA I don't know. (*Sinks on to the couch*)

WESSON You must *tell* me to go.

       Dr Tressider looks at him sideways and shows his teeth, but does
       not speak—Barbara watches the two men in terror   50

BARBARA Perhaps you'd better go—Mama can stay with me.

LADY CHARLCOTE I think Frederick has the right to speak to you alone,
Barbara.

BARBARA (*almost whispering*) But why—?

FREDERICK Are you afraid that I may abduct you?   55

LADY CHARLCOTE No, Frederick, I don't think it is fair to leave her
alone with you.

FREDERICK (*nastily*) Don't you? Perhaps it isn't safe—

LADY CHARLCOTE You might not be responsible for what you did.

FREDERICK So the only place for me is the lunatic asylum.   60

BARBARA If you are like that, Frederick, I don't know what you can
want to speak to me at all for.

FREDERICK It *is* a question for surprise.

BARBARA I'd much rather you *did* treat me as dirt, and left me alone.

WESSON Will you sit down, Lady Charlcote?   65

FREDERICK (*to Wesson*) Will you please take yourself away, while I speak
to my wife?

BARBARA Yes, go, Wesson.

LADY CHARLCOTE I would go for a few minutes, Mr Wesson. It can't do
you any harm. Things will settle themselves then.   70

WESSON (*to Barbara*) Must I?

BARBARA Only to the—to one of the other rooms.

WESSON I'll go to the bedroom, then.

       Exit sullenly

FREDERICK (*taking a seat*) I'm glad you look so well, Barbara.   75

LADY CHARLCOTE You won't do any good that way, Frederick.

FREDERICK (*turning slowly to her*) Perhaps you'll tell me what to say!

LADY CHARLCOTE You needn't behave like a fool, at any rate.

BARBARA I'm afraid you've been ill, Frederick.

FREDERICK Yes—I am ill! I am glad to see you are so well.   80

BARBARA Don't, Frederick—what *is* the good of this—what *is* the good
of it? Let us make the best we can now—

FREDERICK Exactly!

BARBARA Then the only sane thing would be to say what you came to
say and let us get it over.   85

FREDERICK I came for your instructions, of course.

BARBARA It seems rather stupid, don't you think?

FREDERICK I've no doubt I always was stupid—a trusting fool—

BARBARA You know it wasn't like that. Do you really wish to speak
to me?   90

FREDERICK Yes, I think I can honestly say I do. It, no doubt, surprises
you.

BARBARA Then for God's sake don't torture me any longer.

FREDERICK It *would* be a pity! But what I have to say I have to say to my
wife, not to the world at large, or even to my mother-in-law, or your   95
paramour.

BARBARA Perhaps you *had* better leave us alone, Mama.

FREDERICK Hadn't you better consider again, Barbara? Wouldn't that
be giving me too much encouragement? I might take a liberty. I might
even ask you to gallivant with me, like a seductive footman, or   100
dustman. (*There is silence*)

LADY CHARLCOTE I can go into another room. (*Making signs to Barbara*) Where can I go, Barbara?

> *Barbara rises—they go out together—Frederick looks round—*
> *gnaws the ends of his moustache. Re-enter Barbara—she leaves*   105
> *the door open—he glances, sees it, but makes no remark*

BARBARA (*taking her former seat*) Mama is in my bedroom.

FREDERICK Anything to say to me?

BARBARA Don't be horrid with me, Frederick. I *know* I deserve it—

FREDERICK I'll try not to be. (*He sits devouring her with his eyes*) You're   110
in full-dress to-night, madam! Was it a great occasion?

BARBARA No—I put it on—it's the first time.

FREDERICK You look the thing in it. I turned up to see you on your
mettle, by good luck.

BARBARA Don't.   115

FREDERICK Beautiful good luck. War-paint, I suppose!

BARBARA You told me once you'd never be hard on a woman.

FREDERICK I'm sorry if I'm hard on you—that *would* be unjust!

BARBARA Don't talk like that—Frederick.

FREDERICK What shall we talk about—you or me?   120

BARBARA Tell me about yourself—

FREDERICK Ha!—How I suffered, you mean?

BARBARA I know it's been awful for you.

FREDERICK Do you really—I shouldn't have thought it.

BARBARA Oh, but I do! It's nearly driven me cracked sometimes.   125

FREDERICK Ha! It was kind of you.

BARBARA (*going forward impulsively and putting her hand on his knee*) Don't—

FREDERICK I won't—but tell me what—I must—

BARBARA Don't be like this—I can't bear it.   130

FREDERICK You might tell me what you can bear.

BARBARA Why can't you cast me off—why can't you find some other woman—there's Annabel, who adores you—or Lizzie Burroughs—

FREDERICK You think they'd make good successors to you?

BARBARA You might love them better than me—you might! See, I was   135
not faithful to you.

FREDERICK (*laughing*) I wouldn't rub it in, if I were you.

BARBARA (*frightened*) But I'm not!

FREDERICK So you think I might do well to marry again?

BARBARA I thought—I can't bear—to think of you being lonely.   140

FREDERICK And you'd give me a wedding present, I dare say, and give
the woman advice how to fool me.

BARBARA No—no—I won't let you say these things—

FREDERICK I dare say. You were wasted on me, weren't you?

BARBARA You were *good* to me—but you never understood me—   145

FREDERICK I'm sorry! I understood you wanted a decent life, and I
worked hard for you. I understood you wanted some amusement—
you did exactly as you liked—you had everything I had—and had
your own way. I was faithful to you from the day I saw you—and
before that. You might have called me a model husband. I suppose   150
that was my fault.

BARBARA (*crying*) No—it wasn't your fault to be a good husband—
that's why I love you still—in a way—you were so good to me—
but—you weren't near to me—

FREDERICK I think I was as near as ever you'd let me come.   155

BARBARA No—no—can't you remember—when we were first married
—I thought marriage would be a jolly thing—I thought I could have
lovely games with the man. Can you remember, when I climbed to
the top of the cupboard, in Lucerne? I thought you'd look for me,
and laugh, and fetch me down. No, you were terrified. You daren't   160
even come in the room. You stood in the door looking frightened
to death. And I climbed down. And that's how it always was. I had to
climb down.

FREDERICK And so you left me?

BARBARA Yes! I couldn't live with you.   165

FREDERICK Because I didn't drag you by the ankle from the cupboard
    tops!

BARBARA Yes—that's it.

FREDERICK And how long did it take you to find this out?

BARBARA You know very well that I was only introduced to Wesson   170
    about a month before—you knew all about it.

FREDERICK And may I inquire after the predecessors of this clown?

BARBARA Yourself.

FREDERICK I enjoy that honour alone, do I—with the miserable
    clown—   175

BARBARA You were not going to speak of him.

FREDERICK And pray, when did you find out then that I had not—not
    found the real *you*.

BARBARA The first night of our marriage—when I stood on that bal-
    cony and wanted to drown myself—and you were asleep.   180

FREDERICK And afterwards—I suppose you forgot it?

BARBARA Sometimes. You were good to me—and I didn't think then
    there *could* be anything else.

FREDERICK Than what?

BARBARA Than going on as I was—as your wife.   185

FREDERICK And you *never* loved me?

BARBARA Sometimes—when you were so nice to me—

FREDERICK Out of gratitude, as it were, and feeling you *ought* to love me.

BARBARA I always felt I ought to love you.

FREDERICK But could never bring it off. Ha!—thank you for the try, at   190
    any rate.

BARBARA And of course sometimes I hated you.

FREDERICK Naturally.

BARBARA And now it's over.

FREDERICK As you say—it's over.   195
    There is a long silence

FREDERICK (*in a sudden outburst*) Woman, do you know I've given my
    life to you? Do you know, everything I did, everything I thought,
    everywhere I went, was for you? I have worked till I reeled, I was so
    tired. I have been your slave—   200

BARBARA That's it—I didn't want you to be my slave—

FREDERICK I—I—I have done everything. How often have I asked you,
    'What do you want of me?' Why didn't you tell me then? Why didn't
    you say? Why have you deceived me all this while, letting me think
    you loved me?   205

BARBARA I didn't deceive you; (*Crying*) I didn't know myself.

FREDERICK How many times have you had your arms round my neck, and said, 'Do you love me?'—I might well answer, '*Malheureusement*.'° What was that but deceit—

BARBARA It wasn't lying to you, Frederick—you *did* love me, and   210
I wanted you to love me—

FREDERICK What right had you to want me to love you, when you cared not a couple of straws about me?

BARBARA I *did* want you to love me—you were all I had—

FREDERICK Until another came along, and then you threw my love   215
away like a piece of dirty paper wrapping.

BARBARA No—no—I didn't!

FREDERICK What else have you done? You have thrown me away like a bit of paper off a parcel. You got all the goods out of the packet, and threw me away—I gave you everything, my life, everything,   220
and it is not worth the stump of a cigarette, when it comes to—I tell you, this is the end of me. I could work then, but now my brain has gone.

BARBARA No, Frederick, no—you will work again.

FREDERICK I tell you I can no more work now than you can row a boat   225
when you have lost the oars. I am done for—as a man you see me here a ruin. Some nights I sleep, some nights I never close my eyes. I force myself to keep sane. But in the end my brain will go—and then I shall make an end—

BARBARA (*going over to him, kneeling with her hand on his knee, crying*)   230
No—no, Frederick—no—no!

FREDERICK Then I shall go to Wood Norton°—do you remember, where I saw you first—a girl of eighteen with a sash? I shall go to that pine wood where the little grove of larches is, and I shall make an end.

BARBARA (*her head on his knee—weeping*) Oh, what can I do—what can   235
I do?

FREDERICK I've no doubt it all sounds very melodramatic—but it's the truth for me. Then your work will be finished. I have loved you. I would have spilt my blood on every paving stone in Bromley for you, if you had wanted me to—   240

BARBARA But I didn't want you to. I wanted you to come near to me and make me yours and you be mine. But you went on worshipping me instead of loving me—kissing my feet instead of helping me. You put me on a pedestal, and I was miserable.

FREDERICK And you never loved me all the time!   245

BARBARA I did love you—I did love you!

FREDERICK (*his fists clenched—shuddering*) I could strangle you!

BARBARA (*terrified*) Don't—don't—I shall scream! (*She gets up afraid and draws back. He gets hold of one of her arms*)

FREDERICK You devil—you devil—you devil! But you belong to me, do   250
you hear?—you belong to me!

BARBARA (*pushing him away*) Don't—don't—let me go—I shall call
Mama—oh—

> *He releases her—she flings herself face down on the sofa—he sits
> crouching, glaring. Silence for some time*   255

FREDERICK Well, have you been there long enough?

BARBARA (*sitting up*) Yes—long enough to know that it never was any
good, and it never would be any good.

FREDERICK 'It never was any good, and never would be any good'—
what?   260

BARBARA You and me.

FREDERICK You and me! Do you mean to tell me that my life has been a
lie and a falsity?

BARBARA Why?

FREDERICK *You* were my life—you—and you say it was never any good   265
between us.

BARBARA But you had your work. Think, if you had to choose between
me and your work.

FREDERICK You might as well ask an apple-tree to choose between
enjoying the sunshine and growing its own apples: the one depends   270
on the other and is the result of the other.

BARBARA No, Frederick. Why, look how happy you could be with your
work when I was miserable.

FREDERICK But you had no reason to be. I gave you everything you
asked for. What did you want?   275

BARBARA I suppose I wanted something you could not give.

FREDERICK (*glaring at her—after a silence, suddenly*) I had a good mind
to murder you.

BARBARA (*frightened*) Why?

FREDERICK I had a good mind to murder you as you sit there.   280

BARBARA (*frightened*) See—see how you loved me!

FREDERICK How I loved you! Yes—*you* see! You see how I loved you,
you callous devil! Haven't I loved you with every breath I've fetched
—haven't I?

BARBARA But what was the good of loving me if you had all the fun out   285
of it? It didn't seem anything to me because I didn't realize—I didn't
know—

FREDERICK You didn't *love* me!

BARBARA No—well—you should have seen that I did. It doesn't do me

197

any good, if a man *dies* for love of me, unless there is some answer in   290
me, so that it lives in me.

FREDERICK   I ought to have killed myself rather than marry you.

BARBARA   But I couldn't help that, could I?

FREDERICK   No, you could help nothing. You could only throw me away
like waste-paper that had wrapped up a few years of your life.   295

BARBARA   I'm sorry, Frederick. I'll do what I can; I will, really.

FREDERICK   *What* will you do?

BARBARA   Don't you trust me?

FREDERICK   Trust you, yes! You can go on doing as you like with me.

BARBARA   There you are, you see, resigned. Resigned from the very   300
start—resigned to lose. You are, and you always were.

FREDERICK   Very well, you little devil—it seems you were determined—

BARBARA   What?

FREDERICK   To destroy me.

BARBARA (*going and putting her arms round his neck*)   No—no, Frederick.   305
I'd do an awful lot for you—I really would—I have loved you.

FREDERICK   What, for example?

BARBARA   I'd help you with the people in Chislehurst—come and live
for a time in the same house.

FREDERICK (*holding her by the arms and looking in her eyes*)   Will you give   310
up this man and come back to me?

BARBARA   Oh—what's the good of promising, Frederick—I might only
break it again. Don't force me.

FREDERICK   Will you try? Will you try *me* again for three months?

BARBARA   Come and live with you again?   315

FREDERICK   Yes.

BARBARA   As your wife?

FREDERICK   Yes.

BARBARA   Altogether as your wife?

FREDERICK   Yes—or even—at first—   320

BARBARA (*piteously*)   I don't know, Frederick.

FREDERICK   Will you think about it?

BARBARA   But I don't know! What is the good of thinking about it? But
I don't know, Frederick.

FREDERICK   You can make up your mind.   325

BARBARA   But I can't—I can't—it pulls both ways. I don't know, Frederick.

FREDERICK   Will you know better to-morrow—will you come, then,
and tell me—will you?

BARBARA   But I shan't know any better to-morrow. It's now! And I can't
tell. Don't make me decide, Frederick!   330

FREDERICK What?

BARBARA Which way. Don't make me decide! (*She goes and sits on the couch, hiding her face in a cushion*)

FREDERICK (*suddenly flings his arms on the table and sobs*) Oh, good God—I can't bear it!   335

BARBARA (*looks at him, goes and puts her hand on his shoulder*) Don't, Frederick—don't! I *will* make up my mind, I will!

FREDERICK (*his face muffled*) I can't stand it.

BARBARA No, dear. (*He sobs—she touches his hair*) Don't! Don't! You shall—I will do—what I can.   340

FREDERICK (*his face still hidden*) It will kill me, Barbara.

BARBARA No, dear—no, it won't. I must think of something. I will tell you to-morrow. I will come and tell you—

FREDERICK (*his face still hidden*) What?

BARBARA I don't know, dear—but I will see—I will come. Look at   345
me—look at me. (*He lifts his face*) Dear! (*He folds her in his arms—she puts her head back as he kisses her*) There's Mama!

> He listens—hears a sound, snatches his hat and dashes out—
> Barbara turns to the piano—straightens her hair—stands
> waiting. Enter Lady Charlcote   350

LADY CHARLCOTE Has Frederick gone?

BARBARA Yes.

> Enter Wesson

LADY CHARLCOTE What have you decided?

BARBARA I don't know.   355

LADY CHARLCOTE That's no answer. Have you decided nothing?

BARBARA No.

LADY CHARLCOTE I hope he won't go and jump in the lake.

BARBARA I said I'd see him to-morrow.

LADY CHARLCOTE Then he won't be such a fool. How did he behave?   360

BARBARA Oh, don't talk about it, Mama!

LADY CHARLCOTE And are you coming to the Monte Baldo to-morrow then?

BARBARA Yes.

LADY CHARLCOTE What time?   365

BARBARA In the morning—about eleven.

LADY CHARLCOTE And you'll bring him your answer then?

BARBARA Yes.

LADY CHARLCOTE Well, you must decide for the best for yourself. Only don't go and make a double mess of it, that's all.   370

BARBARA How do you mean, a double mess?

LADY CHARLCOTE You'll have to stick to one or the other now, at any
rate—so you'd better stick to the one you can live with, and not to the
one you can do without—for if you get the wrong one, you might as
well drown two people then instead of one.   375

BARBARA I don't know—I shall know to-morrow, Mama. Good night.

LADY CHARLCOTE (*kissing her—crying*) Well—all you can do now is to
make the bed for yourself. Good night! Oh, don't trouble to come
out, Mr Wesson, don't.

> *Wesson follows her. Exit both. Barbara sits down and begins to*   380
> *play a waltz on the piano. Re-enter Wesson*

WESSON Frederick wasn't far off—he hadn't drowned himself.
> *Barbara goes on playing*

WESSON I don't particularly want to hear that piano, Barbara.

BARBARA Don't you? (*Plays a few more bars, then stops*) What *do* you   385
want?

WESSON So you are going to see him to-morrow.

BARBARA I am.

WESSON What for?

BARBARA (*hesitating*) To tell him I'll go back to him.   390
> *She remains with her back to Wesson—he sits at the table. There*
> *is dead silence*

WESSON Did you tell him that to-night?

BARBARA No.

WESSON Why not?   395

BARBARA Because I didn't want to.

WESSON Did you give him hopes of that answer?

BARBARA I don't know.

WESSON You do! Tell me.

BARBARA I say I don't know.   400

WESSON Then you're lying. I don't believe you intended to tell him
that. I believe you say it to make me wild.

BARBARA I don't.

WESSON Then go now.

BARBARA I said I'd go to-morrow.   405

WESSON If you're going back to Frederick in the morning, you're not
going to spend a night under this roof—hear that?

BARBARA Why not? I've spent a good many nights under this roof—
what does one more or less matter?

WESSON While you've been with me here I considered you as a woman   410
who wanted to stick to me as a wife—and as anything else *I don't*
want you.

BARBARA Very much as a wife you considered me at first—you were as unsure of us as ever I was.

WESSON That was at the very first.   415

BARBARA Was it—was it?

WESSON Whether or not—that's what I say now.

BARBARA 'Whether or not!'—you *would* say that. At any rate, Frederick wouldn't say 'whether or not'.

WESSON And you want to go back to him?   420

BARBARA All men are alike. They don't care what a woman wants. They try to get hold of what they want themselves, as if it were a pipe. As for the woman, she's not considered—and so—that's where you make your mistake, gentlemen.

WESSON Want? What *do* you want?   425

BARBARA That's for you to find out.

WESSON What you want is some of the conceit knocking out of you.

BARBARA You do it, Mr Tuppeny-ha'penny.

WESSON If Frederick hadn't been such a damn fool he'd have taken you down a peg or two. Now, you think yourself so blighted high and   430
mighty that nobody's good enough to dangle after you.

BARBARA Only a little puppy-dog that barks at my skirts.

WESSON Very well, then the little puppy-dog *will* bark. Are you going to see Frederick in the morning?

BARBARA Yes.   435

WESSON And are you going to tell him, then, that you're going back to him?

BARBARA I don't know.

WESSON You must know then, because if you are, you're not going to stop the night in this house.   440

BARBARA Pooh! What do I care about your house?

WESSON You know it was really *you* who wanted it, and whose it is.

BARBARA As if *I* care for this house—I'd leave it any minute. I'll leave it now.

WESSON If you're going to go back to Frederick, *leave* it now. I ask you to.   445

BARBARA Oh, very well—that is soon done.

She goes out quickly.

CURTAIN

Act 4

Ten minutes later. Wesson is smoking. Enter Barbara, dressed, with her hat on

BARBARA Here I am, then!

WESSON Are you going straight to Gardone, to the Monte Baldo? 5

BARBARA No—I'm going to the Hotel Cervo.

WESSON But you can't—she knows us, the landlady—and thinks we're man and wife. You can't make that mess. If you're going, go straight to Frederick to-night—I'll see you there.

BARBARA I'm *not* going to Frederick to-night—I'm not going to Gardone—I'm going to the Hotel Cervo. 10

WESSON How much money have you got?

BARBARA None.

WESSON Then I won't give you any.

BARBARA Don't you trouble—I wouldn't take any of your money. 15

WESSON Have you got your night-things in the handbag?

BARBARA Yes.

WESSON Some soap—some hankies?

BARBARA No—forgotten 'em.

WESSON You would. 20

Exit—comes running back in a moment, puts the things in her bag

BARBARA Thank you.

WESSON And your box I'll pack to-morrow. The things you said were mine I shall put in.

BARBARA You needn't. 25

WESSON I shall. I've never given you anything, so you've nothing to return.

BARBARA No—you were always stingy.

WESSON Very well—Frederick isn't.

BARBARA I suppose it's having been brought up so poor, you can't help it. 30

WESSON We won't discuss me now, nor my bringing-up.

BARBARA Oh, all right!

WESSON I consider I owe you, of money you had, about eleven pounds. I'll be stingy and keep one of them. Here's ten out of the forty we'd got.

BARBARA I shan't have them. 35

WESSON You can't go without any money.

BARBARA Yes, I can.

WESSON No, you can't. If you don't have these ten pounds, I'll post them to Frederick to you.

BARBARA All right.   40

WESSON (*feeling in his pocket*) Well, have ten lire, at any rate.

BARBARA No, I won't have anything.

WESSON You ought to be murdered for your obstinacy.

BARBARA Not twice in one night.

WESSON Very well, then—I will come with you down the village, since   45
you're frightened of the men.

BARBARA You needn't—I'm not frightened.

WESSON No—you're too damned high and mighty to possess a single
one of the human virtues or vices, you are! (*A silence*) Do you want to
go, really?   50

BARBARA Yes.

WESSON Liar!—Liar!—you are showing off! (*Snatches the handbag and
flings it into the kitchen*) Fool's idiotic theatrical game. Take that hat off.

BARBARA You're giving your orders.

WESSON All right. (*Seizes the hat, flings it through the door*)   55

BARBARA (*flashing*) What are you doing?

WESSON Stopping you being a fool. Take your coat off.

BARBARA I shall take my coat off when I please. Indeed, *you* needn't
show off, for the minute I want to walk out of this house I shall walk
out, and you nor anybody else will prevent me.   60

WESSON (*taking up his position with his back to the door*) All right—you
want to walk out now, and see!

BARBARA If I want to—

WESSON Want to, then—

BARBARA (*with a laugh of scorn*) Ha—*you* stop me! (*Marches up to him   65
with her breast high. He stands immovable*) Come out! (*He shakes his
head*) Come out!

WESSON I told you I wouldn't.

BARBARA Won't you?

> Seizes him. He grapples with her. They struggle. He forces her   70
> backward, flings her with a smash on to the couch

WESSON You shan't! (*Goes and locks the door—stands at a loss*)

BARBARA (*recovering*) It's very heroic—but I go to-morrow, whether
or not.

WESSON You'll pass the night in this room then. (*He sits down—there is   75
silence for some minutes—at last he looks up, speaks falteringly*) You
don't want to leave me, do you, Barbara? (*No answer*) You *don't* want
to? (*Silence*) Well, whether you think you do or not, I shall never
believe you want to leave me, not really—so there! (*A silence*)

BARBARA A woman couldn't want to leave such a wonder as you, you   80
think.

WESSON   You can't want to leave *me*.

BARBARA   Why not?

WESSON (*sulkily*)   Because I don't believe you can. (*There is a silence*)

BARBARA (*with difficulty*)   A sort of faith performance!   85

    He looks at her steadily, rises, goes and sits beside her

WESSON   Barbican!

BARBARA (*dropping her head on his shoulder with a cry*)   It's so hard on him, Giacomo.

WESSON (*putting his arms round her*)   Never mind, he'll suffer at first,   90
then he'll get better.

BARBARA (*crying*)   He won't.

WESSON   He will—he shall—he shall! And you'll see he will. He'll be all right in the end. You were too big a mouthful for him to swallow, and he was choking.   95

BARBARA   But I make him suffer so.

WESSON (*kissing and kissing her*)   No—it's my fault. You don't want to leave me, do you?

BARBARA   I don't know what to do.

WESSON   Stay with me, Barbican, my darling, and we'll manage that   100
he's all right.

BARBARA   It's not fair when a man goes loving you so much when you don't love him—it makes you feel as if you'd have to go back to him.

WESSON   You can't go back to him—it would be wrong. His love isn't living for you.   105

BARBARA   It isn't, is it, Giacomo?

WESSON   No—kiss me, Barbara, will you? (*She kisses him*) I love you, Barbara.

BARBARA   Do you really love me?

WESSON   *Malheureusement*.   110

BARBARA   He says that.

WESSON   And I don't mean it. I'm glad I love you, even if you torture me into hell.

BARBARA   But do you love me an awful lot?

WESSON   More than enough.   ·115

BARBARA   Really?

WESSON   Truly.

BARBARA   But if he dies, I shall torment the life out of you.

WESSON   You'll do that anyway.

BARBARA (*looking up—taking his face between her hands*)   Shall I?—   120
No!—Say no—say I am a joy to you.

WESSON   You are a living joy to me, you are—especially this evening.

BARBARA (*laughs*) No—but am I really?

WESSON Yes.

BARBARA Kiss me—kiss me—and love me—love me a fearful lot—love   125
me a fearful lot.

WESSON I do. And to-morrow you'll just say to Frederick, 'I can't come
back—divorce me if you love me.' You'll say it, won't you? (*Kissing
her*)

BARBARA Yes.   130

WESSON If it kills him—it won't kill him—but you'll say it?

BARBARA (*hiding her face*) Must I, Giacomo?

WESSON Yes.

BARBARA Then I s'll have to—oh dear! But you'll love me—love me a
lot. (*She clings to him wildly*)   135

WESSON I do—and I will.

BARBARA Love me a fearful lot!

    CURTAIN

TOUCH AND GO

A nice phrase: 'A People's Theatre.'° But what about it? There's no such thing in existence as a People's Theatre: or even on the way to existence, as far as we can tell. The name is chosen, the baby isn't even begotten: nay, the would-be parents aren't married, nor yet courting.

A People's Theatre. Note the indefinite article. It isn't The People's Theatre, but A People's Theatre. Not The People: *il popolo*, *le peuple*, *das Volk*, this monster is the same the world over: Plebs, the proletariat. Not the theatre of Plebs, the proletariat, but the theatre of A People. What people? *Quel peuple donc?*°—A People's Theatre. Translate it into French for yourself.

A People's Theatre. Since we can't produce it, let us deduce it. Major premise: the seats are cheap. Minor premise: the plays are good. Conclusion: A People's Theatre. How much will you give me for my syllogism? Not a slap in the eye, I hope.

We stick to our guns. The seats are cheap. That has a nasty proletarian look about it. But appearances are deceptive. The proletariat isn't poor. Everybody is poor except Capital and Labour. Between these upper and nether millstones great numbers of decent people are squeezed.

The seats are cheap: in decency's name. Nobody wants to swank, to sit in the front of a box like a geranium on a window-sill—'the cynosure of many eyes.'° Nobody wants to profiteer. We all feel that it is as humiliating to pay high prices as to charge them. No man consents in his heart to pay high prices unless he feels that what he pays with his right hand he will get back with his left, either out of the pocket of a man who isn't looking, or out of the envy of the poor neighbour who *is* looking, but can't afford the figure. The seats are cheap. Why should A People, fabulous and lofty giraffe, want to charge or to pay high prices? If it were *the people* now—But it isn't. It isn't Plebs, the proletariat. The seats are cheap.

The plays are good. Pah!—this has a canting smell. Any play is good to the man who likes to look at it. And at that rate *Chu Chin Chow*° is extra-super-good. What about your *good* plays? Whose good? *Pfui* to your goodness!

That minor premise is a bad egg: it will hatch no bird. Good plays? You might as well say mimsy bomtittle plays, you'd be saying as much.

The plays are—don't say good or you'll be beaten. The plays—the plays of A People's Theatre are—oh, heaven, what are they?—not popular nor populous nor plebeian nor proletarian nor folk nor parish plays. None of that adjectival spawn. 40

The only clue-word is People's, for all that. A People's—. Chaste word, it will bring forth no adjective. The plays of A People's Theatre are People's plays. The plays of A People's Theatre are plays about people.

It doesn't look much, at first sight. After all—people! Yes, people! Not *the people*, i.e. Plebs, nor yet the Upper Ten.° People. Neither *Piccoli* 45 nor *Grandi*° in our republic. People.

People, ah God! Not mannequins. Not lords nor proletariats nor bishops nor husbands nor co-respondents° nor virgins nor adulteresses nor uncles nor noses. Not even white rabbits nor presidents. People.

Men who are somebody, not men who are something. Men who 50 *happen* to be bishops or co-respondents, women who happen to be chaste, just as they happen to freckle, because it's one of their innumerable odd qualities. Even men who happen, by the way, to have long noses. But not noses on two legs, not burly pairs of gaiters,° stuffed and voluble, not white meringues of chastity, not incarnations of co- 55 respondence. Not proletariats, petitioners, presidents, noses, bits of fluff. Heavens, what an assortment of bits! And aren't we sick of them!

People, I say. And after all, it's saying something. It's harder to be a human being than to be a president or a bit of fluff. You can be a president, or a bit of fluff, or even a nose, by clockwork. Given a rôle, a 60 *part*, you can play it by clockwork. But you can't have a clockwork human being.

We're dead sick of parts. It's no use your protesting that there is a man behind the nose. We can't see him, and he can't see himself. Nothing but nose. Neither can you make us believe there is a man inside the gaiters. 65 He's never showed his head yet.

It may be, in real life, the gaiters wear the man, as the nose wears Cyrano.° It may be Sir Auckland Geddes and Mr J. H. Thomas° are only clippings from the illustrated press. It may be that a miner is a complicated machine for cutting coal and voting on a ballot-paper. 70

It may be that coal-owners are like the *petit bleu* arrangement,° a system of vacuum tubes for whooshing Bradburys° about from one to the other.

It may be that everybody delights in bits, in parts, that the public insists on noses, gaiters, white rabbits, bits of fluff, automata and gewgaws. If they do, then let 'em. *Chu Chin Chow* for ever! 75

In spite of them all: A People's Theatre. A People's Theatre shows men, and not parts. Not bits, nor bundles of bits. A whole bunch of rôles tied into one won't make an individual. Though gaiters perish, we will have men.

Although most miners may be pick-cum-shovel-cum-ballot 80
implements, and no more, still, among miners there must be two or three
living individuals. The same among the masters. The majority are
suction-tubes for Bradburys. But in this Sodom of Industrialism there
are surely ten men, all told. My poor little withered grain of mustard
seed, I am half afraid to take you across to the seed-testing department! 85

And if there are ten men, there is A People's Theatre.

How many tragic situations did Goethe say were possible? Something like thirty-two.° Which seems a lot. Anyhow, granted that men are
men still, that not all of them are bits, parts, machine-sections, then we
have added another tragic possibility to the list: the Strike situation. As 90
yet no one tackles this situation. It is a sort of Medusa head, which
turns—no, not to stone, but to sloppy treacle. Mr Galsworthy° had a
peep, and sank down towards bathos.°

Granted that men are still men, Labour *v.* Capitalism is a tragic
struggle. If men are no more than implements, it is non-tragic and 95
merely disastrous. In tragedy the man is more than his part. Hamlet is
more than Prince of Denmark, Macbeth is more than murderer of
Duncan. The man is caught in the wheels of his part, his fate, he may be
torn asunder. He may be killed, but the resistant, integral soul in him is
not destroyed. He comes through, though he dies. He goes through with 100
his fate, though death swallows him. And it is in this facing of fate, this
going right through with it, that tragedy lies. Tragedy is not disaster. It
is a disaster when a cart-wheel goes over a frog, but it is not a tragedy.
Tragedy is the working out of some immediate passional problem within
the soul of man. If this passional problem and this working out be absent, 105
then no disaster is a tragedy, not the hugest: not the death of ten million
men. It is only a cart-wheel going over a frog. There must be a supreme
struggle.

In Shakespeare's time it was the people *versus* king storm that was
brewing. Majesty was about to have its head off. Come what might, 110
Hamlet and Macbeth and Goneril and Regan° had to see the business
through.°

Now a new wind is getting up. We call it Labour *versus* Capitalism.
We say it is a mere material struggle, a money-grabbing affair. But this is
only one aspect of it. In so far as men are merely mechanical the struggle 115
is one which, though it may bring disaster and death to millions, is no
more than accident, an accidental collision of forces. But in so far as men
are men, the situation is tragic. It is not really the bone we are fighting

for. We are fighting to have somebody's head off. The conflict is in pure, passional antagonism, turning upon the poles of belief. Majesty was only *hors d'œuvres* to this tragic repast.

So, the strike situation has this dual aspect. First it is a mechanico-material struggle, two mechanical forces pulling asunder from the central object, the bone. All it can result in is the pulling asunder of the fabric of civilization, and even of life, without any creative issue. It is no more than a frog under a cart-wheel. The mechanical forces, rolling on, roll over the body of life and squash it.

The second is the tragic aspect. According to this view, we see more than two dogs fighting for a bone, and life hopping under the Juggernaut wheel. The two dogs are making the bone a pretext for a fight with each other. That old bull-dog, the British capitalist, has got the bone in his teeth. That unsatisfied mongrel, Plebs, the proletariat, shivers with rage not so much at sight of the bone, as at sight of the great wrinkled jowl that holds it. There is the old dog, with his knowing look and his massive grip on the bone: and there is the insatiable mongrel, with his great splay paws. The one is all head and arrogance, the other all paws and grudge. The bone is only the pretext. A first condition of the being of Bully is that he shall hate the prowling great paws of Plebs, whilst Plebs by inherent nature goes mad at the sight of Bully's jowl. 'Drop it!' cries Plebs. 'Hands off!' growls Bully. It is hands against head, the shambling, servile body in a rage of insurrection at last against the wrinkled, heavy head.

Labour not only wants his debt. He wants his pound of flesh.° It is a quandary. In our heart of hearts we must admit the debt. We must admit that it is long overdue. But this last condition—! In vain we study our anatomy to see which part we can best spare.

Where is our Portia, to save us with a timely quibble? We've plenty of Portias. They've recited their heads off—'The quality of mercy is not strained.' But the old Shylock of the proletariat persists. He pops up again, and says, 'All right, I can't have my pound of flesh with the blood. But then you can't keep my pound of flesh with your blood—you owe it me. It is your business to deliver the goods. Deliver it then—with or without blood—deliver it.' Then Portia scratches her head, and thinks again.

What's the solution? There is no solution. But still there is a choice. There's a choice between a mess and a tragedy. If Plebs and Bully hang on one to each end of the bone, and pull for grim life, they will at last tear the bone to atoms: in short, destroy the whole material substance of life, and so perish by accident, no better than a frog under the wheel of destiny. That may be a disaster, but it is only a mess for all that.

On the other hand, if they have a fight to fight they might really drop the bone. Instead of wrangling the bone to bits they might really go straight for one another. They are like hostile parties on board a ship, who both proceed to scuttle the ship so as to sink the other party. Down goes the ship, with all the bally lot on board. A few survivors swim and squeal among the bubbles—and then silence.

It is too much to suppose that the combatants will ever drop the obvious old bone. But it is not too much to imagine that some men might acknowledge the bone to be merely a pretext, another hollow *casus belli.°* If we really could know what we were fighting for, if we could deeply believe in what we were fighting for, then the struggle might have dignity, beauty, satisfaction for us. If it were a profound struggle for something that was coming to life in us, a struggle that we were convinced would bring us to a new freedom, a new life, then it would be a creative activity, a creative activity in which death is a climax in the progression towards new being. And this is tragedy.

Therefore, if we could but comprehend or feel the tragedy in the great Labour struggle, the intrinsic tragedy of having to pass through death to birth, our souls would still know some happiness, the very happiness of creative suffering. Instead of which we pile accident on accident, we tear the fabric of our existence fibre by fibre, we confidently look forward to the time when the whole great structure will come down on our heads. Yet after all that, when we are squirming under the debris, we shall have no more faith or hope or satisfaction than we have now. We shall crawl from under one cart-wheel straight under another.

The essence of tragedy, which is creative crisis, is that a man should go through with his fate, and not dodge it and go bumping into an accident. And the whole business of life, at the great critical periods of mankind, is that men should accept and be one with their tragedy. Therefore we should open our hearts. For one thing, we should have a People's Theatre. Perhaps it would help us in this hour of confusion better than anything.

Hermitage,° June 1919

CHARACTERS

GERALD BARLOW
MR BARLOW, *his father*
OLIVER TURTON
JOB ARTHUR FREER
WILLIE HOUGHTON
ALFRED BREFFITT
WILLIAM, *a butler*
CLERKS, MINERS, *etc.*
ANABEL WRATH
MRS BARLOW
WINIFRED BARLOW
EVA, *a maid*

[*The play is set in the market-place of a large Midlands mining village, serving the local colliery of Barlow and Walsall; in the residence of the Barlow family at Lilley Close; and in the park of a stately home, now the colliery offices*]

Act 1 Scene 1

*Sunday morning. Market-place of a large mining village in the
Midlands. A man addressing a small gang of colliers from the foot
of a stumpy memorial obelisk. Church bells heard. Churchgoers
passing along the outer pavements*

WILLIE HOUGHTON What's the matter with you folks, as I've told you   5
before, and as I shall keep on telling you every now and again, though
it doesn't make a bit of difference, is that you've got no idea of
freedom whatsoever. I've lived in this blessed place for fifty years, and
I've never seen the spark of an idea, nor of any response to an idea,
come out of a single one of you, all the time. I don't know what it is   10
with colliers—whether it's spending so much time in the bowels of
the earth—but they never seem to be able to get their thoughts above
their bellies. If you've got plenty to eat and drink, and a bit over to
keep the missis quiet, you're satisfied. I never saw such a satisfied
bloomin' lot in my life as you Barlow and Walsall's men are, really. Of   15
course you can growse as well as anybody, and you do growse. But you
don't do anything else. You're stuck in a sort of mud of contentment,
and you feel yourselves sinking, but you make no efforts to get out.
You bleat a bit, like sheep in a bog—but you like it, you know. You like
sinking in—you don't have to stand on your own feet then.   20

I'll tell you what'll happen to you chaps. I'll give you a little picture of what you'll be like in the future. Barlow and Walsall's'll make
a number of compounds, such as they keep niggers in in South Africa,°
and there you'll be kept. And every one of you'll have a little brass
collar round his neck, with a number on it. You won't have names any   25
more. And you'll go from the compound to the pit, and from the pit
back again to the compound. You won't be allowed to go outside the
gates, except at week-ends. They'll let you go home to your wives on
Saturday nights, to stop over Sunday. But you'll have to be in again by
half past nine on Sunday night; and if you're late, you'll have your   30
next week-end knocked off. And there you'll be—and you'll be quite
happy. They'll give you plenty to eat, and a can of beer° a day, and a
bit of bacca°—and they'll provide dominoes and skittles for you to
play with. And you'll be the most contented set of men alive.—But
you won't be men. You won't even be animals. You'll go from number   35
one to number three thousand, a lot of numbered slaves—a new sort
of slaves—

VOICE An' wheer shall thee be, Willie?

WILLIE Oh, I shall be outside the palings, laughing at you. I shall have
to laugh, because it'll be your own faults. You'll have nobody but   40
yourself to thank for it. You don't *want* to be men. You'd rather *not*
be free—much rather. You're like those people spoken of in
Shakespeare: 'Oh, how eager these men are to be slaves!' I believe it's
Shakespeare—or the Bible—one or the other—it mostly is—

ANABEL WRATH (*she was passing to church*) It was Tiberius.°   45

WILLIE Eh?

ANABEL Tiberius said it.

WILLIE Tiberius!—Oh, did he? (*Laughs*) Thanks! Well, if Tiberius
said it, there must be something in it. And he only just missed being
in the Bible, anyway. He was a day late, or they'd have had him in.   50
'Oh, how eager these men are to be slaves!'—It's evident the Romans
deserved all they got from Tiberius—and you'll deserve all you get,
every bit of it. But don't you bother, you'll get it. You won't be at the
mercy of Tiberius, you'll be at the mercy of something a jolly sight
worse. Tiberius took the skin off a few Romans, apparently. But   55
you'll have the soul taken out of you—every one of you. And I'd
rather lose my skin than my soul, any day. But perhaps you wouldn't.

VOICE What art makin' for, Willie? Tha seems to say a lot, but tha goes
round it. Tha'rt like a donkey on a gin.° Tha gets ravelled.

WILLIE Yes, that's just it. I am precisely like a donkey on a gin—a   60
donkey that's trying to wind a lot of colliers up to the surface. There's
many a donkey that's brought more colliers than you up to see
daylight, by trotting round.—But do you want to know what I'm
making for? I can soon tell you that. You Barlow and Walsall's men,
you haven't a soul to call your own. Barlow and Walsall's have only to   65
say to one of you, Come, and he cometh; Go, and he goeth, Lie down
and be kicked, and he lieth down and he *is* kicked—and serve him
jolly well right.

VOICE Ay—an' what about it? Tha's got a behind o' thy own, hasn't ter?

WILLIE Do you stand there and ask me what about it, and haven't the   70
sense to alter it? Couldn't you set up a proper Government to-
morrow, if you liked? Couldn't you contrive that the pits belonged
to you, instead of you belonging to the pits, like so many old
pit-ponies that stop down till they are blind, and take to eating
coal-slack for meadow-grass, not knowing the difference? If only   75
you'd learn to think, I'd respect you. As you are, I can't, not if I try
my hardest. All you can think of is to ask for another shilling a day.
That's as far as your imagination carries you. And perhaps you get

sevenpence ha'penny, but pay for it with half-a-crown's worth of
sweat.° The masters aren't fools—as you are. They'll give you   80
two-thirds of what you ask for, but they'll get five-thirds of it back
again—and they'll get it out of your flesh and blood, too, in jolly hard
work. Shylock wasn't in it with them. He only wanted a pound of
flesh. But you cheerfully give up a pound a week, each one of you,
and keep on giving it up.—But you don't seem to see these things.   85
You can't think beyond your dinners and your 'lowance. You think
if you can get another shilling a day you're set up. You make me tired,
I tell you.

JOB ARTHUR FREER We think of others besides ourselves.

WILLIE Hello, Job Arthur—are you there? I didn't recognize you   90
without your frock-coat and silk hat—on the Sabbath.—What was
that you said? You think of something else, besides yourselves?—Oh
ay—I'm glad to hear it. Did you mean your own importance?

> *A motor car, Gerald Barlow driving, Oliver Turton with him, has*
> *pulled up*   95

JOB ARTHUR (*glancing at the car*) No, I didn't.

WILLIE Didn't you, though?—Come, speak up, let us have it. The more
the merrier. You were going to say something.

JOB ARTHUR Nay, you were doing the talking.

WILLIE Yes, so I was, till you interrupted, with a great idea on the tip of   100
your tongue. Come, spit it out. No matter if Mr Barlow hears you.
You know how sorry for you we feel, that you've always got to make
your speeches twice—once to those above, and once to us here below.
I didn't mean the angels and the devils, but never mind. Speak up, Job
Arthur.   105

JOB ARTHUR It's not everybody as has as much to say as you, Mr
Houghton.

WILLIE No, not in the open—that's a fact. Some folks says a great deal
more, in semi-private. You were just going to explain to me, on behalf
of the men, whom you so ably represent and so wisely lead, Job   110
Arthur—we won't say by the nose—you were just going to tell me—
on behalf of the men, of course, not of the masters—that you think of
others, besides yourself. Do you mind explaining *what* others?

JOB ARTHUR Everybody's used to your talk, Mr Houghton, and for
that reason it doesn't make much impression. What I meant to say, in   115
plain words, was that we have to think of what's best for everybody,
not only for ourselves.

WILLIE Oh, I see. What's best for everybody! I see! Well, for myself, I'm
much obliged—there's nothing for us to do, gentlemen, but for all of

us to bow acknowledgments to Mr Job Arthur Freer, who so kindly   120
has *all* our interests at heart.

JOB ARTHUR I don't profess to be a red-rag Socialist. I don't pretend to
think that if the Government had the pits it would be any better for
us. No. What I mean is, that the pits are there, and every man on this
place depends on them, one way or another. They're the cow that   125
gives the milk. And what I mean is, how every man shall have a proper
share of the milk, which is food and living. I don't want to kill the cow
and share up the meat. It's like killing the goose that laid the golden
egg. I want to keep the cow healthy and strong. And the cow is the
pits, and we're the men that depend on the pits.   130

WILLIE Who's the cat that's going to lick the cream?

JOB ARTHUR My position is this—and I state it before masters and
men—that it's our business to strike such a balance between the
interests of the men and the interests of the masters that the pits
remain healthy, and everybody profits.   135

WILLIE You're out for the millennium,° I can see—with Mr Job Arthur
Freer striking the balance. We all see you, Job Arthur, one foot
on either side of the fence, balancing the see-saw, with masters at
one end and men at the other. You'll have to give one side a lot of
pudding.—But go back a bit, to where we were before the motor car   140
took your breath away. When you said, Job Arthur, that you think of
others besides yourself, didn't you mean, as a matter of fact, the office
men? Didn't you mean that the colliers, led—we won't mention
noses—by you, were going to come out in sympathy with the office
clerks, supposing they didn't get the rise in wages which they've   145
asked for—the office clerks? Wasn't that it?

JOB ARTHUR There's been some talk among the men of standing by the
office. I don't know what they'll do. But they'll do it of their own
decision, whatever it is.

WILLIE There's not a shadow of doubt about it, Job Arthur. But it's a   150
funny thing the decisions all have the same foxy smell about them,
Job Arthur.

OLIVER TURTON (*calling from the car*) What was the speech about, in
the first place?

WILLIE I beg pardon?   155

OLIVER What was the address about, to begin with?

WILLIE Oh, the same old hat—Freedom. But partly it's given to annoy
the Unco Guid,° as they pass to their Sabbath banquet of self-
complacency.

OLIVER What *about* Freedom?   160

WILLIE   Very much as usual, I believe. But you should have been here ten minutes sooner, before we began to read the lessons. (*Laughs*)

ANABEL WRATH (*moving forward, and holding out her hand*) You'd merely have been told what Freedom *isn't*: and you know that already. How are you, Oliver?   165

OLIVER   Good God, Anabel!—are you part of the meeting? How long have you been back in England?

ANABEL   Some months, now. My family have moved here, you know.

OLIVER   Your family! Where have they moved from?—from the moon?   170

ANABEL   No, only from Derby.—How are you, Gerald?
       Gerald twists in his seat to give her his hand.

GERALD   I saw you before.

ANABEL   Yes, I know you did.
       Job Arthur has disappeared. The men disperse sheepishly into   175
       groups, to stand and sit on their heels by the walls and the
       causeway edge. Willie Houghton begins to talk to individuals.

OLIVER   Won't you get in and drive on with us a little way?

ANABEL   No, I was going to church.

OLIVER   Going to church! Is that a new habit?   180

ANABEL   Not a habit. But I've been twice since I saw you last.

OLIVER   I see. And that's nearly two years ago. It's an annual thing, like a birthday?

ANABEL   No. I'll go on, then.

OLIVER   You'll be late now.   185

ANABEL   Shall I? It doesn't matter.

OLIVER   We are going to see you again, aren't we?

ANABEL   (*after a pause*) Yes, I hope so, Oliver.

OLIVER   How have you been these two years—well?—happy?

ANABEL   No, neither. How have you?   190

OLIVER   Yes, fairly happy. Have you been ill?

ANABEL   Yes, in France I was very ill.

OLIVER   Your old neuritis?

ANABEL   No. My chest. Pneumonia—oh, a complication.

OLIVER   How sickening! Who looked after you? Is it better?   195

ANABEL   Yes, it's a great deal better.

OLIVER   And what are you doing in England—working?

ANABEL   No, not much.—I won't keep the car here: good-bye.

GERALD   Oh, it's all right.

OLIVER   But, Anabel—we must fix a meeting. I say, wait just a moment.   200
       Could I call on your people? Go into town with me one day. I don't

know whether Gerald intends to see you—whether he intends to ask
you to Lilley Close.

GERALD I—

ANABEL He's no need. I'm fixed up there already.   205

GERALD What do you mean?

ANABEL I am at Lilley Close every day—or most days—to work with
your sister Winifred in the studio.

GERALD What?—why, how's that?

ANABEL Your father asked me. My father was already giving her some   210
lessons.

GERALD And you're at our house every day?

ANABEL Most days.

GERALD Well, I'm—well, I'll be—you managed it very sharp, didn't
you? I've only been away a fortnight.   215

ANABEL Your father asked me—he offered me twelve pounds a month
—I wanted to do something.

GERALD Oh yes, but you didn't hire yourself out at Lilley Close as a sort
of upper servant just for twelve pounds a month.

ANABEL You're wrong—you're wrong. I'm not a sort of upper servant   220
at all—not at all.

GERALD Oh yes, you are, if you're paid twelve pounds a month—three
pounds a week. That's about what father's sick-nurse gets, I believe.
You're a kind of upper servant, like a nurse. You don't do it for twelve
pounds a month. You can make twelve pounds in a day, if you like to   225
work at your little models: I know you can sell your little statuette
things as soon as you make them.

ANABEL But I *can't* make them. I *can't* make them. I've lost the spirit—
the *joie de vivre*°—I don't know what, since I've been ill. I tell you I've
got to earn something.   230

GERALD Nevertheless, you won't make me believe, Anabel, that you've
come and buried yourself in the provinces—*such* provinces—just to
earn father's three pounds a week. Why don't you admit it, that you
came back to try and take up the old threads?

OLIVER Why not, Gerald? Don't you think we ought to take up the old   235
threads?

GERALD I *don't* think we ought to be left without choice. I *don't* think
Anabel ought to come back and thrust herself on me—for that's what
it amounts to, after all—when one remembers what's gone before.

ANABEL I *don't* thrust myself on you at all. I know I'm a fool, a fool, to   240
come back. But I wanted to. I wanted to see you again. Now I know
I've presumed. I've made myself *cheap* to you. I wanted to—I wanted

to. And now I've done it, I won't come to Lilley Close again, nor
anywhere where you are. Tell your father I have gone to France
again—it will be true.   245

GERALD You play tricks on me—and on yourself. You know you do.
You do it for the pure enjoyment of it. You're making a scene here in
this filthy market-place, just for the fun of it. You like to see these
accursed colliers standing eyeing you, and squatting on their heels.
You like to catch me out, here where I'm known, where I've been the   250
object of their eyes since I was born. This is a great *coup de main*° for
you. I knew it the moment I saw you here.

OLIVER After all, we *are* making a scene in the market-place. Get in,
Anabel, and we'll settle the dispute more privately. I'm glad you came
back, anyhow. I'm glad you came right down on us. Get in, and let us   255
run down to Whatmore.

ANABEL No, Oliver. I don't want to run down to Whatmore. I wanted to
see you—I wanted to see Gerald—and I've seen him—and I've heard
him. That will suffice me. We'll make an end of the scene in the
market-place. (*She turns away*)   260

OLIVER I knew it wasn't ended. I knew she would come back and tell us
she'd come. But she's done her bit—now she'll go again. My God,
what a fool of a world!—You go on, Gerald—I'll just go after her and
see it out. (*Calls*) One moment, Anabel.

ANABEL (*calling*) Don't come, Oliver. (*Turns*)   265

GERALD Anabel! (*Blows the horn of the motor car violently and agitat-
edly—she looks round—turns again as if frightened*) God damn the
woman! (*Gets down from the car*) Drive home for me, Oliver.

   CURTAIN

Act 1 Scene 2

*Winifred's studio at Lilley Close. Anabel and Winifred working
at a model in clay*

WINIFRED But isn't it lovely to be in Paris, and to have exhibitions, and
to be famous?

ANABEL Paris *was* a good place. But I was never famous.   5

WINIFRED But your little animals and birds were famous. Jack said so.
You know he brought us that bronze thrush that is singing, that is in
his room. He has only let me see it twice. It's the loveliest thing I've
ever seen. Oh, if I can do anything like that!—I've worshipped it,
I have. Is it your best thing?   10

ANABEL One of the best.

WINIFRED It must be. When I see it, with its beak lifted, singing, something comes loose in my heart, and I feel as if I should cry, and fly up to heaven. Do you know what I mean? Oh, I'm sure you do, or you could never have made that thrush. Father is so glad you've come to show me how to work. He says now I shall have a life-work, and I shall be happy. It's true, too.

ANABEL Yes, till the life-work collapses.

WINIFRED Oh, it can't collapse. I can't believe it could collapse. Do tell me about something else you made, which you loved—something you sculpted. Oh, it makes my heart burn to hear you!—Do you think I might call you Anabel? I should love to. You do call me Winifred already.

ANABEL Yes, do.

WINIFRED Won't you tell me about something else you made— something lovely?

ANABEL Well, I did a small kitten—asleep—with its paws crossed. You know, Winifred, that wonderful look that kittens have, as if they were blown along like a bit of fluff—as if they weighed nothing at all—just wafted about—and yet so *alive*—do you know—?

WINIFRED Darlings—darlings—I love them!

ANABEL Well, my kitten really came off—it had that quality. It looked as if it had just wafted there.

WINIFRED Oh, yes!—oh, I know! And was it in clay?

ANABEL I cut it in soft grey stone as well. I loved my kitten. An Armenian bought her.

WINIFRED And where is she now?

ANABEL I don't know—in Armenia, I suppose, if there is such a place. It would have to be kept under glass, because the stone wouldn't polish—and I didn't want it polished. But I dislike things under glass—don't you?

WINIFRED Yes, I do. We had a golden clock, but Gerald wouldn't have the glass cover, and Daddy wouldn't have it without. So now the clock is in father's room. Gerald often went to Paris. Oliver used to have a studio there. I don't care much for painting—do you?

ANABEL No. I want something I can touch, if it's something outside me.

WINIFRED Yes, isn't it wonderful, when things are substantial. Gerald and Oliver came back yesterday from Yorkshire. You know we have a colliery there.

ANABEL Yes, I believe I've heard.

WINIFRED I want to introduce you to Gerald, to see if you like him. He's good at the bottom, but he's very overbearing and definite.

ANABEL Is he?

WINIFRED Terribly clever in business. He'll get awfully rich.   55

ANABEL Isn't he rich enough already?

WINIFRED Oh yes, because Daddy is rich enough, really. I think if Gerald was a bit different, he'd be really nice. Now he's so *managing*. It's sickening. Do you dislike managing people, Anabel?

ANABEL I dislike them extremely, Winifred.   60

WINIFRED They're such a bore.

ANABEL What does Gerald manage?

WINIFRED Everything. You know he's revolutionized the collieries and the whole Company. He's made a whole new thing of it, so *modern*. Father says he almost wishes he'd let it die out—let the pits be closed.   65 But I suppose things *must* be modernized, don't you think? Though it's very unpeaceful, you know, really.

ANABEL Decidedly unpeaceful, I should say.

WINIFRED The colliers work awfully hard. The pits are quite wonderful now. Father says it's against nature—all this electricity and so   70 on. Gerald adores electricity. Isn't it curious?

ANABEL Very. How are you getting on?

WINIFRED I don't know. It's so hard to make things *balance* as if they were alive. Where *is* the balance in a thing that's alive?

ANABEL The poise? Yes, Winifred—to me, all the secret of life is in   75 that—just the—the inexpressible poise of a living thing, that makes it so different from a dead thing. To me it's the soul, you know—all living things have it—flowers, trees as well. It makes life always marvellous.

WINIFRED Ah, yes!—ah, yes! If only I could put it in my model.   80

ANABEL I think you will. You are a sculptor, Winifred.—Isn't there someone there?

WINIFRED (*running to the door*) Oh, Oliver!

OLIVER Hello, Winnie! Can I come in? This is your sanctum: you can keep us out if you like.   85

WINIFRED Oh, no. Do you know Miss Wrath, Oliver? She's a famous sculptress.

OLIVER Is she? We have met.—Is Winifred going to make a sculptress, do you think?

ANABEL I do.   90

OLIVER   Good! I like your studio, Winnie. Awfully nice up here over the out-buildings. Are you happy in it?

WINIFRED   Yes, I'm perfectly happy—only I shall *never* be able to make real models, Oliver—it's so difficult.

OLIVER   Fine room for a party—give us a studio party one day, Win, and   95
we'll dance.

WINIFRED   (*flying to him*) Yes, Oliver, do let us dance. What shall we dance to?

OLIVER   Dance?—Dance *Vigni-vignons*—we all know that. Ready?

WINIFRED   Yes.   100

> They begin to sing, dancing meanwhile, in a free little ballet-
> manner, a wine-dance, dancing separate and then together
> > De terre en vigne
> > La voilà la jolie vigne,
> > Vigni-vignons—vignons le vin,   105
> > La voilà la jolie vigne au vin,
> > La voilà la jolie vigne.°

OLIVER   Join in—join in, all.

> Anabel joins in; the three dance and move in rhythm

WINIFRED   I love it—I love it! Do *Ma capote a trois boutons*°—you know   110
it, don't you, Anabel? Ready—now—

> They begin to dance to a quick little march-rhythm, all singing
> and dancing till they are out of breath

OLIVER   Oh!—tired!—let us sit down.

WINIFRED   Oliver!—oh, Oliver!—I *love* you and Anabel.   115

OLIVER   Oh, Winifred, I brought you a present—you'll love me more now.

WINIFRED   Yes, I shall. Do give it me.

OLIVER   I left it in the morning-room. I put it on the mantelpiece for you.   120

WINIFRED   Shall I go for it?

OLIVER   There it is, if you want it.

WINIFRED   Yes—do you mind? I won't be long.

> Exit

OLIVER   She's a nice child.   125

ANABEL   A *very* nice child.

OLIVER   Why did you come back, Anabel?

ANABEL   Why does the moon rise, Oliver?

OLIVER   For some mischief or other, so they say.

ANABEL   You think I came back for mischief's sake?   130

OLIVER   Did you?

ANABEL No.

OLIVER Ah!

ANABEL Tell me, Oliver, how is everything now?—how is it with
you?—how is it between us all?   135

OLIVER How is it between us all?—How *isn't* it, is more the mark.

ANABEL Why?

OLIVER You made a fool of us.

ANABEL Of whom?

OLIVER Well—of Gerald particularly—and of me.   140

ANABEL How did I make a fool of you, Oliver?

OLIVER That you know best, Anabel.

ANABEL No, I don't know. Was it ever right between Gerald and me, all
the three years we knew each other —we were together—?

OLIVER Was it all wrong?   145

ANABEL No, not all. But it was terrible. It was terrible, Oliver. You don't
realize. You don't realize how awful passion can be, when it never
resolves, when it never becomes anything else. It is hate, really.

OLIVER What did you want the passion to resolve into?

ANABEL I was blinded—maddened. Gerald stung me and stung me till   150
I was mad. I left him for reason's sake, for sanity's sake. We should
have killed one another.

OLIVER You stung him too, you know—and pretty badly, at the last: you
dehumanized him.

ANABEL When? When I left him, you mean?   155

OLIVER Yes, when you went away with that Norwegian—playing your
game a little too far.

ANABEL Yes, I knew you'd blame me. I knew you'd be against me. But
don't you see, Oliver, you helped to make it impossible for us.

OLIVER Did I? I didn't intend to.   160

ANABEL Ha, ha, Oliver! Your good intentions! They are too good to
bear investigation, my friend. Ah, but for your good and friendly
intentions—

OLIVER You might have been all right?

ANABEL No, no, I don't mean that. But we were a vicious triangle,   165
Oliver—you must admit it.

OLIVER You mean my friendship with Gerald went against you?

ANABEL Yes. And your friendship with me went against Gerald.

OLIVER So I am the devil in the piece.

ANABEL You see, Oliver, Gerald loved you far too well ever to love me   170
altogether. He loved us both. But the Gerald that loved you so dearly,
old, old friends as you were, and *trusted* you, he turned a terrible face

of contempt on me. You don't know, Oliver, the cold edge of Gerald's contempt for me—because he was so secure and strong in his old friendship with you. You don't know his sneering attitude to me in the deepest things—because he shared the deepest things with you. He had a passion for me. But he loved you.

OLIVER Well, he doesn't any more. We went apart after you had gone. The friendship has become almost casual.

ANABEL You see how bitterly you speak.

OLIVER Yet you didn't hate me, Anabel.

ANABEL No, Oliver—I was *awfully* fond of you. I trusted you—and I trust you still. You see I knew how fond Gerald was of you. And I had to respect this feeling. So I *had* to be aware of you: I *had* to be conscious of you: in a way, I had to love you. You understand how I mean? Not with the same fearful love with which I loved Gerald. You seemed to me warm and protecting—like a brother, you know—but a brother one *loves*.

OLIVER And then you hated me?

ANABEL Yes, I had to hate you.

OLIVER And you hated Gerald?

ANABEL Almost to madness—almost to madness.

OLIVER Then you went away with that Norwegian. What of him?

ANABEL What of him? Well, he's dead.

OLIVER Ah! That's why you came back?

ANABEL No, no. I came back because my only hope in life was in coming back. Baard was beautiful—and awful. You know how glisteningly blond he was. Oliver, have you ever watched the polar bears? He was cold as iron when it is so cold that it burns you. Coldness wasn't negative with him. It was positive—and awful beyond expression— like the aurora borealis.

OLIVER I wonder you ever got back.

ANABEL Yes, so do I. I feel as if I'd fallen down a fissure in the ice. Yet I have come back, haven't I?

OLIVER God knows! At least, Anabel, we've gone through too much ever to start the old game again. There'll be no more sticky love between us.

ANABEL No, I think there won't, either.

OLIVER And what of Gerald?

ANABEL I don't know. What do you think of him?

OLIVER I can't think any more. I can only blindly go from day to day, now.

ANABEL So can I. Do you think I was wrong to come back? Do you think I wrong Gerald?

OLIVER No. I'm glad you came. But I feel I can't *know* anything. We must just go on. 215

ANABEL Sometimes I feel I ought never to have come to Gerald again—never—never—never.

OLIVER Just left the gap?—Perhaps, if everything has to come asunder. But I think, if ever there is to be life—hope,—then you had to come 220 back. I always knew it. There is something eternal between you and him; and if there is to be any happiness, it depends on that. But perhaps there is to *be* no more happiness—for our part of the world.

ANABEL (*after a pause*) Yet I feel hope—don't you?

OLIVER Yes, sometimes. 225

ANABEL It seemed to me, especially that winter in Norway,—I can hardly express it,—as if any moment life might give way under one, like thin ice, and one would be more than dead. And then I knew my only hope was here—the only hope.

OLIVER Yes, I believe it. And I believe— 230
        Enter Mrs Barlow

MRS BARLOW Oh, I wanted to speak to you, Oliver.

OLIVER Shall I come across?

MRS BARLOW No, not now. I believe father is coming here with Gerald.

OLIVER Is he going to walk so far? 235

MRS BARLOW He will do it.—I suppose you know Oliver?

ANABEL Yes, we have met before.

MRS BARLOW (*to Oliver*) You didn't mention it. Where have you met Miss Wrath? She's been about the world, I believe.

ANABEL About the world?—no, Mrs Barlow. If one happens to know 240 Paris and London—

MRS BARLOW Paris and London! Well, I don't say you are altogether an adventuress. My husband seems very pleased with you—for Winifred's sake, I suppose—and he's wrapped up in Winifred.

ANABEL Winifred is an artist. 245

MRS BARLOW All my children have the artist in them. They get it from my family. My father went mad in Rome. My family is born with a black fate—they all inherit it.

OLIVER I believe one is master of one's fate sometimes, Mrs Barlow. There are moments of pure choice. 250

MRS BARLOW Between two ways to the same end, no doubt. There's no changing the end.

227

OLIVER I think there is.

MRS BARLOW Yes, you have a *parvenu*'s° presumptuousness somewhere about you.   255

OLIVER Well, better than a blue-blooded fatalism.

MRS BARLOW The fate is in the blood: you can't change the blood.
    Enter Winifred

WINIFRED Oh, thank you, Oliver, for the wolf and the goat, thank you
so much!—The wolf has sprung on the goat, Miss Wrath, and has her   260
by the throat.

ANABEL The wolf?

OLIVER It's a little marble group—Italian—in hard marble.

WINIFRED The wolf—I love the wolf—he pounces so beautifully. His
backbone is so terribly fierce. I don't feel a bit sorry for the goat,   265
somehow.

OLIVER I didn't. She is too much like the wrong sort of clergyman.

WINIFRED Yes—such a stiff, long face. I wish he'd kill her.

MRS BARLOW There's a wish!

WINIFRED Father and Gerald are coming. That's them, I suppose.   270
    Enter Mr Barlow and Gerald

MR BARLOW Ah, good morning—good morning—quite a little gathering! Ah—

OLIVER The steps tire you, Mr Barlow.

MR BARLOW A little—a little—thank you.—Well, Miss Wrath, are you   275
quite comfortable here?

ANABEL Very comfortable, thanks.

GERALD It was clever of you, father, to turn this place into a studio.

MR BARLOW Yes, Gerald. You make the worldly schemes and I the
homely. Yes, it's a delightful place. I shall come here often if the two   280
young ladies will allow me.—By the way, Miss Wrath, I don't know if
you have been introduced to my son Gerald. I beg your pardon. Miss
Wrath, Gerald—my son, Miss Wrath. (*They bow*) Well, we are quite
a gathering, quite a pleasant little gathering. We never expected
anything so delightful a month ago, did we, Winifred, darling?   285

WINIFRED No, daddy, it's much nicer than expectations.

MR BARLOW So it is, dear—to have such exceptional companionship
and such a pleasant retreat. We are very happy to have Miss Wrath
with us—very happy.

GERALD A studio's awfully nice, you know; it is such a retreat. A   290
newspaper has no effect in it—falls quite flat, no matter what the
headlines are.

MR BARLOW Quite true, Gerald, dear. It is a sanctum the world cannot
invade—unlike all other sanctuaries, I am afraid.

GERALD By the way, Oliver—to go back to profanities—the colliers 295
really are coming out in support of the poor, ill-used clerks.

MR BARLOW No, no, Gerald—no, no! Don't be such an alarmist. Let us
leave these subjects before the ladies. No, no: the clerks will have their
increase quite peacefully.

GERALD Yes, dear father—but they can't have it peacefully now. We've 300
been threatened already by the colliers—we've already received an
ultimatum.

MR BARLOW Nonsense, my boy—nonsense! Don't let us split words.
You won't go against the clerks in such a small matter. Always avoid
trouble over small matters. Don't make bad feeling—don't make bad 305
blood.

MRS BARLOW The blood is already rotten in this neighbourhood. What
it needs is letting out. We need a few veins opening, or we shall have
mortification setting in. The blood is black.

MR BARLOW We won't accept your figure of speech literally, dear. No, 310
Gerald, don't go to war over trifles.

GERALD It's just over trifles that one must make war, father. One can
yield gracefully over big matters. But to be bullied over trifles is a sign
of criminal weakness.

MR BARLOW Ah, not so, not so, my boy. When you are as old as I am, you 315
will know the comparative insignificance of these trifles.

GERALD The older *I* get, father, the more such trifles stick in my throat.

MR BARLOW Ah, it is an increasingly irritable disposition in you, my
child. Nothing costs so bitterly, in the end, as a stubborn pride.

MRS BARLOW Except a stubborn humility—and that will cost you 320
more. Avoid humility, beware of stubborn humility: it degrades.
Hark, Gerald—fight! When the occasion comes, fight! If it's one
against five thousand, fight! Don't give them your heart on a dish!
Never! If they want to eat your heart out, make them fight for it, and
then give it them poisoned at last, poisoned with your own blood.— 325
What do you say, young woman?

ANABEL Is it for me to speak, Mrs Barlow?

MRS BARLOW Weren't you asked?

ANABEL Certainly I would *never* give the world my heart on a dish. But
can't there ever be peace—real peace? 330

MRS BARLOW No—not while there is devilish enmity.

MR BARLOW You are wrong, dear, you are wrong. The peace can come,
the peace that passeth all understanding.°

MRS BARLOW That there is already between me and Almighty God.
I am at peace with the God that made me, and made me proud. With 335
men who humiliate me I am at war. Between me and the shameful

229

humble there is war to the end, though they are millions and I am one.
I hate the people. Between my race and them there is war—between
them and me, between them and my children—for ever war, for ever
and ever.   340

MR BARLOW Ah, Henrietta—you have said all this before.

MRS BARLOW And say it again. Fight, Gerald. You have my blood in
you, thank God. Fight for it, Gerald. Spend it as if it were costly,
Gerald, drop by drop. Let no dogs lap it.—Look at your father. He
set his heart on a plate at the door, for the poorest mongrel to eat up.   345
See him now, wasted and crossed out like a mistake—and swear,
Gerald, swear to be true to my blood in you. Never lie down before
the mob, Gerald. Fight it and stab it, and die fighting. It's a lost
hope—but fight!

GERALD Don't say these things here, mother.   350

MRS BARLOW Yes, I will—I will. I'll say them before you, and the child
Winifred—she knows. And before Oliver and the young woman—
they know, too.

MR BARLOW You see, dear, you can never understand that, although
I am weak and wasted, although I may be crossed out from the world   355
like a mistake, I still have peace in my soul, dear, the peace that passeth
all understanding.

MRS BARLOW And what right have you to it? All very well for you to
take peace with you into the other world. What do you leave for your
sons to inherit?   360

MR BARLOW The peace of God, Henrietta, if there is no peace among
men.

MRS BARLOW Then why did you have children? Why weren't you celi-
bate? They have to live among men. If they have no place among men,
why have you put them there? If the peace of God is no more than the   365
peace of death, why are your sons born of you? How can you have
peace with God, if you leave no peace for your sons—no peace, no
pride, no place on earth?

GERALD Nay, mother, nay. You shall never blame father on my behalf.

MRS BARLOW Don't trouble—he is blameless—I, a hulking, half-   370
demented woman, I am *glad* when you blame me. But don't blame me
when I tell you to fight. Don't do that, or you will regret it when you
must die. Ah, your father was stiff and proud enough before men of
better rank than himself. He was overbearing enough with his equals
and his betters. But he humbled himself before the poor, he made me   375
ashamed. He must hear it—he must hear it! Better he should hear it
than die coddling himself with peace. His humility, and my pride,

they have made a nice ruin of each other. Yet he is the man I wanted to marry—he is the man I would marry again. But never, never again would I give way before his goodness. Gerald, if you must be true to your father, be true to me as well. Don't set me down at nothing because I haven't a humble case. 380

GERALD No, mother—no, dear mother. You see, dear mother, I have rather a job between the two halves of myself. When you come to have the wild horses in your own soul, mother, it makes it difficult. 385

MRS BARLOW Never mind, you'll have help.

GERALD Thank you for the assurance, darling.—Father, you don't mind what mother says, I hope. I believe there's some truth in it—don't you?

MR BARLOW I have nothing to say. 390

WINIFRED *I* think there's some truth in it, Daddy. You were always worrying about those horrid colliers, and they didn't care a bit about you. And they *ought* to have cared a million pounds.

MR BARLOW You don't understand, my child.

    CURTAIN 395

Act 2

Scene: evening of the same day. Drawing-room at Lilley Close.
Mr Barlow, Gerald, Winifred, Anabel, Oliver present. Butler
pours coffee

MR BARLOW And you are quite a stranger in these parts, Miss Wrath?

ANABEL Practically. But I was born at Derby.

MR BARLOW I was born in this house—but it was a different affair then:
my father was a farmer, you know. The coal has brought us what
moderate wealth we have. Of course, we were never poor or needy—
farmers, substantial farmers. And I think we were happier so—
yes.—Winnie, dear, hand Miss Wrath the sweets. I hope they're
good. I ordered them from London for you.—Oliver, my boy, have
you everything you like? That's right.—It gives me such pleasure to
see a little festive gathering in this room again. I wish Bertie and
Elinor° might be here. What time is it, Gerald?

GERALD A quarter to nine, father.

MR BARLOW Not late yet. I can sit with you another half-hour. I am
feeling better to-day. Winifred, sing something to us.

WINIFRED Something jolly, father?

MR BARLOW Very jolly, darling.

WINIFRED I'll sing 'The Lincolnshire Poacher', shall I?

MR BARLOW Do, darling, and we'll all join in the chorus.—Will you
join in the chorus, Miss Wrath?

ANABEL I will. It is a good song.

MR BARLOW Yes, isn't it!

WINIFRED All dance for the chorus, as well as singing.
They sing; some pirouette a little for the chorus

MR BARLOW Ah, splendid, splendid! There is nothing like gaiety.

WINIFRED I do love to dance about. I know: let us do a little ballet—
four of us—oh, do!

GERALD What ballet, Winifred?

WINIFRED Any. Eva can play for us. She plays well.

MR BARLOW You won't disturb your mother? Don't disturb Eva if she
is busy with your mother. (*Exit Winifred*) If only I can see Winifred
happy, my heart is at rest: if only I can hope for her to be happy in
her life.

GERALD Oh, Winnie's all right, father—especially now she has Miss
Wrath to initiate her into the mysteries of life and labour.

ANABEL Why are you ironical?

232

MR BARLOW Oh, Miss Wrath, believe me, we all feel that—it is the greatest possible pleasure to me that you have come.   40

GERALD I wasn't ironical, I assure you.

MR BARLOW No, indeed—no, indeed! We have every belief in you.

ANABEL But why should you have?

MR BARLOW Ah, my dear child, allow us the credit of our own discern-ment. And don't take offence at my familiarity. I am afraid I am spoilt   45
since I am an invalid.

    Re-enter Winifred, with Eva

MR BARLOW Come, Eva, you will excuse us for upsetting your evening. Will you be so good as to play something for us to dance to?

EVA Yes, sir. What shall I play?   50

WINIFRED Mozart—I'll find you the piece. Mozart's the saddest musician in the world—but he's the best to dance to.

MR BARLOW Why, how is it you are such a connoisseur in sadness, darling?

GERALD She isn't. She's a flagrant amateur.   55

    Eva plays; they dance a little ballet

MR BARLOW Charming—charming, Miss Wrath: will you allow me to say *Anabel*, we shall all feel so much more at home? Yes—thank you—er—you enter into the spirit of it wonderfully, Anabel, dear. The others are accustomed to play together. But it is not so easy to   60
come in on occasion as you do.

GERALD Oh, Anabel's a genius!—I beg your pardon, Miss Wrath—familiarity is catching.

MR BARLOW Gerald, my boy, don't forget that you are virtually host here.   65

EVA Did you want any more music, sir?

GERALD No, don't stay, Eva. We mustn't tire father.

    Exit Eva

MR BARLOW I am afraid, Anabel, you will have a great deal to excuse in us, in the way of manners. We have never been a formal household.   70
But you have lived in the world of artists: you will understand, I hope.

ANABEL Oh, surely—

MR BARLOW Yes, I know. We have been a turbulent family, and we have had our share of sorrow, even more, perhaps, than of joys. And sorrow makes one indifferent to the conventionalities of life.   75

GERALD Excuse me, father: do you mind if I go and write a letter I have on my conscience?

MR BARLOW No, my boy. (*Exit Gerald*) We have had our share of sorrow and of conflict, Miss Wrath, as you may have gathered.

ANABEL Yes—a little.   80

MR BARLOW The mines were opened when my father was a boy—the first—and I was born late, when he was nearly fifty. So that all my life has been involved with coal and colliers. As a young man, I was gay and thoughtless. But I married young, and we lost our first child through a terrible accident. Two children we have lost through 85
sudden and violent death. (*Winifred goes out unnoticed*) It made me reflect. And when I came to reflect, Anabel, I could not justify my position in life. If I believed in the teachings of the New Testament—which I did, and do—how could I keep two or three thousand men employed underground in the mines, at a wage, let us say, of two 90
pounds a week, whilst I lived in this comfortable house, and took something like two thousand pounds a year—let us name any figure—

ANABEL Yes, of course. But is it money that really matters, Mr Barlow?

MR BARLOW My dear, if you are a working man, it matters. When I went into the homes of my poor fellows, when they were ill or had had 95
accidents—then I knew it mattered. I knew that the great disparity was wrong—even as we are taught that it is wrong.

ANABEL Yes, I believe that the great disparity is a mistake. But take their lives, Mr Barlow. Do you think they would *live* more, if they had more money? Do you think the poor live less than the rich?—is their 100
life emptier?

MR BARLOW Surely their lives would be better, Anabel.

OLIVER All our lives would be better, if we hadn't to hang on in the perpetual tug-of-war, like two donkeys pulling at one carrot. The ghastly tension of possessions, and struggling for possession, spoils 105
life for everybody.

MR BARLOW Yes, I know now, as I knew then, that it was wrong. But how to avoid the wrong? If I gave away the whole of my income, it would merely be an arbitrary dispensation of charity. The money would still be mine to give, and those that received it would probably 110
only be weakened instead of strengthened. And then my wife was accustomed to a certain way of living, a certain establishment. Had I any right to sacrifice her, without her consent?

ANABEL Why, no!

MR BARLOW Again, if I withdrew from the Company, if I retired on a 115
small income, I knew that another man would automatically take my place, and make it probably harder for the men.

ANABEL Of course—while the system stands, if one makes self-sacrifice one only panders to the system, makes it fatter.

MR BARLOW One panders to the system—one panders to the system. 120
And so, you see, the problem is too much. One man cannot alter or

234

affect the system; he can only sacrifice himself to it. Which is the worst thing probably that he can do.

OLIVER Quite. But why feel guilty for the system?—everybody supports it, the poor as much as the rich. If every rich man withdrew from the system, the working classes and socialists would keep it going, every man in the hope of getting rich himself at last. It's the people that are wrong. They want the system much more than the rich do—because they are much more anxious to be rich—never having been rich, poor devils. 125 130

MR BARLOW Just the system. So I decided at last that the best way was to give every private help that lay in my power. I would help my men individually and personally, wherever I could. Not one of them came to me and went away unheard; and there was no distress which could be alleviated that I did not try to alleviate. Yet I am afraid that the greatest distress I never heard of, the most distressed never came to me. They hid their trouble. 135

ANABEL Yes, the decent ones.

MR BARLOW But I wished to help—it was my duty. Still, I think that, on the whole, we were a comfortable and happy community. Barlow and Walsall's men were not unhappy in those days, I believe. We were liberal; the men lived. 140

OLIVER Yes, that is true. Even twenty years ago the place was still jolly.

MR BARLOW And then, when Gerald was a lad of thirteen, came the great lock-out.° We belonged to the Masters' Federation°—I was but one man on the Board. We had to abide by the decision. The mines were closed till the men would accept the reduction.—Well, that cut my life across. We were shutting the men out from work, starving their families, in order to force them to accept a reduction. It may be the condition of trade made it imperative. But, for myself, I would rather have lost everything.—Of course, we did what we could. Food was very cheap—practically given away. We had open kitchen here. And it was mercifully warm summer-time. Nevertheless, there was privation and suffering, and trouble and bitterness. We had the redcoats° down—even to guard this house. And from this window I saw Whatmore head-stocks ablaze, and before I could get to the spot the soldiers had shot two poor fellows. They were not killed, thank God— 145 150 155

OLIVER Ah, but they enjoyed it—they enjoyed it immensely. I remember what grand old sporting weeks they were. It was like a fox-hunt, so lively and gay—bands and tea-parties and excitement everywhere, pit-ponies loose, men all over the countryside— 160

MR BARLOW There was a great deal of suffering which you were too young to appreciate. However, since that year I have had to acknowledge a new situation—a radical if unspoken opposition 165 between masters and men. Since that year we have been split into opposite camps. Whatever I might privately feel, I was one of the owners, one of the masters, and therefore in the opposite camp. To my men I was an oppressor, a representative of injustice and greed. Privately, I like to think that even to this day they bear me no 170 malice, that they have some lingering regard for me. But the master stands before the human being, and the condition of war overrides individuals—they hate the master, even whilst, as a human being, he would be their friend. I recognize the inevitable justice. It is the price one has to pay. 175

ANABEL Yes, it is difficult—very.

MR BARLOW Perhaps I weary you?

ANABEL Oh, no—no.

MR BARLOW Well—then the mines began to pay badly. The seams ran thin and unprofitable, work was short. Either we must close down 180 or introduce a new system, American methods, which I dislike so extremely. Now it really became a case of men working against machines, flesh and blood working against iron, for a livelihood. Still, it had to be done—the whole system revolutionized. Gerald took it in hand—and now I hardly know my own pits, with the great electric 185 plants and strange machinery, and the new coal-cutters—iron men, as the colliers call them—everything running at top speed, utterly dehumanized, inhuman. Well, it had to be done; it was the only alternative to closing down and throwing three thousand men out of work. And Gerald has done it. But I can't bear to see it. The men of 190 this generation are not like my men. They are worn and gloomy; they have a hollow look that I can't bear to see. They are a great grief to me. I remember my men even twenty years ago—a noisy, lively, careless set, who kept the place ringing. Now it is too quiet—too quiet. There is something wrong in the quietness, something unnatural. I feel it is 195 unnatural; I feel afraid of it. And I cannot help feeling guilty.

ANABEL Yes—I understand. It terrifies me.

MR BARLOW Does it?—does it?—Yes.—And as my wife says, I leave it all to Gerald—this terrible situation. But I appeal to God, if anything in my power could have averted it, I would have averted it. I would 200 have made any sacrifice. For it is a great and bitter trouble to me.

ANABEL Ah, well, in death there is no industrial situation. Something must be different there.

MR BARLOW Yes—yes.

OLIVER And you see sacrifice isn't the slightest use. If only people   205
would be sane and decent.

MR BARLOW Yes, indeed.—Would you be so good as to ring, Oliver?
I think I must go to bed.

ANABEL Ah, you have over-tired yourself.

MR BARLOW No, my dear—not over-tired. Excuse me if I have   210
burdened you with all this. It relieves me to speak of it.

ANABEL I realize *how* terrible it is, Mr Barlow—and how helpless one
is.

MR BARLOW Thank you, my dear, for your sympathy.

OLIVER If the people for one minute pulled themselves up and con-   215
quered their mania for money and machine excitement, the whole
thing would be solved.—Would you like me to find Winnie and tell
her to say good-night to you?

MR BARLOW If you would be so kind. (*Exit Oliver*) Can't you find a
sweet that you would like, my dear? Won't you take a little cherry   220
brandy?

　　　Enter butler

ANABEL Thank you.

WILLIAM You will go up, sir?

MR BARLOW Yes, William.   225

WILLIAM You are tired to-night, sir.

MR BARLOW It has come over me just now.

WILLIAM I wish you went up before you became so over-tired, sir.
Would you like Nurse?

MR BARLOW No, I'll go with you, William. Good night, my dear.   230

ANABEL Good night, Mr Barlow. I am so sorry if you are over-tired.
　　　Exit butler and Mr Barlow. Anabel takes a drink and goes to the
　　　fire. Enter Gerald

GERALD Father gone up?

ANABEL Yes.   235

GERALD I thought I heard him. Has he been talking too much?—Poor
father, he will take things to heart.

ANABEL Tragic, really.

GERALD Yes, I suppose it is. But one can get beyond tragedy—beyond
the state of feeling tragical, I mean. Father himself is tragical. One   240
feels he is mistaken—and yet he wouldn't be any different, and be
himself, I suppose. He's sort of crucified on an idea of the working
people. It's rather horrible when he's one's father.—However, apart
from tragedy, how do you like being here, in this house?

ANABEL I like the house. It's rather too comfortable.   245

GERALD Yes. But how do you like being here?

ANABEL How do you like my being in your home?

GERALD Oh, I think you're very decorative.

ANABEL More decorative than comfortable?

GERALD Perhaps. But perhaps you give the necessary finish to the   250
establishment.

ANABEL Like the correct window-curtains?

GERALD Yes, something like that. I say, why did you come, Anabel?
Why did you come slap-bang into the middle of us?—It's not expos-
tulation—I want to know.   255

ANABEL You mean you want to be told.

GERALD Yes, I want to be told.

ANABEL That's rather mean of you. You should savvy, and let it go
without saying.

GERALD Yes, but I don't savvy.   260

ANABEL Then wait till you do.

GERALD No, I want to be told. There's a difference in you, Anabel, that
puts me out, rather. You're sort of softer and sweeter—I'm not sure
whether it isn't a touch of father in you. There's a little sanctified
smudge on your face. Are you really a bit sanctified?   265

ANABEL No, not sanctified. It's true I feel different. I feel I want a new
way of life—something more dignified, more religious, if you like—
anyhow, something *positive*.

GERALD Is it the change of heart, Anabel?

ANABEL Perhaps it is, Gerald.   270

GERALD I m not sure that I like it. Isn't it like a berry that decides to get
very sweet, and goes soft?

ANABEL I don't think so.

GERALD Slightly sanctimonious. I think I liked you better before. I
don't think I like you with this touch of aureole. People seem to me so   275
horribly self-satisfied when they get a change of heart—they take
such a fearful lot of credit to themselves on the strength of it.

ANABEL I don't think I do.—Do you feel no different, Gerald?

GERALD Radically, I can't say I do.—I feel very much more *in*different.

ANABEL What to?   280

GERALD Everything.

ANABEL You're still angry—that's what it is.

GERALD Oh yes, I'm angry. But that is part of my normal state.

ANABEL Why are you angry?

GERALD Is there any reason why I shouldn't be angry? I'm angry 285
     because you treated me—well, so impudently, really—clearing out
     and leaving one to whistle to the empty walls.

ANABEL Don't you think it was time I cleared out, when you became so
     violent, and really dangerous, really like a madman?

GERALD Time or not time, you went—you disappeared and left us high 290
     and dry—and I am still angry.—But I'm not only angry about that.
     I'm angry with the colliers, with Labour for its low-down impu-
     dence—and I'm angry with father for being so ill—and I'm angry
     with mother for looking such a hopeless thing—and I'm angry with
     Oliver because he thinks so much— 295

ANABEL And what are you angry with yourself for?

GERALD I'm angry with myself for being myself—I always was that.
     I was always a curse to myself.

ANABEL And that's why you curse others so much?

GERALD You talk as if butter wouldn't melt in your mouth. 300

ANABEL You see, Gerald, there has to be a change. You'll have to
     change.

GERALD Change of heart?—Well, it won't be to get softer, Anabel.

ANABEL You needn't be softer. But you can be quieter, more sane even.
     There ought to be some part of you that can be quiet and apart from 305
     the world, some part that can be happy and gentle.

GERALD Well, there isn't. I don't pretend to be able to extricate a soft
     sort of John Halifax, Gentleman,° out of the machine I'm mixed up in,
     and keep him to gladden the connubial hearth. I'm angry, and I'm
     angry right through, and I'm not going to play bo–peep with myself, 310
     pretending I'm not.

ANABEL Nobody asks you to. But is there no part of you that can be a bit
     gentle and peaceful and happy with a woman?

GERALD No, there isn't.—I'm not going to smug with you—no, not I.
     You're smug in your coming back. You feel virtuous, and expect me 315
     to rise to it. I won't.

ANABEL Then I'd better have stayed away.

GERALD If you want me to virtue-ize and smug with you,° you had.

ANABEL What *do* you want, then?

GERALD I don't know. I know I don't want *that*. 320

ANABEL Oh, very well. (*Goes to the piano; begins to play*)
     Enter Mrs Barlow

GERALD Hello, mother! Father *has* gone to bed.

MRS BARLOW Oh, I thought he was down here talking. You two alone?

GERALD With the piano for chaperone, mother.   325

MRS BARLOW That's more than I gave you credit for. I haven't come to chaperone you either, Gerald.

GERALD Chaperone *me*, mother! Do you think I need it?

MRS BARLOW If you do, you won't get it. I've come too late to be of any use in that way, as far as I hear.   330

GERALD What have you heard, mother?

MRS BARLOW I heard Oliver and this young woman talking.

GERALD Oh, did you? When? What did they say?

MRS BARLOW Something about married in the sight of heaven, but couldn't keep it up on earth.   335

GERALD I don't understand.

MRS BARLOW That you and this young woman were married in the sight of heaven, or through eternity, or something similar, but that you couldn't make up your minds to it on earth.

GERALD Really! That's very curious, mother.   340

MRS BARLOW Very common occurrence, I believe.

GERALD Yes, so it is. But I don't think you heard quite right, dear. There seems to be some lingering uneasiness in heaven as a matter of fact. We'd quite made up our minds to live apart on earth. But where did you hear this, mother?   345

MRS BARLOW I heard it outside the studio door this morning.

GERALD You mean you happened to be on one side of the door while Oliver and Anabel were talking on the other?

MRS BARLOW You'd make a detective, Gerald—you're so good at putting two and two together. I listened till I'd heard as much as I   350
wanted. I'm not sure I didn't come down here hoping to hear another conversation going on.

GERALD Listen outside the door, darling?

MRS BARLOW There'd be nothing to listen to if I were inside.

GERALD It isn't usually done, you know.   355

MRS BARLOW I listen outside doors when I have occasion to be interested—which isn't often, unfortunately for me.

GERALD But I've a queer feeling that you have a permanent occasion to be interested in me. I only half like it.

MRS BARLOW It's surprising how uninteresting you are, Gerald, for a   360
man of your years. I have not had occasion to listen outside a door, for you, no, not for a great while, believe me.

GERALD I believe you implicitly, darling. But do you happen to know me through and through, and in and out, all my past and present doings, mother? Have you a secret access to my room, and a spy-hole,   365 and all those things? This is uncomfortably thrilling. You take on a new lustre.

MRS BARLOW Your memoirs wouldn't make you famous, my son.

GERALD Infamous, dear?

MRS BARLOW Good heavens, no! What a lot you expect from your very mild sins! You and this young woman have lived together, then?

GERALD Don't say 'this young woman', mother dear—it's slightly vulgar. It isn't for me to compromise Anabel by admitting such a thing, you know.

MRS BARLOW Do you ask me to call her Anabel? I won't.

GERALD Then say 'this person', mother. It's more becoming.

MRS BARLOW I didn't come to speak to you, Gerald. I know you. I came to speak to this young woman.

GERALD 'Person', mother.—Will you curtsey, Anabel? And I'll twist my handkerchief. We shall make a Cruikshank° drawing, if mother makes her hair a little more slovenly.

MRS BARLOW You and Gerald were together for some time?

GERALD Three years, off and on, mother.

MRS BARLOW And then you suddenly dropped my son, and went away?

GERALD To Norway, mother—so I have gathered.

MRS BARLOW And now you have come back because that last one died?

GERALD Is he dead, Anabel? How did he die?

ANABEL He was killed on the ice.

GERALD Oh, God!

MRS BARLOW Now, having had your fill of tragedy, you have come back to be demure and to marry Gerald. Does he thank you?

GERALD You must listen outside the door, mother, to find that out.

MRS BARLOW Well, it's your own affair.

GERALD What a lame summing up, mother—quite unworthy of you.

ANABEL What did you wish to say to me, Mrs Barlow? Please say it.

MRS BARLOW What did I wish to say! Ay, what did I wish to say! What is the use of my saying anything? What am I but a buffoon and a slovenly caricature in the family?

GERALD No, mother dear, don't climb down—please don't. Tell Anabel what you wanted to say.

MRS BARLOW Yes—yes—yes. I came to say—don't be good to my son—don't be good to him.

GERALD Sounds weak, dear—mere contrariness.

MRS BARLOW Don't presume to be good to my son, young woman. I won't have it, even if he will. You hear me?

ANABEL Yes. I won't presume, then.

GERALD May she presume to be bad to me, mother?

MRS BARLOW For that you may look after yourself.—But a woman who was good to him would ruin him in six months, take the manhood out of him. He has a tendency, a secret hankering, to make a gift of himself to somebody. He shan't do it. I warn you. I am not a woman to be despised.   410

ANABEL No—I understand.

MRS BARLOW Only one other thing I ask. If he must fight—and fight he must—let him alone: don't you try to shield him or save him. *Don't interfere*—do you hear?   415

ANABEL Not till I must.

MRS BARLOW *Never.* Learn your place, and keep it. Keep away from him, if you are going to be a wife to him. Don't go too near. And don't let him come too near. Beat him off if he tries. Keep a solitude in your heart even when you love him best. Keep it. If you lose it, you lose   420
everything.

GERALD But that isn't love, mother.

MRS BARLOW What?

GERALD That isn't love.

MRS BARLOW *What?* What do you know of love, you ninny? You only   425
know the feeding-bottle. It's what you want, all of you—to be brought up by hand, and mew about love. Ah, God!—Ah, God!— that you should none of you know the only thing which would make you worth having.

GERALD I don't believe in your only thing, mother. But what is it?   430

MRS BARLOW What you haven't got—the power to be alone.

GERALD Sort of megalomania, you mean?

MRS BARLOW What? Megalomania! What is your *love* but a megalo- mania, flowing over everybody, and everything like spilt water? Mega- lomania! I hate you, you softy! I would *beat* you (*Suddenly advancing   435 on him and beating him fiercely*)—beat you into some manhood— beat you—

GERALD Stop, mother—keep off.

MRS BARLOW It's the men who need beating nowadays, not the children. Beat the softness out of him, young woman. It's the only   440 way, if you love him enough—if you love him enough.

GERALD You hear, Anabel?

> *Speak roughly to your little boy,*
> *And beat him when he sneezes.*°

MRS BARLOW (*catching up a large old fan, and smashing it about his head*)   445
You softy—you piffler—you will never have had enough! Ah, you

should be thrust in the fire, you should, to have the softness and the brittleness burnt out of you!

> *The door opens—Oliver Turton enters, followed by Job Arthur Freer. Mrs Barlow is still attacking Gerald. She turns, infuriated*   450

Go out! Go out! What do you mean by coming in unannounced? Take him upstairs—take that fellow into the library, Oliver Turton.°

GERALD Mother, you improve our already pretty reputation. Already they say you are mad.

MRS BARLOW (*ringing violently*) Let me be mad then. I am mad—   455
driven mad. One day I shall kill you, Gerald.

GERALD You won't, mother, because I shan't let you.

MRS BARLOW Let me!—let me! As if I should wait for you to let me!

GERALD I am a match for you even in violence, come to that.

MRS BARLOW A match! A damp match. A wet match.   460

> *Enter butler*

WILLIAM You rang, madam?

MRS BARLOW Clear up those bits.—Where are you going to see that white-faced fellow? Here?

GERALD I think so.   465

MRS BARLOW You will *still* have them coming to the house, will you? You will still let them trample in our private rooms, will you? Bah! I ought to leave you to your own devices.

> *Exit*

GERALD When you've done that, William, ask Mr Freer to come down   470
here.

WILLIAM Yes, sir.

> *A pause. Exit William*

GERALD So-o-o. You've had another glimpse of the family life.

ANABEL Yes. Rather—disturbing.   475

GERALD Not at all, when you're used to it. Mother isn't as mad as she pretends to be.

ANABEL I don't think she's mad at all. I think she has most desperate courage.

GERALD 'Courage' is good. That's a new term for it.   480

ANABEL Yes, courage. When a man says 'courage' he means the courage to die. A woman means the courage to live. That's what women hate men most for; that they haven't the courage to live.

GERALD Mother takes her courage into both hands rather late.

ANABEL We're a little late ourselves.   485

GERALD We are, rather. By the way, you seem to have had plenty of the courage of death—you've played a pretty deathly game, it seems to me—both when I knew you and afterwards, you've had your finger pretty deep in the death-pie.

ANABEL That's why I want a change of—of—   490

GERALD Of heart?—Better take mother's tip, and try the poker.

ANABEL I will.

GERALD Ha—corraggio!°

ANABEL Yes—corraggio!

GERALD Corraggiaccio!°   495

ANABEL Corraggione!°

GERALD Cock-a-doodle-doo!

Enter Oliver and Freer

Oh, come in. Don't be afraid; it's a charade. (*Anabel rises*) No, don't go, Anabel. Corraggio! Take a seat, Mr Freer.   500

JOB ARTHUR Sounds like a sneezing game, doesn't it?

GERALD It is. Do you know the famous rhyme:

Speak roughly to your little boy,
And beat him when he sneezes?

JOB ARTHUR No, I can't say I do.   505

GERALD My mother does. Will you have anything to drink? Will you help yourself?

JOB ARTHUR Well—no—I don't think I'll have anything, thanks.

GERALD A cherry brandy?—Yes?—Anabel, what's yours?

ANABEL Did I see Kümmel?°   510

GERALD You did. (*They all take drinks*) What's the latest, Mr Freer?

JOB ARTHUR The latest? Well, I don't know, I'm sure—

GERALD Oh, yes. Trot it out. We're quite private.

JOB ARTHUR Well—I don't know. There's several things.

GERALD The more the merrier.   515

JOB ARTHUR I'm not so sure. The men are in a very funny temper, Mr Barlow—very funny.

GERALD Coincidence—so am I. Not surprising, is it?

JOB ARTHUR The men, perhaps not.

GERALD What else, Job Arthur?   520

JOB ARTHUR You know the men have decided to stand by the office men?

GERALD Yes.

JOB ARTHUR They've agreed to come out next Monday.

GERALD Have they?

JOB ARTHUR Yes; there was no stopping them. They decided for it like   525
one man.

GERALD How was that?

JOB ARTHUR That's what surprises me. They're a jolly sight more certain over this than they've ever been over their own interests.

GERALD All their love for the office clerks coming out in a rush?   530

JOB ARTHUR Well, I don't know about love; but that's how it is.

GERALD What is it, if it isn't love?

JOB ARTHUR I can't say. They're in a funny temper. It's hard to make out.

GERALD A funny temper, are they? Then I suppose we ought to laugh.

JOB ARTHUR No, I don't think it's a laughing matter. They're coming   535
out on Monday for certain.

GERALD Yes—so are daffodils.

JOB ARTHUR Beg pardon?

GERALD Daffodils.

JOB ARTHUR No, I don't follow what you mean.   540

GERALD Don't you? But I thought Alfred Breffitt and William Straw
were not very popular.

JOB ARTHUR No, they aren't—not in themselves. But it's the principle
of the thing—so it seems.

GERALD What principle?   545

JOB ARTHUR Why, all sticking together, for one thing—all Barlow and
Walsall's men holding by one another.

GERALD United we stand?

JOB ARTHUR That's it. And then it's the strong defending the weak as
well. There's three thousand colliers standing up for thirty-odd   550
office men. I must say I think it's sporting myself.

GERALD You do, do you? United we stand, divided we fall. What do
they stand for, really? What is it?

JOB ARTHUR Well—for their right to a living wage. That's how I see it.

GERALD For their right to a living wage! Just that?   555

JOB ARTHUR Yes, sir—that's how I see it.

GERALD Well, that doesn't seem so preposterously difficult, does it?

JOB ARTHUR Why, that's what I think myself, Mr Gerald. It's such a
little thing.

GERALD Quite. I suppose the men themselves are to judge what is a   560
living wage?

JOB ARTHUR Oh, I think they're quite reasonable, you know.

GERALD Oh, yes, eminently reasonable. Reason's their strong point.—
And if they get their increase they'll be quite contented?

JOB ARTHUR Yes, as far as I know, they will.   565

GERALD As far as you know? Why, is there something you don't know?
—something you're not sure about?

JOB ARTHUR No—I don't think so. I think they'll be quite satisfied this
time.

GERALD Why this time? Is there going to be a next time—every-day-   570
has-its-to-morrow kind of thing?

JOB ARTHUR I don't know about that. It's a funny world, Mr Barlow.

GERALD Yes, I quite believe it. How do you see it funny?

JOB ARTHUR Oh, I don't know. Everything's in a funny state.

GERALD What do you mean by everything?   575

JOB ARTHUR Well—I mean things in general—Labour, for example.

GERALD You think Labour's in a funny state, do you? What do you
    think it wants? What do you think, personally?

JOB ARTHUR Well, in my own mind, I think it wants a bit of its own
    back.   580

GERALD And how does it mean to get it?

JOB ARTHUR Ha! that's not so easy to say. But it means to have it, in the
    long run.

GERALD You mean by increasing demands for higher wages?

JOB ARTHUR Yes, perhaps that's one road.   585

GERALD Do you see any other?

JOB ARTHUR Not just for the present.

GERALD But later on?

JOB ARTHUR I can't say about that. The men will be quiet enough for a
    bit, if it's all right about the office men, you know.   590

GERALD Probably. But have Barlow and Walsall's men any special griev-
    ance apart from the rest of the miners?

JOB ARTHUR I don't know. They've no liking for you, you know, sir.

GERALD Why?

JOB ARTHUR They think you've got a down on them.   595

GERALD Why should they?

JOB ARTHUR I don't know, sir; but they do.

GERALD So they have a personal feeling against me? You don't think all
    the colliers are the same, all over the country?

JOB ARTHUR I think there's a good deal of feeling—   600

GERALD Of wanting their own back?

JOB ARTHUR That's it.

GERALD But what can they do? I don't see what they can do. They can
    go out on strike—but they've done that before, and the owners, at a
    pinch, can stand it better than they can. As for the ruin of the   605
    industry, if they do ruin it, it falls heaviest on them. In fact, it leaves
    them destitute. There's nothing they can do, you know, that doesn't
    hit them worse than it hits us.

JOB ARTHUR I know there's something in that. But if they had a strong
    man to head them, you see—   610

GERALD Yes, I've heard a lot about that strong man—but I've never
    come across any signs of him, you know. I don't believe in one strong
    man appearing out of so many little men. All men are pretty big in an

age, or in a movement, which produces a really big man. And Labour is a great swarm of hopelessly little men. That's how I see it. 615

JOB ARTHUR I m not so sure about that.

GERALD I am. Labour is a thing that can't have a head. It's a sort of unwieldy monster that's bound to run its skull against the wall sooner or later, and knock out what bit of brain it's got. You see, you need wit and courage and real understanding if you're going to do 620 anything positive. And Labour has none of these things—certainly it shows no sign of them.

JOB ARTHUR Yes, when it has a chance, I think you'll see plenty of courage and plenty of understanding.

GERALD It always has a chance. And where one sees a bit of courage, 625 there's no understanding; and where there's some understanding, there's absolutely no courage. It's hopeless, you know—it would be far best if they'd all give it up, and try a new line.

JOB ARTHUR I don't think they will.

GERALD No, I don't either. They'll make a mess, and when they've 630 made it, they'll never get out of it. They can't—they're too stupid.

JOB ARTHUR They've never had a try yet.

GERALD They're trying every day. They just simply couldn't control modern industry—they haven't the intelligence. They've no *life* intelligence. The owners may have little enough, but Labour has 635 none. They're just mechanical little things that can make one or two motions, and they're done. They've no more idea of life than a lawn-mower has.

JOB ARTHUR It remains to be seen.

GERALD No, it doesn't. It's perfectly obvious—there's nothing remains 640 to be seen. All that Labour is capable of, is smashing things up. And even for that I don't believe it has either energy or the courage or the bit of necessary passion, or slap-dash—call it whatever you will. However, we'll see.

JOB ARTHUR Yes, sir. Perhaps you see now why you're not so very 645 popular, Mr Gerald.

GERALD We can't all be popular, Job Arthur. You're very high up in popularity, I believe.

JOB ARTHUR Not so very. They listen to me a bit. But you never know when they'll let you down. I know they'll let me down one day—so it 650 won't be a surprise.

GERALD I should think not.

JOB ARTHUR But about the office men, Mr Gerald. You think it'll be all right?

GERALD Oh, yes, that'll be all right. 655

JOB ARTHUR Easiest for this time, anyhow, sir. We don't want bloodshed, do we?

GERALD I shouldn't mind at all. It might clear the way to something.
But I have absolutely no belief in the power of Labour even to bring
about anything so positive as bloodshed.   660

JOB ARTHUR I don't know about that—I don't know.—Well.

GERALD Have another drink before you go.—Yes, do. Help yourself.

JOB ARTHUR Well—if you're so pressing. (*Helps himself*) Here's luck,
all!

ALL Thanks.   665

GERALD Take a cigar—there's the box. Go on—take a handful—fill
your case.

JOB ARTHUR They're a great luxury nowadays, aren't they? Almost
beyond a man like me.

GERALD Yes, that's the worst of not being a bloated capitalist. Never   670
mind, you'll be a Cabinet Minister some day.—Oh, all right—I'll
open the door for you.

JOB ARTHUR Oh, don't trouble. Good night—good night.
        Exit Job Arthur and Gerald

OLIVER Oh God, what a world to live in!   675

ANABEL I rather liked him. What is he?

OLIVER Checkweighman°—local secretary for the Miners' Federation—
plays the violin well, although he was a collier, and it spoilt his hands.
They're a musical family.

ANABEL But isn't he rather nice?   680

OLIVER I don't like him. But I confess he's a study.° He's the modern
Judas.

ANABEL Don't you think he likes Gerald?

OLIVER I'm sure he does. The way he suns himself here—like a cat
purring in his luxuriation.   685

ANABEL Yes, I don't mind it. It shows a certain sensitiveness and a
certain taste.

OLIVER Yes, he has both—touch of the artist, as Mrs Barlow says. He
loves refinement, culture, breeding, all those things—loves them—
and a presence, a fine free manner.   690

ANABEL But that is nice in him.

OLIVER Quite. But what he loves, and what he admires, and what
he aspires to, he *must* betray. It's his fatality. He lives for the moment
when he can kiss Gerald in the Garden of Olives,° or wherever it was.

ANABEL But Gerald shouldn't be kissed.   695

OLIVER That's what I say.

ANABEL And that's what his mother means as well, I suppose.
    Enter Gerald
GERALD Well—you've heard the voice of the people.
ANABEL He isn't the people.   700
GERALD I think he is, myself—the epitome.
OLIVER No, he's a special type.
GERALD Ineffectual, don't you think?
ANABEL How pleased you are, Gerald! How pleased you are with your-
    self! You love the turn with him.   705
GERALD It's rather stimulating, you know.
ANABEL It oughtn't to be, then.
OLIVER He's your Judas, and you love him.
GERALD Nothing so deep. He's just a sort of Æolian harp° that sings to
    the temper of the wind. I find him amusing.   710
ANABEL I think it's boring.
OLIVER And I think it's nasty.
GERALD I believe you're both jealous of him. What do you think of the
    British working man, Oliver?
OLIVER It seems to me he's in nearly as bad a way as the British   715
    employer: he's nearly as much beside the point.
GERALD What point?
OLIVER Oh, just life.
GERALD That's too vague, my boy. Do you think they'll ever make a
    bust-up?   720
OLIVER I can't tell. I don't see any good in it, if they do.
GERALD It might clear the way—and it might block the way for ever:
    depends what comes through. But, sincerely, I don't think they've
    got it in them.
ANABEL They may have something better.   725
GERALD That suggestion doesn't interest me, Anabel. Ah well, we shall
    see what we shall see. Have a whisky and soda with me, Oliver, and let
    the troubled course of this evening run to a smooth close. It's quite
    like old times. Aren't you smoking, Anabel?
ANABEL No, thanks.   730
GERALD I believe you're a reformed character. So it won't be like old
    times, after all.
ANABEL I don't want old times. I want new ones.
GERALD Wait till Job Arthur has risen like Antichrist, and proclaimed
    the resurrection of the gods.—Do you see Job Arthur proclaiming   735
    Dionysus and Aphrodite?°
ANABEL It bores me. I don't like your mood. Good night.

GERALD Oh, don't go.

ANABEL Yes, good night.

   Exit   740

OLIVER She's *not* reformed, Gerald. She's the same old moral character—moral to the last bit of her, really—as she always was.

GERALD Is that what it is?—But one must be moral.

OLIVER Oh, yes. Oliver Cromwell° wasn't as moral as Anabel is nor such an iconoclast.   745

GERALD Poor old Anabel!

OLIVER How she hates the dark gods!

GERALD And yet they cast a spell over her. Poor old Anabel! Well, Oliver, is Bacchus the father of whisky?

OLIVER I don't know.—I don't like you either. You seem to smile all 750
over yourself. It's objectionable. Good night.

GERALD Oh, look here, this is censorious.

OLIVER You smile to yourself.

   Exit Oliver.

   CURTAIN   755

Act 3 Scene 1

An old park. Early evening. In the background a low Georgian
hall, which has been turned into offices for the Company, shows
windows already lighted. Gerald and Anabel walk along the path

ANABEL How beautiful this old park is!

GERALD Yes, it is beautiful—seems so far away from everywhere, if one
doesn't remember that the hall is turned into offices.—No one has
lived here since I was a little boy. I remember going to a Christmas
party at the Walsalls'.

ANABEL Has it been shut up so long?

GERALD The Walsalls didn't like it—too near the ugliness. They were
county,° you know—we never were: father never gave mother a
chance, there. And besides, the place is damp, cellars full of water.

ANABEL Even now?

GERALD No, not now—they've been drained. But the place would
be too damp for a dwelling-house. It's all right as offices. They burn
enormous fires. The rooms are quite charming. This is what happens
to the stately homes of England—they buzz with inky clerks, or their
equivalent. Stateliness is on its last legs.

ANABEL Yes, it grieves me—though I should be bored if I had to be
stately, I think.—Isn't it beautiful in this light, like an eighteenth-
century aquatint? I'm sure no age was as ugly as this, since the world
began.

GERALD For pure ugliness, certainly not. And I believe none has been
so filthy to live in.—Let us sit down a minute, shall we? and watch the
rooks fly home. It always stirs sad, sentimental feelings in me.

ANABEL So it does in me.—Listen! one can hear the coal-carts on the
road—and the brook—and the dull noise of the town—and the
beating of New London pit—and voices—and the rooks—and yet it
is so still. We seem so still here, don't we?

GERALD Yes.

ANABEL Don't you think we've been wrong?

GERALD How?

ANABEL In the way we've lived—and the way we've loved.

GERALD It hasn't been heaven, has it? Yet, I don't know that we've been
wrong, Anabel. We had it to go through.

ANABEL Perhaps.—And, yes, we've been wrong too.

GERALD Probably. Only, I don't feel it like that.

ANABEL   Then I think you ought. You ought to feel you've been wrong.

GERALD   Yes, probably. Only, I don't. I can't help it. I think we've gone the way we had to go, following our own natures.

ANABEL   And where has it landed us?

GERALD   Here.

ANABEL   And where is that?

GERALD   Just on this bench in the park, looking at the evening.

ANABEL   But what next?

GERALD   God knows! Why trouble?

ANABEL   One must trouble. I want to feel sure.

GERALD   What of?

ANABEL   Of you—and of myself.

GERALD   Then *be* sure.

ANABEL   But I can't. Think of the past—what it's been.

GERALD   This isn't the past.

ANABEL   But what is it? Is there anything sure in it? Is there any real happiness?

GERALD   Why not?

ANABEL   But how can you ask? Think of what our life has been.

GERALD   I don't want to.

ANABEL   No, you don't. But what *do* you want?

GERALD   I'm all right, you know, sitting here like this.

ANABEL   But one can't sit here for ever, can one?

GERALD   I don't want to.

ANABEL   And what will you do when we leave here?

GERALD   God knows! Don't worry me. Be still a bit.

ANABEL   But *I'm* worried. You don't love me.

GERALD   I won't argue it.

ANABEL   And I'm not happy.

GERALD   Why not, Anabel?

ANABEL   Because you don't love me—and I can't forget.

GERALD   I do love you—and to-night I've forgotten.

ANABEL   Then make me forget, too. Make me happy.

GERALD   I *can't* make you—and you know it.

ANABEL   Yes, you can. It's your business to make me happy. I've made you happy.

GERALD   You want to make me unhappy.

ANABEL   I *do* think you're the last word in selfishness. If I say I can't forget, you merely say, '*I've* forgotten'; and if I say I'm unhappy, all *you* can answer is that I want to make *you* unhappy. I don't in the least. I want to be happy myself. But you don't help me.

252

GERALD There is no help for it, you see. If you *were* happy with me
here you'd be happy. As you aren't, nothing will make you—not   80
genuinely.

ANABEL And that's all you care.

GERALD No—I wish we could both be happy at the same moment. But
apparently we can't.

ANABEL And why not?—Because you're selfish, and think of nothing   85
but yourself and your own feelings.

GERALD If it is so, it is so.

ANABEL Then we shall never be happy.

GERALD Then we shan't. (*A pause*)

ANABEL Then what are we going to do?   90

GERALD Do?

ANABEL Do you want me to be with you?

GERALD Yes.

ANABEL Are you sure?

GERALD Yes.   95

ANABEL Then why don't you want me to be happy?

GERALD If you'd only *be* happy, here and now—

ANABEL How can I?

GERALD How can't you?—You've got a devil inside you.

ANABEL Then make me not have a devil.   100

GERALD I've known you long enough—and known myself long enough
—to know I can make you nothing at all, Anabel: neither can you
make me. If the happiness isn't there—well, we shall have to wait for
it, like a dispensation. It probably means we shall have to hate each
other a little more.—I suppose hate is a real process.   105

ANABEL Yes, I know you believe more in hate than in love.

GERALD Nobody is more weary of hate than I am—and yet we can't fix
our own hour, when we shall leave off hating and fighting. It has to
work itself out in us.

ANABEL But I don't *want* to hate and fight with you any more. I don't   110
believe in it—not any more.

GERALD It's a cleansing process—like Aristotle's Katharsis.° We shall
hate ourselves clean at last, I suppose.

ANABEL Why aren't you clean now? Why can't you love? (*He laughs*) Do
you love me?   115

GERALD Yes.

ANABEL Do you want to be with me for ever?

GERALD Yes.

ANABEL Sure?

GERALD Quite sure.   120

ANABEL Why are you so cool about it?

GERALD I'm not. I'm only sure—which you are not.

ANABEL Yes, I am—I *want* to be married to you.

GERALD I know you want me to want you to be married to me.
But whether off your own bat you have a positive desire that way, I'm   125
not sure. You keep something back—some sort of female reservation—like a dagger up your sleeve. You want to see me in transports
of love for you.

ANABEL How can you say so? There—you see—there—this is the man
that pretends to love me, and then says I keep a dagger up my sleeve.   130
You liar!

GERALD I do love you—and you do keep a dagger up your sleeve—
some devilish little female reservation which spies at me from a
distance, in your soul, all the time, as if I were an enemy.

ANABEL How *can* you say so?—Doesn't it show what you must be your-   135
self? Doesn't it show?—What is there in your soul?

GERALD I don't know.

ANABEL Love, pure love?—Do you pretend it's love?

GERALD I'm so tired of this.

ANABEL So am I, dead tired: you self-deceiving, self-complacent thing.   140
Ha!—aren't you just the same. You haven't altered one scrap, not a
scrap.

GERALD All right—you are always free to change yourself.

ANABEL I *have* changed, I *am* better, I *do* love you—I love you wholly
and unselfishly—I do—and I want a good new life with you.   145

GERALD You're terribly wrapped up in your new goodness. I wish you'd
make up your mind to be downright bad.

ANABEL Ha!—Do you?—You'd soon see. You'd soon see where you'd
be if—There's somebody coming. (*Rises*)

GERALD Never mind; it's the clerks leaving work, I suppose. Sit still.   150

ANABEL Won't you go?

GERALD No. (*A man draws near, followed by another*) Good evening.

CLERK Good evening, sir. (*Passes on*) Good evening, Mr Barlow.

ANABEL They are afraid.

GERALD I suppose their consciences are uneasy about this strike.   155

ANABEL Did you come to sit here just to catch them, like a spider
waiting for them?

GERALD No. I wanted to speak to Breffitt.

ANABEL I believe you're capable of any horridness.

GERALD All right, you believe it. (*Two more figures approach*) Good   160
  evening.

CLERKS Good night, sir. (*One passes, one stops*) Good evening, Mr
  Barlow. Er—did you want to see Mr Breffitt, sir?

GERALD Not particularly.

CLERK Oh! He'll be out directly, sir—if you'd like me to go back and tell   165
  him you wanted him.

GERALD No, thank you.

CLERK Good night, sir. Excuse me asking.

GERALD Good night.

ANABEL Who is Mr Breffitt?   170

GERALD He is the chief clerk—and cashier—one of father's old pillars
  of society.

ANABEL Don't you like him?

GERALD Not much.

ANABEL Why?—You seem to dislike very easily.   175

GERALD Oh, they all used to try to snub me, these old buffers. They
  detest me like poison, because I am different from father.

ANABEL I believe you enjoy being detested.

GERALD I do. (*Another clerk approaches—hesitates—stops*)

CLERK Good evening, sir. Good evening, Mr Barlow. Er—did you want   180
  anybody at the office, sir? We're just closing.

GERALD No, I didn't want anybody.

CLERK Oh, no, sir. I see. Er—by the way, sir—er—I hope you don't
  think this—er—bother about an increase—this strike threat—
  started in the office.   185

GERALD Where did it start?

CLERK I should think it started—where it usually starts, Mr Barlow—
  among a few loud-mouthed people who think they can do as they like
  with the men. They're only using the office men as a cry—that's all.
  They've no interest in us. They want to show their power.—That's   190
  how it is, sir.

GERALD Oh, yes.

CLERK We're powerless, if they like to make a cry out of us.

GERALD Quite.

CLERK We're as much put out about it as anybody.   195

GERALD Of course.

CLERK Yes—well—good night, sir.
      Clerks draw near—there is a sound of loud young voices and
      bicycle bells. Bicycles sweep past

CLERKS Good night, sir.—Good night, sir.   200

GERALD Good night.—They're very bucked to see me sitting here with a woman—a young lady as they'll say. I guess your name will be flying round to-morrow. They stop partly to have a good look at you. Do they know you, do you think?

ANABEL Sure.   205

CLERKS Mr Breffitt's just coming, sir.—Good night, sir.—Good night, sir. (*Another bicycle passes*)

ANABEL The bicycles don't see us.—Isn't it rather hateful to be a master? The attitude of them all is so ugly. I can quite see that it makes you rather a bully.   210

GERALD I suppose it does. (*Figure of a large man approaches*)

BREFFITT Oh—ah—it's Mr Gerald!—I couldn't make out who it was.—Were you coming up to the office, sir? Do you want me to go back with you?

GERALD No, thank you—I just wanted a word with you about this   215
agitation. It'll do just as well here. It's a pity it started—that the office should have set it going, Breffitt.

BREFFITT It's none of the office's doing, I think you'll find, Mr Gerald. The office men did nothing but ask for a just advance— at any rate, times and prices being what they are, I consider it a fair advance. If   220
the men took it up, it's because they've got a set of loud-mouthed blatherers and agitators among them like Job Arthur Freer, who deserve to be hung—and hanging they'd get, if I could have the judging of them.

GERALD Well—it's very unfortunate—because we can't give the clerks   225
their increase now, you know.

BREFFITT Can't you?—can't you? I can't see that it would be anything out of the way, if I say what I think.

GERALD No. They won't get any increase now. It shouldn't have been allowed to become a public cry with the colliers. We can't give in now.   230

BREFFITT Have the Board decided that?

GERALD They have—on my advice.

BREFFITT Hm! then the men will come out.

GERALD We will see.

BREFFITT It's trouble for nothing—it's trouble that could be avoided.   235
The clerks could have their advance, and it would hurt nobody.

GERALD Too late now.—I suppose if the men come out, the clerks will come out with them?

BREFFITT They'll have to—they'll have to.

GERALD If they do, we may then make certain alterations in the office 240
staff which have needed making for some time.

BREFFITT Very good—very good. I know what you mean.—I don't
know how your father bears all this, Mr Gerald.

GERALD We keep it from him as much as possible.—You'll let the clerks
know the decision. And if they stay out with the men, I'll go over the 245
list of the staff with you. It has needed revising for a long time.

BREFFITT I know what you mean—I know what you mean—I believe I
understand the firm's interest in my department. I ought, after forty
years studying it. I've studied the firm's interests for forty years, Mr
Gerald. I'm not likely to forget them now. 250

GERALD Of course.

BREFFITT But I think it's a mistake—I think it's a mistake, and I'm
bound to say it, to let a great deal of trouble rise for a very small cause.
The clerks might have had what they reasonably asked for.

GERALD Well, it's too late now. 255

BREFFITT I suppose it is—I suppose it is. I hope you'll remember, sir,
that I've put the interest of the firm before everything—before every
consideration.

GERALD Of course, Breffitt.

BREFFITT But you've not had any liking for the office staff, I'm afraid, 260
sir—not since your father put you amongst us for a few months.—
Well, sir, we shall weather this gale, I hope, as we've weathered those
in the past. Times don't become better, do they? Men are an un-
grateful lot, and these agitators should be lynched. They would, if I
had my way. 265

GERALD Yes, of course. Don't wait.

BREFFITT Good night to you.

　　　　Exit

GERALD Good night.

ANABEL He's the last, apparently. 270

GERALD We'll hope so.

ANABEL He puts you in a fury.

GERALD It's his manner. My father spoilt them—abominable old
limpets. And they're so self-righteous. They think I'm a sort of
criminal who has instigated this new devilish system which runs 275
everything so close and cuts it so fine—as if they hadn't made this
inevitable by their shameless carelessness and wastefulness in the
past. He may well boast of his forty years—forty years' crass, stupid
wastefulness.

> *Two or three more clerks pass, talking till they approach the seat,*   280
> *then becoming silent after bidding good night*

ANABEL   But aren't you a bit sorry for them?

GERALD   Why? If they're poor, what does it matter in a world of chaos?

ANABEL   And aren't you an obstinate ass not to give them the bit they
want? It's mere stupid obstinacy.   285

GERALD   It may be. I call it policy.

ANABEL   Men always do call their obstinacy policy.

GERALD   Well, I don't care what happens. I wish things would come to a
head. I only fear they won't.

ANABEL   Aren't you rather wicked?—*Asking* for strife?   290

GERALD   I hope I am. It's quite a relief to me to feel that I may be wicked.
I fear I'm not. I can see them all anticipating victory, in their low-
down fashion wanting to crow their low-down crowings. I'm afraid
I feel it's a righteous cause, to cut a lot of little combs before I die.

ANABEL   But if they're in the right in what they want?   295

GERALD   In the right—in the right!—They're just greedy, incompetent, stupid, gloating in a sense of the worst sort of power. They're
like vicious children, who would like to kill their parents so that they
could have the run of the larder. The rest is just cant.

ANABEL   If you're the parent in the case, I must say you flow over with   300
loving-kindness for them.

GERALD   I don't—I detest them. I only hope they will fight. If they
would, I'd have some respect for them. But you'll see what it will be.

ANABEL   I wish I needn't, for it's very sickening.

GERALD   Sickening beyond expression.   305

ANABEL   I wish we could go right away.

GERALD   So do I—if one could get oneself out of this. But one can't.
It's the same wherever you have industrialism—and you have
industrialism everywhere, whether it's Timbuctoo or Paraguay or
Antananarivo.   310

ANABEL   No, it isn't: you exaggerate.

JOB ARTHUR (*suddenly approaching from the other side*) Good evening,
Mr Barlow. I heard you were in here. Could I have a word with you?

GERALD   Get on with it, then.

JOB ARTHUR   Is it right that you won't meet the clerks?   315

GERALD   Yes.

JOB ARTHUR   Not in any way?

GERALD   Not in any way whatsoever.

JOB ARTHUR   But—I thought I understood from you the other night—

GERALD   It's all the same what you understood.   320

JOB ARTHUR Then you take it back, sir?

GERALD I take nothing back, because I gave nothing.

JOB ARTHUR Oh, excuse me, excuse me, sir. You said it would be all right about the clerks. This lady heard you say it.

GERALD Don't you call witnesses against me.—Besides, what does it 325 matter to you? What in the name of—

JOB ARTHUR Well, sir, you said it would be all right, and I went on that—

GERALD You went on that! Where did you go to?

JOB ARTHUR The men'll be out on Monday. 330

GERALD So shall I.

JOB ARTHUR Oh, yes, but—where's it going to end?

GERALD Do you want me to prophesy? When did I set up for a public prophet?

JOB ARTHUR I don't know, sir. But perhaps you're doing more than you 335 know. There's a funny feeling just now among the men.

GERALD So I've heard before. Why should I concern myself with their feelings? Am I to cry when every collier bumps his funny-bone—or to laugh?

JOB ARTHUR It's no laughing matter, you see. 340

GERALD And I'm sure it's no crying matter—unless you want to cry, do you see?

JOB ARTHUR Ah, but, very likely, it wouldn't be me who would cry.— You don't know what might happen, now.

GERALD I'm waiting for something to happen. I should like something 345 to happen—very much—very much indeed.

JOB ARTHUR Yes, but perhaps you'd be sorry if it did happen.

GERALD Is that a warning or a threat?

JOB ARTHUR I don't know—it might be a bit of both. What I mean to say— 350

GERALD (*suddenly seizing him by the scruff of the neck and shaking him*) What do you mean to say?—I mean you to say less, do you see?—a great deal less—do you see? You've run on with your saying long enough: that clock had better run down. So stop your sayings—stop your sayings, I tell you—or you'll have them shaken out of you— 355 shaken out of you—shaken out of you, do you see? (*Suddenly flings him aside*)

> *Job Arthur, staggering, falls*

ANABEL Oh no!—oh, no!

GERALD Now get up, Job Arthur; and get up wiser than you went down. 360 You've played your little game and your little tricks and made your

little sayings long enough. You're going to stop now. We've had quite
enough of strong men of your stamp, Job Arthur—quite enough—
such Labour leaders as you.

JOB ARTHUR You'll be sorry, Mr Barlow—you'll be sorry. You'll wish   365
you'd not attacked me.

GERALD Don't you trouble about me and my sorrow. Mind your own.

JOB ARTHUR You will—you'll be sorry. You'll be sorry for what you've
done. You'll wish you'd never begun this.

GERALD Begun—begun?—I'd like to finish, too, that I would. I'd like   370
to finish with you, too—I warn *you*.

JOB ARTHUR I warn you—I warn you. You won't go on much longer.
Every parish has its own vermin.

GERALD Vermin?

JOB ARTHUR Every parish has its own vermin; it lies with every parish   375
to destroy its own. We shan't have a clean parish till we've destroyed
the vermin we've got.

GERALD Vermin? The fool's raving. Vermin!—Another phrase-maker,
by God! Another phrase-maker to lead the people.—Vermin? What
vermin? I know quite well what *I* mean by vermin, Job Arthur. But   380
what do you mean? Vermin? Explain yourself.

JOB ARTHUR Yes, vermin. Vermin is what lives on other people's lives,
living on their lives and profiting by it. We've got 'em in every
parish—vermin, I say—that live on the sweat and blood of the
people—live on it, and get rich on it—get rich through living on   385
other people's lives, the lives of the working men—living on the
bodies of the working men—that's vermin—if it isn't, what is it? And
every parish must destroy its own—every parish must destroy its
own vermin.

GERALD The phrase, my God, the phrase.   390

JOB ARTHUR Phrase or no phrase, there it is, and face it out if you
can. There it is—there's not one in every parish—there's more than
one—there's a number—

GERALD (*suddenly kicking him*) Go! (*Kicks him*) Go! (*Kicks him*) Go! (*Job
Arthur falls*) Get out! (*Kicks him*) Get out, I say! Get out, I tell you!   395
Get out! Get out!—Vermin!—Vermin!—I'll vermin you! I'll put my
foot through your phrases. Get up, I say, get up and go—*go*!

JOB ARTHUR It'll be you as'll go, this time.

GERALD What? What?—By God! I'll kick you out of this park like a
rotten bundle if you don't get up and go.   400

ANABEL No, Gerald, no. Don't forget yourself. It's enough now. It's
enough now.—Come away. Do come away. Come away—leave him—

JOB ARTHUR (*still on the ground*) It's your turn to go. It's you as'll go, this time.

GERALD (*looking at him*) One can't even tread on you.   405

ANABEL Don't, Gerald, don't—don't look at him.—Don't say any more, you Job Arthur.—Come away, Gerald. Come away—come—do come.

GERALD (*turning*) *That* a human being! My God!—But he's right—it's I who go. It's we who go, Anabel. He's still there.—My God! a human   410 being!

     CURTAIN

Act 3 Scene 2

Market-place as in Act 1. Willie Houghton, addressing a large crowd of men from the foot of the obelisk

WILLIE And now you're out on strike—now you've been out for a week pretty nearly, what further are you? I heard a great deal of talk about what you were going to do. Well, what *are* you going to do? You don't   5 know. You've not the smallest idea. You haven't any idea whatsoever. You've got your leaders. Now then, Job Arthur, throw a little light on the way in front, will you: for it seems to me we're lost in a bog. Which way are we to steer? Come—give the word, and let's gee-up.

JOB ARTHUR You ask me which way we are to go. I say we can't go our   10 own way, because of the obstacles that lie in front. You've got to remove the obstacles from the way.

WILLIE So said Balaam's ass.° But you're not an ass—beg pardon; and you're not Balaam—you're Job.° And we've all got to be little Jobs, learning how to spell patience backwards. We've lost our jobs and   15 we've found a Job. It's picking up a scorpion when you're looking for an egg.—Tell us what you propose doing. . . . Remove an obstacle from the way! What obstacle? And whose way?

JOB ARTHUR I think it's pretty plain what the obstacle is.

WILLIE Oh ay. Tell us then.   20

JOB ARTHUR The obstacle to Labour is Capital.

WILLIE And how are we going to put salt on Capital's tail?

JOB ARTHUR By Labour we mean us working men; and by Capital we mean those that derive benefit from us, take the cream off us and leave us the skim.   25

WILLIE Oh yes.

JOB ARTHUR So that, if you're going to remove the obstacle, you've got to remove the masters, and all that belongs to them. Does everybody agree with me?

VOICES (*loud*) Ah, we do—yes—we do that—we do an' a'—yi—yi—   30
that's it!

WILLIE Agreed unanimously. But how are we going to do it? Do you propose to send for Williamson's furniture van, to pack them in? I should think one pantechnicon would do, just for this parish. I'll drive. Who'll be the vanmen to lift and carry?   35

JOB ARTHUR It's no use fooling. You've fooled for thirty years, and we're no further. What's got to be done will have to be begun. It's for every man to sweep in front of his own doorstep. You can't call your neighbours dirty till you've washed your own face. Every parish has got its own vermin, and it's the business of every parish to get rid of   40
its own.

VOICES That's it—that's it—that's the ticket—that's the style!

WILLIE And are you going to comb 'em out, or do you propose to use Keating's?°

VOICES Shut it! Shut it up! Stop thy face! Hold thy gab!—Go on, Job   45
Arthur.

JOB ARTHUR How it's got to be done is for us all to decide. I'm not one for violence, except it's a force-put.° But it's like this. We've been travelling for years to where we stand now—and here the road stops. There's only room for one at a time on this path. There's a precipice   50
below and a rock-face above. And in front of us stand the masters. Now there's three things we can do. We can either throw ourselves over the precipice; or we can lie down and let the masters walk over us; or we can *get on*.

WILLIE Yes. That's all right. But how are you going to get on?   55

JOB ARTHUR Well—we've either got to throw the obstacle down the cliff—or walk over it.

VOICES Ay—ay—ay—yes—that's a fact.

WILLIE I quite follow you, Job Arthur. You've either got to do for the masters—or else just remove them, and put them somewhere else.   60

VOICES Ged rid on 'em—drop 'em down the shaft—sink 'em—ha' done wi' 'em—drop 'em down the shaft—bust the beggars—what do you do wi' vermin?

WILLIE Supposing you begin. Supposing you take Gerald Barlow, and hang him up from this lamp-post, with a piece of coal in his mouth for   65
a sacrament—

VOICES Ay—serve him right—serve the beggar right! Shove it down 's throttle—ay!

WILLIE Supposing you do it—supposing you've done it—and supposing you aren't caught and punished—even supposing that—what   70
are you going to do next? *That's* the point.

JOB ARTHUR We know what we're going to do. Once we can get our
hands free, we know what we're going to do.

WILLIE Yes, so do I. You're either going to make *such* a mess that we
shall never get out of it—which I don't think you will do, for the   75
English working man is the soul of obedience and order, and he'd
behave himself to-morrow as if he was at Sunday school, no matter
what he does to-day.—No, what you'll do, Job Arthur, you'll set up
another lot of masters, such a jolly sight worse than what we've
got now. I'd rather be mastered by Gerald Barlow, if it comes to   80
mastering, than by Job Arthur Freer—oh, *such* a lot! You'll be far less
free with Job Arthur for your boss than ever you were with Gerald
Barlow. You'll be far more degraded.—In fact, though I've preached
socialism in the market-place for thirty years—if you're going to start
killing the masters to set yourselves up for bosses—why, kill me along   85
with the masters. For I'd rather die with somebody who has one tiny
little spark of decency left—though it *is* a little tiny spark—than live
to triumph with those that have none.

VOICES Shut thy face, Houghton—shut it up—shut him up—hustle
the beggar! Hoi!—hoi-ee!—whoo!—whoam-it, whoam-it!—whoo!—   90
bow-wow!—wet-whiskers!

WILLIE And it's no use you making fools of yourselves— (*His words are
heard through an ugly, jeering, cold commotion*)

VOICE (*loudly*) He's comin'.

VOICES Who?   95

VOICE Barlow.—See 's motor?—comin' up—sithee?

WILLIE If you've any sense left—(*Suddenly and violently disappears*)

VOICES Sorry!—he's comin'—'s comin'—sorry, ah! Who's in?—
That's Turton drivin'—yi, he's behind wi' a woman—ah, he's
comin'—he'll none go back—hold on. Sorry!—wheer's 'e comin'?—   100
up from Lodnor—ay—

    *The cries die down—the motor car slowly comes into sight, Oliver
driving, Gerald and Anabel behind. The men stand in a mass in
the way*

OLIVER Mind yourself, there. (*Laughter*)   105

GERALD Go ahead, Oliver.

VOICE What's yer 'urry?

    *Crowd sways and surges on the car. Oliver is suddenly dragged
out. Gerald stands up—he, too, is seized from behind—he
wrestles—is torn out of his great-coat—then falls—disappears.*   110

263

Loud cries—'Hi!—hoi!—hoi-ee!'—*all the while. The car*
shakes and presses uneasily

VOICE Stop the blazin' motor, somebody.

VOICE Here y' are!—hold a minute. (*A man jumps in and stops the*
engine—he drops in the driver's seat)   115

COLLIER (*outside the car*) Step down, miss.

ANABEL I am Mrs Barlow.

COLLIER Missis, then. (*Laugh*) Step down—lead 'er forrard. Take 'em
forrard—take 'em forrard.

JOB ARTHUR Ay, make a road.   120

GERALD You're makin' a proper fool of yourself now, Freer.

JOB ARTHUR You've brought it on yourself. *You've* made fools of
plenty of men.

COLLIERS Come on, now—come on! Whoa!—whoa!—he's a jibber°—
go pretty now, go pretty!   125

VOICES (*suddenly*) Lay hold o' Houghton—nab 'im—seize 'im—
rats!—rats!—bring 'im forrard!

ANABEL (*in a loud, clear voice*) I never knew anything so *ridiculous*.

VOICES (*falsetto*) Ridiculous! Oh, ridiculous! Mind the step, dear!—I'm
Mrs Barlow!—Oh, are you?—Tweet—tweet!   130

JOB ARTHUR Make a space, boys, make a space. (*He stands with prisoners*
in a cleared space before the obelisk) Now—now—quiet a minute—we
want to ask a few questions of these gentlemen.

VOICES Quiet!—Quiet!—Sh-h-h! Sh-h-h!—Answer pretty—answer
pretty now!—Quiet!—Shh-h-h!   135

JOB ARTHUR We want to ask you, Mr Gerald Barlow, why you have
given occasion for this present trouble?

GERALD You are a fool.

VOICES Oh!—oh!—naughty Barlow!—naughty baa-lamb—answer
pretty—answer pretty—be good baa-lamb—baa—baa!—answer   140
pretty when gentleman asks you.

JOB ARTHUR Quiet a bit. Sh-h-h!—We put this plain question to you,
Mr Barlow. Why did you refuse to give the clerks this just and fair
advance, when you knew that by refusing you would throw three
thousand men out of employment?   145

GERALD You are a fool, I say.

VOICES Oh!—oh!—won't do—won't do, Barlow—wrong answer—
wrong answer—be good baa-lamb—naughty boy—naughty boy!

JOB ARTHUR Quiet a bit—now!—If three thousand men ask you a just,
straightforward question, do you consider they've no right to an   150
answer?

GERALD I would answer you with my foot.

VOICES (*amid a threatening scuffle*) Da-di-da! Hark ye—hark ye! Oh—whoa—whoa a bit!—won't do!—won't do!—naughty—naughty—say you're sorry—say you're sorry—kneel and say you're sorry— 155 kneel and beg pardon!

JOB ARTHUR Hold on a bit—keep clear!

VOICES Make him kneel—make him kneel—on his knees with him!

JOB ARTHUR I think you'd better kneel down.

> *The crowd press on Gerald—he struggles—they hit him behind* 160
> *the knees, force him down*

OLIVER This is shameful and unnecessary.

VOICES All of 'em—on your knees—all of 'em—on their knees!

> *They seize Oliver and Willie and Anabel, hustling. Anabel kneels*
> *quietly—the others struggle* 165

WILLIE Well, of all the damned, dirty, cowardly—

VOICES Shut up, Houghton—shut him up—squeeze him!

OLIVER Get off me—let me alone—I'll kneel.

VOICES Good little doggies—nice doggies—kneel and beg pardon—yap-yap—answer—make him answer! 170

JOB ARTHUR (*holding up his hand for silence*) It would be better if you answered straight off, Barlow. We want to know why you prevented that advance?

VOICES (*after a pause*) Nip his neck! Make him yelp!

OLIVER Let me answer, then.—Because it's worse, perhaps, to be 175 bullied by three thousand men than by one man.

VOICES Oh!—oh!—dog keeps barking—stuff his mouth—stop him up—here's a bit of paper—answer, Barlow—nip his neck—stuff his mug—make him yelp—cork the bottle!

> *They press a lump of newspaper into Oliver's mouth, and bear* 180
> *down on Gerald*

JOB ARTHUR Quiet—quiet—quiet—a minute, everybody. We give him a minute—we give him a minute to answer.

VOICES Give him a minute—a holy minute—say your prayers, Barlow—you've got a minute—tick-tick, says the clock—time him! 185

JOB ARTHUR Keep quiet.

WILLIE Of all the damned, cowardly—

VOICES Sh-h-h!—Squeeze him—throttle him! Silence is golden, Houghton.—Close the shutters, Willie's dead.—Dry up, wet-whiskers! 190

JOB ARTHUR You've fifteen seconds.

VOICES There's a long, long trail a-winding—

JOB ARTHUR The minute's up.—We ask you again, Gerald Barlow,
why you refused a just and fair demand, when you know it was
against the wishes of three thousand men all as good as yourself?   195

VOICES And a sight better—I don't think—we're not all vermin—
we're not all crawlers, living off the sweat of other folks—we're not all
parish vermin—parish vermin.

JOB ARTHUR And on what grounds do you think you have no occasion
to answer the straightforward question we put you here?   200

ANABEL (*after a pause*) Answer them, Gerald. What's the use of pro-
longing this?

GERALD I've nothing to answer.

VOICES Nothing to answer—Gerald, darling—Gerald, duckie—oh,
lovey-dovey—I've nothing to answer—no, by God—no, by God, he   205
hasna—nowt to answer—ma'e him find summat, then—answer for
him—gi'e him 's answer—let him ha'e it—go on—mum—mum—
lovey-dovey—rub his nose in it—kiss the dirt, ducky—bend him
down—rub his nose in—he's saying something—oh no, he isn't—
sorry I spoke—bend him down!   210

JOB ARTHUR Quiet a bit—quiet, everybody—he's got to answer—keep
quiet.—Now—(*A silence*) Now then, Barlow, will you answer, or
won't you? (*Silence*)

ANABEL Answer them, Gerald—never mind.

VOICES Sh-h-h! Sh-h-h! (*Silence*)   215

JOB ARTHUR You won't answer, Barlow?

VOICE Down the beggar!

VOICES Down him—put his nose down—flatten him!
    The crowd surges and begins to howl—they sway dangerously—
    Gerald is spread-eagled on the ground, face down   220

JOB ARTHUR Back—back—back a minute—back—back! (*They recoil*)

WILLIE I *hope* there's a God in heaven.

VOICES Put him down—flatten him!
    Willie is flattened on the ground

JOB ARTHUR Now then—now then—if you won't answer, Barlow,   225
I can't stand here for you any more.—Take your feet off him, boys,
and turn him over. Turn him over—let us look at him. Let us see if
he *can* speak. (*They turn him over, with another scuffle*) Now then,
Barlow—you can see the sky above you. Now do you think you're
going to play with three thousand men, with their lives and with their   230
souls?—now do you think you're going to answer them with your
foot?—do you—do you?

The crowd has begun to sway and heave dangerously, with a low,
muffled roar, above which is heard Job Arthur's voice. As he
ceases, the roar breaks into a yell—the crowd heaves   235

VOICES Down him—crack the vermin—on top of him—put your foot
on the vermin!

ANABEL (*with a loud, piercing cry, suddenly starting up*) Ah no! Ah no!
Ah-h-h-h no-o-o-o! Ah-h-h-h no-o-o-o! Ah-h-h-h no-o-o-o!
No-o-o-o! No-o-o-o! No-o! No-o-o!—Ah-h-h-h!—it's enough, it's   240
enough, it's enough! It's enough—he's a man as you are. He's a man
as you are. He's a man as you are. He's a man as you are. (*Weeps—a*
breath of silence)

OLIVER Let us stop now—let us stop now. Let me stand up. (*Silence*)
I want to stand up. (*A muffled noise*)   245

VOICE Let him get up. (*Oliver rises*)

OLIVER Be quiet. Be quiet.—Now—choose! Choose! Choose! Choose
what you will do! Only choose! Choose!—it will be irrevocable. (*A*
moment's pause) Thank God we haven't gone too far.—Gerald, get
up. (*Men still hold him down*)   250

JOB ARTHUR Isn't he to answer us? Isn't he going to answer us?

OLIVER Yes, he shall answer you. He shall answer you. But let him stand
up. No more of this. Let him stand up. He must stand up. (*Men still*
hold Gerald down. Oliver takes hold of their hands and removes them)
Let go—let go now. Yes, let go—yes—I ask you to let go. (*Slowly,*   255
sullenly, the men let go. Gerald is free, but he does not move) There—get
up, Gerald! Get up! You aren't hurt, are you? You must get up—
it's no use. We're doing our best—you must do yours. When things
are like this, we have to put up with what we get. (*Gerald rises slowly*
and faces the mob. They roar dully) You ask why the clerks didn't   260
get this increase? Wait! Wait! Do you still wish for any answer, Mr
Freer?

JOB ARTHUR Yes, that's what we've been waiting for.

OLIVER Then answer, Gerald.

GERALD They've trodden on my face.   265

OLIVER No matter. Job Arthur will easily answer that you've trodden
on their souls. Don't start an altercation. (*The crowd is beginning to*
roar)

GERALD You want to know why the clerks didn't get their rise?—
Because you interfered and attempted to bully about it, do you see.   270
That's why.

VOICES You want bullying.—You'll get bullying, you will.

267

OLIVER Can't you see it's no good, either side? It's no mortal use. We
might as well all die to-morrow, or to-day, or this minute, as go on
bullying one another, one side bullying the other side, and the other   275
side bullying back. We'd *better* all die.

WILLIE And a great deal better. I'm damned if I'll take sides with anybody against anything, after this. If I'm to die, I'll die by myself. As
for living, it seems impossible.

JOB ARTHUR Have the men nothing to be said for their side?   280

OLIVER They have a great deal—but not *everything*, you see.

JOB ARTHUR Haven't they been wronged? And *aren't* they wronged?

OLIVER They have—and they are. But haven't they been wrong themselves, too?—and aren't they wrong now?

JOB ARTHUR How?   285

OLIVER What about this affair? Do you call it right?

JOB ARTHUR Haven't we been driven to it?

OLIVER Partly. And haven't you driven the masters to it, as well?

JOB ARTHUR I don't see that.

OLIVER Can't you see that it takes two to make a quarrel? And as long as   290
each party hangs on to its own end of the stick, and struggles to get
full hold of the stick, the quarrel will continue. It will continue till
you've killed one another. And even then, what better shall you be?
What better would you be, really, if you'd killed Gerald Barlow just
now? You wouldn't, you know. We're all human beings, after all. And   295
why can't we try really to leave off struggling against one another, and
set up a new state of things?

JOB ARTHUR That's all very well, you see, while you've got the goods.

OLIVER I've got very little, I assure you.

JOB ARTHUR Well, if you haven't, those you mix with have. They've got   300
the money, and the power, and they intend to keep it.

OLIVER As for power, somebody must have it, you know. It only rests
with you to put it into the hands of the best men, the men you *really*
believe in.—And as for money, it's life, it's living that matters, not
simply having money.   305

JOB ARTHUR You can't live without money.

OLIVER I know that. And therefore why can't we have the decency to
agree simply about money—just agree to dispose of it so that all men
could live their own lives.

JOB ARTHUR That's what we want to do. But the others, such as Gerald   310
Barlow, they keep the money—*and* the power.

OLIVER You see, if you wanted to arrange things so that money flowed
more naturally, so that it flowed naturally to every man, according to

his needs, I think we could all soon agree. But you don't. What you want is to take it away from one set and give it to another—or keep it yourselves. 315

JOB ARTHUR We want every man to have his proper share.

OLIVER I'm sure *I* do. I want every man to be able to live and be free. But we shall never manage it by fighting over the money. If you want what is natural and good, I'm sure the owners would soon agree with you. 320

JOB ARTHUR What? Gerald Barlow agree with us?

OLIVER Why not? I believe so.

JOB ARTHUR You ask him.

OLIVER Do you think, Gerald, that if the men really wanted a whole, better way, you would agree with them? 325

GERALD I want a better way myself—but not their way.

JOB ARTHUR There, you see!

VOICES Ah-h! look you!—That's him—that's him all over.

OLIVER You want a better way—but not his way: he wants a better way—but not your way. Why can't you both drop your buts, and 330 simply say you want a better way, and believe yourselves and one another when you say it? Why can't you?

GERALD Look here! I'm quite as tired of my way of life as you are of yours. If you make me believe you want something better, then I assure you I do: I want what you want. But Job Arthur Freer's not the 335 man to lead you to anything better. You can tell what people want by the leaders they choose, do you see? You choose leaders whom I respect, and I'll respect you, do you see? As it is, I don't. And now I'm going.

VOICES Who says?—Oh ay!—Who says goin'? 340

GERALD Yes, I'm going. About this affair here we'll cry quits; no more said about it. About a new way of life, a better way all round—I tell you I want it and need it as much as ever you do. I don't care about money really. But I'm never going to be bullied.

VOICE Who doesn't care about money? 345

GERALD I don't. I think we ought to be able to alter the whole system—but not by bullying, not because one lot wants what the other has got.

VOICE No, because you've got everything.

GERALD Where's my coat? Now then, step out of the way.

They move towards the car. 350

CURTAIN

EXPLANATORY NOTES

A Collier's Friday Night

1.2–3 *oven side of the stove*: the traditional kitchen 'range' would have one or more ovens adjacent to the grate, with doors opening to the front and boiling and simmering plates above.

7–8 *edition . . . green and gilt*: probably the three volumes of the *Historical and Dramatic Works* of the German writer (1729–81) available in translation in the 'green and gilt' binding of Bohn's Standard Library.

19 *Reeve's silver trade-mark*: the greyhound crest of the well-established manufacturer of boxes of water colours and other paints.

25 *World's Famous Literature*: a twenty-volume anthology, published in 1899, and known to have been owned by Lawrence's brother.

27 *Nuttall's dictionary*: inexpensive and widely used single-volume English dictionary.

33 *Windsor chair*: 'a kind of wooden chair with the back formed of upright rod-like pieces surmounted by a cross-piece, and often with arms' (*OED*).

36 *Stead's Christmas Numbers*: special issues of popular journals, such as those published by W. T. Stead, would often include a print or cheap colour reproduction suitable for framing.

39–40 *The New Age*: a Fabian socialist weekly edited by A. R. Orage.

60 *gaby*: muddled but garrulous person.

61 *register*: list recording the names and attendance of pupils at a school.

86 *potted meat*: meat preserved, often as a paste for spreading, in a sealed jar.

98–9 *The Scarlet Pimpernel*: best-selling novel (1905) by Baroness Orczy.

113 *Selson*: local form of Selston, a colliery two miles from Eastwood.

136 *'prunes and prisms' manner*: artificially genteel way of speaking.

143 *bacon sawyer*: employee in a grocer's shop who cuts up bacon into joints and rashers.

147 *Carooso*: Nellie's pronunciation of the 'heart-throb' Italian tenor, Enrico Caruso.

148 *Gibson bend*: female pose in the manner of the 'Gibson girls', portrayals of idealized womanhood by the American artist Charles Dana Gibson.

159 *slikey*: slick, crafty.

178 *dun . . . dunna*: dialect forms of 'do' and 'do not' respectively (although, confusingly, 'dun' in some contexts also denotes 'do not').

199   *dotty 'un*: dirty one.

235   *lard paper*: wrapper for lard or other fat, retained for use in greasing baking pans to prevent sticking.

240   *hoss*: horse.

247   *pottering the fire*: giving the fire a succession of riddling pokes.

258   *panchion*: a wide, shallow pan used in bread-making.

266   *mun*: dialect form of 'must' (cf note to line 178, above).

360   *bobby*: bantering group.

372   *seven-and-six*: see 'Note on the Currency', p. 282 below.

375   *Piers the Ploughman*: allegorical poem by William Langland (1303–90), often used as a 'set text' in the study of Middle English.

      Horace: Roman poet and critic (65–8 BC).

389   *Little*: referring forward to the diminutive on the following line.

390   *Mütterchen*: 'little mother' (German).

392   *chough*: compulsive chatterer.

393   *nap*: game of cards.

397   *Burke*: Edmund Burke (1729–97), the Whig philosopher and statesman.

406   *Ovid*: Latin poet (43 BC–AD 17), author of *Arts of Love* and *Metamorphoses*.

426–7 *peacock and thistle*: that is, an heraldic crest, indicating noble ancestry.

432   *Matoushka*: Ernest now affects the Russian form of 'little mother'.

463   *draughtin'*: that is, making a draught with her continuous movement.

470   *back*: bet (or back up, substantiate).

486–7 *Swinburne's dead*: the poet A. G. Swinburne died on 10 April 1909. This newspaper report apparently 'fixes' the action shortly after this date.

490   *lading-can*: vessel for scooping up (and sometimes for measuring) water or other liquids.

529   *bested*: done better than (here, ' arrived before').

530   *I'n bet*: 'I've done better than.'

545   *Onoto*: well-known brand of fountain-pen.

555   *'butty'*: leader of a small team of miners responsible for working an allocated seam of coal, or 'stall', and for distributing the money earned by his team.

560–1 *day men*: the hired members of the 'butty's' team (see note preceding).

564   *Ready Reckoner*: set of mathematical tables for simple calculations.

2.17 *Ow's gerrin' some iv'ry day or tow*: 'She's getting some every day or two.'

 18   *Grieg*: see note to 2.69–70, below.

 20   *The Maiden's Prayer*: piano piece of 1856, very popular with amateurs.

 50   *Twenty-eight shillings*: see 'Note on the Currency', p. 282 below.

55 *club*: generic term for insurance schemes, friendly societies, and other mutual forms of protection against a worker's sickness or unemployment.

58 *score*: record of purchases on credit, often of drink and 'scored' on a slate.

68 *Norfolk costume*: casual, sporting suit of jacket and knee-breeches.

69–70 *Anitra's Tanz . . . Ase's Tod*: parts of the *Peer Gynt* suite by the Norwegian composer Edvard Grieg (1843–1907).

183 *tam-o'-shanter*: soft, circular, wide-brimmed woollen bonnet.

209 *white cake*: here, a flat-shaped loaf of bread.

283 *soak*: here, to allow the heat to spread evenly through the bread.

423 *Francis Thompson's Shelley*: recently published monograph on the Romantic poet, from which Lawrence noted Shelley's liking for childish playthings such as paper boats.

440 *such a flat*: so dull.

444 *Baudelaire*: French poet (1821–67), from whose works Ernest proceeds to quote (see notes following).

456 *Maîtresse des Maîtresses*: phrase from first line of Baudelaire's poem (see note following).

459 *Le Balcon*: poem by Baudelaire.

471 *The Albatross*: *L'Albatros*, another poem by Baudelaire.

493 *lawk*: vulgar form of 'Lord'.

499 *'ormin'*: awkward, gauche.

503 *Garn*: vulgar form of 'Go on!', intended ironically.

507 *'dead certs'*: certainties to win (racing term).

518 *drowning-mouse engines*: kind of patent mousetraps.

527 *revenant à son mouton*: form of the French idiom indicating 'returning to the subject', sometimes found anglicized as 'getting back to one's muttons'.

536 *the Dark, or the Athletics*: Ernest's private terms for College girls.

547 *Erewhonian*: here, another of Ernest's categories of College girl, presumably earnest and gloomy, after Samuel Butler's dystopian novel *Erewhon* (1872).

549 *'Sigh no more, ladies'*: line from a song in Shakespeare's *Much Ado about Nothing*, 2.3.

581 *Inter. list*: list of candidates in the College's Intermediate Examination.

601–2 *Vous m'agacez . . . au diable*: 'You set my nerves on edge. Go to the Devil.'

674 *nutmeg-grater*: kitchen implement with rough, raised surface for scraping nutmegs.

713 *'adsum'*: 'I am here', phrase widely used in this Latin form when answering a school roll-call.

767 *lum*: colloquial contraction of 'Lord love me!'

3.3 *drawn-thread work*: 'ornamental work done in textile fabrics by drawing out some of the threads of warp and woof, so as to form patterns, with or without the addition of needlework, or other accessories' (*OED*).

15 *fagged*: extremely fatigued.

30 *net*: shopping bag.

82 *Old Lad*: that is, the Devil himself.

93 *scroddy*: meagre, scrawny.

399 *jockey*: swindler, impostor.

402 *sliving*: mean, deceitful.

406 *chelp*: impudent chatter.

416 *Waterbury watch*: cheap but sturdy brand of fob-watch, for everyday use. The Father also has a 'silver watch' (l. 421) which he keeps wound for 'best'.

480 *Exhibition*: possibly the Royal Academy winter exhibition of 1909.

Frank Brangwyn: artist (1867–1956) prominent in the 'art nouveau' movement, but earlier associated with impressionism.

481 *Impressionism*: artistic movement originating in late nineteenth-century France, concerned with capturing overall tone and effect rather than with literalism of detail. Cf. note following.

484 *Pre-Raphaelitism*: artistic 'brotherhood' in mid nineteenth-century England concerned with exact observation of natural detail. Cf. preceding note.

548 *Herod's Farm*: that is, where Maggie Pearson lives—Lawrence's renaming of Haggs Farm, the home of Jessie Chambers.

641–4 *Rose, red rose . . . Amen!*: the poem is apparently Lawrence's invention.

676 *'raker'*: device for keeping large lumps of coal from burning too fast, thus preventing a fire from going out overnight.

The Widowing of Mrs Holroyd

1.1.14 *headstocks*: the framework over a mine-shaft, housing the pulleys for the cables which hoist the lift-cage up and down the shaft.

26 *swarfed*: covered with swarf, or fine grits—in this case, of coal dust.

53 *swarf it up*: get it dirtied with coal-dust.

102 *lamp-glass*: a cylinder of glass, open at the top and fitting into the rim of an oil-lamp at the bottom, used to regulate the flame and protect it from draughts.

128 *dog's-nose*: beer topped with a measure of spirits—in this case, as we learn at 1.202, 'a small whiskey'.

139 *cackling*: stupidly chattering.

140 *taken up*: arrested.

141 *road*: way.

171 *Selvidge to selvidge*: with the woven-side edges abutting.

1.2.20 *fronts*: stands face to face with.

 94 *thumper*: 'whopping', large of its kind.

113 *claver*: gossipy mouth.

192–3 *jug-handle coiffure*: hair-style with long side curls like the handles of a jug.

238 *pull a mug*: make a face.

253 *Yi*: yes now.

297 *down th' line*: down the railway track.

340 *fow*: bad-tempered.

2.22 *thaigh*: you (singular: thou).

 57 *smoke-room*: one of the smaller bars in a public house.

88–9 *It's him tha cuts thy cloth by*: he's the one whose advice you follow.

117 *flimsy jack*: weak and idle fellow.

126 *slivin'*: sneaking.

143 *door-jamb*: side-piece of the door.

200 *It's more mark than mar*: it looks worse than it is.

213 *ladling can*: measuring jug for drawing liquid, in this case hot water.

225 *the drawn sword between us*: metaphor indicating an unbreachable divide between lovers—in this case, the physical presence of Holroyd.

3.6 *irons*: presumably here indicating not the fire-irons, but the spare flat-irons being heated to replace the one presently in use after it has cooled down.

 15 *steal the baby*: reputedly the habit of a tinker, which is Jack's role in his game with Minnie.

 80 *snap*: food for the pit, and its container.

149 *bright daisies*: loose girls.

203 *ravishing*: with abandoned delight.

217 *butties*: works as a butty (see note to *A Collier's Friday Night*, 1.555, above).

224 *bantle*: group of men, crew.

225 *stall*: the seam of coal worked by a butty and his daymen.

227 *stint*: set amount of work to be performed in a shift.

229 *bottom*: that is, the bottom of the shaft, whence the lift-cage ascends to the surface.

246 *mosh*: pulped and mangled (mush).

252 *night deputy*: the under-manager responsible for the night shift.

275 *fan engine*: the engine driving the ventilation system.

  driving engine: the engine controlling the lift-cage in the shaft.

276 *skirr of brakes*: sound of the brakes being applied to the cables of the lift-cage.

277 *chair*: the lift-cage.

346 *the lumps fly broadcast*: the sugar lumps scatter in all directions.

377 *after-damp*: poisonous gas formed after a pit explosion. (None has occurred in this case, but Rigley may be trying to suggest that Holroyd lost consciousness, in order to ease the women's pain.)

393 *By Guy*: by God.

394 *'ings*: that is, hangs.

405 *holin' a stint*: a shift spent clearing space to give access to a seam of coal.

565 *taking*: captivating, attractive.

603 *maun*: must.

The Daughter-in-Law

1.1.1 *Windsor chairs*: see note to *A Collier's Friday Night*, 1.33.

16 *th' office*: the colliery manager's office.

21 *fourteen shillin' a week*: see 'Note on the Currency', p. 282 below.

30 *hutch up*: move over.
   gammy: lame.

55 *wringer*: crow-bar, wrecking tool.

55 *pick-heft*: handle of a pick-axe.

57 *I' th' stall, at snap time*: in the seam being worked, during a meal break.

65 *sta'*: stall (see preceding note).

72 *bully-ragging*: intimidating, verbally bullying or teasing.

73 *chappil man*: member of a nonconformist chapel, likely to be scrupulous (Joe feels over-scrupulous) about giving honest answers.

77 *linkin'*: looking.

87 *clat-farted*: gossiped, spoken too readily.

91 *slaver*: drivelling chatter.

95 *thripenny bit*: see 'Note on the Currency', p. 282 below.

96 *clunch*: stiff, lumpish clay, often found in coal seams.

106–7 *scrape yer tabs*: clean out your ears.

125 *ten shillin's a week*: see 'Note on the Currency', p. 282 below.

126 *club-money*: sick pay from the funds of an insurance company or friendly society, to which Joe contributes.

132 *slutherers*: slackers, idlers.

162 *a guinea a week*: see 'Note on the Currency', p. 282 below.

164 *slave on th' roads*: work on the tunnels in the mines (rather than the coal face).

168–9 *widders' coals*: coal allowed to miners' widows free or at reduced price.

169 *leadin'*: coal from very fine seams, not likely to be of the highest quality.

   four-an'-eight: see 'Note on the Currency', p. 282 below.

171–2 *I'd ma'e . . . rowdy*: 'I'd beat a ruddy complexion into his flanks.'

178 *iron-men*: coal-cutting machines, recently introduced from America.

181 *American Cutters*: see preceding note.

192 *werritted*: worried.

230 *scraightin'*: weeping.

259–60 *cast yer bread on th' wathers*: ironic allusion to the biblical proverb in *Ecclesiastes*, 11.1.

274 *jack up*: ruin the lives of.

290–1 *come-day . . . Sunday*: proverbial, of a lazy working-man going through the motions till the 'day of rest'.

295 *slormed*: crept sullenly away.

303–4 *fudged and haffled*: made evasions and excuses.

315 *chancy*: dialect form of 'choosy'.

331 *mormin' on*: muddling on.

356 *bitted an' bobbed*: cut up and chewed over.

386 *th' notice was in at th' registrar*: the announcement of intention to marry, as required by law, had been given to the local Registrar.

396 *racket an' tacket*: noise and upheaval.

500 *chelp an' chunter*: argument and complaining.

525 *addled*: hard-earned.

542 *flig*: pleased, spry.

1.2.2 *cottage style*: in the 'arts and crafts' style then fashionable for the moderately affluent.

   3 *delft*: superior form of earthenware, originating in Holland.

16–17 *Union medal*: the local Miners' Association badge,

   32 *throng*: in a hurry.

   58 *thy cloth . . . blackymoor*: your tablecloth will be soiled with coal dust (like a blackamoor, or black-skinned Ethiopian).

125 *Good laws*: dialect form of 'Good Lord!'

128 *proper scale*: the nationally agreed rates of pay.

147 *Sluther*: work idly and carelessly.

150 *back*: bet.

158 *mardin'*: softening.

188 *hawksed*: hauled.

308 *clat-fart*: inveterate gossip.

334 *while*: in this context, 'until'.

355 *wallit*: literally, wall-eyed—hence dim-sighted, incompetent.

383 *shifting shirt*: clean shirt, for after work.

403 *chalked of a line*: white as a sheet.

423 *doited*: daft, soft in the head.

      mort: a great deal.

433–4 *neither nice nor near*: neither too posh nor too mean.

493 *th' Co-op*: the village branch of the local Co-operative Society, where members obtained a dividend ('divi') on purchases.

528 *shine*: shindig, row.

2.83–4 *What I addle's my own*: what I earn is my own.

282 *sawney*: simpleton.

336 *short commons*: limited supplies.

      ten bob a wik: ten shillings a week. See 'Note on the Currency', p. 282 below.

3.10 *th' Midland station*: the local station of the Midland Railway Company.

29 *mormin'*: muddling.

      bletherin' and boozin': idly chattering and drinking.

52 *th' statutes ground*: the place where the 'statute fair' (held by virtue of an ancient statute) was annually held.

54 *Lord Roberts to Candyhar*: the reference is to Lord Roberts's famous march in the Afghan War of 1878–80, and the victory at Kandihar which followed.

61–2 *Black Watch*: the British Highland Regiment.

81–2 *there's more blort than bustle*: there's more talk than action.

100 *What's a gait*: what's going on?

140 *free dinners*: provided by the church at times of economic deprivation.

150 *scrawdrags*: idlers, hangers on.

240 *in collier's britches, instead o' a stool-arsed Jack's*: wearing a pitman's trousers instead of the suit worn by a sedentary clerk.

260 *orts and slarts*: the leftovers of a meal, often subsequently served up cold.

297 *bobby*: euphemistic for 'bloody'.

382 *on strap*: on credit.

415 *bobby-dazzler*: striking piece of dress or (here) personal decoration.

436 *Co-op almanack*: decorative calendar given away to members by the local Co-op (see note to 1.2.493 above).

465 *soup-tickets*: vouchers entitling the poor to use of a soup-kitchen.

4.38 *winding engines*: the engines used to raise and lower the lift-cage in the shaft.

57–8 *spite*: here, revenge, as line 72 below makes clear.

125 *sluther*: here, muddled entrance.

The Fight for Barbara

1.14 *Questa*: this one? (Italian).

16 *Abondante misura*: give us a generous measure (Italian).

17 *Come*: what?

18 *Abondante misura latte*: give us a generous measure of milk (Italian).

19 *Si*: yes (Italian).

23 *Vous apprenez anglais—voi—inglese*: you're learning English—you—English (French, Italian).

24 *O—non—niente inglese*: oh no, not English at all (Italian).

25 *fa tempo cattivo*: rotten weather we're having (Italian).

26 *Tempo cattivo—si*: rotten weather, yes (Italian).

30 *giorno che giorno*: today—what day is it? (Italian).

31 *Oggi? Domenica*: today? It's Sunday (Italian).

32 *Domenica!—dimanche—Sonntag*: Sunday (respectively in Italian, French, and German).

37 *Buon giorno, Signore*: good morning, sir (Italian).

40 *'Put me among the girls'*: music-hall song, first performed in 1907.

46 *Giacometti*: Barbara's diminutive of the Italian form of 'James', Giacomo.

124 *butty collier*: see note to *A Collier's Friday Night*, 1.555.

128–9 *Apollo Belvedere*: copy of a Greek statue of the God of Poetry and of the Sun, on display in the Vatican Museum.

134 *Antinous*: a famously handsome favourite of the Roman Emperor Hadrian.

Endymion: in Greek mythology, a well-favoured youth, beloved of the moon goddess, Semele.

140 *Pimlico or Bloomsbury*: residential districts close to central London, at that time suggestive of respectable poverty and shabby gentility respectively.

156 *Judy*: girl of loose morals.

159 *teenty*: tiny.

160 *scroddy*: puny, shoddy.

196 *bregger*: public-school slang for 'breakfast'—so used ironically by Wesson?

313 *Buon giorno*: good morning (Italian).

315 *Piove*: is it raining? (Italian).

317 *e il lago*: and the lake? (Italian).

318 *È burrascoso*: it's stormy (Italian).

319 *tempo cattivo per voi*: rotten weather for you (Italian).

322 *ha vitello*: is there any veal? (Italian).

323 *Si—si—quanto*: yes, yes—how much would you like? (Italian).

325 *Mezzo chilo*: half a kilo (Italian).

327 *Grazia—buon giorno*: thank you—good morning (Italian).

391 *La posta*: here's the post (Italian).

417 *Harrogate*: spa town in Yorkshire, much favoured for convalescence.

438 *daggeroso*: Lawrence's own Italianate form for a dagger kept in readiness.

510 *I kiss the rod*: proverbial, indicating willingness to accept punishment.

2.38 *Till death do us part*: one of the vows in the Anglican marriage service.

141 *Gardone*: northern Italian town on the shores of Lake Garda.

168 *vin du pays*: local wine.

174 *Brescia*: northern Italian town at the foot of the Alps.

174–5 *Oh, thank you*: since Lady Charlcote has refused refreshment, this presumably indicates that she has been handed her coat and gloves.

3.1.228–32 *Desdemona . . . sycamore tree*: the allusion is to Shakespeare's tragedy, in which the jealous Othello kills his wronged wife Desdemona, who in IV.iii has sung the 'willow song' from which the words in l. 232 are taken.

3.2.19 *'Blue Danube'*: popular waltz tune of 1867 by Johann Strauss II (1825–99).

209 *Malheureusement*: unhappily, sadly (French).

232 *Wood Norton*: village in the north of Norfolk.

Touch and Go

PREFACE. 1 *People's Theatre*: although much used in generic and other specific senses since, the term here refers to the People's Theatre Society formed in 1919 by the socialist writer Douglas Goldring (1887–1960). The Society was successful in publishing a series of 'Plays for a People's Theatre' (of which *Touch and Go* was the second, after Goldring's own *The Fight for Freedom*); but it failed in its attempts to have them staged.

9 *Quel peuple donc*: which people, then? (French).

21–2 *the cynosure of many eyes*: attracting the admiration of many—a misquotation from Milton's poem, 'L'Allegro', l. 80.

32 *Chu Chin Chow*: a musical which opened in 1916 and went on to achieve the then longest run (2,238 performances) in the history of the London theatre.

Like the later record-breaker, *The Mousetrap*, it was often cited as an archetype of meretricious success.

45   *Upper Ten*: that is, the upper ten per cent or wealthiest strata of society.

45–6   *Neither Piccoli nor Grandi*: neither the little people nor the great ones.

48   *co-respondents*: 'other parties' to be served with a legal petition—often for divorce, the co-respondent being the alleged adulterer.

54   *burly pairs of gaiters*: bishops of the 'muscular Christian' persuasion.

68   *Cyrano*: the eponymous hero of Edmond Rostand's *Cyrano de Bergerac* (1897), who was distinguished by an excessively long nose.

Sir Auckland Geddes and Mr J. H. Thomas: Conservative and Labour politicians respectively. In 1919 the former was President of the Board of Trade, the latter General Secretary of the National Union of Railwaymen.

71   *petit bleu arrangement*: French term (as Lawrence proceeds to explain) for 'a system of vacuum tubes' through which money and documents were transferred between departments in some shops and offices.

72   *Bradburys*: English currency notes, so-called from the signature they bore of the then Permanent Secretary to the Treasury, Sir John Bradbury.

87–8   *How many . . . thirty-two*: in fact, the German poet Goethe was recalling the claim of the Italian playwright Gozzi, that there were 'thirty-six tragic situations', whereas his own compatriot Schiller 'believed there were more'.

92   *Mr Galsworthy*: the English novelist and playwright, John Galsworthy (1867–1933), whose play *Strife* (1909) concerned a strike in a tin-plate works.

93   *bathos*: a descent from the sublime to the ridiculous.

109–12   *In Shakespeare's time . . . business through*: a reference to the execution of King Charles I just a generation after Shakespeare wrote his tragedies.

111   *Goneril and Regan*: the king's eldest daughters in Shakespeare's *King Lear*.

143   *pound of flesh*: the penalty demanded by Shylock when Antonio defaults on his debt in Shakespeare's *The Merchant of Venice*.

169   *casus belli*: cause of a war.

193   *Hermitage*: village in Berkshire where the Lawrences spent time in the later war years, and where Lawrence completed revisions to *Touch and Go*.

1.1.23   *compounds . . . South Africa*: concentration camps established by the English for non-combatant South Africans during the Boer War (1899–1902).

32   *can of beer*: the bulk container used to carry draught beer from the stillage for immediate dispense.

33   *bacca*: tobacco.

45   *Tiberius*: Anabel correctly reattributes Willie's quotation to the Roman Emperor Tiberius Claudius Nero (42 BC–AD 37).

59   *gin*: here, device for hoisting heavy weights by means of ropes coiled round a winding mechanism, often worked by donkey-power.

77–80 *shilling a day ... half-a-crown's worth of sweat*: see 'Note on the Currency', p. 282 below.

136 *millennium*: in this context, suggesting the coming of an ideal society.

158 *Unco Guid*: the hypocritically religious, or 'rigidly righteous', as Robert Burns (1759–96) subtitled his poem, 'Address to the Unco Guid'.

229 *joie de vivre*: 'joy in living' (French).

251 *coup de main*: surprise attack (French).

1.2.103–7 *De terre ... jolie vigne*: popular French drinking song, which may be roughly translated: 'From the earth to the vine/What a lovely vine/Let us cling to the wine like the vine/The vine that gives us the wine/What a lovely vine.'

110 *Ma capote a trois boutons*: 'My cloak has three buttons', first line of a French round song.

254 *parvenu*: upstart aspiring to a higher social status.

333 *peace ... understanding*: biblical reference, to Philippians, 4.7.

2.13–14 *Bertie and Elinor*: presumably two of the Barlows' older children.

20 *Lincolnshire Poacher*: English folk song.

145 *great lock-out*: the masters' enforced exclusion of pitmen from the mines following their resistance to an attempt to reduce wages in 1893.

Masters' Federation: the Coal Owners' Federation, responsible for imposing the 'great lock-out' (see preceding note).

155 *redcoats*: regular soldiers.

308 *John Halifax, Gentleman*: title of a novel of 1856 by Mrs Craik (1826–87). The natural gentility of its eponymous hero brings him prosperity despite his humble origins.

318 *smug with you*: put on a smug expression for you.

380 *Cruikshank*: nineteenth-century cartoonist and illustrator (1792–1878), especially remembered for his portrayals of low life.

443–4 *Speak roughly ... he sneezes*: slightly misquoted opening of the 'lullaby' sung by the Duchess in Lewis Carroll's *Alice in Wonderland* (1865).

452 *take that fellow ... Oliver Turton*: this should clearly also be taken as a stage direction. Oliver and Freer re-enter at l. 497.

493 *corraggio*: courage (Italian).

495 *Corraggiaccio*: not much courage (Italian).

496 *Corraggione*: lots of courage (Italian).

510 *Kümmel*: cumin-flavoured liqueur of German origin.

677 *Checkweighman*: the union official responsible for checking the miners' output on their own behalf.

681 *study*: here, an object worthy of study.

694 *Garden of Olives*: where Judas betrayed Jesus with a kiss.

709 *Æolian harp*: 'a stringed instrument adapted to produce musical sounds on exposure to a current of air' (*OED*).

736 *Dionysus and Aphrodite*: Greek deities, respectively of wine and of love.

744 *Oliver Cromwell*: English ruler during the Protectorate, here cited as an exemplar of puritanism.

3.1.11 *county*: that is, of the upper class which 'led' local society.

112 *Aristotle's Katharsis*: the concept introduced in the *Poetics* of the ancient Greek philosopher and pedagogue Aristotle, summarized elusively as the capacity of tragedy 'through pity and fear to effect a purgation of those emotions'.

3.2.13 *Balaam's ass*: according to Numbers, xxii, 28–30, the ass who refused to budge because an angel stood in its path.

14 *Job*: the Old Testament prophet, here used to exemplify patience.

44 *Keating's*: a brand of household insecticide which had become generic of its kind.

48 *force-put*: 'an action rendered unavoidable by circumstances' (*OED*).

124 *jibber*: one who 'jibs' or stops short (usually a horse at a fence).

Note on the Currency

Before the decimalization of the British currency in 1971, the pound sterling was divided into twenty shillings, and each shilling into twelve pence, so that there were 240 pence to the pound. Coins included the penny and halfpenny pieces — the latter pronounced *hay'p'ny*, as in 'sevenpence ha'penny' (*Touch and Go*, 1.1.79); a threepenny coin usually known as a 'thripenny bit' (*The Daughter-in-Law*, 1.1.95); a sixpence (or 'tanner'); a shilling piece (or 'bob'); a florin, worth two shillings (or 'two bob'); and a 'half-crown' coin, worth two shillings and sixpence (the almost obsolescent crown being itself worth five shillings). Paper currency (the 'Bradburys' mentioned in the Preface to *Touch and Go*, 72), was just coming in to replace the higher-value ten-shilling (half-sovereign) and pound (sovereign, or colloquially 'quid') coins. 'Four an' eight' (*The Daughter-in-Law*, 1.1.169) was verbal shorthand for four shillings and eightpence, and 'seven-and-six' (*A Collier's Friday Night*, 1.372) indicated seven shillings and sixpence—multiples of half-crowns being common in pricing. Amounts between one and five pounds were often expressed in shillings, as with 'twenty-eight shillings' (*A Collier's Friday Night*, 2.50), representing one pound, eight shillings. 'Guineas' (*The Daughter-in-Law*, 1.1.162) were multiples of one pound, one shilling, widely in use for professional fees.